Apache Jakarta and Beyond

Apache Jakarta and Beyond: A Java Programmer's Introduction

Larne Pekowsky

Jan 2005

Addison-Wesley

Upper Saddle River, NJ • Boston • Indianapolis • San Francisco
New York • Toronto • Montreal • London • Munich • Paris
Madrid • Capetown • Sydney • Tokyo • Singapore • Mexico City

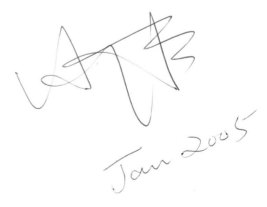

The publisher offers excellent discounts on this book when ordered in quantity for bulk purchases or special sales, which may include electronic versions and/or custom covers and content particular to your business, training goals, marketing focus, and branding interests. For more information, please contact:

U.S. Corporate and Government Sales
(800) 382-3419
corpsales@pearsontechgroup.com

For sales outside the U.S., please contact:

International Sales
international@pearsoned.com

Visit us on the Web: www.awprofessional.com

Library of Congress Cataloging-in-Publication Data:

Pekowsky, Larne, 1966-
Apache Jakarta and beyond: a Java programmer's introduction / Larne Pekowsky.
p. cm.
Includes bibliographical references and index.
ISBN 0-321-23771-4 (pbk. : alk. paper)
1. Java (Computer program language) 2. Open source software. I. Title.

QA76.73.J38P44 2004
005.13'3—dc22

2004021825

ISBN 0-321-23771-4

Text printed in the United States on recycled paper at Courier in Stoughton, Massachusetts.
First printing, December 2004

This one is for my parents.

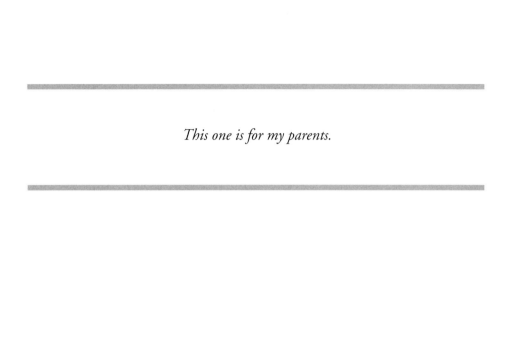

Contents

Preface

This book is about developing more effectively and more efficiently. There are many ways to do this: development paradigms, data structures and design patterns, intimate familiarity with the language of choice, and learning from other good developers, to name just a few. One option is so ubiquitous that it is seldom discussed in detail: using existing code to simplify the task at hand.

What will become evident over the course of this book is that learning to use tools effectively also helps in many other ways. Some tools are designed around a development paradigm and make the adoption of that paradigm simple and natural. Some tools facilitate the use of particular data structures or are designed around specific design patterns. Some tools use Java in interesting and novel ways.

The last category—the opportunity to learn from other developers—is not included in most toolkits. This is only one of many ways that open source offers additional benefits. All the tools in this book are helpful in their own right, and Chapter 1 discusses how the open source model has contributed to their high quality and usefulness. Beyond the direct utility of the tools is a feature that is hard to qualify. When using any of these packages a developer has not only a first-rate tool but a great deal of high-quality source code to study and learn from as well.

Who Should Read This Book?

This book is geared toward Java developers—those who sit in front of Java code every day, tirelessly constructing new applications, whether for their own use or that of their employer. Every tool in this book is useful for Web development, but only a few are Web-specific. Developers of client applications, Web applications, Web services, and all other manner of Java developers will find a wealth of information on these pages.

Technical managers, even up to the CTO level, can also benefit from this book. People who are responsible for steering entire teams in the most productive directions will find strong allies in open source tools.

Organization

Chapters 2 through 20 each cover a tool or group of related tools. Chapters 2 and 3 discuss tools that are entirely external to the application being developed. These tools provide environments and utilities that simplify the process of development itself.

Chapters 4 through 7 discuss testing tools, some of which require programming and some that do not. Testing is a critically important part of development that is too often overlooked. The tools covered in this book can help change that.

Chapters 8 through 16 discuss code packages that solve or simplify common problems. Many programs face common issues such as logging, working with databases, searching through text, and others. The tools covered in these chapters offer attractive alternatives to writing code from scratch to solve these problems.

Chapters 17 through 20 focus on tools for the Web. Chapter 17 starts with Tomcat, a powerful server for deploying Web applications. The remaining chapters cover toolkits that provide additional functionality and frameworks.

A Few Words on Development Environments

Because all the tools discussed are written in Java, they will run on any system with a JDK (Java Development Kit). All anyone needs to use these tools is a computer, a JDK, and an editor. However, having a good environment available will make development faster and more pleasant. There is no universally accepted concept of an "ideal" environment. To a large extent this will be determined by personal taste and often company policies. However, the following elements are recommended:

JDK 1.4. Most of the tools in this book will work with earlier versions of Java, but 1.4 offers so much more that there is no good reason not to adopt it.

A good text editor. Note that a text editor is just that—a program that edits text. Many integrated development environments come with powerful editors (such as Eclipse, discussed in Chapter 2). Many word processors can also edit plain text. There are times, however, when one needs to quickly open a configuration file, make a tweak or two, and save it. In these cases something small and light that starts up quickly yet provides enough editing features can be invaluable. Vi is a good candidate. It is available on almost all Unix systems, and a version for Windows is available from http://www.bulbous.freeserve.co.uk/vim16.html.

Source control management. This is essential in large groups where several people may be working on a project simultaneously. Even individuals may have a need to quickly revert to earlier versions of code. Everyone heads down the wrong road once in a while. A good candidate is CVS, the Concurrent Versions System. It certainly doesn't hurt that it is also open source. CVS is available from http://www.cvshome.org/.

A backup tool. Nothing is worse than losing a week's worth of work to a hard disk failure. CVS can also serve to automatically back up files, but there are also other options. Rsynch is a simple but solid choice, available from http://samba.anu.edu.au/rsync/.

Jikes. Jikes is a Java compiler from IBM that is *significantly* faster than javac. In the course of a day a developer may compile hundreds of files or a few files several dozens of times. It only makes sense to waste as little time as possible by making these compilations quick. Jikes is available from http://www.research.ibm.com/jikes/.

A good shell/command-line interpreter. Graphical user interfaces are wonderful for certain kinds of applications, but for many others a command line is both faster and more powerful. It is usually much easier to type a command like `java TestClass` than it is to use an IDE to click through a hierarchy of available classes, load the class, then switch to another window to provide runtime parameters, then select a particular menu option to run the program, and finally switch to another view to see the results. Most of the examples in this book are meant to be invoked from a command line.

Windows users can bring up the venerable DOS prompt, but there are better alternatives that support features such as command histories, command editing, and advanced scripting. Bash or csh are excellent choices, and they are available on Windows as part of Cygwin, from http://www.cygwin.com/.

It should be stressed that none of these tools is essential to using this book, but readers may find them handy.

Acknowledgments

First and foremost I thank my many friends—those I know in person and those I only know online—for their support and encouragement.

It has been my very great pleasure to work with some of the brightest and most dedicated people in New York at both CapitalThinking and Netomat. Although there are too many to name, my thanks to all of them for helping to keep technology fun and exciting enough to write about. Almost every consideration regarding the use of open source software in the real world that appears in this book came out of projects my colleagues and I worked on.

Many thanks and high praise to all the developers behind the tools and programs used in this book at Apache, Jakarta, and elsewhere. Their decision to make such high-quality tools free and open source deserves a round of applause from every Java developer.

All the code in this book was developed on a FreeBSD system, and I owe a debt of gratitude to everyone behind both the operating system and the Java ports.

I also thank everyone who took the time to read over the manuscript and make suggestions. The final result is profoundly better for their efforts.

This book would be nothing but a collection of unread bits on my hard drive if not for everyone at Addison-Wesley, including Ann Sellers, Ebony Haight, and many others whom I may not have been lucky enough to work with directly.

Finally, I thank the artists who created the music that kept me company while I was writing. Many of their names appear in examples scattered throughout the text.

CHAPTER 1

Introduction

Before entering the world of open source tools it makes sense to pause and consider what exactly constitutes a "tool" and what "open source" means. This will provide the reader with a context for examining these tools, and it may define ways to use them more effectively.

1.1 On Tools

When you think of a *tool,* you probably picture something like a hammer or a screwdriver—a device that aids in the process of turning raw materials into a finished product. This construction metaphor is useful because the ultimate goal is to make something new out of a collection of algorithms and ideas and Java classes. However, the strict sense of *tool* is applicable only to a Java compiler. To make the definition useful it will have to be expanded. For the purposes of this book a tool will be anything that makes development easier, regardless of how it does so. Applying this definition to the construction of physical objects suggests many new kinds of tools.

A screw, nail, or prebuilt component may be a tool. Certainly one would not want to undertake a project without them. The equivalent in Java terms might be individual classes.

A robotic assembly line greatly simplifies the process of repeatedly building new objects once the first has been built. The Java equivalent of an assembly line is something like Ant (covered in Chapter 2), which automates the process of assembling classes and other data into an application.

An entire workshop can even be a tool by providing a place and resources in which to build new things. The Java equivalent is an integrated development environment, such as Eclipse, covered in Chapter 3.

Most manufacturing facilities have devices that test the finished products. These can be as simple as a chamber in which objects are repeatedly dropped in order to see how much stress they can take, or they can be as elaborate as automobile crash tests. Such facilities simplify development in a number of ways: by ensuring that individual pieces work, that they work together as expected, and that the result is stable and robust. Java, too, has testing tools, covered in Chapters 4 through 7.

Prefabricated components can also be tools. Someone building a remote-controlled car is more likely to buy an off-the-shelf motor than build one from scratch. It is even possible to build quite elaborate systems by simply connecting prebuilt components. Indeed, this is how most desktop computers are built. Java comes with many such components in the form of the core library, but there are many common needs that are not covered by this library. Chapters 8 through 16 introduce new components.

Finally, something like a breadboard can aid development by providing a framework on top of which a project will be built. Chapters 17 through 20 discuss frameworks for building Web applications.

1.2 On Open Source

The question of what "open source" really means is in many ways an obscure one. There is no universally recognized body that is empowered to define the term. There is not even global consensus that it is a useful term.

A first reasonable attempt at a definition is as follows: A product is open source if the full source code comes included with the product. To put it another way, a set of classes could be considered open if the .java files are provided along with the .class or .jar files.

This definition implies that, at any time, a working version of the product can be reconstructed by compiling the source files, just as the original provider would have done in preparing the class or jar files. The definitional subtleties arise when considering what else the recipient can do with the source code besides compiling it as-is. Is the recipient allowed to make changes to the source code and compile that? Is the recipient allowed to incorporate the source code into its own products? Is the recipient allowed to give original or modified source code to other people?

Each developer who decides to provide source code with their products is free to answer these questions as they see fit. Typically the answers are codified as a license to which the recipient must agree. Even the point at which the agreement happens is subject to variation. Some licenses must be accepted to use the software; others need only be accepted to redistribute the software.

Open source is more than a label that may or may not apply to a particular piece of software. It is also a way to think about development, a philosophy, and, perhaps, a movement. The definitions get even muddier here; a brief history should help clarify them. Please note that this history is very abbreviated, and each of the participants will likely tell it a little differently. See some of the Further Reading at the end of this chapter for more information.

In the early 1980s a developer at MIT named Richard Stallman was facing an ethical dilemma. He felt that if he liked a program he had a moral obligation to share it with other people who might also like it. This sharing would of necessity include not only the program itself but also the source. He has often compared the situation to a recipe: If someone likes certain cookies, they should be free to give some cookies to others to enjoy. But maybe the original recipe uses walnuts, and a lot of people are allergic to nuts. The recipe can be modified to omit nuts, and in the end a lot more people can enjoy the cookies.

The Unix system and tools he was using at the time did not have this property of being sharable. So he gathered a group of volunteers and started the Free Software Foundation (FSF), whose initial goal was the creation of a complete replacement for Unix, called GNU, that would be distributed in accordance with his ethics and ideology.

At no point was this described as "open source," because the openness of the source was a consequence, not a goal. Instead the term "free" was used, and as is often stressed, this refers to liberty, not price. A user of free software is permitted to do anything at all with that software, except restrict other users from doing the same. This idea was encoded as the GPL, the General Public License, under which all FSF code is released.

By 1991 a great many of the elements that comprise a complete Unix system had been completed. The one major piece still missing was the core of the system, also called the "kernel." The GNU project had been working on a kernel called the HURD, which would incorporate a number of cutting-edge concepts in operating system design. Today the HURD is usable, and it continues to be developed, but it was not nearly ready in 1991.

Around that time a programmer named Linus Torvalds developed his own kernel, which while initially not as cutting edge as the HURD, was stable and complete. Torvalds chose to release this kernel under the terms of the GPL, which enabled it to be used in conjunction with the other elements the GNU project had already developed. The resulting complete system became widely known as Linux, although some, including Stallman, feel that the name GNU/Linux is more appropriate because everything but the kernel originated as part of GNU.[1]

The rise of the GNU/Linux system is nothing less than remarkable, and it is now replacing products from long-established companies like Sun and Microsoft in many places. However, much of its rise can be attributed to pragmatic rather than ideological reasons. Many believe that these reasons are directly attributable to the openness of the source. It is claimed that having the source available makes bug fixes faster and more reliable, makes features easier to add, and makes the whole system easier to customize for particular purposes.

These pragmatic motivations for using and contributing to open source were written up in a document called *The Cathedral and the Bazaar* by Eric S. Raymond. This document had a huge impact. Suddenly people who would never agree with Richard Stallman's ideals saw other reasons to get involved. The number of open source projects, and licenses, exploded exponentially.

This new interest in open source quickly led to the formation of the Open Source Initiative (OSI), which acts as a grassroots campaign for the support of open source. Among other things OSI has drawn up a statement of what constitutes "open source" and maintains a list of what licenses qualify. The FSF also maintains a list of what licenses qualify as free. While neither of these sources is universally accepted, they are the closest thing to standards bodies that exist.

At this point there are still tensions between the "free software" and "open source" communities, even as they work on projects together. Their differences are worth considering, and every developer who benefits from free or open source software should at least consider them and decide for themselves which—if either—view they support and will live by.

These issues will not be discussed again in this book, beyond pointing out that all the code in this book is released under licenses that qualify as "open source" according to OSI and "free" according to the FSF. However, not every license is compatible with the GPL, which may be regarded as the definitive free software license.[2]

The benefits of open source software are particularly relevant in the context of tools. The source code of a tool may itself be considered another tool—pieces and algorithms may be extracted and used in other contexts, reducing development time. It is also possible, if not always easy, to modify a tool for a particular purpose. It is as if a screwdriver can be adapted to use on an unusual screw instead of having to buy a

---

[1] The convention extends to other systems containing the GNU tools and a kernel. For example, systems using the HURD would be called GNU/HURD.

[2] In particular the Apache 2.0 license, which covers all Apache and Jakarta code released after January 2004, is not compatible with the GPL.

new screwdriver. There are many examples throughout this book of how these ideas are realized in practice.

1.3 The Apache Software Foundation and the Jakarta Project

Much of the software on which the Internet is constructed has always been open source, even before anyone called it that. One of the most important of these was a Web server written at the University of Illinois, which saw the Web from its infancy through 1995 or so. At that point development on this server stopped, and a number of Web masters informally picked it up and started adding new features. Note that this was only possible because the original source code was open. The result was called Apache, a play on words because it was "a patchy" server. To this day Apache is the most frequently used Web server by a sizable margin. It is no longer patchy and is among the most solid and robust code available.

As Apache grew, a number of related projects developed around it, and the Apache Software Foundation was eventually formed to organize and support them all.

Among these related projects was Tomcat, the reference implementation of Sun's first Servlet and JavaServer Pages specifications. Tomcat grew into a full-featured Web server in its own right, and some of its features are discussed in Chapter 17. History repeated itself during the development of Tomcat, and a number of sub- and related projects grew up around it. These were eventually grouped under the name "Jakarta."

There was a time when Jakarta could be thought of as the Java arm of Apache, but that is no longer strictly true. While every Jakarta project is written in Java, many Apache Java projects are no longer part of Jakarta. Apache has continued to grow and now includes subcategories for XML, databases, logging, and much more. Several Jakarta projects have been moved to these new hierarchies or, in some cases, given their own.

1.4 On Application Development

The final element that must be considered before looking at the tools is the general process of development. This will help clarify a number of ways in which a tool can fit into a project.

Engineering is an inherently difficult enterprise; clearly no one person could build a bridge, plane, or skyscraper. The same is true of software engineering beyond fairly small projects. Often a project is so big and complex that it simply cannot all fit into a single human brain.

For a large project to be manageable it must be split into smaller pieces. This is true when there are many members of a team working on the same project so that each knows what part of the whole they will create. It is even true when a project is being undertaken by a single person because it allows the developer to concentrate on one thing at a time. Usually the smaller pieces are easier to design, build, and test, and once built, the individual components can be updated or changed without worrying about how that change will affect the rest of the system.

While using toolkits can be a great time saver, it does require some additional thought at the beginning when deciding how to split up a project. This is because some attention must be given to what pieces the toolkit can provide. If this is not done properly, it may turn out that there is some overlap between what is being developed and what the tool provides. Besides being inefficient, this can lead to problems when integrating the tools into the rest of the code.

Metaphorically, if the whole project is to build a cube, one particular tool may look like a pyramid. This then defines the shape for the remainder of the project that the in-house developers must build.

1.4.1 Modularity in Java

One obvious way to divide a project is by splitting it into individual classes. Classes are Java's natural unit of work and may be thought of as Lego blocks that are ultimately connected together to build the final product. Each individual block can be written by one person or a small team without needing to know the details of how the other blocks work. Each block can also be individually tested to ensure that it exhibits the correct behavior. All that is needed for this approach to work is to ensure that the "connectors" of each block, which typically means the public methods, are stable and well documented.

Indeed, this is how many toolkits work. It is very common for a toolkit to consist of a large collection of classes or, metaphorically, a set of blocks with a variety of shapes and colors. When faced with the need to create one such block, one can save time by using an already-existing block provided as part of a toolkit.

This idea of using existing blocks goes well beyond the question of toolkit use. Such code reuse is fundamental to the whole idea of object-oriented programming. The Java core libraries provide many such blocks. Good developers will try to generalize their tasks and so create additional general-purpose blocks, and other blocks will come as part of toolkits.

What has been called "blocks" would more correctly be called JavaBeans. At one level beans are just classes whose methods conform to certain naming conventions. A bean can expose a property by providing a method that sets the property and/or a method that obtains the current value. For example, a bean might have a property called "color" and corresponding methods called `getColor()` and `setColor()`. A bean can also designate itself as the source of any number of events that can be registered with other classes that will react to such events.

Note that the notion of bean properties is fairly abstract. They may be simple values, such as a name or color or price, which can be represented as a Java primitive type. A property may also be some compound value represented as another bean or even an array of beans. Beyond this, invoking a get or set method may perform any operation that can be done in Java, from sending an e-mail to updating a database to accessing an external Web page. None of these things are properties in the dictionary sense, but the notion of properties is a useful way of unifying access to beans or toolkits composed of beans.

As powerful as classes are, Java's *interfaces* are even more powerful. A class represents what a component *is,* but an interface specifies what a component *does.* This idea is often referred to as "programming by contract," and it is discussed in many good books on object-oriented programming, including *The Object of Data Abstraction and Structures (Using Java)* by David Riley.

The interface concept is powerful for two reasons. First, a single object may do several things, which is why any class may implement any number of interfaces. More significantly, interfaces provide for a very loose connection between components. While a loose connection may sound like a bad thing, in fact it allows for a great deal of flexibility.

One common design pattern that captures this flexibility is called a *factory.* A factory is a class whose job is to build an instance of a class that implements an interface. Typically there will be many possible implementations to choose from, and the factory will decide which to use based on some configuration file or internal logic.

Such factories are a natural integration point for using toolkits, and this integration can take two forms. The common model where user code calls out to the toolkit can be slightly modified by using a factory as an intermediary. It is also possible to turn this model "inside out." Many of the tools in this book provide complete frameworks into which users plug some of their own code. Often this is accomplished by creating a class that implements an interface provided by the toolkit and then notifying a factory about the presence of this class. When the framework runs, the factory will create an instance of the class, and one of the interface methods will then be invoked automatically.

This is even how servlets work: The configuration files used by application servers associate a URL or URL pattern with a servlet. Internally when a request comes into the server, something akin to a factory uses the configuration information to determine which class that implements the servlet interface should be invoked, and the request is then passed to this servlet.

1.4.2 Model/View/Controller

Beyond the division into such fine-grained units such as classes and interfaces, it often makes sense to divide projects into major functional units. After all, this is the way most physical engineering is done. When building a car one team is likely to be responsible for the engine, another for the electronics that control everything, and a third with the exterior. These are natural ways to divide up the work, partly because each piece is somewhat independent of the others but also because very different skills are required for each.

There is no set recipe for the way in which a software project should be divided, but there is an important pattern that has emerged over time that advocates identifying three major pieces. The first piece will be responsible for modeling the problem to be solved, so it is called the *model.* This model might be a virtual shopping cart for an online catalog, a database representing a CD collection, or a set of equations representing some complex scientific simulation. In each case, the model contains all the information about how the data is internally stored and the operations that may be performed on that data.

The second piece is responsible for allowing users to interact with this data. This could be a desktop application written in Java using the Swing API (application programming interface), or it could be an applet, or a class that generates HTML, or even a program that controls a huge electronic billboard. The code for this piece contains everything needed in order to navigate through the data, display the values, modify the display as needed, and possibly allow the user to make changes to the model. Ideally, the presentation should also be aesthetically pleasing and intuitive to use. This piece is known as the *view.*

Finally, the third piece acts to mediate between the first two. Although the view allows the user to request particular data, it will not itself load that data into the model. In addition, some data may be restricted to certain users. This kind of information should not reside in either the model or the view. So the third piece, called the *controller,* is responsible for controlling the model based on instructions from the view, and it may also tell the view to hide certain information based on data in the model.

Once these three pieces have been defined, the only remaining work is to ensure that they all fit together and can interoperate. This is done by providing well-defined interfaces between each pair of components. The view will know how to get data from the model, the controller will know how to configure the view and the model, and so on.

Splitting the work in this way is known as the *model/view/controller* paradigm, and it is very powerful. Generally it is used in the context of Web applications, where beans play the role of the model, Java Server Pages and servlets act as the view, and typically a master servlet acts as the controller. Many of the toolkits to be examined are also organized along model/view/controller lines. Some assist in the construction of one of these elements, while others provide entire frameworks comprising integrated implementations of all three into which developers can plug their own code.

This completes the groundwork for this book. In what follows keep in mind the general concept of tools, the motivations and benefits behind open source, and the ways in which tools can integrate with the larger application. And now, on to the tools!

1.5 Further Reading

- The GNU Manifesto: http://www.gnu.org/gnu/manifesto.html
- The Open Source Initiative home page: http://opensource.org/
- The Cathedral and the Bazaar: http://www.catb.org/esr/writings/cathedral-bazaar/cathedral-bazaar/
- A history of Apache: http://httpd.apache.org/ABOUT_APACHE.html

CHAPTER 2

Ant

The process by which a collection of files is turned into a running program or deployable Web application can be surprisingly complex. Java files must be compiled into class files, but typically this is just one step in a much more involved process. Prior to compilation, Java files may need to be retrieved from a remote location or generated based on some set of rules. Following compilation, code may need to be tested, and following testing, the classes and auxiliary resources may need to be packaged into jar or war (Web application resource) files. The complete set of actions that must be performed, and the dependencies between them, is called the **build process.**

Unix-like operating systems have for some time had a tool called "make" that automates build processes. Make is used in almost all projects written in C or C++, ranging from games to entire operating systems. More recently make has been made available on Windows.

Despite make's ubiquitousness, it has many problems. Make is notoriously finicky about the syntax of its configuration files; even something as innocuous as the use of a space instead of a tab can cause make to fail. Despite the portability of the make program itself, much of what it does is accomplished by invoking external programs that may only be available on certain kinds of systems. This prevents make scripts from being portable, and it means that it is not easy to build the same program on both Windows and Unix.

The solution to both these problems is Ant, which its creator, James Duncan Davidson, describes as "make, without make's wrinkles." While it is likely Davidson is referring to make's complexity, one must also consider that wrinkles are a sign of old age, and make is quite old in computer terms. Ant, being younger, is able to take advantage of newer technology. One of these is Java itself. Ant is 100 percent pure Java and hence is automatically available on any platform with a Java VM. Ant uses XML, another relatively new technology, for its configuration files. This provides a simple, uniform, and standard format with which to configure build processes.

2.1 Introduction to Ant

Ant is concerned with the fundamental entities called **tasks;** the tasks to perform are collected in a **build file.** A task may be thought of as a single operation that corresponds roughly to a single command issued at a DOS or Unix shell prompt. Tasks may take parameters just as shell commands may take arguments. Unlike command arguments, task parameters are all named. This avoids the confusing issues of syntax and ordering that accompany shell commands and, by extension, make commands.

Tasks are specified in a build file as XML nodes where the name of the node indicates the task to be performed and the attributes specify parameters to the task. The simplest task is called `echo` and it may be used from within an build file as

```
<echo message="Hello world!"/>
```

Ant provides tasks that manage compilation, file operations, archiving, and a great deal more. We will examine many of these shortly. Programmers can also create new tasks; this ability is discussed at the end of this chapter.

Tasks are grouped into units called **targets,** which have a name and an optional description. Within a target, tasks are executed sequentially. A target that echos several consecutive messages could be written as

```
<target name="sample"
        description="A basic target">
  <echo message="This is a simple target"/>
  <echo message="It just echos several messages"/>
  <echo message="Not very exciting so far"/>
</target>
```

All targets are contained within the top-level node of the build file, called the **project.** The project specifies the default target to run, which may be overridden when Ant is started. The project may also include a name and description.

A complete and valid build file would result from placing the preceding `sample` target within a project tag, such as

```
<project default="sample">
  ...
</project>
```

By default Ant will look for a file called `build.xml` when it is run. If `build.xml` contains the preceding project, then Ant can be invoked by issuing the command

```
ant.bat
```

under Windows or

```
ant
```

under any variant of Unix, including Mac OS X. The result will be several lines of output

```
Buildfile: build.xml

sample:
     [echo] This is a simple target
     [echo] It just echos several messages
     [echo] Not very exciting so far

BUILD SUCCESSFUL
Total time: 5 seconds
```

This output announces the build file that Ant is using, which, as mentioned, is `build.xml` by default. It then announces the target that is being run, which is `sample` here. Each of the `echo` tasks in the `sample` target then runs and produces a line of output. Note that Ant prepends the name of the task to any output from that task, which can help clarify exactly what is happening. Finally, Ant announces that the build was successful, meaning that all tasks executed correctly, and announces how long the build took.[1]

[1] Five seconds may seem like a long time to print three lines of text. Much of this is the time required for the Java Virtual Machine (VM) to start up, the Ant classes to load, and the build file to be parsed. For larger projects this overhead will quickly diminish to insignificance, and overall Ant will be much faster than performing the corresponding actions by hand.

2.2 Dependencies

Stringing together tasks within a target solves part of the problem of a complex build process. A target could run one task to generate any needed Java files, then another to compile them, another to collect the resulting class files into an archive, and so on.

Ant provides a much more powerful and hence more commonly used mechanism for connecting tasks, called **dependencies.** Task B is said to depend on task A if A must complete successfully in order for B to run. One task may depend on many others and may be depended on by many others. Dependencies are represented within a build file by adding the depends attribute to a target, as in

```
<target name="B" depends="A">
  ...
</target>
```

If one target depends on multiple other targets, their names appear separated by commas in the depends attribute.

A hierarchy of dependencies implies an order in which tasks will be executed, but it is a logical ordering rather than the explicit one given by placing multiple tasks in a target. Conceptually the programmer specifies what each individual target needs in order to do its job, and Ant figures out an ordering in which to execute the targets such that these requirements are met.

To illustrate the idea of dependencies, consider a set of abstract targets designated A, B, C, and D with the relationships illustrated in Figure 2.1. In this figure an arrow

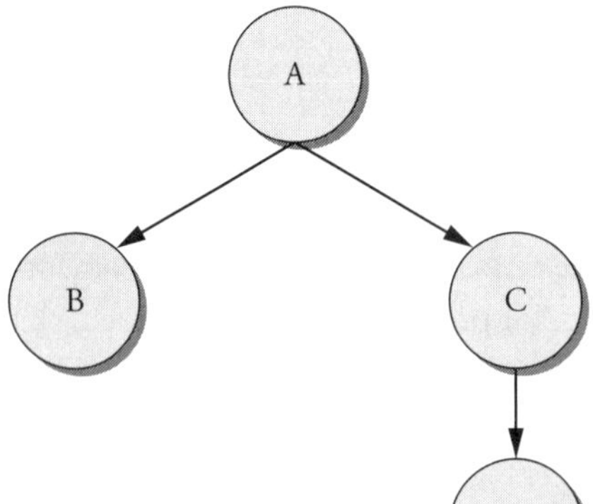

Figure 2.1. Task dependencies.

between two tasks indicates that the task at the tail depends on the task at the head—for example $A \rightarrow B$ means that `A` depends on `B`.

By having each of these tasks echo its name it is possible to see how Ant arranges execution to satisfy dependencies. The build file is shown in Listing 2.1.

Listing 2.1 Dependencies between tasks

```
<?xml version="1.0"?>

<project default="sampleA">

  <target name="sampleA" depends="sampleB,sampleC">
    <echo message="This is a simple target A"/>
  </target>

  <target name="sampleB">
    <echo message="This is a simple target B"/>
  </target>

  <target name="sampleC" depends="sampleD">
    <echo message="This is a simple target C"/>
  </target>

  <target name="sampleD">
    <echo message="This is a simple target D"/>
  </target>
</project>
```

When this build file is run, Ant will produce the following output:

```
Buildfile: build.xml

sampleB:
     [echo] This is a simple target B

sampleD:
     [echo] This is a simple target D
```

```
sampleC:
     [echo] This is a simple target C

sampleA:
     [echo] This is a simple target A

BUILD SUCCESSFUL
Total time: 9 seconds
```

This shows that `B` was run first, then `D`, then `C`, and finally `A`. Ant has some flexibility in the precise order in which it executed the targets, as long as `B` and `C` happened before `A` and `D` happened before `C`. If `B` also depended on `D`, this order would be further constrained. By changing the target definition for `B` to `<target name="sampleB" depends="sampleD">` the order would be restricted to either `DBCA` or `DCBA`.

2.3 Sets of Files as Task Arguments

Most parameters to tasks are provided as name/value pairs in the XML (Extensible Markup Language) node specifying the task. Some parameters are too complex to be represented by such pairs and must be provided as XML nodes within the task node.

The most common instance of this is specifying a set of files on which a task should act. For example, when compiling Java files typically the compilation should run over all .java files in all subdirectories within a given top-level directory. When generating javadocs it may be useful to omit certain directories—for example, those containing Java files that have been automatically generated by some other process. When building a Java file, usually only class files are included, but there may be special instances where images or other resources must also be included in the archive.

Ant provides a sophisticated mechanism for specifying sets of files. Normally this mechanism is used in conjunction with one of the built-in tasks, such as the one that performs compilation. To better see how this mechanism works independently of the tasks that use it, a minimal new task will be introduced. This task, called `ls`, processes a set of files by listing the full name of each. The last section in this chapter shows how the `ls` task was created and how other user-created tasks can access the same kind of information.

Along with the `ls` task the following examples will use the hypothetical directory structure shown in Figure 2.2; Listing 2.2 shows the initial build file.

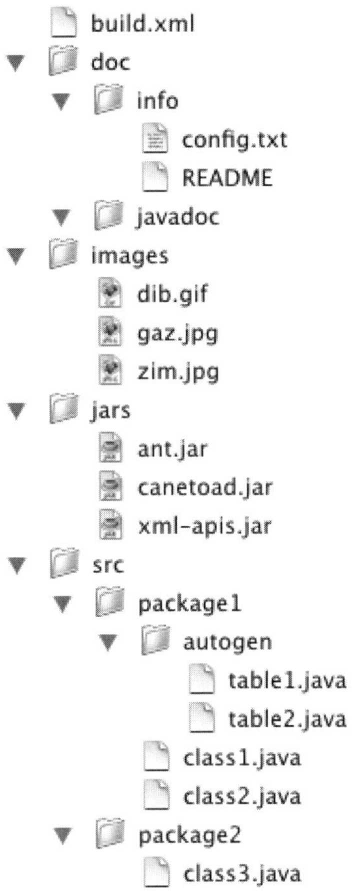

Figure 2.2. A sample directory.

Listing 2.2 A build file for exploring filesets

```
<project default="fileList">

  <taskdef name="ls"
           classname="com.awl.toolbook.chapter02.LsTask"/>

  <target name="fileList">
    <ls>
      <fileset dir="."/>
    </ls>
  </target>
</project>
```

The first new element in this buildfile is the `taskdef` element at line two. This notifies Ant of the custom task by specifying the class that implements it and the name by which it can be used in targets.

When the `ls` task is used, it has no attributes, but it does have an inner node, `fileset`. `fileset` is the basic element used to construct lists of files; the only required attribute is `dir`, which in this example is set to "." indicating the current directory. With no other restrictions this will build a list containing every file and subdirectory within the specified `dir`. When Ant is run with this build file, it will produce the following output:

```
fileList:
       [ls] build.xml
       [ls] src/package1/autogen/table1.java
       [ls] src/package1/autogen/table1.class
       [ls] src/package1/autogen/table2.java
       [ls] src/package1/autogen/table2.class
       [ls] src/package1/class1.java
       [ls] src/package1/class1.class
       [ls] src/package1/class2.java
       [ls] src/package1/class2.class
       [ls] src/package2/class3.java
       [ls] src/package2/class3.class
       [ls] images/zim.jpg
       [ls] images/dib.gif
       [ls] images/gaz.jpg
       [ls] doc/info/README
       [ls] doc/info/config.txt
       [ls] jars/ant.jar
       [ls] jars/xml-apis.jar

BUILD SUCCESSFUL
Total time: 3 seconds
```

2.3.1 Including and Excluding Sets of Files

The set of files in a `fileset` can be finely controlled through use of the `include` and `exclude` elements. These elements work as their names imply when given individual files. If a `fileset` contains only `include` elements, then only the included files will be used. If the `ls` task in Listing 2.2 were replaced with

```
<ls>
  <fileset dir=".">
    <include name="src/package1/autogen/table1.java"/>
    <include name="images/zim.jpg"/>
  </fileset>
</ls>
```

then Ant would output

```
fileList:
       [ls] src/package1/autogen/table1.java
       [ls] images/zim.jpg
```

If a `fileset` contains only `exclude` elements, then the files named in these elements will be omitted from the list. Replacing the two `include` elements in the preceding example with `<exclude name="doc/info/README"/>` will output everything in the original list except for the README file.

It is also possible to specify `include` and `exclude` elements as attributes in the `fileset` node instead of as separate nested nodes. In this usage all elements appear in a single attribute separated by spaces. Using this syntax, the preceding example would be rewritten as

```
<fileset dir="."
  includes="src/package1/autogen/table1.java
            images/zim.jpg"/>
```

For the sake of clarity this book will only use the nested form, although the two are functionally equivalent.

2.3.2 Patterns

The `include` and `exclude` elements become even more powerful through the use of **patterns.** These patterns resemble the wildcards used in DOS and Unix shells. For example,

```
<fileset dir=".">
  <include name="src/package1/*.java"/>
</fileset>
```

will return all the java files in `package1`:

```
fileList:
       [ls] src/package1/class1.java
       [ls] src/package1/class2.java
```

Two consecutive asterisks in a pattern means "any number of directories," so `<include name="**/*.java"/>` will get all Java files throughout the project

```
fileList:
       [ls] src/package1/autogen/table1.java
       [ls] src/package1/autogen/table2.java
       [ls] src/package1/class1.java
       [ls] src/package1/class2.java
       [ls] src/package2/class3.java
```

It is possible to combine `include` and `exclude` elements, as in

```
<fileset dir=".">
  <include name="**/*.java"/>
  <exclude name="**/autogen/*.java"/>
</fileset>
```

which would remove all the files from the `autogen` directory in the preceding list.

Ant does not process combinations of `include` and `exclude` elements sequentially; the order could be switched in the preceding example and the result would be the same. Rather, Ant works by matching all the patterns against the complete set of files. Any file that matches any of the `includes` and does not match any of the `excludes` is placed in the final list.

2.3.3 Other Tools to Build File Sets

It is possible to build sets of files based on criteria other than the names of the files. A set of files that contain a given string can be obtained with the `contains` element, which takes as an attribute the text to locate.[2] Note that the string may not be a wildcard pattern or regular expression.[3]

---

[2] Be warned that this may be very slow because Ant will need to open and read every file.

[3] Regular expressions are discussed in Chapter 13.

This fileset specification

```
<fileset dir=".">
  <contains text="Hello"/>
</fileset>
```

would return the following file list:

```
fileList:
       [ls] build.xml
       [ls] src/package2/class3.java
       [ls] doc/info/README
```

It should not be surprising that the text "Hello" was deliberately placed in the `README` and `class3.java` files in order to demonstrate the functionality of the `contains` element. The presence of `build.xml` is more of a surprise because there is clearly no instance of "Hello" in Listing 2.2. However, if Listing 2.2 were modified to include the `contains` element, then "Hello" *would* be present in the file—in the very `contains` element that looks for "Hello." Therefore, `build.xml` has been added to this file list for the sake of realism.

The `contains` element combines with `include` in an obvious way; a file will make it to the final list if it is both in one of the included directories and it contains the specified text. For example, the preceding list could be restricted to just the `README` file by only including the documentation directories

```
<fileset dir=".">
  <include name="doc/**/*"/>
  <contains text="Hello"/>
</fileset>
```

Likewise, multiple `contains` elements in the same `fileset` provides a means to select only files that contain multiple specified strings.

2.4 Global Variables

It is likely that many tasks within a project will need identical configuration values. Ant provides the means to define such values in global variables rather than requiring the developer to duplicate them in many places throughout a file.

Many definitions can be made global by placing the definition at the top level of the file and adding an identifier. The `fileset` definition that obtains all Java files could be made global and used by the `ls` task as follows:

```
<fileset dir="." id="defaultFiles">
  <include name="**/*.java"/>
</fileset>

<target name="fileList">
  <ls>
    <fileset refid="defaultFiles"/>
  </ls>
</target>
```

The global `fileset` definition looks like any of the nested definitions seen so far, but it adds an `id`, which here is `defaultFiles`. There is nothing special about this name, and any legal identifier can be used. The target then uses this `fileset` through the `refid` attribute within its nested `fileset`.

A `fileset` initially constructed by referencing a global `fileset` can be further manipulated by nesting any of the elements examined previously. A target that operates only on handwritten files could filter `defaultFiles` as

```
<fileset refid="defaultFiles">
  <exclude name="**/autogen/*.java"/>
</fileset>
```

It is even possible for global `filesets` to reference and modify other `filesets`. This ability leads to a common technique where one global `fileset` will define a base set of files and directories, and subsequent definitions and targets will modify this set as needed. For example, a compile target might use `defaultFiles` as is, and a target that generates documentation might use the `fileset` with autogenerated files removed.

Errors to Watch For

Global variables cannot be redefined. The first definition that Ant encounters will be used throughout the project.

2.5 Paths

Paths are somewhat like filesets except the elements in a fileset are meant to be accessed sequentially, whereas paths conceptually concatenate all their elements into a single unit. The obvious example of a path is the CLASSPATH used by Java, and Ant provides a special `classpath` element that allows targets within a built script to use explicitly provided CLASSPATHs. Ant also provides a more general `path` element that is used for many purposes.

Both the `classpath` and `path` elements look a lot like `filesets` except they are constructed from sets of `pathelements` instead of `includes`. A CLASSPATH for the hypothetical project in Figure 2.2 might be constructed as

```
<classpath>
  <pathelement path="src"/>
  <pathelement path="jars/canetoad.jar"/>
  <pathelement path="jars/xml-apis.jar"/>
</classpath>
```

In addition to building `paths` from single `pathelements`, `paths` can also be built from `filesets`, as in the following:

```
<fileset id="alljars">
  <include name="**/*.jar"/>
</fileset>

<classpath>
  <pathelement path="src"/>
  <fileset refid="alljars"/>
</classpath>
```

which builds a CLASSPATH consisting of all the jars and the `src` directory.

Note that variables such as CLASSPATH are valid only within the build file where they are defined. There is no way for any Java program to change the global CLASSPATH that is used when other Java programs start running.

The `filesets` within `paths` may also have nested elements, and `paths` may have identifiers by which they can be used in other `paths`. Ant is a very logical program and in general behaves as expected. If it seems like it should be possible to combine any of the constructs that have been presented so far, then the odds are that they can indeed be combined.

2.6 Properties

If a build file hard-codes the location of a directory in a `fileset` or `path`, the build file may not work on a computer other than the one on which it was created. It may also be necessary to fix such build files if a directory structure ever changes over the life of a project. These may or may not be concerns, depending on the nature of the project. A project that is meant to be released in source form, such as Ant itself, must be able to be compiled on any machine, including those with different operating systems. On the other hand, a project that will be used only within a company or by an individual can safely assume directories will always be where they were initially.

Ant provides a mechanism called **properties** by which build files can obtain information about the environment in which they are running. Properties can come from many places; the simplest is to define a property within the build file. In this case the property acts as a simple variable:

```
<property name="source_directory" value="src"/>
```

Once such a property has been defined, it can be used anywhere else in the build file by surrounding the given `name` within braces preceded by a dollar sign.

```
<classpath>
  <pathelement path="${source_directory}"/>
  <fileset refid="alljars"/>
</classpath>
```

This will result in a CLASSPATH including all jar files and the `src` directory, just as in the preceding `classpath` example.

Errors to Watch For

An expression that references a nonexistent property will evaluate as a literal. If the `fileset` in the previous example attempted to include `${sourc_directory}` instead of `${source_directory}`, then Ant would look for files in a directory called "$sourc_directory" instead of in "src." This can lead to problems that will be difficult to diagnose, such as files mysteriously failing to compile or errors about classes missing from the CLASSPATH.

It is more useful for the values of properties to come from outside the build file, and Ant provides a number of ways to do this. First, properties can be stored in separate property files. For example, if the following line is present in a file called proptest.properties

```
text.value=This is a build property
```

then it may be loaded and used within a build file as

```
<project default="sampleA">

  <property file="proptest.properties"/>

  <target name="sampleA">
    <echo message="${text.value}"/>
  </target>
</project>
```

There is also a means to import values from the **environment** as properties. The environment is the set of bindings from the Unix or DOS shell from where Ant was invoked. Typically this includes such values as JAVA_HOME—the location where the JDK (Java Development Kit) is installed—but it may also include any other values.

To use environment values, first the environment itself must be made available as a property though the special environment attribute.

```
<property environment="env"/>
```

The name env is not special, although it is traditional.

Once the environment has been imported, values may be obtained by appending the name of the environment variable to the name assigned to the environment. <echo message="${env.JAVA_HOME}"/> would echo the location where the JDK is installed, and

```
<classpath>
  <pathelement path="${env.JAVA_HOME}/jre/lib/rt.jar"/>
</classpath>
```

will add the Java runtime classes to the CLASSPATH on any computer, regardless of operating system or location of the JDK. This jar file is usually added to the

CLASSPATH automatically when Java starts up, but the principle is sound and can be used to access other files and directories in a general way.

2.6.1 Checking for Properties

While some environment variables like JAVA_HOME will always be set, a build file will often need additional variables to be set by the person running the build. A common example arises when compiling Web applications, and the compiler needs to know the location of the jar files containing the `javax.servlet` packages. Often these will be provided by Tomcat (discussed in Chapter 18), in which case the build file needs to know where Tomcat is installed. This information is usually present in a environment variable called TOMCAT_HOME, but there is no way to be sure in advance that this variable is set.

Ant can check for the presence of a property with the `fail` task, which takes the name of the property to require and a message to display when that property is not set. For example,

```
<fail message="Please set TOMCAT HOME"
      unless="env.TOMCAT_HOME"/>
```

will produce the following output if TOMCAT_HOME is not set in the environment

```
BUILD FAILED
file:build.xml:14: Please set TOMCAT_HOME
```

The `fail` task will typically be used from a target that is low on the chain of dependencies, ensuring it will be evaluated early in the build process.

2.7 Command-Line Arguments

By default, when Ant is started from the command line, it will look for a file called `build.xml` in the current directory, start processing from the `default` target of the `project`, and produce output messages in the format seen throughout this chapter. All of these behaviors can be modified by passing Ant appropriate flags when it starts up. Ant takes options in Unix format, with the name of each option prepended by a dash (-) and with spaces between each option and any arguments to that option.

When started with `-buildfile`, `-file`, or just `-f`, followed by the name of the file, Ant will use the specified file instead of `build.xml`. The file name may be a complete path or relative to the current directory. It is important to note that when the build file is in a directory other than the one from which Ant is run, then all paths in the build file will be relative to the location of the build file. So if a user's current directory is "/home" and that user runs `ant -f /projects/sample/samplebuild.xml`, then any references to "."—such as in the `dir` attribute of a `fileset`—will refer to the "/projects/sample" directory.

When started with `-find` and the name of a file, Ant will look for a build file with the given name in the current directory, then the parent directory, and so on until it finds the file or reaches the root of the file system. In the latter case, Ant will abort with an error message. This option allows many projects or subprojects to use the same build file.

Ant can be made to run a target other than the default by giving the name of the target on the command line. If several target names are provided, Ant will run each in the order it appears on the command line. Target names must appear as the last command line arguments.

It is common for one build file to have separate targets to assemble and compile all the code for a project, test the final project, and package it up for distribution. Often the default task will be the one that runs the compilation because that is what developers spend most of their time doing. Once all the code has compiled to the developers' satisfaction, he or she may run `ant.bat test` or `ant.bat deploy`. In addition the `deploy` target will likely depend on the `test` target, which in turn will depend on the `compile` target. The `deploy` target therefore represents the complete build process, and the other targets provide a handy way to jump in at some intermediate point and run only what is needed.

Properties can also be provided on the command line, using `-D` followed immediately by the name of the property to set, then an equals sign (`=`) and the value—for example, `-DTOMCAT_HOME=/usr/local/tomcat`. Property values provided in this way are accessed directly by name, without the environment name and dot that accompany environment properties. Ant can ensure that needed command line properties have been provided with the `fail` task, just as with environment properties.

Ant also accepts additional flags that will not be covered here, a full list can be obtained by running

```
ant -help
```

2.8 Built-In Tasks

Ant comes equipped with many useful tasks, too many to list comprehensively here. The following list includes several of the most common that are likely to appear in any realistic build file, as well as several others that give a flavor for what Ant can do out of the box.

2.8.1 AntCall

AntCall invokes one target from another. While Ant can always figure out the order in which targets should be invoked, based on dependency information, there may be logical relationships between targets that cannot be described in terms of dependencies. In those cases, targets can explicitly call each other via the AntCall task.

Attributes:

target: The name of the target within the same build file to invoke. Required.

Example:

```
<project default="callOther">

  <target name="other">
    <echo message="I have been called"/>
  </target>

  <target name="callOther">
    <antcall target="other"/>

  </target>
</project>
```

Produces the following output

```
callOther:

other:
     [echo] I have been called
```

Note that the other task is announced just as if Ant had invoked it directly.

2.8.2 Copy

Copy copies a file or directory. Copy is one of may tasks Ant provides that manipulate files. As the name implies, Copy can copy a single file to another file, or a file into a directory, or a whole `FileSet` from one place to another, preserving the directory structure.

Attributes:

file: The name of a file to copy. Required, unless a nested `fileset` is provided.
tofile: The name of the copied file. This attribute is only valid when copying a single file.
todir: The name of the directory into which the file or file set should be copied. One of `tofile` or `todir` must be provided.

Example:

```
<target name="copyFile">
  <copy file="images/gaz.jpg" tofile="image1.jpg"/>
</target>

<target name="copyDir">
  <copy todir="image_backup">
    <fileset dir="images"/>
  </copy>
</target>
```

The `copyFile` target will copy `images/gaz.jpg` to `image1.jpg` in the current directory. `copyDir` will copy every file in the `images` directory to the `image_backup` directory.

2.8.3 Delete

`Delete` deletes files or directories. Conceptually this is much like the `Copy` task except it deletes files. Most build files will have a target called "clean" that deletes all generated files. That target will often consist of a series of `Delete` tasks: one to delete class files, another to delete generated documentation, and so on.

Attributes:

file: The file to delete.
dir: The directory to delete. Either `file`, `dir`, or a nested `fileset` must be provided.

Example:

```
<target name="deleteFile">
  <delete file="image1.jpg"/>
</target>

<target name="cleanDir">
  <delete>
    <fileset dir="image_backup"/>
  </delete>
</target>
```

`deleteFile` and `deleteDir` will delete the files copied by the `copyFile` and `copyDir` tasks, respectively. Note that `deleteDir` deletes the contents of the `image_backup` directory but does not remove the directory itself.

2.8.4 Exec

`Exec` runs an external program. There are rare occasions where a build file may need to run a program to accomplish its task. For example, an automated build system might need to page the lead programmer when a build fails. There will be a program on the system to send pages, which may be impractical to port to Java.

Attributes:

executable: The name of the program to run, possibly including the full path to the program if it is in a nonstandard place. Required.

Arguments to the program are provided by special nested elements called `arg`. `arg` takes several forms; see the Ant documentation for details. The most common form includes all the arguments as a single line because they would be typed at a command prompt. For example, the hypothetical page operation might look like

```
<exec executable="/usr/local/pager/bin/page">
  <arg line="-text 'build failed' -target=lead@company.com"/>
</exec>
```

2.8.5 Get

`Get` retrieves a file from a URL. There are many reasons why a build file might need to do this: It may need to download the latest version of a jar file, include the current version of an image as a resource, or even grab the source it is about to compile.

Attributes:

src: The URL. Required.
dest: The name of the file in which the retrieved data should be stored. Required.

Example:

```
<target name="getSlash">
  <get src="http://www.slashdot.org/" dest="index.html"/>
</target>
```

will grab the current home page from `www.slashdot.org` and save it as `index.html` in the current directory.

2.8.6 Jar

`Jar` creates a Java archive file. Ant provides tasks to create numerous kinds of archive files, but jars are certainly the most common. At a minimum any of these tasks will need to know the name of the file to create and the set of files to store. `jar` also includes special options to build manifests; see the Ant documentation for details.

Attributes:

destfile: The name of the file to create. Required.
basedir: The top-level directory to include in the archive. With no other arguments an archive containing this directory and all subdirectories will be created. Required, unless a nested `fileset` is provided.

Includes:

A space-separated list of files, directories, or patterns to include, just as in the `includes` attribute of the `fileset` element.

Excludes:

A space-separated list of files, directories, or patterns to exclude, just as in the `excludes` attribute of the `fileset` element.

Many tasks follow this pattern of allowing a combination of `basedir`, `includes`, and `excludes` as attributes. Such tasks are called **implicit filesets.** All of the following are equivalent:

```
<jar destfile="src.jar" basedir="." includes="**/*java"/>

<jar destfile="src.jar">
  <filset dir="." includes="**/*java"/>
</jar>

<jar destfile="src.jar">
  <filset dir=".">
    <include="**/*java"/>
  </fileset>
</jar>
```

All of these will create a file called `src.jar` containing the Java files from any directory within the current one. The notable feature of jar files is that they have a special directory called `META-INF` containing information about what is in the file. If the `src.jar` file were exampled by running the command `unzip -t src.jar`, the output would be as follows:

```
Archive:  src.jar
    testing: META-INF/                 OK
    testing: META-INF/MANIFEST.MF      OK
    testing: example_dir/              OK
    testing: example_dir/src/          OK
    testing: example_dir/src/package1/   OK
    testing: example_dir/src/package1/autogen/   OK
    testing: example_dir/src/package1/autogen/table1.java   OK
    testing: example_dir/src/package1/autogen/table2.java   OK
    testing: example_dir/src/package1/class1.java   OK
    testing: example_dir/src/package1/class2.java   OK
    testing: example_dir/src/package2/   OK
    testing: example_dir/src/package2/class3.java   OK
```

Notice all the files and directories are present, along with the special `META-INF` directory that the `jar` task has created automatically.

2.8.7 Java

`Java` runs a Java program either within the virtual machine in which Ant is running or externally. The motivation for this task is similar to that for the `Exec` task. Sometimes it may be necessary to run some Java code that would be too difficult to turn into a task.

Attributes:

classname: The name of the class to run. This class must define a `public static void main(String[])` method.

jar: The name of the jar to run. One of `classname` or `jar` must be provided.

fork: Whether to run the program in a separate VM. Defaults to `false`.

Example:

```
<target name="hello">
  <java classname="com.awl.toolbook.chapter02.Hello"/>
</target>
```

will produce

```
hello:
     [java] Hello, world
```

Note that the output is preceded by the task name.

2.8.8 Javac

`Javac` compiles Java files. The set of files to compile comprises a fileset, which may be specified either explicitly with a nested `fileset` element or implicitly by naming a top-level directory and specifying `includes` and `excludes` as attributes.

Note that Ant will not compile every file in the resulting fileset, only those that have been updated since the last time they were compiled. This can occasionally cause confusion when compiling files that reside on a remote server. If the clocks on the server and local machine are out of sync, Ant may generate messages about the source files having been modified in the future, or it may not recognize that files have been modified.

Attributes:

srdir: The top-level source directory. Required.

destdir: The directory into which class files should be written. Defaults to `srcdir`.

includes: The set of files, directories, or patterns to include.

excludes: The set of files, directories, or patterns to exclude.

classpath: The classpath to use for compilation.

classpathref: A reference to a `classpath` defined elsewhere in the file.

Example:

```
<target name="compile">
  <javac srcdir="src"/>
</target>
```

will compile all the Java files in the example used throughout this chapter. Ant will report this as follows:

```
compile:
    [javac] Compiling 5 source files

BUILD SUCCESSFUL
```

Any compilation errors will be reported and will cause the build to fail.

2.8.9 Javadoc

`Javadoc` generates javadoc-style documentation. The javadoc generator contains a huge number of options for how to format and construct documentation. See the documentation for javadoc or Ant for details.

Attributes:

destdir: The directory into which generated documentation should be written.
classpath: The classpath to use to resolve references found in classes.
classpathref: A reference to a `classpath` defined elsewhere in the file.
sourcepath: The path of source files for which documentation should be generated.
sourcepathref: A reference to a `path` element defined elsewhere in the file.
sourcefiles: A list of individual files for which documentation should be generated. One of `sourcepath`, `sourcepathref`, `sourcefiles` or a nested `fileset` must be provided.

Example:

```
<target name="buildDocs">
  <javadoc destdir="docs"
           packagenames="package1,package2"
           sourcepath="src"/>
</target>
```

will generate documentation for all classes in the `package1` and `package2` packages.

2.8.10 A More Complete Example

Listing 2.3 shows a simple but complete build file as might be used for the hypothetical project used in this chapter.

Listing 2.3 A complete build file

```
<project default="compile">
  <target name="buildJar" depends="compile, copy">
    <jar destfile="project.jar"
         basedir="deploy"
         manifest="mainClass"/>
  </target>

  <target name="compile" depends="setup">
    <javac srcdir="src" destdir="deploy"/>
  </target>

  <target name="setup">
    <mkdir dir="deploy"/>
  </target>

  <target name="copy">
    <copy todir="deploy/images">
      <fileset dir="images"/>
    </copy>
  </target>

  <target name="buildDocs">
    <javadoc destdir="docs"
             packagenames="package1,package2"
             sourcepath="src"/>
  </target>
```

Listing 2.3 A complete build file *(continued)*

```
  <target name="clean">
    <delete>
      <fileset dir="deploy"/>
      <fileset dir="src">
        <include name="**/*.class"/>
      </fileset>
    </delete>
  </target>
</project>
```

The ultimate goal of this build file is to prepare a jar file containing the compiled code along with the images that are presumably used or displayed by the program. This process happens in several steps.

The default target is `compile`, because that is what developers spend the most time doing. Here the `javac` task builds class files in a separate directory, `deploy`, which is used to hold all the files that make up the finished program. It would also be possible to copy all the class files after they had been compiled.

Another target called `copy` uses the `copy` task to move the images into the same `deploy` directory.

Once all the files are in place the jar file can be assembled, which is done by the `buildJar` target. Here a `manifest` attribute is used, which names a file to use as the `MANIFEST.MF` in the special `META-INF` directory. The `mainClass` file contains a single line:

```
Main-Class: package1.class1
```

Placing this line in the manifest enables the resulting jar file to be executable—in other words, that user could run `java -jar project.jar` and the `main()` method of the `package1.class1` class would be invoked.

2.9 Creating New Tasks

Many examples in this chapter used the custom `ls` task. A build file can use a custom task by importing it with the `taskdef` element that associates a name for the task with a class, as can be seen in Listing 2.2. Creating a new task is simply a matter of writing this implementation class, which will extend `Task` from the `org.apache.tools.ant` package.

All the potentially difficult aspects of writing a task are managed by either the `Task` base class or Ant itself with the help of some introspection. Task developers can concentrate on making their tasks perform the necessary actions.

The entry point for a task is a method called `execute()`, which takes no arguments, and this is the only method that a task must provide. This method is called by Ant when the task is reached within a target. Listing 2.4 shows the simplest possible task.

Listing 2.4 A simple custom task

```
package com.awl.toolbook.chapter02;

import org.apache.tools.ant.*;

public class DemoTask extends Task {
    public void execute() {
        System.out.println("Hello, ant!");
    }
}
```

This task could be used by a build file in the obvious way

```
<project default="demo">
  <taskdef name="demoTask"
           classname="com.awl.toolbook.chapter02.DemoTask"/>
  <target name="demo">
    <demoTask/>
  </target>
</project>
```

which will produce the expected output when run

```
demo:
 [demoTask] Hello, ant!
```

Options to tasks that may be provided by build files are treated as JavaBean properties. The implementing class needs to provide a `set` method for each option. Ant will take care of invoking this method with provided values, as well as converting from strings to the appropriate types as needed. These features are demonstrated in Listing 2.5, which takes two options, a `message` to display and a `repeatCount` giving the number of times to repeat the message.

Listing 2.5 A custom task with properties

```
package com.awl.toolbook.chapter02;

import org.apache.tools.ant.*;

public class SimpleEchoTask extends Task {
    private int repeatCount = 1;
    public void setRepeatCount(int count) {
        repeatCount = count;
    }

    private String message = null;
    public void setMessage(String message) {
        this.message = message;
    }

    public void execute() throws BuildException {
        if(message == null) {
            throw new BuildException(
                        "Please specify a message");
        }

        for(int i=0;i<repeatCount;i++) {
            System.out.println(i + ".  " + message);
        }
    }
}
```

This could be used from a build file as

```
<simpleEcho message="Hello" repeatCount="8"/>
```

Note that Ant automatically converts the `repeatCount` to an integer. To quote the Ant manual: "It's really this simple!"

Listing 2.5 introduces another new feature, the `BuildException`. Tasks may throw this exception when they have not been given necessary configuration information as is done here or because they were unable to complete for any external reason. In either case, the build will immediately terminate with a "build failed" message that will include the text used to construct the `BuildException`.

Handling filesets is only slightly more difficult than handling primitive values. Instead of providing a `set` method, the task class provides an `addFileset()` method, which takes as an argument a `FileSet` from the `org.apache.tools.ant.types` package. This `addFilset()` method will be called once for each fileset constructed from the set in the build file. The task should hold on to each `FileSet` until the `execute()` method is called.

Within the `execute()` method sets of files are obtained from each `FileSet` through use of a `DirectoryScanner`. The `DirectoryScanner` will look through a directory or set of directories and select files based on the given `include`, `exclude`, `contains`, and other selection elements, and can return an array of matching file names. Task developers do not need to worry about the details of how this filtering happens. Ant takes care of all that within the `DirectoryScanner`.

This is sufficient information to write the `ls` task that has been used in this chapter, and it is shown in Listing 2.6.

Listing 2.6 The directory listing task

```
package com.awl.toolbook.chapter02;

import org.apache.tools.ant.*;
import org.apache.tools.ant.types.FileSet;
import org.apache.tools.ant.util.FileUtils;
import java.util.Vector;
import java.io.File;

public class LsTask extends Task {
    private boolean showSize = false;
    public boolean getShowSize() {return showSize;}
    public void setShowSize(boolean showSize) {
        this.showSize = showSize;
    }

    private Vector fileSets  = new Vector();
    private FileUtils fileUtils;

    public void addFileset(FileSet set) {
        fileSets.addElement(set);
    }
```

Listing 2.6 The directory listing task *(continued)*

```
    public void execute() throws BuildException {
        if(fileSets.size() == 0) {
            throw
                new BuildException(
                "Please specify at least one fileset.");
        }

        for(int i=0;i<fileSets.size();i++) {
            FileSet fileset =
                (FileSet) fileSets.elementAt(i);
            DirectoryScanner scanner =
                fileset.getDirectoryScanner(project);

            File baseDir = fileset.getDir(project);

            // Handle the files in this fileset
            String files[] = scanner.getIncludedFiles();
            for(int j=0;j<files.length;j++) {
                handleFile(baseDir,files[j]);
            }
        }
    }

    private void handleFile(File baseDir,String f) {
        File file = new File(baseDir,f);

        if(showSize) {
            System.out.println(f +
                               "(" + f.length() +
                               " bytes)");
        } else {
            System.out.println(f);
        }
    }
}
```

As explained, the `addFileset()` method simply stores the provided `FileSet` in a `Vector` for later use by `execute()`. `execute()` traverses this vector and for each element obtains a set of files through a `DirectoryScanner`. Each `DirectoryScanner` needs to know what project it is a part of to obtain certain global information. This is accomplished by passing the `project` variable, which is defined in the base `Task` class.

2.10 Beyond This Book

Ant has several dozen tasks, available either built in or as part of a standard package of supplementary tasks. Some of these are used in later chapters of this book when discussing how to integrate Ant with other tools. It is worth the time to read over the list of tasks that comes with the Ant documentation. Many may turn out to be useful in ways that could surprise you.

As comprehensive as the set of tasks is, most large projects will end up requiring one or two custom tasks. The information in this chapter should help you create just about any needed custom task. The Ant documentation contains information on a number of classes that custom tasks can use. In addition to `FileSets`, there are also related classes called `FileList` and `DirList` that may be useful on occasion. Ant also provides a number of base classes in addition to `Task` that are meant to be extended. These contain additional functionality that may simplify the development of certain kinds of tasks, such as those that deal with archives.

Of course, because Ant is open source, all the code for all the built-in tasks are readily available. If an existing task has some useful functionality, don't hesitate to import the code into a new task.

2.11 Summary

Tool: Ant
Purpose: Simplifies build processes
Version covered: 1.6.1
Home page: http://ant.apache.org/
License: The Apache Software License
Further Reading: *Ant: The Definitive Guide*, by Jesse E. Tilly and Eric M. Burke, O'Reilly, 2002.

CHAPTER 3

Eclipse

It is certainly possible to write Java programs using nothing more than the JDK and "vi" on Unix or "notepad" on Windows, but doing so is a rather arduous process. While most readers are likely familiar with the development process, it is worth listing the steps in some detail to discover where the inefficiencies lie. To that end, consider a typical development session using only an editor and the JDK:

1. Code is written in the editor.
2. The editor is suspended, or focus moved to another window, and javac is run.
3. Numerous errors will likely be produced, such as syntactic errors like missing semicolons or braces, semantic errors like incorrect types, and missing or mistyped classes and methods.
4. The editor is resumed, and one by one a sequence of keystrokes is used to access the troublesome lines as reported by javac.
5. The syntax errors are relatively easily fixed, although it is easy to lose one's place in an undifferentiated mass of white-on-black text.
6. The semantic errors are more difficult. Often the editor needs to be suspended or exited to look up some Javadoc information. Navigating this information may itself be time consuming, requiring many clicks in a browser to get to the right point.
7. Repeat steps 1–6 until the code compiles cleanly. This may take a while.

8. Finally, the program is run. In practice the best possible outcome of a first run is often a runtime exception. At least the exception reports a specific line number to examine. Return to step 4.
9. Once the program runs cleanly, it may still produce incorrect answers. The developer then has two options: start adding `println()` statements throughout the code to track intermediate state or fire up jdb, the Java debugger included with the JDK. Neither option is particularly attractive.

It is possible to simplify some of these steps just by using a more sophisticated editor. Many editors color-code Java syntax, automatically assist in formatting, and make it easier to navigate around and between source files. Even with a better editor, the fundamental problems remain. Most of these problems reduce to a single issue: that five different programs are used (the editor, compiler, javadoc browser, debugger, and the program being constructed) at different steps of the process. Because each of these programs is run independently, there is no way that one program can inform or simplify the process of using the others. For example, if the compiler and the editor were aware of each other, the compiler could notify the editor of the line numbers at which errors occurred, and the editor could position itself at the right place automatically.

The recognition that using five programs to accomplish one task is essentially inefficient has lead to the development of **Integrated Development Environments,** or IDEs. IDEs can trace their roots all the way back to the Symbolics Lisp Machines of the early 1980s. The concept became more widespread with programs like Borland's "Turbo Pascal" and more recently Microsoft's suite of development tools such as "Visual Basic," "Visual C++," and so on.

Throughout this history IDEs have had to walk a fine line. If an IDE is too bloated or slow, it may be more painful to use than simple command line tools. If an IDE tries to do too much, it may require users to adopt a development methodology with which they are not comfortable or happy. If an IDE is too simple, lightweight, or general, it may provide no significant benefit over simpler tools.

One approach to this problem is to design the IDE as a framework or platform into which new functionality can be imported. This approach works very well for IDEs that are themselves written in Java, since new functionality can be implemented as classes that are loaded dynamically. By implementing certain interfaces these class can fit seamlessly into the IDE and interact with other components already present. For example, a component that checks source code for syntax can integrate with the component that allows the user to edit files. Every time a new character is entered the syntax component can ensure that the file is still valid.

There are many IDEs and IDE platforms for Java, and many of these are free and open source. These include NetBeans (http://www.netbeans.org) and JDEE, which runs within the Emacs editor (http://jdee.sunsite.dk). The purpose of this chapter is not to recommend any of these over any other. Every developer has different tastes and requirements and may find one better suited for his or her use than the others. For example, NetBeans is written in 100 percent pure Java, and JDEE works with Emacs.

What this chapter will do is present Eclipse, a very powerful IDE from IBM that is justifiably getting a lot of attention. Most of Eclipse is written in Java, which makes it easy to add new components and functionality. However, the front end does not use Java's AWT (Abstract Windowing Toolkit) or Swing classes, but rather a toolkit called SWT (Standard Widget Toolkit), which is written in a combination of Java and C. The portions written in C makes the system very fast and responsive, but at the loss of Java's "write once, run anywhere" power. However, the full Eclipse system is available for most common operating systems, including Windows, Linux, Solaris, and OS X.[1] Note that because each version uses native graphics Eclipse will appear slightly differently on each platform. The screenshots in this chapter come from the Linux/GTK version, which should nearly match the appearance on any Unix variant. Other platforms will all have the same controls and abilities but will differ slightly in details.

3.1 Getting Started with Eclipse

To see Eclipse in action it will be used to create a very simple program that computes the factorial of a number provided as an argument.[2]

The first time Eclipse is run the user will be presented with the screen in Figure 3.1.

From this welcome screen a user can explore eclipse through the provided overview, tutorials, and samples, and new users should definitely take the time to do this. Eclipse proper is accessed through the Workbench icon, which brings up the screen shown in Figure 3.2.

The **workbench,** the main Eclipse window, is divided into a number of **views.** Each view acts as a miniature window, with its own title at the upper left and close box at the upper right. Views can also be moved and resized within the workspace. The collection of views active at a given time along with associated menu items constitutes a perspective. The full set of tools available, designed for working with a particular class of language and project, is called the workspace.

---

[1]Note for FreeBSD users: Eclipse 2.1.3 is in the ports collection, and 3.0.0 should follow shortly. In the meantime both the Linux/motif and Linux/GTK versions of Eclipse can be run on FreeBSD by installing the appropriate Linux Libraries and a Linux version of the JDK. More complete instructions appear on the CD-ROM.

[2]The factorial of a number is the product of all numbers between one and that number. The factorial of four is $4 * 3 * 2 * 1 = 24$.

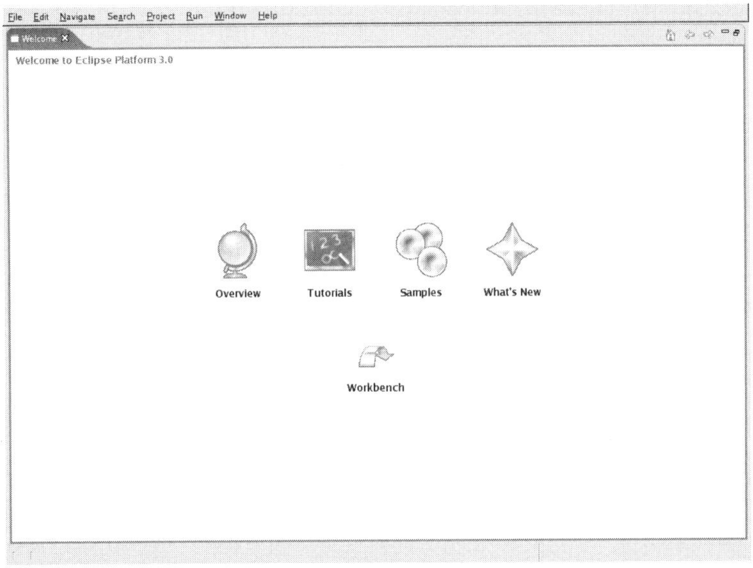

Figure 3.1. The Eclipse startup screen.

Eclipse groups code and related resources together into projects, much the same way that Ant groups all the tasks necessary to build a target into a project. Eclipse maintains information about projects in special files, allowing users to switch between them effortlessly. It is also easy to create a new project, which is the first step to using

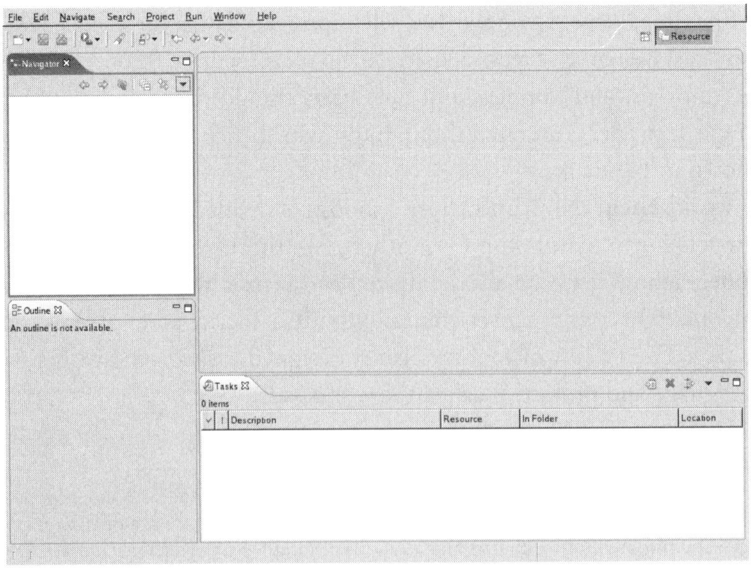

Figure 3.2. The Eclipse startup screen.

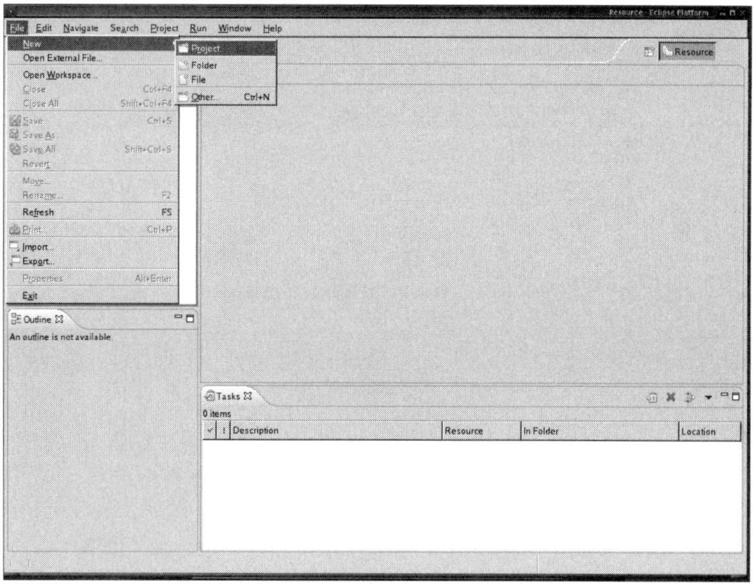

Figure 3.3. The project creation menu.

Eclipse. This is accomplished through the "new" option of the "file" menu, as shown in Figure 3.3.

From the initial perspective it is also possible to create a new folder or file. Eclipse has the ability to associate editors with file types, so when creating a Word file on Windows, Word will come up embedded within Eclipse. This is another example of how Eclipse functions as an IDE platform—by allowing it to serve as the integration point for numerous applications, not just those bundled with Eclipse initially.[3]

Selecting the "Project" option brings up the Project creation wizard, as shown in Figure 3.4.

On the left side of this wizard are three options. The "Java" option is the one of immediate interest. Clicking it brings up the Java project template on the right. Clicking "next" at the bottom continues the project creation process with the dialog shown in Figure 3.5.

This screen allows the project to be named; here the name "factorial" has been filled in. It is possible to define various types of Java projects, each of which will start with a different set of contents. As no new project templates have been defined, the only available option is "default," which will serve most projects quite well.

---

[3]Some users may prefer to use Eclipse to manage resources such as Word documents, but use an editor outside Eclipse to edit them. Eclipse allows this style of usage as well.

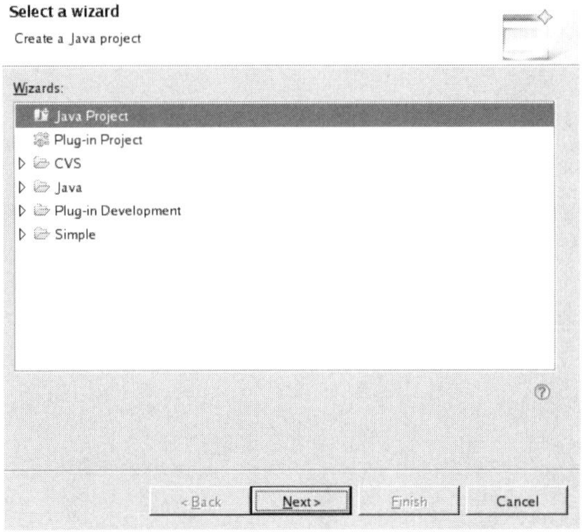

Figure 3.4. The project creation wizard.

From here the "next" button would allow certain default values to be overridden and additional options specified. For the sample project the defaults are fine, so the "finish" button will be used to create the project and start working with it.

Eclipse associates Java projects with a Java perspective, a set of views with information relevant to Java development. On initially creating a project Eclipse will ask

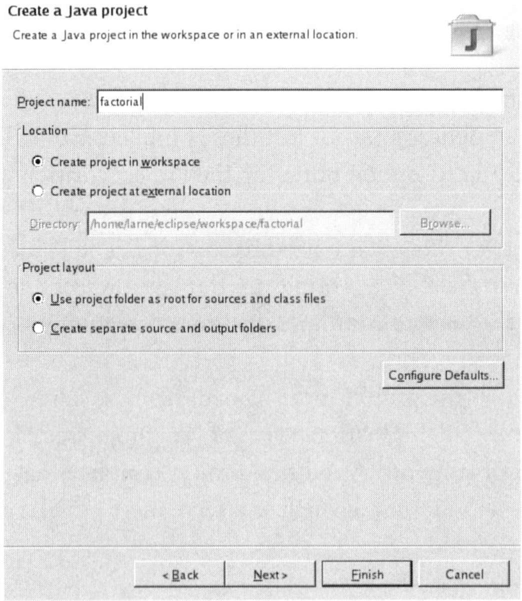

Figure 3.5. The project creation wizard, part 2.

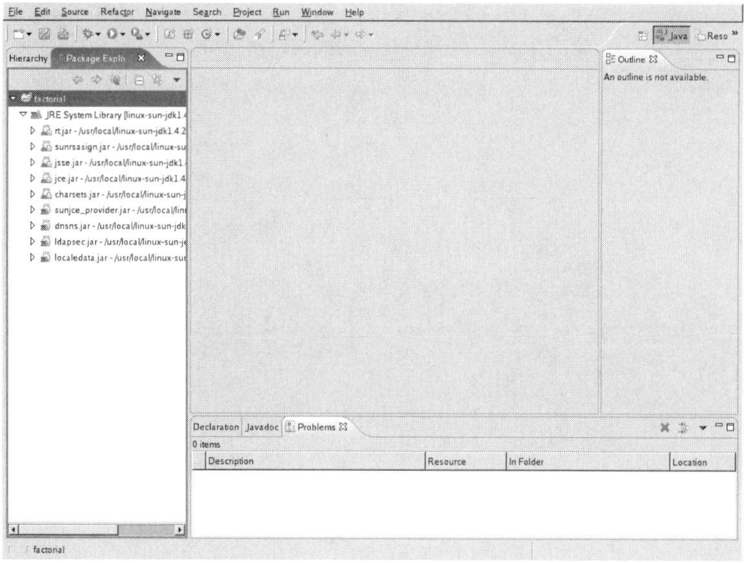

Figure 3.6. The Java perspective.

whether it should switch to the Java perspective. Clicking on the "yes" button will return the user to the workbench, shown in Figure 3.6.

On the left is the Package Explorer, which allows a developer to browse through all the classes available to the current project. By default Eclipse imports the standard Java run time consisting of the core classes in rt.jar, the internationalization classes in i18n.jar, and various cryptography classes in sunrsasign.jar. It is possible to navigate through these jars, packages, and classes in the standard way for such a tree view. An arrow can be clicked to expand an item or clicked again to recollapse a list back into a single line. For example, it is possible to open rt.jar, then the java.util package, and finally the `Vector` class to get the view presented in Figure 3.7.

Double-clicking a class or method will bring up the source code in the editor view, which appears in the center of the Java perspective.[4]

It is a relatively little known fact that the portion of the standard run time that is written in Java is included in source form with the JDK—in an archive called src.jar. This is where Eclipse gets the source when a class is double-clicked. If a method is clicked, the editor view will go directly to the definition of that method.

It is more likely a developer will wish to start off the new project with a new class rather than edit a core Java class. This can be accomplished from the file menu,

[4]Source editing is not available when using a JRE (Java Runtime Environment). A full JDK (Java Development Kit) is required for this feature.

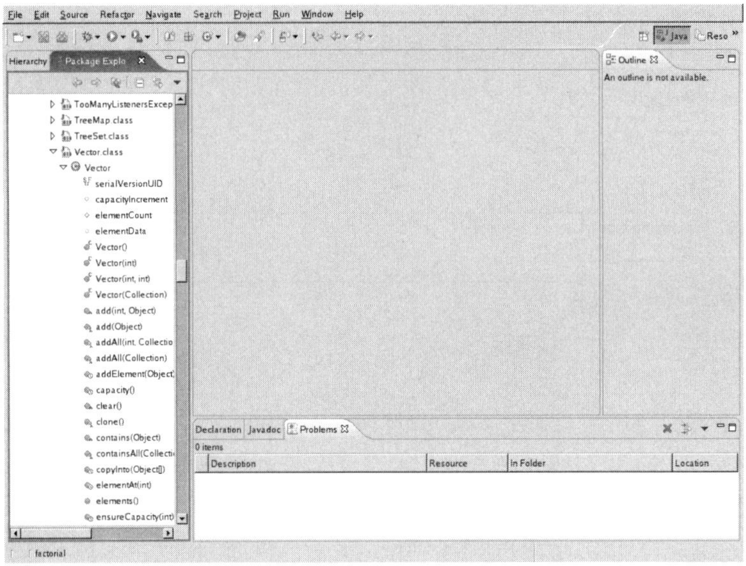

Figure 3.7. Using the Package Explorer.

which now lists additional options as part of the Java perspective. This is shown in Figure 3.8.

The most notable new feature is the ability to create a new class or interface, in addition to being able to create a new project or general file. In one sense a class or

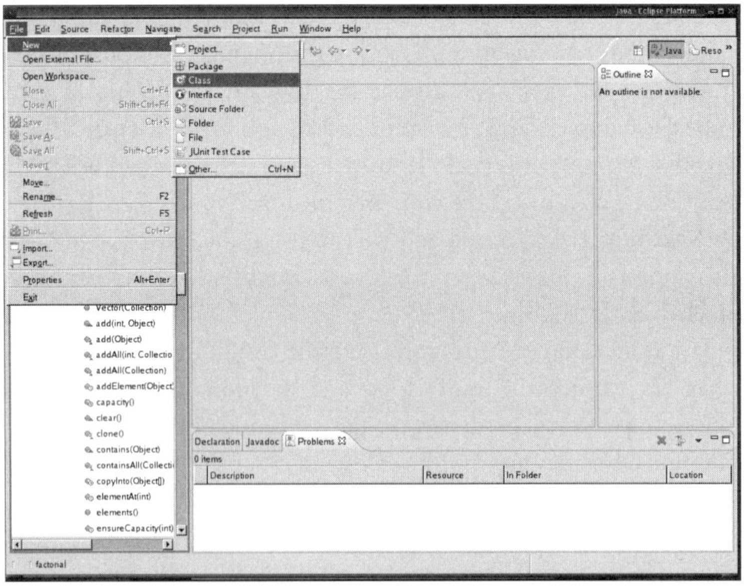

Figure 3.8. The expanded file menu.

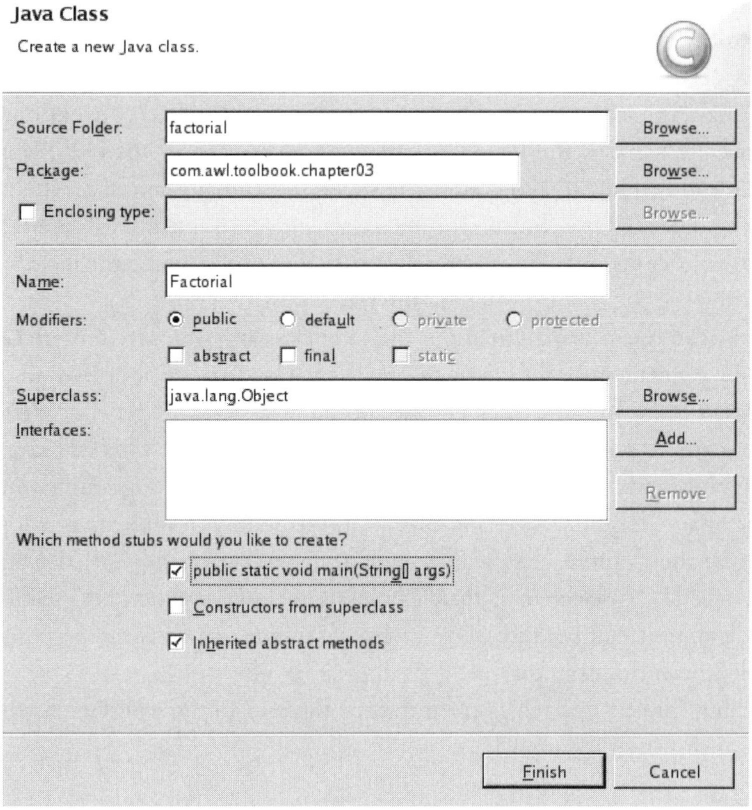

Figure 3.9. The class creation wizard.

interface is just a file, but from a developer's perspective a class's role as Java code is far more important than its role as data on a disk, and so Eclipse treats classes specially. This special treatment can be seen in the class creation dialog, which comes up when a new class is created; it is shown in Figure 3.9.

This wizard allows many aspects of the class to be specified before the class is edited, which in turn will allow Eclipse to automatically generate a lot of the skeletal parts of a class that typically must be written by hand before the real work can begin. At the top of the class creation wizard is an option that allows the user to specify the folder where the class file will be created. By default this is set to the folder for the project, which here is "factorial."

Below that is a box where the package can be specified. Clicking on "Browse" would bring up another dialog like the Package Explorer, which would allow the developer to review existing packages. In this case the package does not yet exist, so the name is manually entered in the text box.

Below the package option is a section where attributes of the class can be specified. The first of these is the name, which has been filled out with "Factorial." There is nothing special about this name to either Java or Eclipse. The entry point to a program need not have the same name as the project, but it is a standard convention.

Below the name is the set of modifiers to be applied to the class, along with boxes that can be filled out to specify the superclass and any interfaces the class will implement. The "Browse" button for superclass and "Add" button for interfaces both bring up explorer dialogs, eliminating the possibility of mistyping the name of a class or forgetting the package in which an interface lives.

Eclipse can use information about the superclass and supported interfaces to automatically generate stubs for methods, and the option to do so appears at the bottom of the class wizard. In most cases Eclipse should be allowed to generate stubs for all interface methods and any abstract methods in the superclass. This will save a lot of tedious typing, and it will also eliminate the possibility of the programmer mistyping the name of a method or forgetting that an implementation must be provided.

Because the factorial class will be run from the command line, the button to generate `main()` is selected. Eclipse can also provide constructors as indicated by the middle option, but because `Object` has no interesting constructors, this option is not relevant in this example.

Clicking "finish" from this screen returns the user to the workbench with some changes, as shown in Figure 3.10.

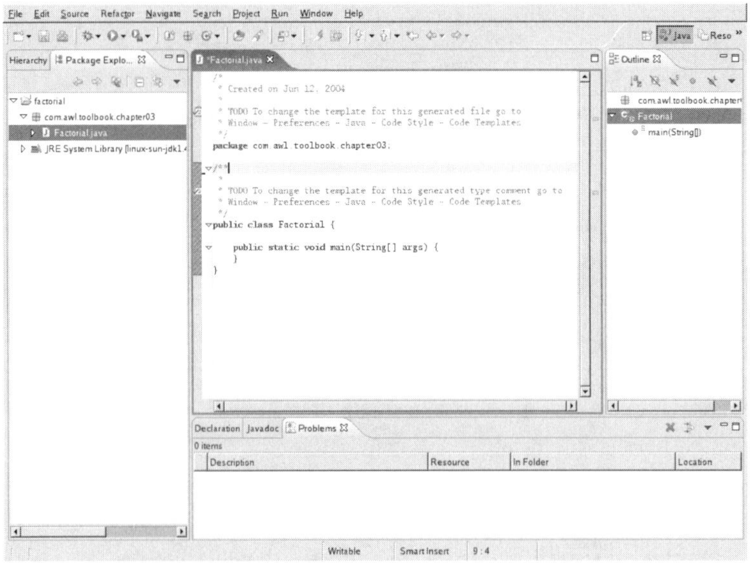

Figure 3.10. The workbench, ready to work on a class.

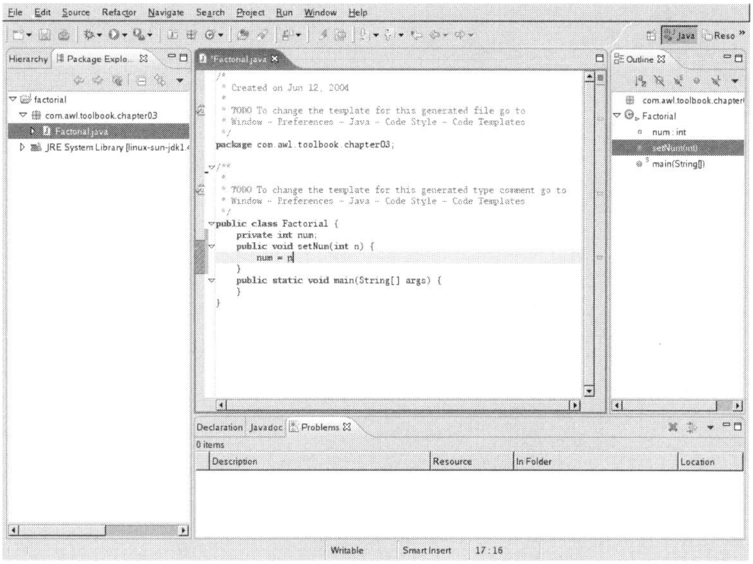

Figure 3.11. Eclipse warning of a syntactic error.

Notice that all of the class infrastructure has been created, saving the developer from a bit of tedious typing and ready to get on with exciting job of programming. The package explorer has also changed, positioning itself at the new class. Likewise the "outline" view, which has thus far been empty, now shows a high-level overview of the class being edited. Clicking on a method name in this view would take the editor directly to that method. When editing multiple files all will be shown in the "outline" view, and it is possible to simultaneously switch files and go to a specific point in that file by clicking on a method.

The javadoc that gets inserted at the top of each new class is completely configurable. Most companies will have standards as to what this should contain.

Eclipse really comes into its own in the next step once the developer is ready to start creating source code. In Figure 3.11 some code has been added to the `Factorial` class.[5]

Something is syntactically wrong with what has been written so far, and Eclipse flags this with a small box immediately to the right of the editor view. To obtain more information about the error, the developer need only place the mouse pointer over this box, and a pop-up will be displayed with more information, as shown in Figure 3.12.

[5]It should be pointed out that the use of an instance variable and set method is not the way such a simple mathematical function would ever be written in practice; any real-world factorial method would take the number as an argument. However, the purpose of this chapter is to illustrate the features of Eclipse, and some of these can be better demonstrated by use of this slightly artificial construct.

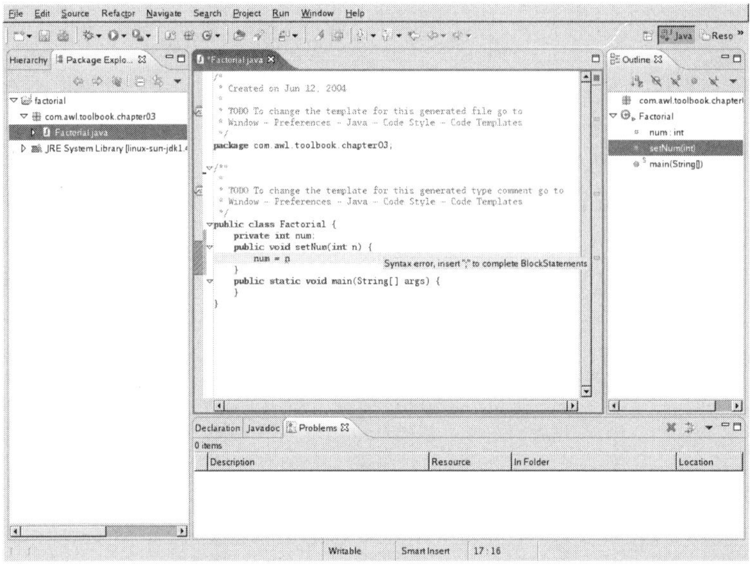

Figure 3.12. More detail about the error.

This can be a tremendous time saver. Instead of waiting for the compiler to find such errors, Eclipse can find them as they happen, and the developer can fix them immediately. This can completely eliminate several compile-edit cycles. Eclipse can also find semantic errors, as shown in Figure 3.13.

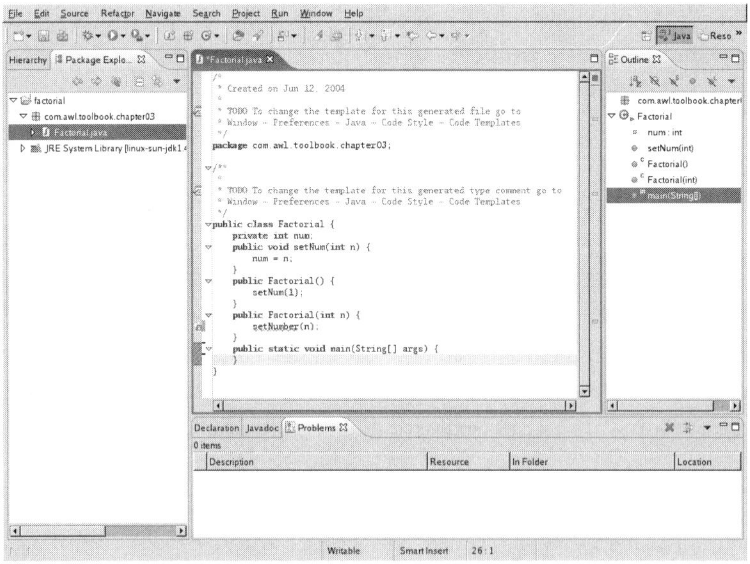

Figure 3.13. Eclipse warning of semantic error.

The error is indicated by a small circle with an X that appears on the left of the editor view. As with syntactic errors more detail can be obtained by placing the mouse pointer over the error icon, as shown in Figure 3.14.

Eclipse has correctly identified that the code references an unknown method. Unlike the syntactic error Eclipse can do more than just flag the error—it can even help the developer to fix it. Clicking on the error icon raises two pop-up messages, as shown in Figure 3.15.

Eclipse presents two ways to resolve this error: either create the `setNumber()` method as used or change it to `setNum()`. If there were multiple possible matches, Eclipse would present them all, and they could be navigated by the mouse or arrow keys. The second pop-up message to the left gives a little more information about what the currently selected option would do. As a further convenience, Eclipse will mark the default option with a green arrow. This can be selected by simply hitting the Enter key.

Incidentally, this whole problem could have been avoided by allowing Eclipse to generate the accessors automatically, which can be done via an option under the "source" menu. When selected, Eclipse will show all the currently defined private variables and allow the developer to specify the ones for which accessors should be built. Eclipse will even add javadoc stubs for each generated method.

There are many others kinds of error that Eclipse can catch and help fix as the code is being written. Rather than list them here, the best way to discover them is

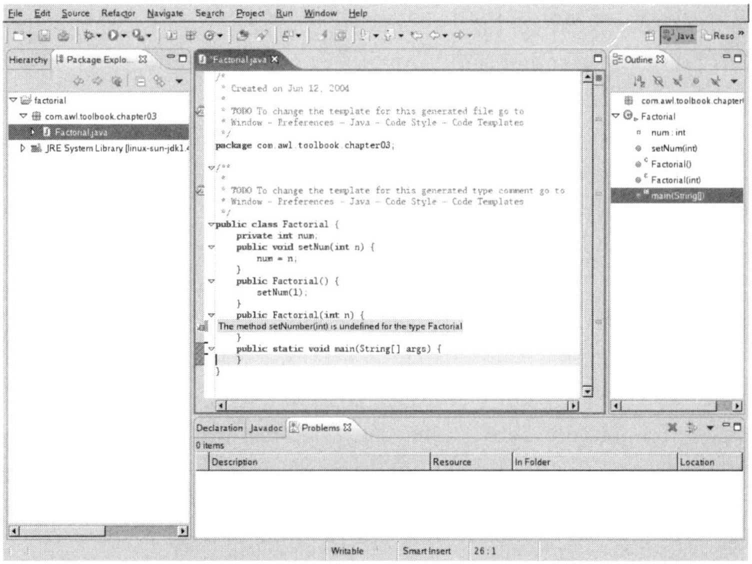

Figure 3.14. More information on the error.

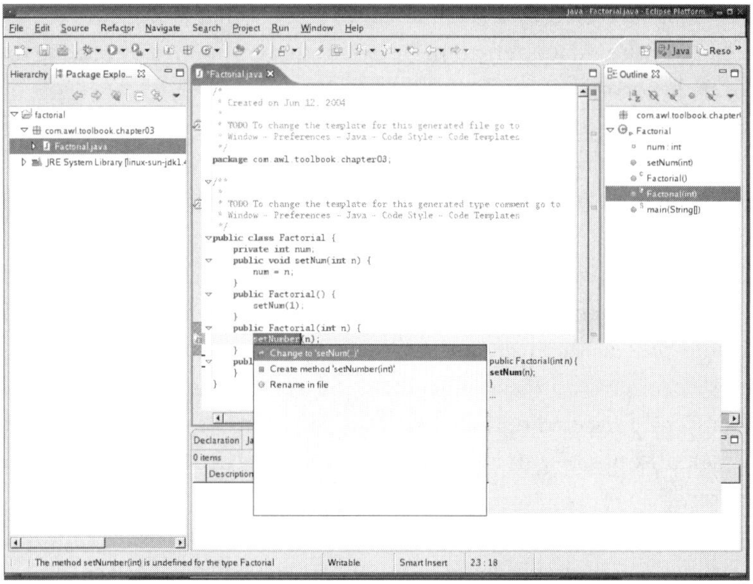

Figure 3.15. Options for fixing the error.

to use Eclipse for a while. It is often surprising just how good Eclipse is at catching things that might otherwise fester in code until it is compiled.

Eclipse's knowledge of every available class, method, and signature is useful in many ways besides allowing edit-time error detection. Eclipse can recognize when the first part of the name of a class or method has been typed and offer possible completions. This is illustrated in Figure 3.16.

At this point more code has been written and development has moved to the `main()` method. The first thing that needs to be done here is to process the arguments by converting the first argument to an integer. Perhaps the developer remembers that there is a static method in the `Integer` class that does this but does not remember what it is called. By typing "Integer" and pressing the space bar while holding down the "control" key, Eclipse will pop up the two views shown in Figure 3.17.[6]

The view on the right lists all the fields and methods in the Integer class, which can be navigated in the usual way. The view on the left shows the Javadoc for the currently selected item. No more switching to a browser to find a method or get the details. It can all be done within Eclipse.

The more Eclipse knows about what the developer wants, the more it can narrow the range of options. By adding a "p" after the dot, Eclipse will show only the methods in `Integer` that start with a p, as shown in Figure 3.17.

---

[6]Often pausing after typing the period will have the same effect.

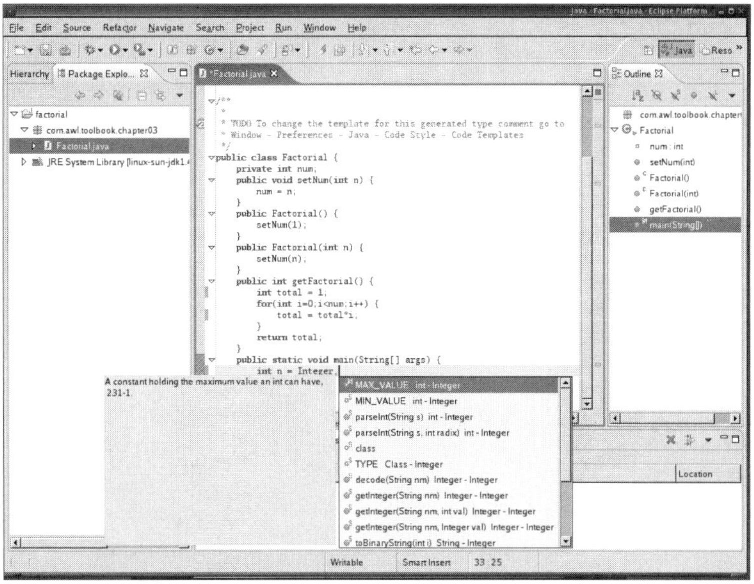

Figure 3.16. Name completion.

It is worth noting that Eclipse can provide the same functionality to local variables. If the program had defined an `Integer` named `theInt`, then as soon as "theInt" had been typed, Eclipse would provide the same options as shown in Figure 3.15.

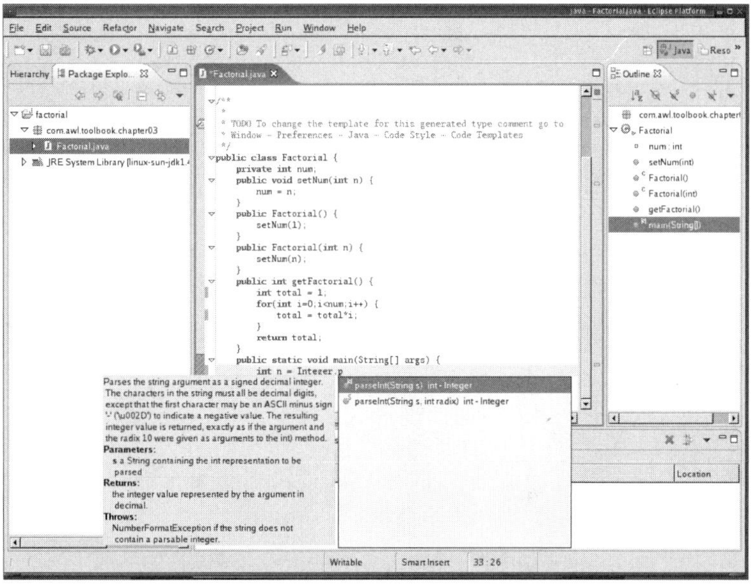

Figure 3.17. A restricted name completion.

With this last bit of help from Eclipse, the program is now completed. It is shown in Listing 3.1.

Listing 3.1 The factorial program

```
/*
 * Created on Jun 23, 2003
 *
 * To change the template for this generated file go to
 * Window>Preferences>Java>Code Generation>Code and
 * Comments
 */
package com.awl.toolbook.chapter03;

/**
 *
 * To change the template for this generated type comment
 * go to Window>Preferences>Java>Code Generation>Code and
 * Comments
 */
public class Factorial {
    private int num;
    public void setNum(int n) {
        num = n;
    }
    public Factorial() {
        setNum(1);
    }
    public Factorial(int n) {
        setNum(n);
    }
    public int getFactorial() {
        int total = 1;
        for(int i=0;i<num;i++) {
            total = total * i;
        }
        return total;
    }
    public static void main(String[] args) {
        int n = Integer.parseInt(args[0]);
```

```
            Factorial f = new Factorial(n);
            System.out.println(f.getFactorial());
        }
    }
```

The program is now ready to be compiled and tested, both of which can be done within Eclipse by selecting the "Run" option from the Run menu, as shown in Figure 3.18.

Running a program from Eclipse brings up a dialog that allows the user to configure how the program will be run. This dialog is shown in Figure 3.19.

Eclipse knows how to run several types of program, as illustrated by the frame on the left of Figure 3.19. Of interest at the moment is the ability to run stand-alone Java applications. When the "application" option is selected, it expands into a list of all classes with `main()` methods currently loaded in Eclipse. At the moment this means only the `Factorial` class.

Once this class has been selected the frame on the right presents numerous options. The "main" tab on the right specifies the project and class to run; these are both automatically populated with default values. Other tabs allow the user to specify which Java run time should be used, which can be useful for testing a program against multiple versions or implementations of Java. Another tab allows the classpath to be set if it is different from the one used to compile the program, and so on. For the

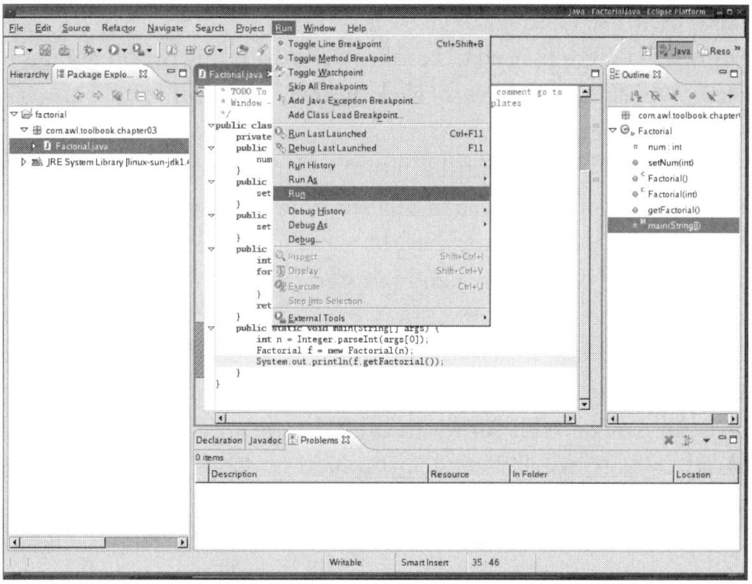

Figure 3.18. The Run menu.

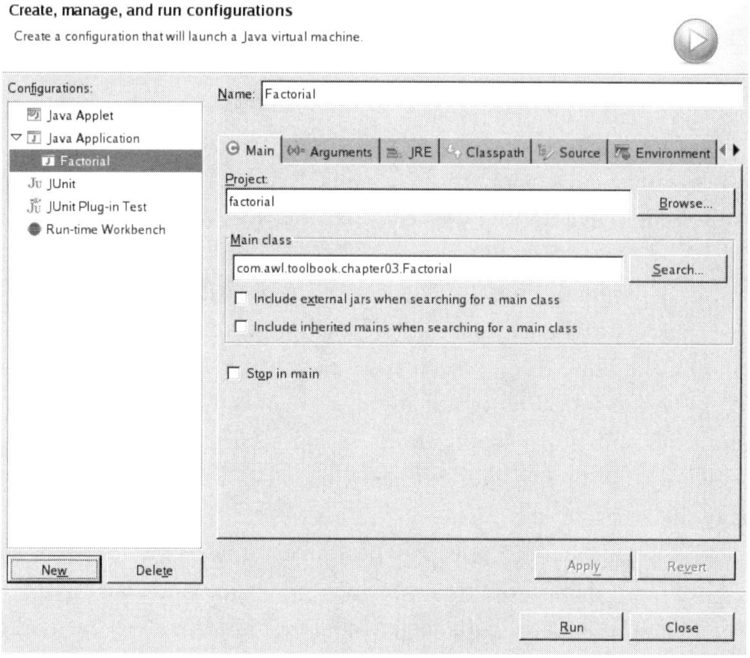

Figure 3.19. The run dialog.

purpose of this demo the default values for all these options can be used, and there is no need to use these tabs.

The only step that does need to be taken before running the program is to supply an argument, which can be done by clicking the "argument" tab. This changes the dialog as shown in Figure 3.20.

A value of 10 has been provided as a runtime argument. VM arguments are such things as the amount of heap space to allocate, none of which need to be specified for this demo program. Once the values have been provided, clicking "Run" at the bottom of the dialog will run the program and return the user to the Eclipse workbench, as shown in Figure 3.21.

Note that the task view at the bottom of the screen has been replaced by the output of the program. There is a problem with this output: The factorial of 10 should certainly not be zero! Although the program compiled cleanly and runs, it clearly has a bug. Fortunately Eclipse incorporates a debugger that can help find it.

To use this debugger, first a breakpoint is placed in the program by double-clicking the appropriate line of source code in the editor. A breakpoint is just what it sounds like: a point in the program where execution will halt when debugged. Since it seems likely that the problem is somewhere in the `getFactorial()` method,

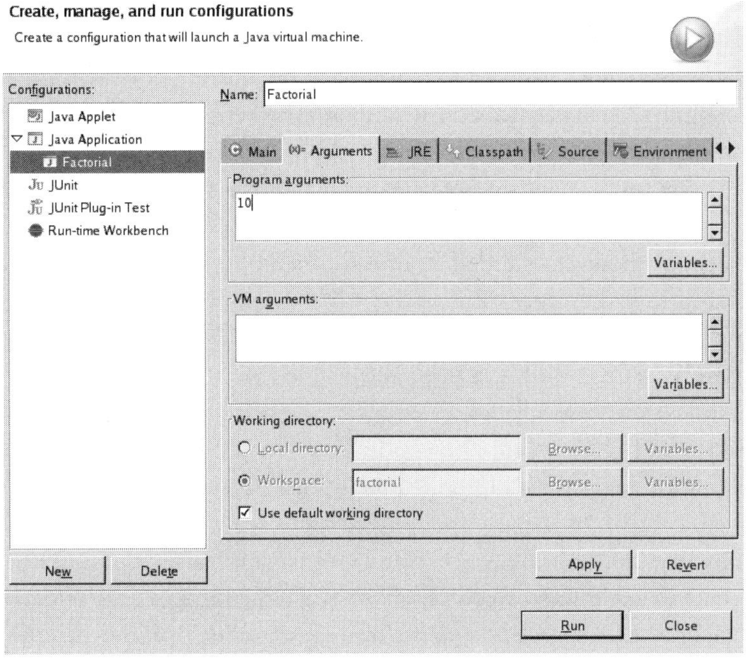

Figure 3.20. Providing runtime arguments.

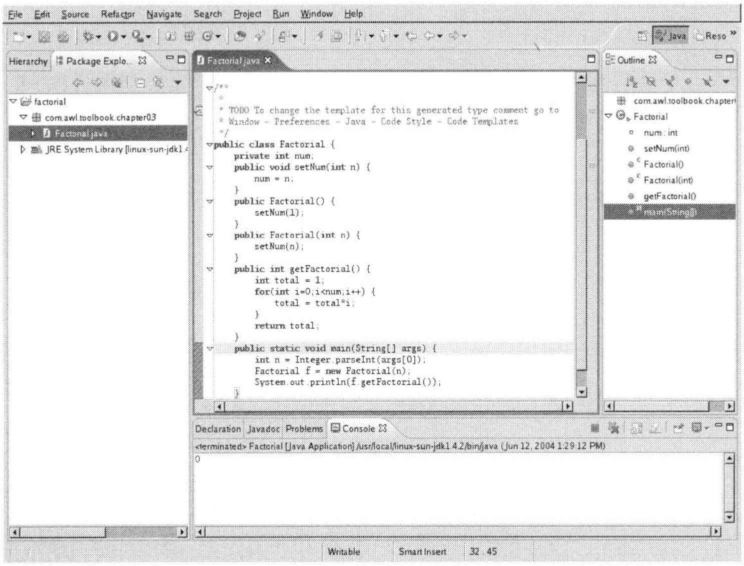

Figure 3.21. The workbench after running the program.

the breakpoint will be set right at the entry point of that method. The breakpoint is indicated by a small dot to the left of relevant line, as shown in Figure 3.22.

Next the debugger is invoked by returning to the Run menu shown in Figure 3.18 and selecting the "debug last launched" option. This starts the program and switches Eclipse to the debugger perspective, shown in Figure 3.23.

The editor, outline, and console views remain in this perspective, although they have been moved and rearranged. They are joined by two new views. The view labeled "debug" shows the state of all threads, including a call stack. In Figure 3.23 this indicates that the program is in `Factorial.getFactorial()` at line 26 and that `getFactorial()` was called from `Factorial.main()` at line 35. The cursor in the editor view is also placed in `getFactorial()` at line 26.

The other new view is labeled "variables," and it appears at the upper right of the workbench. The view shows the values of all variables currently in scope. Since the breakpoint is set at the entry point, `total` has not yet been defined.

Along the top of the "debug" frame are several icons with arrows, which represent the actions that can be taken once a program has hit a breakpoint. The first two both execute a single line of code but differ in how they treat that line if it is a method invocation. The first button performs a "step over," which treats the method invocation as a single operation. The second performs a "step into" that will take the debugger into the method, the editor view will switch to that method if source code is available, and the developer can proceed to examine that method's code in a similar step-by-step fashion.

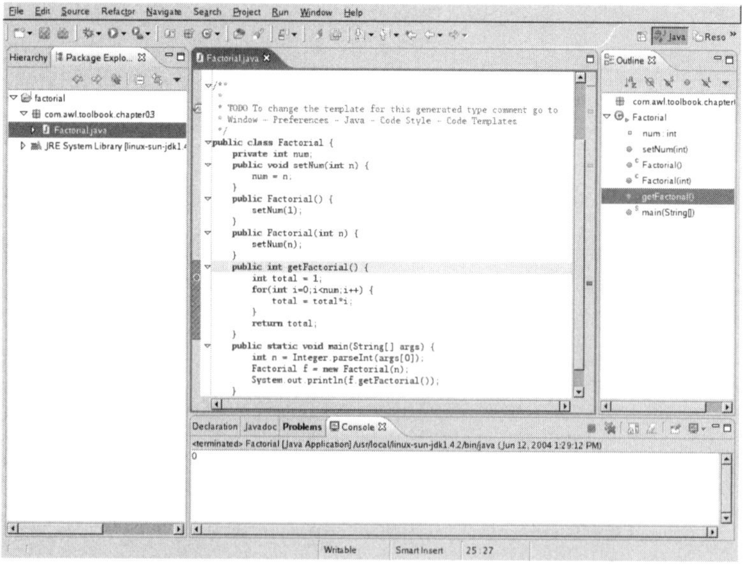

Figure 3.22. The editor view with a breakpoint set.

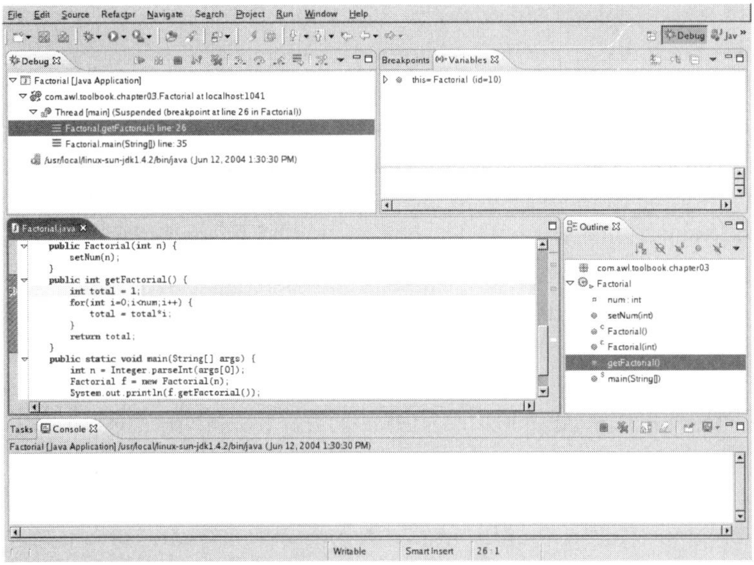

Figure 3.23. The debugger perspective.

Everything is now ready to find and exterminate the bug by examining exactly what `getFactorial()` is doing. When the single-step button is clicked, the program executes line 27 and the "debug" view changes to reflect this. Line 27 defines the `total` variable, and the "variable" view also changes accordingly, as shown in Figure 3.24. Figure 3.24 also shows an expanded view of `this` that illustrates another

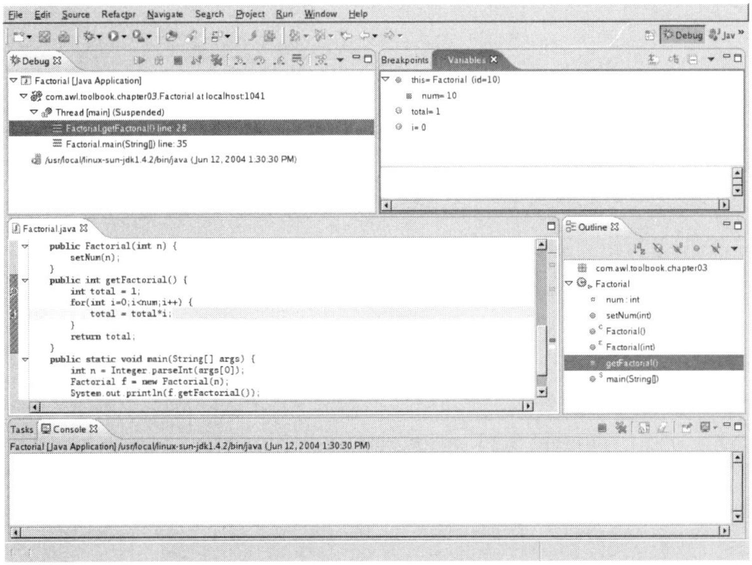

Figure 3.24. After executing a statement.

ability of Eclipse. Objects and arrays can be navigated in the "variable" view, making it possible to examine entire hierarchies of data effortlessly.

When the "step into" button is clicked again execution moves to the `for` loop. This also defines the variable `i`, which shows up in the "variable" view as expected with an initial value of 0. Clicking "step into" one more time executes the assignment to `total`, leading to the display in Figure 3.25.

Although it may not be clear in Figure 3.25, when a variable changes value, Eclipse changes the color in the "variable" view to alert the developer to the change. In this case, it draws attention to the fact that `total` is now zero. The bug has been found! By starting the loop at zero the program multiplies `total` by zero in the first iteration. Subsequently, since zero times any number is zero, the value remains unchanged. This fix is simple: run from 1 to `num` instead of from 0 to `num-1`.

This change can be made in the editor even while in the debugger perspective, and the program can be rerun from the Run menu one more time, leading to the triumphant screen in Figure 3.26.

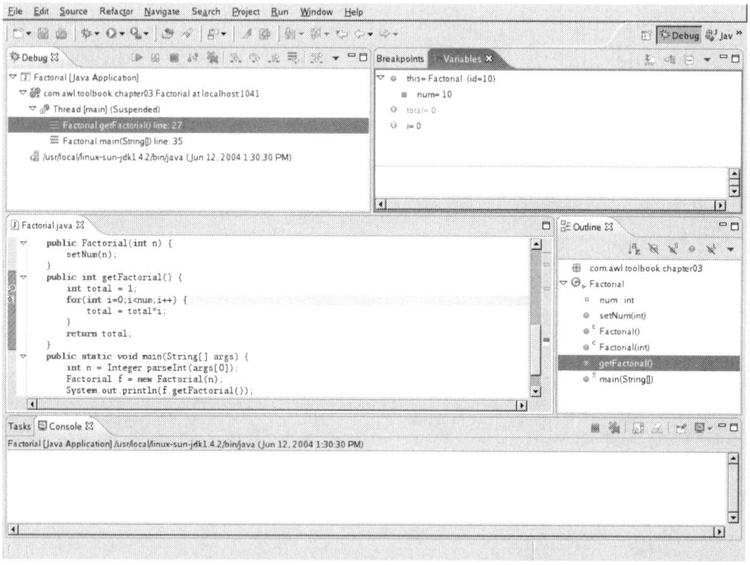

Figure 3.25. After executing the assignment.

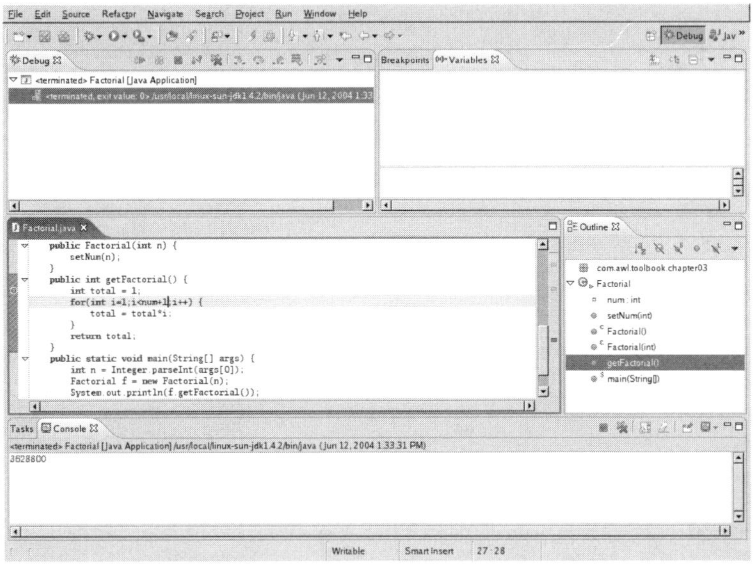

Figure 3.26. Success!.

3.2 Using Ant with Eclipse

By default when "Run" or "Debug" are selected from the Run menu, Eclipse will compile all files that have changed before starting the program. Often, this is a sufficient build process during the edit/compile/debug cycle. When a more complex build is needed, either preceding a release or as part of a standard test build, Eclipse can call out to Ant to do the build. All the other capabilities remain in place, so during a debugging session Eclipse can call Ant to do the build and then stop at the appropriate breakpoint and continue as normal.

To use Ant, select the "External Tools" option from the Run menu shown in Figure 3.18. This will bring up the dialog shown in Figure 3.27.

This dialog allows the developer to select a build file—here the sample build file from Listing 2.1 has been specified. Once Eclipse has been told about an Ant build file, it can determine the set of targets provided by the build file and offer the developer the option of which ones to run. This information is accessible from the "targets" tab shown in Figure 3.27, which brings up the screen shown in Figure 3.28.

Once the set of targets has been selected, the "External tools" menu will have a submenu with the name of this build profile; selecting that item will run the build.

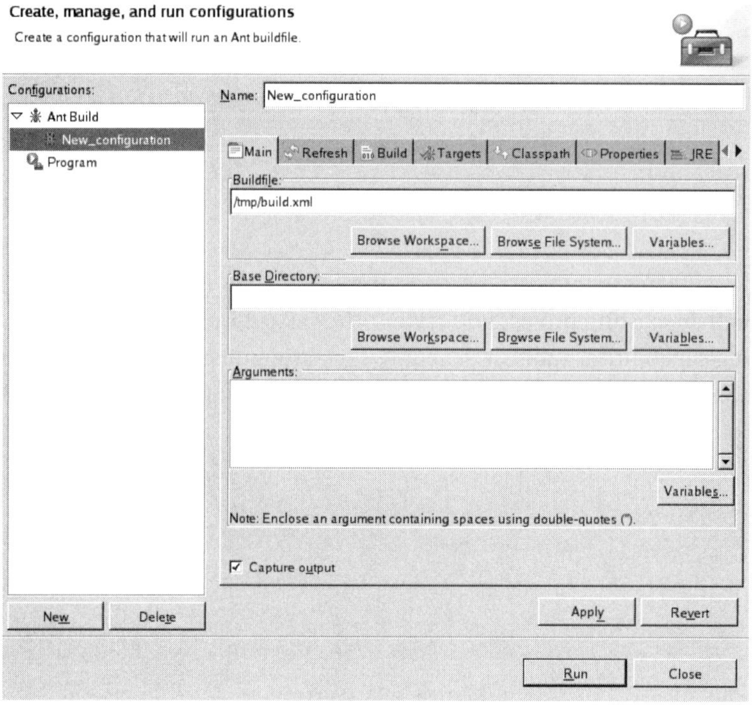

Figure 3.27. The External build tools dialog.

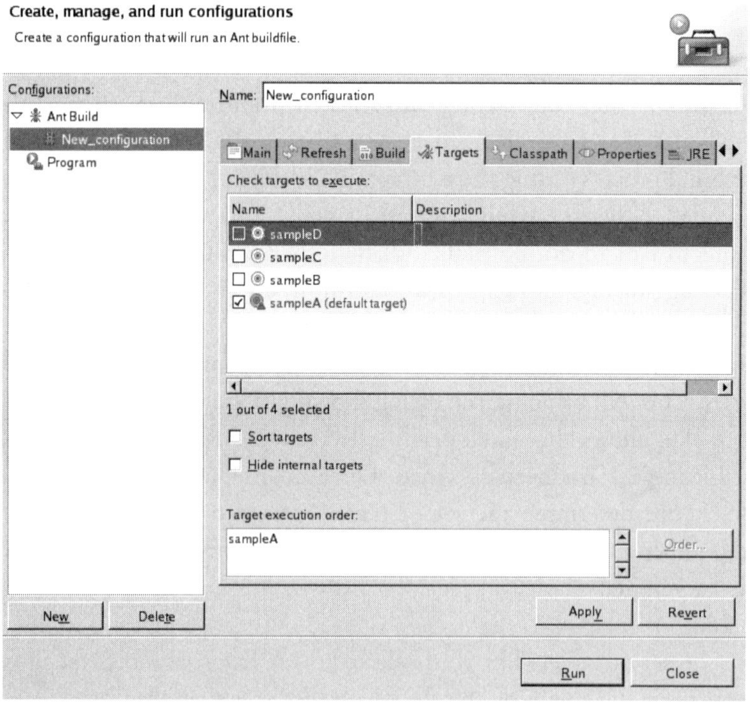

Figure 3.28. The list of available targets.

3.3 Beyond This Book

The information presented in this chapter covers most of how Eclipse would be used in daily development. Eclipse has many other capabilities, some of which can be inferred from the numerous menus and tabs that were seen in the figures but not explored. The best way to discover these capabilities is to take Eclipse for a test drive. Load an existing project and try out the various options, experiment with the refactoring capabilities, and just generally click around and try everything out.

Although Eclipse has been used as as a Java IDE throughout this chapter, it is really much more. It is a platform into which various tools and views can be plugged, providing a central integration point. A set of views for C++ development are already available, and it is expected other languages will follow. There is also a set of views intended to make Eclipse useful as a tool to build Web services, although as of this writing this effort is quite young.

3.4 Summary

Tool: Eclipse
Purpose: Integrated Development Environment
Version covered: 2.0.0
Home page: http://www.eclipse.org
License: CPL (Common Public License)
Further Reading: *The Java Developer's Guide to Eclipse,* by Sherry Shavor et al., Addison-Wesley, 2003.

CHAPTER 4

Testing with JUnit

Sooner or later all code will be tested. In the worst possible case this testing is done by an end user who uncovers a bug and becomes justifiably upset. It is therefore in everyone's interest that testing be done as early as possible and under tightly controlled conditions.

No large program can do without extensive manual testing, and no large company can do without an intelligent and dedicated quality assurance staff. For reasons that are difficult to quantify, humans are remarkably good at finding unforeseen problems in untested code. It is also true that developers are often not the best people to find problems with their own code.

This certainly does not mean that developers should not test their code, but it does suggest that developers should do a different kind of testing than quality assurance (QA) teams. If QA tests the finished product, then programmers should test the code as it is being developed. The leads to the concept of continuous integration, a model in which after every change to the system the entire system is retested. Doing this kind of testing manual would be extremely time consuming, and furthermore manual testing would replicate, rather than enhance, the testing done by QA. There is therefore a need for automated testing, testing of the code at various levels by other code. With such a tool developers can make changes and then quickly run the tests to ensure that bugs have been fixed and previously working functionality has not been damaged.

There are many toolkits available that assist in developing automated tests. Three of these will be the focus of this and the next two chapters. There are many issues surrounding automated testing that persist regardless of the toolkit used, and these will also be addressed in a limited way as they arise. Understanding these issues is essential in order to use testing toolkits effectively.

4.1 An Introduction to Automated Testing

One of the most widely used testing toolkits is called JUnit, and it will be introduced shortly. Before getting to JUnit, it is worth considering the motivation behind the development of such a tool.

A developer initially testing a program is likely to do something similar to what was done with the factorial program developed in Chapter 3. That example was tested by running the program with a "typical" input and making sure it worked. We will examine what constitutes a good set of inputs to test against soon, but for now just consider the process by which testing is done.

After repeating this kind of test many times, it may occur to the developer that one of the things computers are good at is performing time-consuming, repetitive tasks so that humans don't need to. This suggests writing a second program to test the first, which might be done as in Listing 4.1.

Listing 4.1 A simple automated tester

```
package com.awl.toolbook.chapter04;

import com.awl.toolbook.chapter03.Factorial;

public class FactTest {
    public void testFact() {
        Factorial f = new Factorial(10);
        if(f.getFactorial() == 3628800) {
            System.out.println("Test succeeded");
        } else {
            System.out.println("Test failed");
        }
    }
    public static void main(String argv[]) {
        FactTest ft = new FactTest();
        ft.testFact();
    }
}
```

Listing 4.1 is certainly not the simplest possible test program. It would have been possible to run the test within `main()` or to make `testFact()` static and thus avoid the constructor. These shortcuts were avoided to treat `TestFact` as a full-fledged Java program.

It is straightforward to derive more sophisticated test programs from Listing 4.1. One possibility would be to make the test more comprehensive by testing the behavior when given a negative number. This is a classic example of the kind of test that might often be overlooked. A developer who was asked to write a factorial program is likely to know that the factorial function is only defined for positive integers and so would not think to test a negative value. However, an end user might be curious as to what the factorial of a negative number is, or a more complex program might compute some intermediate value that could be negative and then use `Fact` to compute the factorial of that value.

Adding such a test can most easily be accomplished by adding another method to `FactTest` that will closely resemble `testFact()`. The only question is what value should be compared against the result of `getFactorial()` to determine whether the test succeeded.

As written, `getFactorial()` will return `1` when given a negative value. This is wrong in the worst possible way because it produces an answer that looks reasonable but is meaningless. A better behavior would be for `Factorial` to explicitly reject negative values, which can be accomplished by having `setNum()` throw an `IllegalArgumentException` when called with a negative value. A few additional steps will need to be made to accommodate this change. The result is shown in Listing 4.2. Notice how considerations about how a program should be tested can in turn affect how the code is written, which in turn makes that code more robust.

Listing 4.2 The revised Factorial class

```
/*
 * Created on Jun 23, 2003
 *
 * To change the template for this generated file go to
 * Window>Preferences>Java>Code Generation>Code and
 * Comments
 */
package com.awl.toolbook.chapter04;

/**
 *
 * To change the template for this generated type comment
```

Listing 4.2 The revised Factorial class *(continued)*

```
 * go to
 * Window>Preferences>Java>Code Generation>Code and
 * Comments
 */
public class Factorial {
    private int num;
    public void setNum(int n)
        throws IllegalArgumentException
    {
        if(n < 1) {
            throw new IllegalArgumentException(
       "Factorial is only defined for positive integers");
        }
        num = n;
    }

    public Factorial() {
        try {
            setNum(1);
        } catch (IllegalArgumentException e) {}
    }

    public Factorial(int n)
        throws IllegalArgumentException
    {
                setNum(n);
    }

    public int getFactorial() {
        int total = 1;
        for(int i=1;i<num+1;i++) {
            total = total * i;
        }
        return total;
    }
```

```
        public static void main(String[] args) {
            int n = Integer.parseInt(args[0]);
            Factorial f = new Factorial(n);
            System.out.println(f.getFactorial());
        }
    }
```

With `Factorial` suitably modified the second test can be written and `main()` modified to invoke it. The new code is shown in Listing 4.3.

Listing 4.3 A second test

```
public void testFactNegative() {
     try {
         Factorial f = new Factorial(-1);
         System.out.println("Test failed");
     } catch (IllegalArgumentException e) {
         System.out.println("Test succeeded");
     }
 }

public static void main(String argv[]) {
    FactTest2 ft = new FactTest2();
    ft.testFact();
    ft.testFactNegative();
}
```

4.2 JUnit—A Testing Framework

There are several ways to generalize the code from Listings 4.1 and 4.2. Rather than invoke each test in `main()` it would be possible to use introspection to dynamically discover and invoke all methods whose names start with the prefix "test." This would split the functionality of `FactTest` into two classes: one with a set of methods specific to testing the factorial program and one completely general test runner.

The way in which success and failure messages are reported could be moved into the test runner to further abstract the process. It would then be necessary to provide a means for the test methods to communicate their status to the test runner. One possibility would be to make them return a `boolean`, but a more general possibility would be to have test methods throw an exception on a test failure. Specifically, this makes it possible to create methods that will take the value to be tested and the desired value as arguments and throw the failure exception if they do not match. Such a method is called an assertion because it asserts that some condition must be true.[1] It is possible to create similar methods to check conditions other than equality such as inequality, ranges, and so on. Use of the assertion methods can avoid the need to write a lot of `if` statements, all of which would do essentially the same thing. Even more code can be eliminated by placing all the assertion methods in a base class and having the test classes extend that base.

The system just described consists of a general test runner, an exception to indicate test failure, and a set of assertion methods. This system has been realized in a toolkit called JUnit, one of the most popular and useful open source tools ever developed. The base JUnit class is called `TestCase`, and by using this class Listing 4.2 can be transformed into Listing 4.4.

Listing 4.4 A test program that uses JUnit

```
package com.awl.toolbook.chapter04;

import junit.framework.*;

public class FactUnit extends TestCase {
    public void testFact() throws Exception {
        Factorial f = new Factorial(10);
        assertEquals(3628800,f.getFactorial());
    }

    public void testFactNegative() {
        try {
            Factorial f = new Factorial(-1);
            fail("Constructor accepted negative value");
        } catch (IllegalArgumentException e) {
            assertTrue(true);
        }
    }
}
```

The `TestFact()` method is now almost trivial. The use of the assertion has significantly reduced the length of the code. There is also no need to explicitly check

[1]These assertions should not be confused with the assert keyword introduced in J2SE 1.4, although they do serve similar purposes.

for the `IllegalArgumentException` in this method because if it is thrown the test will fail. This would be appropriate if `Factorial()` does not accept the perfectly valid value 10. Note that the expected value appears as the first argument in `assertEquals`. This will allow JUnit to distinguish between the actual and expected results when they are different.

The exception still needs to be checked in `testFactNegative()` because the test is meant to ensure that it is thrown. Note the idiom used here: The line meant to generate the exception is followed by a `fail()` call. If the exception is not thrown, control will pass to this line and the failure will be reported. If the exception is correctly thrown, the `assertTrue(true)` line will be called. This line is a very clear way to declare that the test has succeeded.

JUnit's generalized test runner can now run these tests. JUnit offers two ways to do this: a no-frills version that runs in terminals and a prettier version that uses Swing. The console version can be run with the following command:

```
java junit.textui.TestRunner \
     com.awl.toolbook.chapter04.FactUnit
```

and it will produce the following output

```
..
Time: 0.013

OK (2 tests)
```

Each dot represents a test being run. Note that JUnit makes no promises about the order in which tests will be run, so there is no way to associate a particular dot with a particular test. This also means that each test must be completely self-contained and cannot rely on a previous test, leaving an object or variable in a particular state.

Once all tests have been run, JUnit prints a synopsis containing how long the tests took, the number of tests run, and a status, which in this case is the reassuring "OK."

The graphical version is invoked in much the same way:

```
java junit.swingui.TestRunner \
     com.awl.toolbook.chapter04.FactUnit
```

This command brings up the window shown in Figure 4.1.

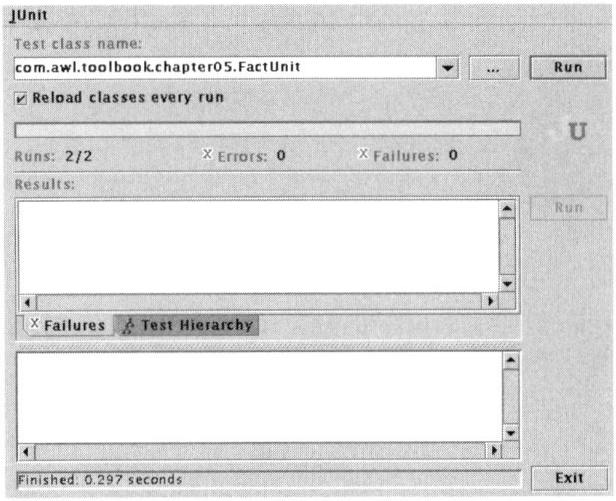

Figure 4.1. The JUnit GUI.

At the top of this window the name of the current test class is displayed. The button labeled "..." can find other test classes to run, although it does so by listing all available classes with the word "Test" in their name whether they are JUnit test classes or not. The "Run" button will run all tests in the currently selected test class.

Normally a running Java program will not pick up the new version of any classes that have become available since the program started. When checked, the "Reload classes every run" checkbox alters this behavior and tells JUnit that it should load the latest available version of any class it needs—both test classes and the classes that are being tested. This is extremely convenient because it means that when a test fails the developer can change the code, recompile, and then click "Run" again without needing to restart JUnit. However, there are many subtleties involved in Java's class loader, and often programs will implement their own loaders, which further complicates the issue. The result is that sometimes relying on JUnit to automatically reload may introduce new problems that can be difficult to find. When in doubt check whether tests behave differently when JUnit is restarted than when classes are reloaded.

Below the checkbox is the most important feature of the JUnit GUI (graphical user interface): the status bar. This bar shows the percentage of tests that have been run. More importantly, although it is reproduced in black and white in this book, the status bar remains a comforting green as long as all tests have succeeded, and it turns a warning red as soon as a single test has failed. This is the reason behind the JUnit motto "Keep the bar green to keep the code clean!"

Below the status bar is an indicator of the number of tests run, the number of unexpected exceptions (reported as "errors"), and the number of assertion failures. Either an error or failure will turn the status bar red.

Although one would hope to see only successful results from JUnit it is also instructional to see how JUnit behaves when tests fail. When the test value of 3628800 is changed to zero in Listing 4.4 the command line version of JUnit produces the following (reformatted slightly to fit the printed page):

```
.F.
Time: 0.029
There was 1 failure:
1) testFact(com.awl.toolbook.chapter04.FactUnit)
   junit.framework.AssertionFailedError:
   expected:<0> but was:<3628800>

         at FactUnit.testFact(FactUnit.java:8)
         ... remainder of thread dump ...

FAILURES!!!
Tests run: 2,  Failures: 1,  Errors: 0
```

This time there is an "F" mixed in with dots, indicating a failure. The total failure count is reported, along with more details and a thread dump for each one. The equivalent display in the GUI is shown in Figure 4.2.

The failure and error messages are reported in the top window; the thread dumps appear in the lower window. More information can be obtained by clicking the "Test Hierarchy" tab, which switches the view as shown in Figure 4.3. This view shows the set of classes that contained tests and which tests within those classes succeeded and which failed.

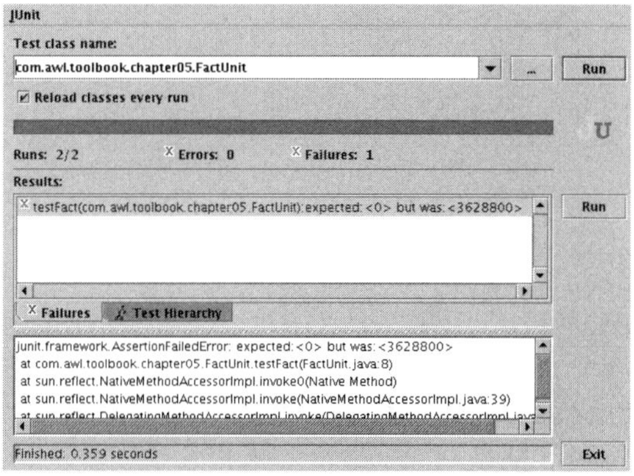

Figure 4.2. The JUnit GUI with a failure.

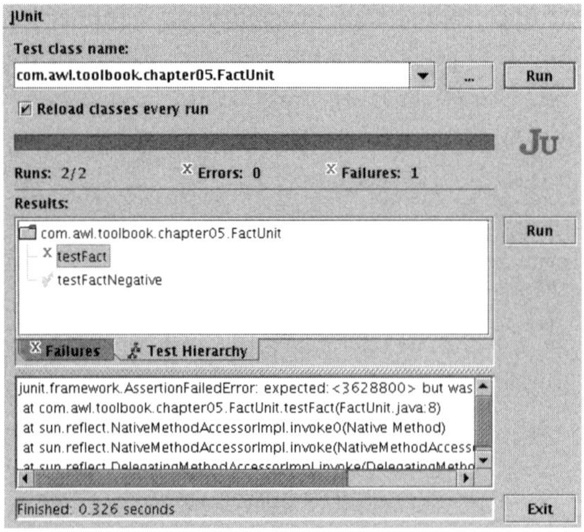

Figure 4.3. The JUnit test hierarchy view.

4.3 More on JUnit

The previous discussion covers just about everything most users will need to know about JUnit. There are, however, just a few remaining details.

If a test class provides a method called `setUp()`, that method will be called before each of the tests are run. This method can be used to put global values or resources such as database connections into states that exercise the test in question. Likewise, a method called `tearDown()` will be called after each test has run and can close or free global resources.

Test classes can be grouped into test suites, as illustrated in Listing 4.5.

Listing 4.5 A test suite

```
package com.awl.toolbook.chapter04;

import junit.framework.*;

public class FactSuite extends TestSuite {
    public FactSuite() {
        super();
        addTestSuite(FactUnit.class);
    }
```

```
        public static Test suite() {
            return new FactSuite();
        }
    }
```

The `addTestSuite()` method adds all the tests in the specified test class. If this example had more tests, each would have been added with a separate call to `addTestSuite()`. It is also possible to add a single test with the `addTest()` method. For example, the constructor could have added only the `testFact()` test by calling

```
addTest(new FactUnit("testFact"));
```

There are a few variations to the basic pattern shown in Listing 4.5. Any class with a static method called `suite()` that returns an instance of `TestSuite` can be given to JUnit, and all the tests in the suite will be run. This is true even if the class does not extend `TestSuite`. The advantage of extending `TestSuite` and building up the suite in the constructor is that the resulting class can be added to a larger agregation of test suites. In this case, another test suite could have added `FactSuite` by calling

```
addTestSuite(FactSuite.class);
```

This ability leads to a very common pattern. Typically in a large project every class will have a parallel test class, and every package will have a test suite that includes all of these test classes. Then every major functional unit of the project will have a test suite that includes all the test suites from its constituent packages, and the whole project will have a master test suite that includes all the test suites of the major components. This allows testing at several levels. A developer creating or fixing a class can test just that class, speeding up the debugging cycle. Once the developer is satisfied with the behavior of that class, he or she can ensure that the rest of the package has not been damaged by the introduced changes, and so on up to the whole project.

4.4 How and What to Test

JUnit itself is a fairly simple system, as the preceding sections have shown. In a sense JUnit is little more than a handful of utility classes to simplify the creation of tests and another set of classes to run tests and display the results. The secret to successful and useful testing lies not in an overly elaborate, overly complex testing framework but in how the framework is used. The question of how to test effectively is surprisingly complex, and there is not room for a full treatment here. Although it is certainly possible to run useful automated testing without subscribing to any design methodologies, such testing is often considered in the context of what is called extreme programming. There are many books and Web sites on extreme programming, each of which will address the issue of effective testing.

In lieu of a full analysis, here are general guidelines that should be useful.

Test every class.

Every class should have a corresponding test class that will typically live in a parallel directory. For example, tests for classes in the `com.awl.toolbook. chapter04` package should live in `tests.com.awl.toolbook.chapter04`. This makes it very easy for Ant to omit these directories when bundling the system for deployment; just add `excludes="tests/*"` to the appropriate target.

These test classes should have at least one test for every public method in the class they are meant to test. There are limits to this; conventional wisdom is that simple accessors do not need to be tested. Any method that may be considered part of the API exposed by that class should definitely be tested.

Write tests before writing code.

This may seem backward, but it makes a great deal of sense. Writing the tests first will require thinking through issues such as what methods should be public, what combinations of values each method should expect, how malformed or invalid input should be handled, and so on. It is certainly possible to think through these issues without writing tests, but the advantage of doing it as part of the testing process is that the tests become both a formal specification and a means to ensure that the specification has been satisfied.

Add a test whenever a bug is found.

Whenever a bug has been found the first step should be to create a new test that exhibits the bug. Then run the test suite and watch the JUnit progress bar turn red; this will confirm that the error condition has been captured. When the bug is fixed and the bar turns green, there is a level of assurance that that particular problem will never plague the system again.

Note that a bug may manifest at several layers of the code. At the outermost layer, an end user has probably provided some input and received an incorrect response, which may take the form of an incorrect value or an exception. This condition should be tested. In addition the bug will ultimately be the result of incorrect code in one or more methods of one or more classes. Each of these methods should have a new test or an extension of an existing test that exhibits the problem.

Adding tests when bugs are found is a good way to introduce automated testing to existing systems for which no tests were initially written. It can be a major hassle to go back and revisit large amounts of code to add tests (another reason to write tests before code). Adding tests for each bug will slowly build up a respectable test suite, and the parts of the system that are working don't pressingly need tests.

Testing saves time!

Often developers under a tight schedule feel they do not have time to write lots of extra test classes. However, even in the absence of automated testing tools the code still needs to be tested. Doing it manually every time a change is made cannot possibly be faster in the long run.

More importantly, it is very common in large systems that a fix for one bug will introduce another. This can result in a horrendous "one step forward, two steps back" mode of development, which always seems to happen just before a project is due. With automated testing there is much more of a guarantee that changes will not make anything worse.

Test early and often.

It is better to change one line of code and discover that one test has broken than to spend six hours writing code to discover that the new code has broken twenty tests. In the latter case it will be very difficult to back trace through the code to find the cause of each failure, whereas in the first case it is easy to track the influence of the one modified line.

Compilation and testing take time, and if development really had to pause to test after every line, nothing would get done. A balance between the overhead of compilation and testing and the need to keep development momentum going is needed, and it will come with experience.

Tests should be fast.

This is a corollary of the previous point. A test that takes one second will get run more than sixty times as often as one that takes a minute. Using the GUI version of JUnit can help here; by clicking "Reload classes every run" and leaving the GUI active, the time needed to restart JUnit is eliminated.

Select good sample values.

There is not much to be gained by testing `Factorial` on both 10 and 11. If one of these works, the other will as well due to the nature of the function. On the other hand, the correct behavior of `Factorial` for numbers greater than one is very different from correct behavior for numbers less than one. This is a specific instance of the more general question of choosing appropriate test values.

One extreme position, called white-box testing, advocates writing tests that are guaranteed to exercise every line of code. For example, if a conditional branches based on whether some variable is less than 10, then a white-box test would have one test where the variable is less than 10 and another where the variable is 10 or greater. This can hugely multiply the number of tests,[2] which can significantly slow down the testing process. This also breaks the rule about writing tests before code because it requires testing based on the implementation of the class rather than the specified behavior.

Generally, although not always, it is reasonable to think in terms of representative values. Consider what kinds of values will give different kinds of results. Also consider what values are "pathological" and should be trapped, such as values that will result in a division by zero or indexing into an empty array.

Each test should leave a clean slate.

Recall that JUnit does not guarantee the order in which tests will be run. Consequently each test needs to be responsible for setting up any state that it needs to test against and should clean up after itself.

Testing database code requires special approaches.

The preceding requirement can be especially problematic when databases are involved, in which case the full state may consist of every row in every table. Problems may manifest only when there are exactly 100 rows of data or other equally specific conditions.

Such situations may be difficult to test for a number of reasons. If an entire development staff is sharing a database, it may be impossible to keep the database quiet long enough to run the tests. If a test tries to put itself into a clean state, it may wipe out large amounts of data needed by another developer.

There is no solution to this problem that will work in all cases. One possibility is to give each developer his or her own database to test against, possibly using a small simple database like Hsqld (see Chapter 10). Note, however, that testing against a database other than the one used in production may result in code that works in development but fails in production.

The problem of requiring specific sets of test data can be addressed by storing data files external to the test and having the test call out to a database utility to load data from a file.

[2]Roughly, there are likely to be 2^n tests, where n is the number of conditionals.

Another possibility is to take the program as far as generating the SQL (Structured Query Language) that will be issued to the database and checking that SQL against expected strings without necessarily executing it.

4.5 Integrating JUnit with Ant

Ant has a task called `junit` that allows testing to be done as part of the build process. Typically any deployment target will have a dependency on the testing target so that if any tests fail, the deployment will not happen.

The `junit` task is not one of Ant's core tasks; rather it is considered an "optional" task. Formerly, the optional tasks were collected in a separate jar file, called optional.jar, that had to be downloaded separately from the Ant distribution. This is no longer the case; optional tasks are now included with the standard Ant system, although a great deal of documentation still refers to "optional.jar."

The difference between a "main" task and an "optional" one is that each of the "optional" tasks require one or more third-party jars in order to work. The `junit` task, not surprisingly, requires JUnit.jar. This jar can be manually added to the CLASSPATH, or it can be placed in the "lib" directory within the directory where Ant was installed.

Errors to Watch For

If Ant cannot find junit.jar for any reason, the resulting error message still recommends installing optional.jar.

There are numerous options to `junit` that control which tests should be run, how they should be run, and how the results should be presented. The only parameter that is absolutely needed is the name of the test class or test suite to run. For example,

```
<target name="test" depends="compile">
  <junit>
    <test name="com.awl.toolbook.chapter04.FactSuite"/>
  </junit>
</target>
```

will silently run the tests in `FactSuite`. Whether or not the tests are successful the build will continue after the JUnit target completes. This is the correct behavior if the dependent task will do something with the test results, such as formatting them or mailing them to an administrator. Continuing regardless of status may not be the right thing to do if dependent tasks will continue the build, such as deploying the application. In that case, adding `haltonfailure="on"` will stop the build if a failure or error occurs.

The `junit` task can be given a formatter that will specify the set of data to be reported and the format in which it should be presented. This can be used if more detail about the tests is needed beyond a simple success or failure. Changing the target definition to

```
<junit>
  <test name="com.awl.toolbook.chapter04.FactSuite"
        outfile="results/FactSuite"/>
  <formatter type="plain"/>
</junit>
```

will print a one-line summary after all the tests run, and the full JUnit output will be found in a file called FactSuite.txt in the results directory.

More sophisticated formatting is also available. By changing `type="plain"` to `type="xml"` a detailed report will be generated in FactSuite.xml, resembling the following:

```
<?xml version="1.0" encoding="UTF-8" ?>
<testsuite
    errors="0"
    failures="0"
    name="com.awl.toolbook.chapter04.FactSuite"
    tests="2"
    time="0.372">
  <properties>
  ...
  </properties>

  <testcase
    classname="com.awl.toolbook.chapter04.FactUnit"
    name="testFact"
    time="0.012">
  </testcase>
  <testcase
```

```
      classname="com.awl.toolbook.chapter04.FactUnit"
      name="testFactNegative"
      time="0.0010">
    </testcase>
  </testsuite>
```

The `properties` section contains a huge amount of information including every property available to the system. This information has been omitted in the interest of space.

Although the XML output contains more detail than the standard format, it is still not optimally formatted. Ant also provides a task called `JUnitReport` that uses XSLT (Extensible Stylesheet Transformation) to convert the generated XML into any desired format, typically HTML. Its use is straightforward: The task needs to be told which files to use as input, how to format them, and where the results should be placed.

```
<target name="format" depends="test">
  <junitreport>
    <fileset dir="./results">
      <include name="*.xml"/>
    </fileset>
    <report format="frames" todir="./results/html"/>
  </junitreport>
</target>
```

This target will collect all the xml files in the "results" directory, each of which might have been generated by a different test. It will use a predefined style, called "frames," that is included with Ant to build the HTML. It is also possible to use a custom stylesheet. The results will be placed in the "results/html" directory and will look like Figure 4.4.

4.5.1 Integrating JUnit with Eclipse

Eclipse provides special facilities to run JUnit tests. From the Run menu (see Figure 3.18) it is possible to run either a single test or every test within the current project, as shown in Figure 4.5.

When a JUnit test is run, Eclipse switches to the JUnit perspective to show the results. Figure 4.6 shows this perspective. The test that was run here is the modified version that is expecting zero instead of the correct value in order to illustrate what a

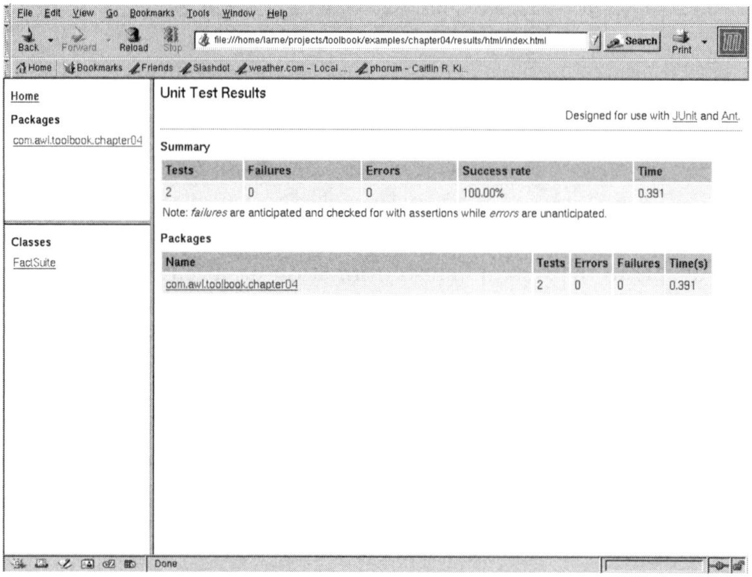

Figure 4.4. The generated test report.

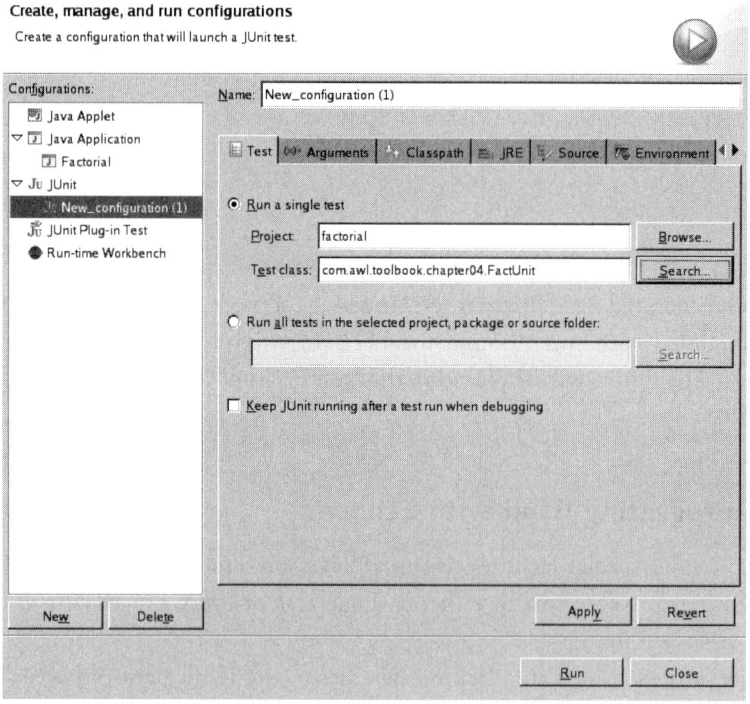

Figure 4.5. Running JUnit tests from Eclipse.

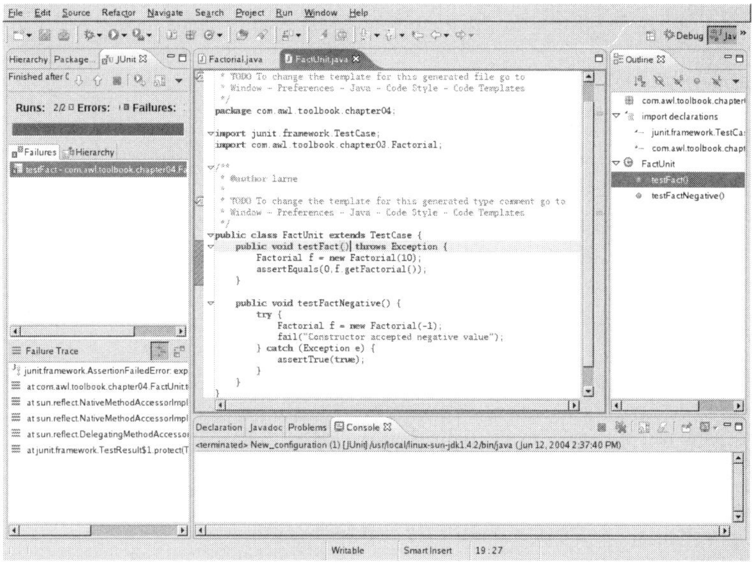

Figure 4.6. The JUnit perspective.

test failure looks like. Any of the lines in the "failure trace" frame can be clicked to bring the editor to the corresponding file and line.

4.6 Summary

Tool: JUnit
Purpose: Automated testing
Version covered: 3.8.1
Home page: http://junit.sourceforge.net/
License: CPL (Common Public License)
Further Reading:

- http://www.junit.org/—A very comprehensive site on using JUnit.
- http://www.extremeprogramming.org/—Information about extreme programming, one cornerstone of which is automated testing.
- There is a very active and useful mailing list that can be joined at http://groups.yahoo.com/group/junit/.

CHAPTER 5

Testing Web Sites with HTTPUnit

The ability to test Java classes with a tool like JUnit is of great utility and importance. Because many applications are deployed as Web sites, it would also be tremendously useful to automate the testing of such applications. Manual testing of Web sites consists of a user interacting with the site through a browser, so any automated testing tool should mimic this interaction as closely as possible.

JUnit can be used as a first step toward this ideal testing tool. Writing a JUnit test is a matter of writing a Java class, so anything that can be expressed in Java can be tested. Listing 5.1 demonstrates this flexibility by showing a JUnit test that ensures that the string "Hello" appears on the first page of the application.

Listing 5.1 A test for a Web page

```
package com.awl.toolbook.chapter05;

import junit.framework.*;
import java.io.*;
import java.net.*;

public class SimpleWebTest extends TestCase {
    public void testPage() throws Exception {
        URL url = new URL(
        "http://localhost:8080/toolbook/" +
```

Listing 5.1 A test for a Web page *(continued)*

```
            "chapter05/sample.jsp");

        InputStream in     = url.openStream();
        byte data[]        = new byte[1024];
        StringBuffer buffy = new StringBuffer();
        int count;

        while((count = in.read(data)) > 0) {
            buffy.append(new String(data,0,count));
        }
        in.close();

        assertTrue(buffy.toString().indexOf("Hello") != 0);
    }
}
```

This example works, but it is clearly less than optimal. There are nine lines of code for one single line of meaningful testing, which is a poor ratio. The kinds of test that can be done this way are also very limited. There is no easy way to test for structural elements on a page such as the presence of a particular link, form, or button. Testing a page that uses JavaScript is completely out of the question.

5.1 An Introduction to HTTPUnit

The problem of testing Web sites is so ubiquitous and so important that a set of tools called HTTPUnit[1] has evolved on top of JUnit. HTTPUnit provides a number of classes that model a conversation between a browser and a server. These classes allow code to programmatically request pages, click on links, fill out and submit forms, and a number of other useful things. Listing 5.2 shows how HTTPUnit eliminates all the overhead that is present in Listing 5.1.

Listing 5.2 A simple HTTPUnit test

```
package com.awl.toolbook.chapter05;

import junit.framework.*;
```

[1]The name comes from Hypertext Transfer Protocol, the protocol used between Web servers and clients.

```
import com.meterware.httpunit.*;

public class WebTest1 extends TestCase {
    public void testGet() throws Exception {
        WebConversation wc = new WebConversation();
        WebRequest req     = new GetMethodWebRequest(
  "http://localhost:8080/toolbook/chapter05/sample.jsp");
        WebResponse res    = wc.getResponse(req);

        assertTrue(res.getText().indexOf("Hello") != -1);
    }
}
```

Listing 5.2 starts as most HTTPUnit tests will: by constructing a `WebConversation`, which is the class that mediates communication between the client and server. Next, a `GetMethodWebRequest` is constructed to simulate a browser using the HTTP GET method to request a page. The `WebConversation` uses this request to get a response from the server, which is stored as `res`. From here the text of the page can be obtained and used as a string, just as in Listing 5.1.

Note that `WebTest1` extends `TestCase`, so it may be run the same way that the examples in Chapter 4 were run. HTTPUnit exists as a set of add-on classes to JUnit, so all the points made about how and what to test still hold.

5.2 A More Sophisticated Example

Consider a simple Web-based calculator consisting of three pages. The first page consists of nothing more than a greeting and a link to the second page, in a display of poor user interface design. This page is shown in Listing 5.3.

Listing 5.3 The first page

```
<html>
<body>
<h1>Hello</h1>
<a href="calc2.html">Proceed to the application</a>
</body>
</html>
```

The second page contains some instructions and a form with two inputs for numbers. Some JavaScript on this page will ensure that both fields are filled in and that the provided values are numbers. This page is shown in Listing 5.4.

Listing 5.4 The second page

```
<html>
<head>
  <script language="JavaScript">
function checkValues() {
  var theForm = document.form1;
  var elt0    = theForm.elements[0].value;
  var elt1    = theForm.elements[1].value;
  var ok      = true;

  if(elt0 == '') {
    alert("Please provide a value for the first number");
    ok = false;
  } else if(elt1 == '') {
    alert("Please provide a value for the second number");
    ok = false;
  } else {
    for(i=0;ok && i<elt0.length;i++) {
      ok = elt0.charAt(i) >= '0' && elt0.charAt(i) <= '9';
    }

    if(!ok) {
      alert("The first input does not appear to be a number");
    } else {
      for(i=0;ok && i<elt1.length;i++) {
        ok = elt1.charAt(i) >= '0' && elt1.charAt(i) <= '9';
      }

      if(!ok) {
       alert("The second input does not appear to be a number");
      }
    }
  }

  return ok;
}
  </script>

<body>
```

```
Enter two number below, then click to compute the sum<p>

<form name="form1"
      action="calc3.jsp"
      method="POST"
      onSubmit="return checkValues();">

 First number: <input type="text" name="number1"><br>
 Second number: <input type="text" name="number2"><br>

<input type="submit" name="submit" value="Click to add">
</form>

</body>
</html>
```

Submitting the form in Listing 5.4 will take the user to the third page where the sum of the numbers will be displayed, as shown in Listing 5.5.

Listing 5.5 The third page

```
<%@ taglib prefix="c"
    uri="http://java.sun.com/jstl/core" %>

<html>
<body>

The sum is:
<c:out value="${param.number1 + param.number2}"/>

</body>
</html>
```

Listing 5.5 uses features of the Java Standard Tag Library to perform the addition. The details of how this works are unimportant for the moment, and the JSTL is covered in detail in Chapter 18.

There are three features on page one that should be tested: that the text "Hello" appears in the appropriate place, that the link is provided, and that the link goes to the second page.

The test for the greeting could be done using string comparisons, as was done in Listings 5.1 and 5.2. Using HTTPUnit, it is possible to do better than this; the structure of the document can be examined as a DOM (Document Object Model). This makes it possible not only to find the string but to identify the tag in which it appears and the location of that tag within the document as a whole.

Similarly the link could be found by looking for the appropriate anchor tag in the text, and the href could be checked to ensure it points to the correct place. This approach, however, would not live up to HTTPUnit's goal of acting like a browser. Instead, HTTPUnit provides a method called `getLinkWith()` to find links containing specified text, along with another method called `click()` that simulates the clicking of a link.

The use of DOM and links is demonstrated in Listing 5.6, which shows the test for the welcome page.

Listing 5.6 Testing the first page

```
private static String firstPage =
"http://localhost:8080/toolbook/chapter05/calc1.html";

private static String secondPage =
"http://localhost:8080/toolbook/chapter05/calc2.html";

public void testPage1() throws Exception {
    WebConversation wc = new WebConversation();
    WebRequest req     =
        new GetMethodWebRequest(firstPage);
    WebResponse res    = wc.getResponse(req);
    Document doc       = res.getDOM();
    Node html          = doc.getFirstChild();
    Node body          = findNode(html,"body");
    Node h1            = findNode(body,"h1");
    Node text          = h1.getFirstChild();

    assertEquals("Hello",text.getNodeValue());

    WebLink link       = res.getLinkWith("Proceed");

    assertNotNull("Link not found",link);

    link.click();
```

```
        res = wc.getCurrentPage();

        assertEquals(res.getURL().toString(),secondPage);
    }

    private Node findNode(Node n,String name) {
        NodeList kids = n.getChildNodes();
        for(int i=0;i<kids.getLength();i++) {
            if(kids.item(i).getNodeName().
               equalsIgnoreCase(name))
            {
                return kids.item(i);
            }
        }
        return null;
    }
```

The first portion of Listing 5.6 is very similar to previous examples up to the point where the `getDOM()` method is used instead of `getText()`. Once the DOM has been obtained, it is traversed through the use of an auxiliary method, `findNode()`. The general use of DOM is beyond the scope of this book, but this code should give a taste of what programming with DOM is like. Every `Node` has a number of children, and methods are available to traverse these children as well as determine their names, values, and other attributes. Listing 5.6 uses these methods to find the `h1` tag and ensure that the text within it is "Hello."

Finding and following the link is even easier. First `getLinkWith()` is used to find the link, and `assertNotNull()` is used to ensure it has been found. Then the `click()` method is used as described. After clicking the link, the `WebConversation` object is used to obtain the resulting page just as when explicitly providing a URL to a `WebRequest`. Various features of the resulting page can be tested once the page has been obtained, including its URL.

There are a number of things that could go wrong in this test that are not explicitly checked. If the link points to a page that does not exist, an exception will be thrown when it is clicked. In that case JUnit will report a test error instead of a test failure, but that is a perfectly reasonable outcome because it does convey the problem.

Testing the second and third pages presents a number of new challenges. First, a mechanism is needed to fill out and submit the form, and it should come as no surprise that HTTPUnit provides such methods. The first of these methods is `getForms()`, which returns an array of `WebForm` objects, which encapsulate each of the forms on the page. WebForm provides a setParameter() method that sets a value in the form by the name of the field. A submit() method that submits the form is also available. Like click(), the submit() method results in a new page being loaded.

Using these methods, a simple test of page 2 could be done with the code in listing 5.7.

Listing 5.7 Using HTTPUnit to test a form

```
public void testPage2() throws Exception {
    WebConversation wc = new WebConversation();
    WebRequest req     =
        new GetMethodWebRequest(secondPage);
    WebResponse res    = wc.getResponse(req);
    WebForm form       = res.getForms()[0];

    form.setParameter("number1","8");
    form.setParameter("number2","12");
    form.submit();

    res = wc.getCurrentPage();
    assertEquals(res.getURL().toString(),thirdPage);
    assertTrue(res.getText().indexOf("20") != -1);
}
```

There are a number of implicit tests in Listing 5.7. If the form does not exist or does not contain any of the named parameters, an exception will be thrown, which will result in a test error. Two explicit tests are performed: one that ensures the form goes to to the correct page and one that ensures the correct sum has been computed. This latter test is done with a simple string rather than by traversing the DOM. This is sufficient for such a simple page.

Although Listing 5.7 checks one mode of the application, it does not test the **failure modes,** the behavior of the form when invalid input is provided. To do so, it will be necessary to test the JavaScript, and once again HTTPUnit makes this possible. HTTPUnit contains a JavaScript interpreter that traps events such as onSubmit() and onLoad(), as well as many others. Interactive features of JavaScript, such as alerts, are available through a number of new methods in the WebConversation class. One of these methods, popNextAlert(), retrieves the text of the next pending alert and clears that alert from the queue. If the second setParameter() call in

Listing 5.7 were omitted, the error could be tested with a simple line of code:

```
assertEquals(
   "Please provide a value for the second number",
   wc.popNextAlert());
```

As an aside, note that the `assertEquals()` method first seen in Chapter 4 provides some nice features when dealing with strings. If the strings do not match, `assertEquals()` will show where and how they diverge, rather than showing the entire text of both strings. For example, if the JavaScript incorrectly matched inputs with messages, the error reported would be

```
There was 1 failure:
1) junit.framework.ComparisonFailure:
   expected:<...second...> but was:<...first...>
```

HTTPUnit's JavaScript abilities are used in conjunction with some utility methods in Listing 5.8, which tests all the failure modes of the calculator pages.

Listing 5.8 Testing the second page

```
public void testPage2() throws Exception {
    WebConversation wc = new WebConversation();
    WebRequest req     =
        new GetMethodWebRequest(secondPage);
    WebResponse res    = wc.getResponse(req);
    WebForm form       = res.getForms()[0];

    // Test the various failure modes

    tryScript(wc,form,"10",null,
    "Please provide a value for the second number");

    tryScript(wc,form,null,"8",
    "Please provide a value for the first number");

    tryScript(wc,form,"notANumber","8",
    "The first input does not appear to be a number");
```

Listing 5.8 Testing the second page *(continued)*

```
    tryScript(wc,form,"8","notANumber",
    "The second input does not appear to be a number");

    // Test a sucessful run
    runForm(form,"8","10");
    assertNull("An error was incorrectly generated",
               wc.getNextAlert());
    res = wc.getCurrentPage();
    assertTrue(res.getText().indexOf("18") != -1);
}

private void tryScript(WebConversation wc,
                       WebForm form,
                       String val1,
                       String val2,
                       String message)
    throws Exception
{
    runForm(form,val1,val2);

    WebResponse res = wc.getCurrentPage();

    assertEquals(message,wc.popNextAlert());
}


private void runForm(WebForm form,
                     String val1,
                     String val2)
    throws Exception
{

    form.removeParameter("number1");
    form.removeParameter("number2");

    if(val1 != null) {
        form.setParameter("number1",val1);
    }
```

```
        if(val2 != null) {
            form.setParameter("number2",val2);
        }

        form.submit();
    }
```

Although Listing 5.8 is longer than Listing 5.7, it is no more complicated. The `runForm()` method is used to run the form with different inputs, and `tryScript` runs the form and checks for a given alert message. These methods avoid the overhead of manually calling the form for each set of inputs.

It is somewhat a matter of preference whether multiple tests should be done in one method as is done in Listing 5.8. It would certainly be possible to place each `tryForm()` in a separate test method. One rule of thumb is that multiple variations on the same basic test can reasonably be placed in one method.

5.3 Testing with ServletRunner

By emulating a browser HTTPUnit can test servlets, JavaServer pages, flat HTML pages, server-side includes, and anything else a Web server can utilize. Such emulation is also, in some sense, the most "honest" way to test a site. The downside of such testing is that starting up Tomcat or another Web server may be time consuming, especially if it must be restarted to accommodate changes. This is in direct opposition to the "tests must be fast" principle.

HTTPUnit provides a compromise between completeness and speed in the form of a utility called ServletUnit, which allows the testing of servlets without needing to deploy them in an application server. Conceptually this is not difficult. The servlet API requires implementations of a number of interfaces such as `HttpServletRequest` and `RequestDispatcher`. Any container that provides these classes can load and invoke servlets, and the servlets will respond exactly as they would if run in an application server. In practice, of course, implementing all these classes is no small feat. The result of all this hard work has been made available as ServletRunner.jar.

To demonstrate this functionality a servlet will first be needed for testing. Listing 5.9 shows a servlet that acts as yet another calculator. It will display a form with two inputs for numbers, and if the form has been filled out, it will display the sum.

Listing 5.9 The calculator servlet

```
package com.awl.toolbook.chapter05;

import java.io.IOException;
import java.io.PrintWriter;
import javax.servlet.*;
import javax.servlet.http.*;


public class CalcServlet extends HttpServlet {
    public void doGet(HttpServletRequest req,
                      HttpServletResponse res)
        throws IOException,ServletException
    {
        handle(req,res);
    }


    public void doPost(HttpServletRequest req,
                       HttpServletResponse res)
        throws IOException,ServletException
    {
        handle(req,res);
    }


    public void handle(HttpServletRequest req,
                       HttpServletResponse res)
        throws IOException,ServletException
    {
        res.setStatus(res.SC_OK);
        res.setContentType("text/html");
        PrintWriter out = res.getWriter();

        out.println("<html>");
        out.println("<body>");
        out.println("Provide two numbers below, and ");
        out.println("the sum will be computed<p>");
```

```
        out.println("<form action=\"CalcServlet\" " +
                    "method=\"get\">");
        out.print("  Number 1: ");
        out.println("<input type=\"text\" " +
                    "name=\"number1\"><br>");
        out.print("  Number 2: ");
        out.println("<input type=\"text\" " +
                    "name=\"number2\"><br>");
        out.println("<input type=\"submit\" name=\"Add\"" +
                    " value=\"Add\">");
        out.println("</form>");

        out.println(add(req));

        out.println("</body>");
        out.println("</html>");
        out.close();
    }

    public String add(HttpServletRequest req) {
        String num1 = req.getParameter("number1");
        String num2 = req.getParameter("number2");

        if(num1 != null && num2 != null) {
            try {
                int n1 = Integer.parseInt(num1);
                int n2 = Integer.parseInt(num2);
                return "The sum is " + (n1 + n2);
            } catch (Exception e) {
            }
        }

        return "";
    }
}
```

Testing the initial page using ServletRunner is almost the same as testing against a Web server. The code is shown in Listing 5.10.

Listing 5.10 Testing the start page

```
public void testStart() throws Exception {
    ServletRunner sr = new ServletRunner("web.xml");
    ServletUnitClient client = sr.newClient();
    WebResponse response     = client.getResponse(
           "http://localhost/CalcServlet");
    String text              = response.getText();

    assertTrue(
      text.indexOf("Provide two numbers") != -1);
}
```

Rather than initializing a `WebConversation` and using it to get a response, Listing 5.10 initializes a `ServletRunner` and uses it to get a `ServletUnitClient` and then uses the client to get the response. Once the response has been obtained, its use is identical to previous examples.

The `ServletRunner` is initialized with a `web.xml` file,[2] which is a subset of the full `web.xml` used to configure a Web application under Tomcat. In this case `web.xml` will have nothing but an entry for the servlet and a mapping of that servlet to the "/CalcServlet" URL.

Testing forms works a little differently under ServletUnit because there is no longer a `WebConversation` to mediate the interaction. The technique is illustrated in Listing 5.11.

Listing 5.11 Testing the form

```
public void testSubmit() throws Exception {
    ServletRunner sr = new ServletRunner("web.xml");
    ServletUnitClient client = sr.newClient();
    WebResponse response     = client.getResponse(
           "http://localhost/CalcServlet");

    WebForm form       = response.getForms()[0];
    WebRequest request = form.getRequest("Add","Add");

    request.setParameter("number1","8");
    request.setParameter("number2","50");
```

[2]See Chapter 17 for more about `web.xml` and Tomcat configuration.

```
        response        = client.getResponse(request);
        String text     = response.getText();

        assertTrue(text.indexOf("58") != -1);
    }
```

Here a `WebRequest` is obtained from the `form`. This `WebRequest` encapsulates the request that would result from clicking the specified submit button. Additional parameters are then added to the `WebRequest` rather than directly to the `form`. The `client` then obtains the response to this request, which is then processed normally.

5.4 Beyond This Book

HTTPUnit has many additional features, including support for cookies and other elements of HTTP. See the documentation for complete details.

5.5 Summary

Tool: HTTPUnit
Purpose: Automated testing of Web applications
Version covered: 1.5.4
Home page: http://httpunit.sourceforge.net/
License: Custom license that claims to permit unrestricted use and redistribution provided the copyright notice and license are included. See the included license file for details.
Further Reading: http://java.sun.com/j2se/1.4.2/docs/api/org/w3c/dom/package-summary.html—Documents the Java API for traversing DOM.

CHAPTER 6

Further Web Testing with Jakarta Cactus

Testing with HTTPUnit is a great way to simulate a user's perspective of a Web application. However, such testing often does not give a complete picture of what is happening *within* the system. HTTPUnit can report that a page did not function as expected but can give no direct clues as to why it failed. Such failures may be be directly attributable to incorrect HTML, but more often failures have their origins in code within a servlet or scoped bean.

This is one of the motivations behind Cactus, another testing suite that is built on top of JUnit.

6.1 An Introduction to Cactus

When testing a Web application with HTTPUnit the testing code sits entirely outside the server being tested. The only interaction between the code doing the testing and the code being tested is the HTTP request and response, as shown in Figure 6.1.

By contrast Cactus provides an "in-container strategy," meaning a portion of the code doing the testing resides within the application. This portion is a servlet called the **redirector,** and it acts as the central point of all Cactus activity.

The fact that the redirector is a servlet has two immediate consequences. First, there is a simple and obvious way in which the redirector is placed within the application server; it is installed like any other servlet. This can be accomplished with the

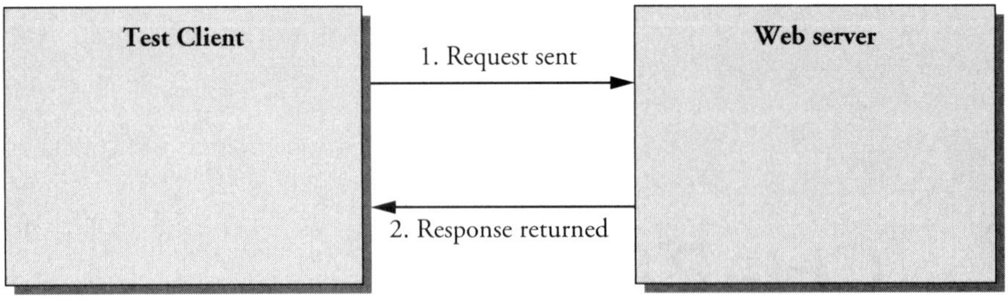

Figure 6.1. Simple HTTP testing.

following entries in web.xml, the application's configuration file:[1]

```
<servlet>
  <servlet-name>
    ServletRedirector
  </servlet-name>
  <servlet-class>
    org.apache.cactus.server.ServletTestRedirector
  </servlet-class>
</servlet>

<servlet-mapping>
  <servlet-name>ServletRedirector</servlet-name>
  <url-pattern>/ServletRedirector</url-pattern>
</servlet-mapping>
```

Note that the servlet mapping must place the redirector at the top level of the application, or it would not be possible to map the servlet to "/chapter06/ServletRedirector." The servlet to be tested, however, may reside anywhere.

The second implication of having the redirector be a servlet is that it provides a natural way for an external program to invoke a test. The external program can make a regular HTTP request to the appropriate URL—`/ServletRedirector`, in this case—and on receiving such a request the redirector will run the tests. The broad outline of this process is illustrated in Figure 6.2, which will be refined shortly. Figure 6.2 gives a sense of how Cactus works, but the picture is not yet complete. So far nothing has been said about the client. Since JUnit provides such a useful and flexible framework, the Cactus client will be constructed on top of it. This means

[1]The web.xml file is discussed in more detail in Chapter 17.

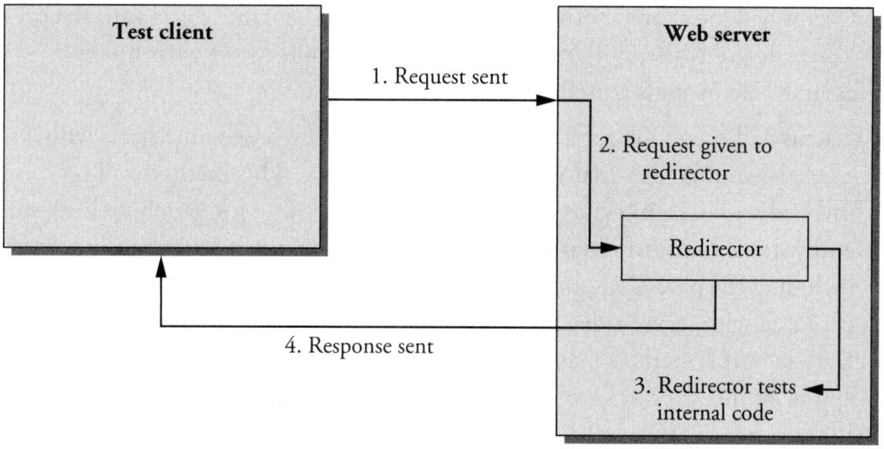

Figure 6.2. Internal testing.

that Cactus test cases will look much like JUnit and HTTPUnit test cases; they will be individual Java classes with specially named methods that a test runner will dynamically discover and invoke.

There are a number of ways in which the client could know which server and which URL to contact in order to invoke the redirector. Cactus looks for this information in a file called `cactus.properties`, which must be placed somewhere in the CLASSPATH on the client side. The `cactus.properties` file for this example contains the following:

```
cactus.contextURL = http://localhost:8080/toolbook
cactus.servletRedirectorName = ServletRedirector
```

Moving right in Figure 6.2, the next point of clarification is the communication channel between the client and the redirector. When HTTPUnit wants to test a page, it sends a request containing the URL, query string, POST data, and other elements intended for the page to be tested. When Cactus wants to test a page, the URL will be the URL for the redirector, not for the page or servlet to be tested. There must, therefore, be a mechanism for the client to tell the redirector how to run the test. This is done through an auxiliary class called a **WebRequest.**

The full process by which a Cactus test runs is listed here, and it will be illustrated shortly in the context of an actual test case.

1. The JUnit `TestRunner` will construct an instance of the test class, just as it would do for any other test case. This instance will be referred to as the **client instance.**

2. Cactus will look for a method in the test class whose name starts with the prefix `test`, just as with any JUnit-based test. For the purpose of what follows, assume Cactus finds a method called `testTest1`.
3. Cactus will then look for a corresponding method whose name starts with `begin`—in this case, that would be `beginTest1`. This method will be invoked with a `WebRequest` object. The `WebRequest` is purely a client-side entity. It contains information about the request that will be sent to the server, including the base URL, parameters, cookies, and so forth. It should not be confused with server-side classes such as `HttpServletRequest`. The `beginTest1` method may set parameters in the `WebRequest` that will appear in the `HttpRequest` of the class being tested.
4. Information in the `cactus.properties` file is used to construct a URL to the redirector on the server.
5. An HTTP request is made to this URL, including all the parameters and other information loaded into the `WebRequest` by the `beginTest1` method. In this way the parameters set in the `WebRequest` on the client side are transparently placed in the `HttpServletRequest` on the server side.
6. The redirector constructs a *second* instance of the test class, which will be referred to as the **server instance.**
7. The redirector will set various fields in the server instance that are defined in the test class. Most importantly, the redirector will set the `request` variable to be the current `HttpServletRequest`.
8. Like any JUnit test, the `setup()` method of the server instance is invoked if it is defined.
9. The redirector invokes the `testTest1` method of the server instance. Note that if there are multiple `test` methods, only the one found in step (1) will be invoked at this time. Tests can use the `request` and other servlet-related objects that were set in step (6).
10. The teardown() method is called on the server instance, if it exists.
11. The redirector bundles up information about the response.
12. The test result is sent back to the client along with the response information built in step (11). This information is used to construct a `WebResponse` object, and if the client instance has an `endTest1` method corresponding to the `testTest1` method, it will be called with this object. The `endTest1` method can be used to check status codes, cookies, or anything else the server instance might have set in the `response`.

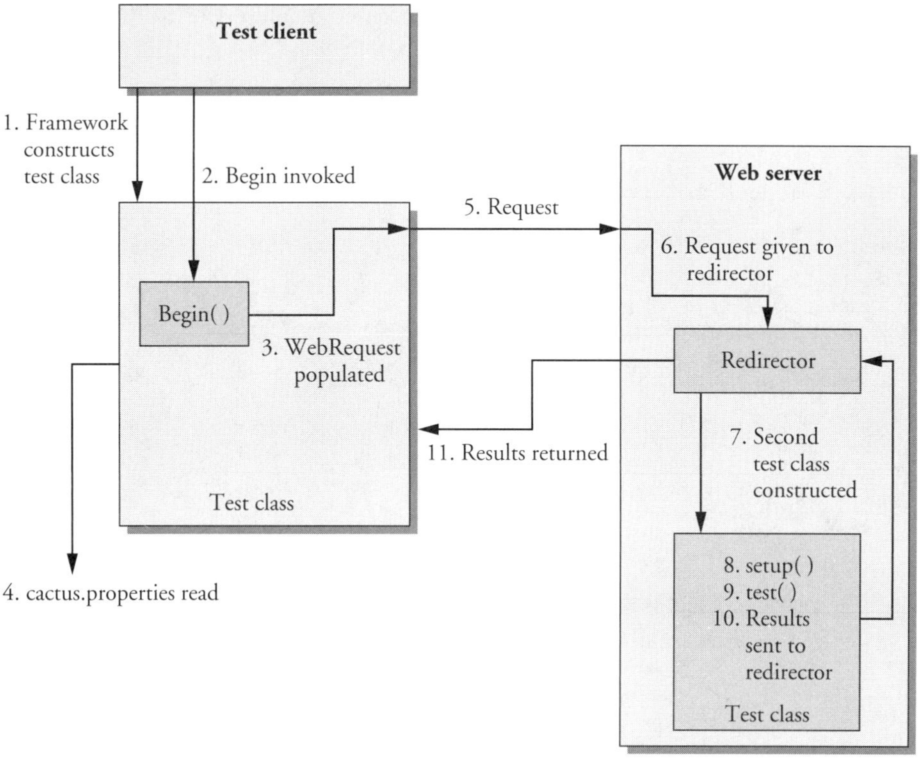

Figure 6.3. Testing with Cactus.

Items 2 through 12 are repeated once for each test, so if a test class defines `testTest2` and `testTest3` methods, then there will be three requests to the server, three server instances constructed, `setup()` will be called three times, and so on. This process is illustrated in Figure 6.3.

6.2 Writing and Running Cactus Tests

Although the detailed description in the preceding section may sound quite complicated, in practice writing Cactus tests is quite easy. With the redirector properly installed in a Web application and the `cactus.properties` file in the CLASSPATH, everything is in place. Individual tests cases are written as Java classes in a manner very similar to the way JUnit and HTTPUnit tests are written. In particular no code is needed in a Cactus test to interface with the redirector, just as JUnit tests do not need code to work with the test runner. In both cases the surrounding test framework invokes the tests based on introspection.

To illustrate these concepts a class will be presented that tests the calculator servlet from Listing 5.9. This test is shown in Listing 6.1.

Listing 6.1 A Cactus test

```
package com.awl.toolbook.chapter06;

import junit.framework.Test;
import junit.framework.TestSuite;

import org.apache.cactus.ServletTestCase;
import org.apache.cactus.WebRequest;

import com.awl.toolbook.chapter05.CalcServlet;

public class CalcServletTest extends ServletTestCase {
    public CalcServletTest(String theName) {
        super(theName);
    }

    public static Test suite() {
        return new TestSuite(CalcServletTest.class);
    }

    public void beginAdditionOK(WebRequest webRequest) {
        webRequest.addParameter("number1", "8");
        webRequest.addParameter("number2", "16");
    }

    public void testAdditionOK() {
        CalcServlet servlet = new CalcServlet();
        assertEquals("The sum is 24",
                     servlet.add(request));
    }
}
```

On the surface this class closely resembles any other JUnit class. The first difference is that it extends `ServletTestCase` from the Cactus packages. The second thing to notice is that in addition to the `testAdditionOK()` method, there is a similarly named beginAdditionOK(). Both of these methods play an important role that will be examined in more detail shortly.

The most important thing about Listing 6.1 is that it tests the servlet's add() method directly, with a genuine request object. When run this will be a full Web container request that can be used to get a session, cookies, examine other aspects of the application, and many other things that could not be done with the simplified request provided by ServletRunner.

A number of properties must be configured on the server side before the test can be run. The redirector servlet must be installed as previously noted. Numerous jar files must also be available and will traditionally be placed in the WEB_INF/lib directory of the Web application to be tested. These files include the following:

cactus-1.6.1.jar

commons-httpclient-2.0.jar
commons-logging-1.0.3.jar
junit-3.8.1.jar
aspectjrt-1.1.1.jar

Once all the preceding have been set up and Tomcat has been started, the simplest way to run a Cactus test is from the command line, where it looks much like running any other JUnit test.

```
java junit.textui.TestRunner \
     com.awl.toolbook.chapter06.CalcServletTest
```

which results in output that looks just like any other test.

```
.
Time: 1.256

OK (1 tests)
```

The Swing UI could have been used just as easily.

6.2.1 Testing through a Browser

One of the things the Web is good at is providing attractive, easy-to-use, and distributed front ends to complex systems. While issuing the command to start a Cactus test is not too burdensome, it is certainly not as easy as going to Web page. The command line version also requires a complete installation of Java on the client side. While the dots or green bar provide a nice at-a-glance view, they are not as informative or readable as a detailed breakdown when one or more tests fail. For these reasons Cactus provides a Web-based front end.

The idea behind this front end is a second servlet that plays the role of the client in the preceding discussion. The use of the word *client* here may be a bit confusing. A servlet is a server-side entity, almost by definition. However, it is also possible for a servlet to initiate an HTTP conversation, in which case it also acts as a client. In this case the HTTP conversation will be to the redirector on the same server. It may seem strange for a Web server to make a request to itself, but there is certainly no reason this could not or should not be done.

The new servlet is called `ServetTestRunner`. It can be added to a Web application or a global Tomcat configuration by adding the following to the appropriate `web.xml`.

```
<servlet>
  <servlet-name>
    ServletTestRunner
  </servlet-name>
  <servlet-class>
    org.apache.cactus.server.runner.ServletTestRunner
  </servlet-class>
</servlet>

<servlet-mapping>
  <servlet-name>ServletTestRunner</servlet-name>
  <url-pattern>/ServletTestRunner</url-pattern>
</servlet-mapping>
```

A test can be invoked by pointing a browser at the servlet URL and including a parameter specifying which test to run. To run the calculator test, the following URL would be used (this should all be on a single line, but to make it fit on the printed page, it must be broken up):

```
http://localhost:8080/toolbook/ServletTestRunner?
suite=com.awl.toolbook.chapter06.CalcServletTest
```

This URL can be saved as a bookmark or used as a link from another page, or a form could even be used to select from among many available tests. This provides

Figure 6.4. Cactus results as XML.

the means to run tests from any computer without needing a JDK or knowledge of Java. The output of this servlet as seen in a browser is shown in Figure 6.4.

In many ways this output closely resembles the XML produced by the JUnit task from Ant. As with the Ant output, it would be preferable to make this more readable and attractive, and once again the solution is XSLT. The XML can be converted into HTML by telling the `ServletTestRunner` to use a stylesheet provided with Cactus.

```
http://localhost:8080/toolbook/ServletTestRunner?
suite=com.awl.toolbook.chapter06.CalcServletTest
&xsl=/toolbook/chapter06/cactus-report.xsl
```

This results in the display shown in Figure 6.5. This closely resembles the HTML built by the `JUnitReport` task because the `cactus-report.xsl` stylesheet is closely based on the Ant stylesheet.

Note that there is nothing magical happening here, the test runner simply adds a stylesheet reference to the generated XML, as in

```
<?xml-stylesheet
  type="text/xsl"
  href="/toolbook/chapter06/cactus-report.xsl"?>
```

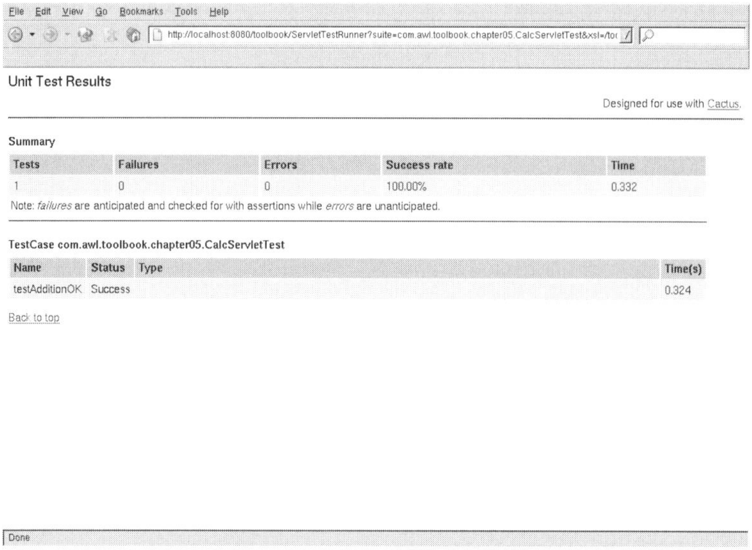

Figure 6.5. Cactus results as HTML.

The translation and rendering is done entirely on the client side. It is therefore possible to specify any xsl file, even one that resides on another server.

While most modern browsers are capable of performing XSLT transformations, Cactus provides a mechanism for performing this translation on the server side, which can be enabled by adding the following parameter to the servlet definition in `web.xml`:

```
<init-param>
  <param-name>xsl-stylesheet</param-name>
  <param-value>styles/cactus-report.xsl</param-value>
</init-param>
```

To invoke a server-side translation from the browser, replace the `xsl=` portion of the URL with `transform=yes`.

6.3 Using Cactus with Eclipse

As mentioned in Chapter 3 Eclipse is far more than an IDE; it is a sophisticated environment whose functionality can be expanded through the use of plugins. Two such plugins are provided with Cactus to simplify the use of Cactus from within Eclipse.

Note that it is not strictly necessary to use these plugins in order to run Cactus tests from Eclipse. Since Cactus tests are ultimately extensions of JUnit tests, the standard method of running JUnit tests as covered in Chapter 4 can be used. The downside of doing so is that the servlet to be tested and related assets must be manually packaged into a Web application, installed under Tomcat or another application server, and the server must be started manually before running the tests. The goal of the Cactus plugins is to automate and simplify as much of this as possible.

The first plugin, webapp, handles much of this through a process dubbed "cactification." This consists of building a Web application, which includes all the necessary Cactus jars and a `web.xml` modified to include the relevant proxy servlets. The second plugin, "runner," deploys this Web application in the appropriate container, starts the container automatically, and runs the test.

Errors to Watch For

At the time of this writing, cactification was not working. The documentation states:

The Eclipse plugin is a work in progress. In the past it was working, but since we moved to the new Ant integration, it has been broken. This requires a rewrite of the plugin code to fix. In the meantime, we have removed the plugin download.

However, this is expected to be fixed shortly, and the information presented in this section is not expected to change.

The Cactus plugins can be enabled by copying them into the "plugins" directory in the Eclipse installation and restarting Eclipse. Under the "project" menu there is an option to set global properties. One of these is Web Application, which allows the developer to specify a set of resources and name a war file into which the application should be built. This feature is independent of Cactus, but Cactus will use this information to determine the target for cactification. The Web Application dialog is shown in Figure 6.6.

The next step is to configure the Cactus-specific properties. This is done through the "preferences" dialog, to which the Cactus plugins will have added several options. The first screen allows the user to specify the URL and context for the application, which will be used both in cactification and when running the tests. This dialog can be accessed from the "window" menu and is shown in Figure 6.7.

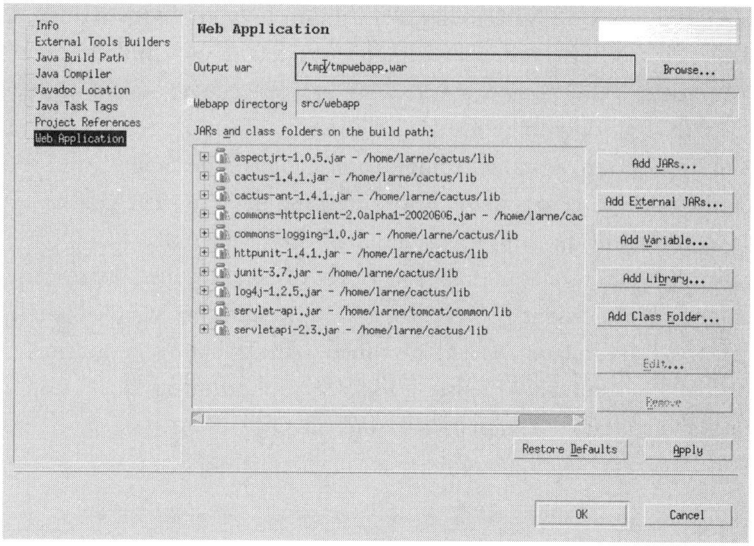

Figure 6.6. The Web Application dialog.

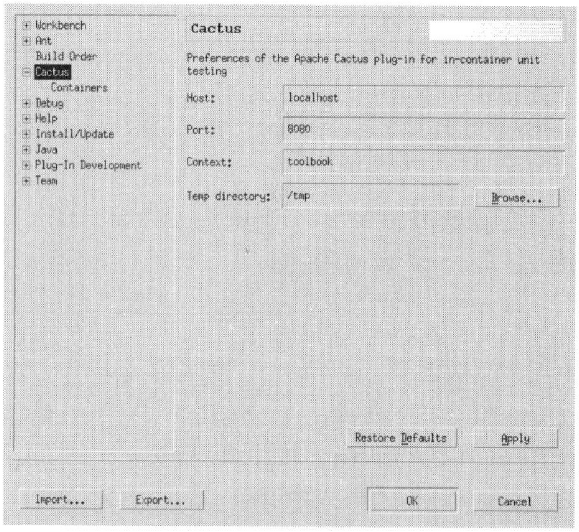

Figure 6.7. Further configuration.

The second option screen is used to specify the container that will be used to run the application. This dialog is shown in Figure 6.8. By default Cactus will attempt to use Jetty, a lightweight servlet and JSP container, although it is possible to configure it to use Tomcat or other application servers. Although Jetty is an open -source project it is not covered in this book.

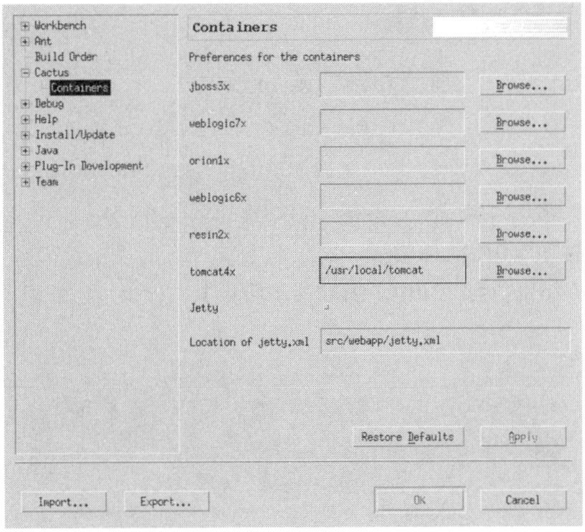

Figure 6.8. Cactus container options.

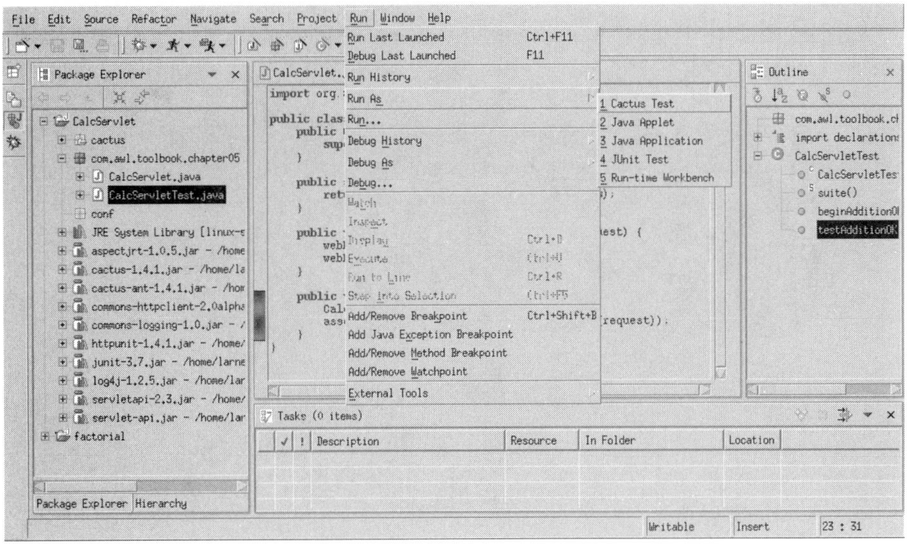

Figure 6.9. The new run option.

Finally, the "runner" plugin adds a new option to the "Run" menu, as shown in Figure 6.9.

When this option is selected, all needed compilations will be performed, the war file will be built and deployed, Tomcat will be started, and the tests will be run. The results are displayed using the same perspective used for JUnit tests.

6.4 Beyond This Book

One easy way to introduce Cactus into a testing environment is to use it in conjunction with HTTPUnit. An HTTPUnit test can ensure that a page responds as expected, and a subsequent Cactus test can ensure that the page has left a session object in the correct state. These tests can be run as part of the same suite, thanks to the fact that both testing tools build on JUnit.

Cactus also provides the ability to test EJBs (Enterprise Java Beans). See the Web site for more details.

6.5 Summary

Tool: Cactus
Purpose: Automated testing of Web applications
Version covered: 1.6.1
Home page: http://jakarta.apache.org/cactus/
License: The Apache Software License, Version 2.0
Further Reading:

- Readers interested in Jetty, the default container used by Cactus, can find more information on Jetty from its homepage at http://jetty.mortbay.com/jetty/.
- There is a wiki devoted to Cactus at http://wiki.apache.org/jakarta-cactus/FrontPage.

CHAPTER 7

Stress Testing with Jakarta JMeter

All of the previous testing tools were meant to determine whether code works as expected. JMeter addresses the different but equally important issue of *how well* code works, particularly in a server context. Server-based applications exist in extreme environments where they may remain active for very long periods of time and be used by potentially vast numbers of people simultaneously. JMeter provides tools to measure long-term performance and test behavior under heavy usage.

Normally JMeter does not require any Java programming. JMeter tests are constructed by connecting predefined elements and providing them with parameters. This makes JMeter very simple and painless to use.

7.1 Using JMeter

JMeter is not only a testing framework but also a sophisticated GUI for constructing tests. After running `jmeter` on Unix or `jmeter.bat` on Windows the user will be presented with the screen in Figure 7.1.

Tests are organized in units called test plans, not be confused with the human QA activities that are a part of development projects and that are also called test plans. JMeter test plans are constructed by adding elements to the framework, which is done through the "add" option of the "edit" menu, as shown in Figure 7.2.

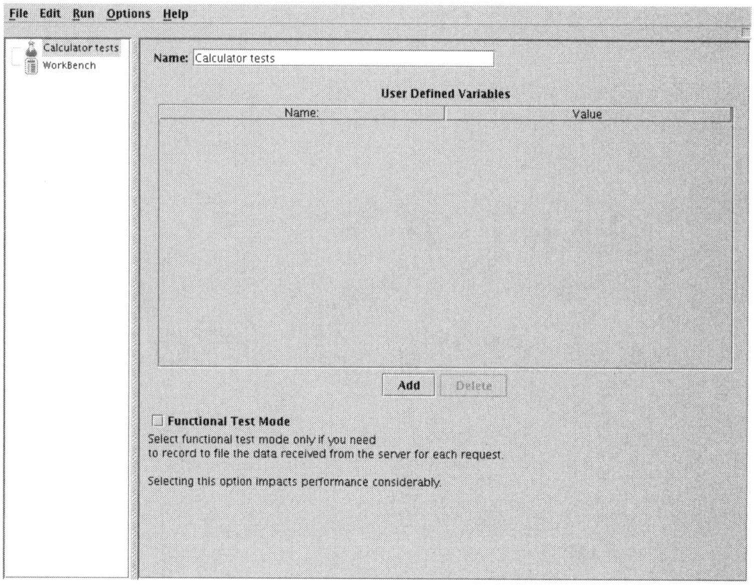

Figure 7.1. The JMeter startup screen.

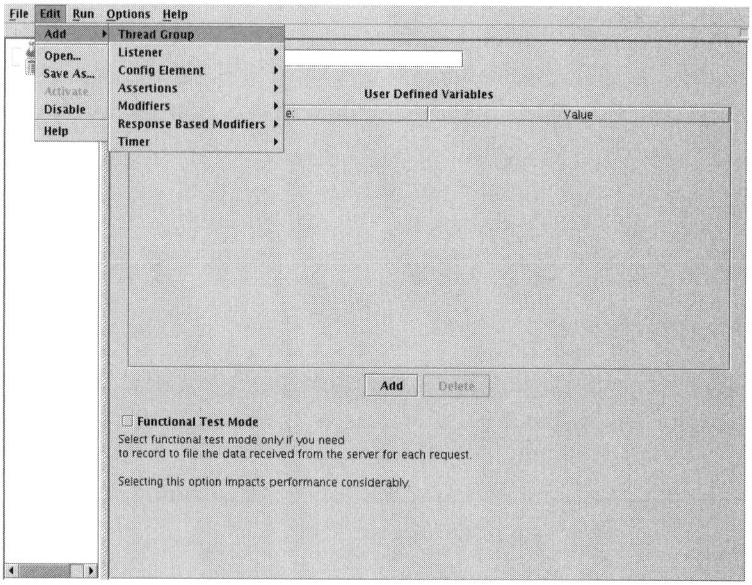

Figure 7.2. The JMeter add menu.

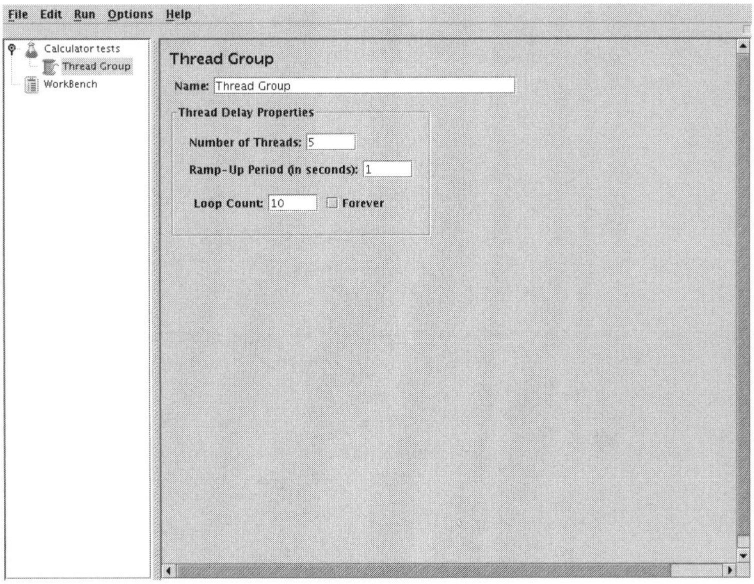

Figure 7.3. The thread group configuration.

This process begins by adding a **thread group,** which is an entity that maintains a set of threads. Each thread will independently run the entire test suite and will look like a separate client to the server being tested. This is the simplest way that JMeter provides load testing; it can simulate many independent clients—as many as the client machine and Java virtual machine can handle. The thread group configuration screen is shown in Figure 7.3.

Here it is specified that five threads are to be started, and each one should run the tests ten times. It is also possible to run the tests indefinitely by clicking "forever." The ramp-up time indicates how long it will take to start all the threads. The value of one second provided here means that each thread will be started one-fifth of a second after the previous one.

Now that the thread group has been defined, it is possible to specify what each thread should do, which is also done through the "Add" menu. This menu is context-sensitive and will present valid options based on the selected element in the left frame. Although the entries change, the overall look does not, and so the menu will not be shown again.

The simplest way to add a test is to add a **sampler** to the thread group. Samplers may be thought of as individual clients; they are objects that make a request to a server. Many kinds of samplers are available, including ones to test Web servers, databases, and FTP servers. The configuration screen for the sampler that tests Web servers is shown in Figure 7.4.

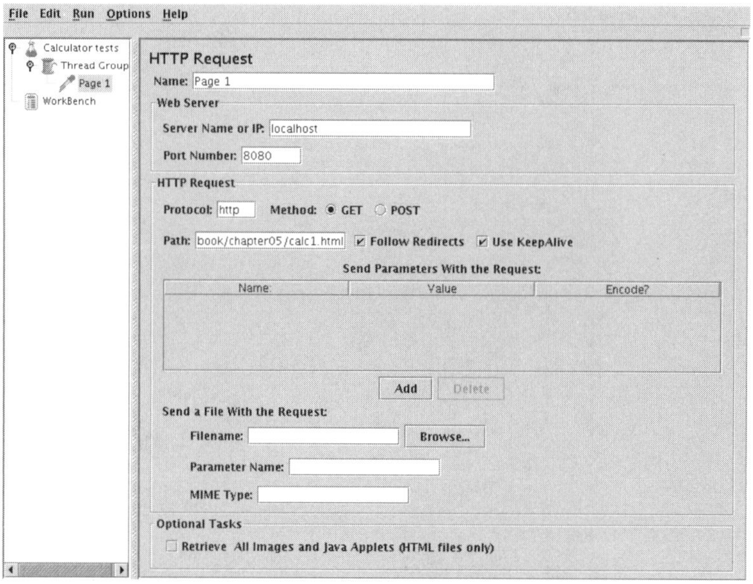

Figure 7.4. The HTTP sampler configuration.

This screen allows the user to specify the host and port to test, along with the type of request and the URL path. It is also possible to add form parameters, including file uploads.

This sampler will be used to test page one of the calculator application from Listing 5.3. Note that the sampler itself does not test anything; it simply requests the page. The testing is done by another element called an **assertion,** many kinds of which are provided. There is a duration assertion that requires a response within a specified time. There is also a size assertion that requires that the response contains a specified number of bytes. Finally, there is a response assertion that can look through the response for a pattern or patterns. Any combination of these can be used; it would be possible to require that a Web application responds quickly, that the response is the correct length, and that the response contains an expected string.

Assertions are added to samplers through the "Add" menu, and the configuration screen for the response assertion is shown in Figure 7.5.

This is functionally similar to the HTTPUnit test from Listing 5.6. The combination of the sampler and the assertion will request the first page of the calculator and ensure that the string "Hello" is present.

This may seem to be much easier than writing an HTTPUnit class, but it is important to keep in mind that JMeter and HTTPUnit tests have different goals. HTTPUnit is meant to ensure that a page works as expected and to perform this check as quickly as possible so that it may be run often. Conversely the JMeter test

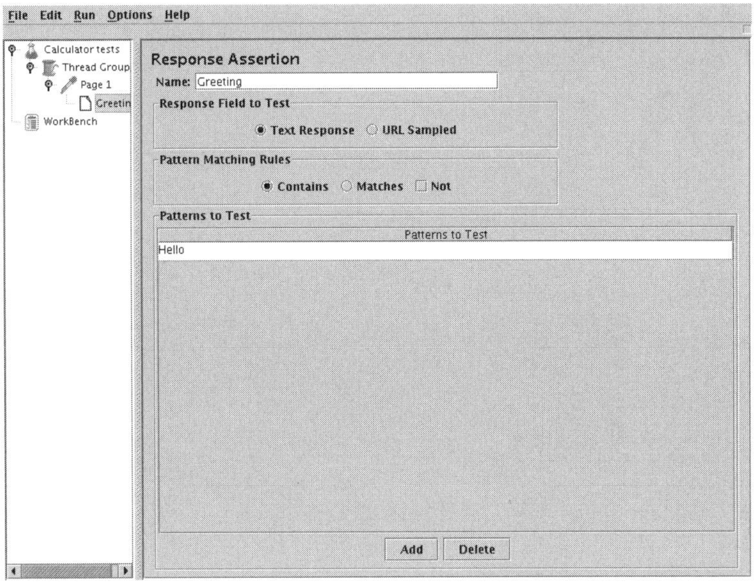

Figure 7.5. The response configuration.

is meant to ensure that the page continues to work properly and respond quickly under extended heavy load and must be run over a long period of time in order to get accurate results. Both kinds of test are important, and HTTPUnit and JMeter should therefore be thought of as complimentary.

Another important difference is that JMeter makes no attempt to provide a browser-like environment. It is possible to test form-driven pages, but it is not as straightforward as obtaining an object representing the form, filling it in, and submitting it. Instead, form parameters must be manually provided to the URL being tested. For example, page three of the calculator could be tested by providing values for `number1` and `number2` in another sampler, as shown in Figure 7.6. This sampler will use a response assertion to check that "59" appears on the resulting page.

The final ingredient is a means to monitor the results, which JMeter calls a **listener.** Listeners can be attached to many points within a test plan. Attaching a listener to a sampler will display the results for that sampler only, whereas attaching a listener to a thread group will merge the results from all samplers.

Once the listener has been defined, the test can be started from the "Run" menu. The results are then displayed by the listener, as shown in Figure 7.7.

Note that 100 tests were performed. This is because the thread group allocates the specified number of threads for each sampler—hence 2 tests times 5 threads times 10 runs equals 100 tests.

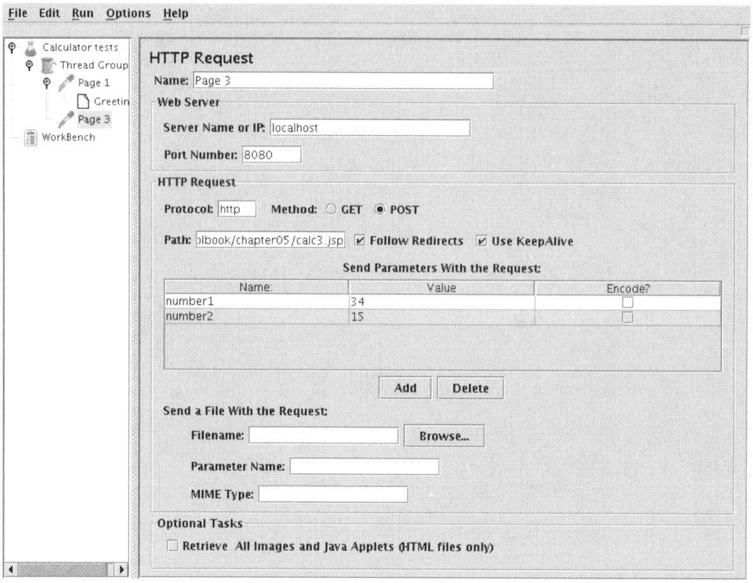

Figure 7.6. Testing the result of the form.

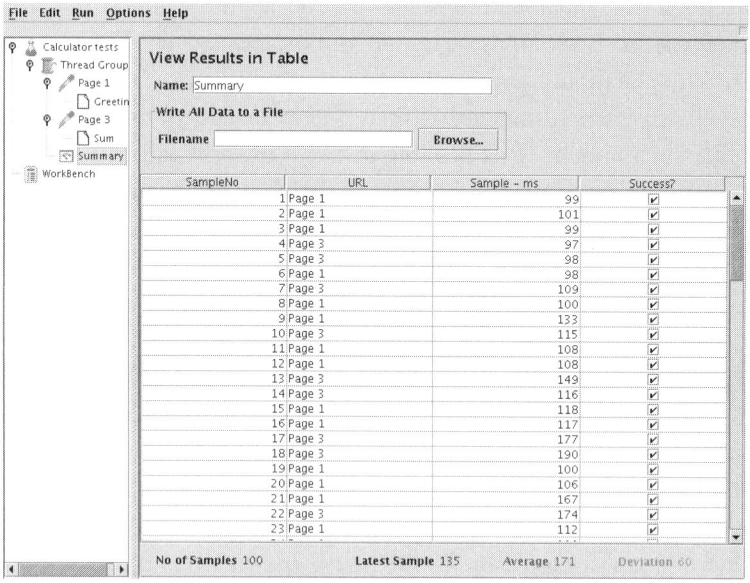

Figure 7.7. The test results.

Once tests have been defined they can be saved so that they may be reused later. This is done through the `Save` or `Save as` options in the `file` menu. JMeter uses an XML representation that can be hand-edited, although doing so is usually neither necessary nor advised. The CD-ROM accompanying this book contains the XML for the tests that have been defined to this point.

7.2 Distributed Testing

Load testing inadvertently puts stress on two computers. Not only do the incoming requests push the limits of the server, but all the test threads and data verification and result presentation puts a heavy burden on the machine doing the testing. One implication of this is that the testing machine may run short of resources before the server does, leading to inaccurate results. This is especially true if the server is being hosted on a production-class machine with lots of memory and multiple processors.

The solution is to run the same test from multiple computers all testing against the same server. This reduces the burden on any one computer while allowing a more rigorous overall test. This also provides a more realistic test, as in the real world multiple users from many computers will be hitting the server simultaneously. It is not at all inconceivable that a system will exhibit different behavior when handling requests from many computers than it would when handling the same number of requests from a single computer.

Manually starting a test from several computers is a burden, even if a system like X windows or PC Anywhere is used to allow all control to happen from one computer. Besides the cumbersome need to start the tests on all these machines, the resulting logs and other reports will need to be gathered and combined once the test has completed. JMeter addresses these problems by providing for distributed testing.

To use distributed testing one or more instances of JMeter will be started in **server mode,** which is done by adding the `-s` option on the command line. These are the instances of JMeter, which will perform the tests, so calling them "server instances" may be slightly misleading. They act as clients against the Web application to be tested, but they act as servers to a master instance of JMeter, which will tell them when to start and stop testing.

Server instances may be left running indefinitely. When they are not engaged in testing, they will consume very few resources on their host computer.

The JMeter instance from which the tests will be controlled must be made aware of the other instances. This can be done from the command line by use of the `-Jremote_hosts=` option, which takes a comma-separated list of computer names or IP addresses. Alternately, the list of JMeter servers can be placed in the `jmeter.properties` file, which lives in the `bin` directory of the JMeter installation. Within this file is a line containing `remote_hosts=`, again a comma-separated list of servers can be provided.

In either case once remote hosts have been defined, the "Run" menu from the JMeter GUI will contain options for "remote start" and "remote end," both of which will have a submenu listing all the defined hosts. When a remote host is started, the test plan will first be sent to that host, so there is no need to define the test plan once on each host. Similarly, the results from all hosts will be aggregated by any listeners and can be viewed from the controlling JMeter instance. In a sense each remote thread will look like part of the thread group of the controlling instance.

7.3 More Sophisticated Test Plans

Often pages cannot be tested individually but must be accessed in a particular order. The archetypal example of this is a site that requires the user to log in. Typically an entry page must be used to log in, after which the user is given a cookie that grants access to subsequent pages. Using the features of JMeter encountered so far it would be possible to test the login page with one sampler, but the best that could be done with other pages would be to determine how long it takes for the request to be rejected and the user sent back to the login page. The necessity for a test like this should not be underestimated; every mode of a site should be stress tested, just as every mode should be functionally tested. This still leaves the problem of how to test the behavior of protected pages.

JMeter's solution to this problem takes the form of **logic controllers.** A logic controller is an entity that groups samplers and controls how they are invoked. One possibility is to interleave a set of requests. It would have been possible to use a controller to alternate requests to the first and third pages of the calculator. This would have meant a total of five threads would have been allocated, rather than five for each sampler for a total of ten. This would have provided a more efficient use of JMeter at the cost of not testing the behavior of the system in the presence of simultaneous requests to different pages.

A better use of logic controllers is to make one initial request to a login page, obtain the cookie, and then make many requests against the desired page.

Although it is not directly relevant to the issue of logic controllers, it is worth noting that there is another way in which pages may be protected. Some sites still use HTTP-based authentication, where the Web server itself is configured to restrict access, rather than the application. A nonauthenticated user requesting such a page will get a browser pop-up where he or she may provide their username and password. This kind of authentication has become less popular over recent years for a few reasons. First, this kind of authentication provides an awkward user experience because it is impossible to make the pop-up look like part of the site. Second, it can be difficult to configure, especially for applications that need very fine-grained control over how resources are protected. Nevertheless, JMeter can still test such pages by adding an HTTP Authentication manager to the thread group via the "Config element" menu.

7.4 Using JMeter with Ant

JMeter was originally designed to be used interactively through a graphic interface, as has been done in this chapter. However, as previous chapters have illustrated testing becomes even more useful when it is included in the normal build cycle. Therefore, a means to integrate JMeter into Ant has been provided from http://www.programmerplanet.org/ant-jmeter/. Although this is not part of the official JMeter distribution, it works quite well and quite easily.

The code needed to call JMeter from Ant is distributed as a jar file, ant-jmeter.jar, which can be placed in the standard Ant libs directory or manually added to the CLASSPATH. This jar file provides a custom Ant task called `JMeterTask` which works much like those discussed in 2. Listing 7.1 contains a build.xml file that uses this new task.

Listing 7.1 An Ant build file that invokes JMeter

```
<project name="JMeter demo"  default="format" basedir=".">

<taskdef
    name="jmeter"
    classname=
    "org.programmerplanet.ant.taskdefs.jmeter.JMeterTask"/>

<target name="test">
  <jmeter
    jmeterhome="${toolbook.home}/jakarta-jmeter-2.0.1"
    testplan="demotest.jmx"
    resultlog="demotest.jtl"/>
</target>

<target name="format" depends="test">
  <xslt
    in="demotest.jtl"
    out="demotest.html"
    style="jmeter-results-report.xsl"/>
</target>

</project>
```

First, the custom task is loaded. Next, the `jmeter` target uses this task to run the tests. The `jmeterhome` attribute specifies where JMeter is installed. Here this location is given relative to the toolbook home, which should name the directory where the CD-ROM contents have been placed. The `demotest.jmx` file contains the test definitions in XML form, and `resultlog` specifies the name of a file where the results should be written.

When Ant is invoked as

```
ant -Dtoolbook.home=C:toolbook test
```

(replacing the value of `toolbook.home` as appropriate), it will generate the following output:

```
Buildfile: build.xml

test:
    [jmeter] Executing test plan: demotest.jmx
    [jmeter] Created the tree successfully
    [jmeter] Starting the test
    [jmeter] Tidying up ...
    [jmeter] ... end of run


BUILD SUCCESSFUL
Total time: 18 seconds
```

Note that the success, failure, and performance results are not reported here but are all placed in `demotest.jtl`. This is another XML file. Usually this file will be quite verbose and difficult to read, so an XSLT template such as the one discussed in Chapter 4 has been provided to process the results into a more readable form. This is done by the `format` task, which leaves the result in `demotest.html`. This file may be viewed in a browser, and the results will look like Figure 7.8.

7.5 How to Stress Test

To use JMeter effectively a good deal of thought must be given to what should be tested and how the results should be interpreted. There is no short answer, but an excellent guiding principle is that tests should anticipate how the system will be realistically be used. If a system is likely to be used by only a few people at a time,

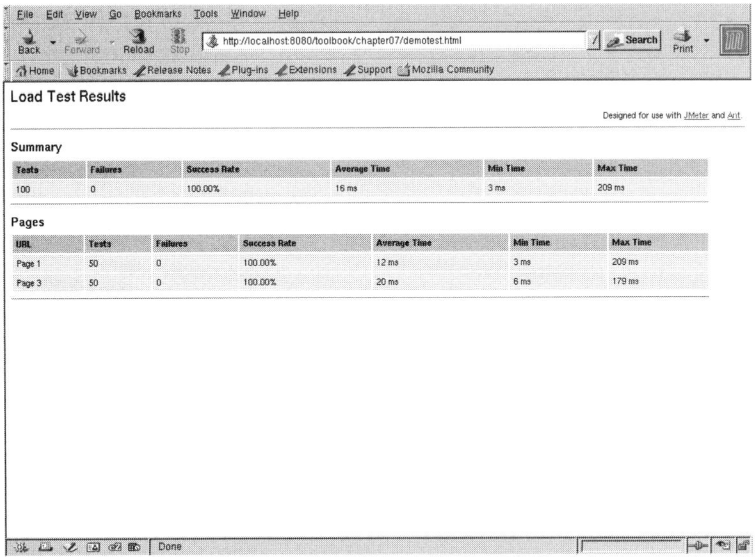

Load Test Results

Designed for use with JMeter and Ant.

Summary

Tests	Failures	Success Rate	Average Time	Min Time	Max Time
100	0	100.00%	16 ms	3 ms	209 ms

Pages

URL	Tests	Failures	Success Rate	Average Time	Min Time	Max Time
Page 1	50	0	100.00%	12 ms	3 ms	209 ms
Page 3	50	0	100.00%	20 ms	6 ms	179 ms

Figure 7.8. HTML results of a JMeter test.

there is no need to hit it with thousands of threads. If there are certain times of day when the load is expected to increase, then the expected peak load should be simulated. A safety margin should always be factored in, which could be anything from 10 percent to 300 percent, based on the kind of fluctuations that are expected. This margin will provide an extra level of comfort that the system will stay up on an unexpectedly busy day.

It is also necessary to consider what users will be doing on a system, as well as how many of them there will be. In the calculator application users will more commonly be submitting numbers to be added than loading the welcome page. Therefore, more threads should be hitting the result page, with a few simultaneously hitting the welcome and input pages.

Tests should be run from multiple machines and, if possible, from machines with different operating systems. Using several machines creates a more realistic test as well as ensuring that each JMeter instance is running at full speed. It is possible that different operating systems will have slight quirks in their network implementations. As remarkable as it may seem, under heavy loads it is possible for these quirks to affect behavior on the server.

Although all the tests in this book have run for a limited number of iterations, a better test would be to let the system run for hours or even days. Sometimes an application will very slowly consume resources, and it may not run out until many thousands of requests have been handled.

Some consideration is also required to determine what constitutes a successful test. The success of all text assertions is a good start, but a page that takes a minute to render is almost as useless to an end user as one that does not render at all. The use of a timing assertion can ensure not only that pages work but that they work well.

For systems that will need to handle very large amounts of traffic it may be necessary to build in some type of graceful performance degradation. Perhaps beyond a certain level of activity the system will need to display pages recommending that users come back later. Tests would then need to be written that ensure that every concurrent request beyond the threshold results in this message. Creating such a test may be difficult, but one way to approach it would be to add two assertions to the sampler, one expecting the normal page and one expecting the delay message. If the threshold is 200 simultaneous requests, then under a load of 300 threads, the former assertion should fail about 33 percent of the time. The exact number of failures should match the number of times the second assertion succeeds.

7.6 Beyond This Book

Although JMeter is written in Java, it executes no code on the server and therefore may be used to test Web application written in Perl or any other language. It may even be used to test how well Web servers serve static content such as flat HTML and images.

JMeter is capable of doing much more than testing Web pages. It is also possible to test database queries by specifying JDBC connection info, a SQL command, and the expected results. Often a significant portion of an application's time is spent accessing the database, so performance testing the database components in isolation is often a good step toward improving overall performance.

Although JMeter comes with a rich set of logic controllers, timers, and other components, there is always the possibility that some functionality will be needed that JMeter does not provide. Because JMeter is open source, such functionality could always be added to the base system by modifying or extending the source code. Fortunately this potentially difficult solution is not needed, as JMeter is extensible. Just as the Ant developers foresaw the need to dynamically add new tasks, JMeter allows new elements to be defined and loaded.

The steps to add a feature to JMeter are rather similar to those for adding a new task to Ant. The base system provides a number of interfaces including `Timer`, `SampleListener`, `ConfigElement`, and so on. A new component needs to implement the appropriate interface, most of which are rather simple. Components will also typically implement the `JMeterComponentModel` interface, which will allow them to be used from the GUI. Finally, all custom components should be placed in a file called "ApacheJMeter.jar" and this jar placed in the classpath. JMeter will automatically find the classes and place them in the appropriate menus.

In practice, creating the GUI is likely to be the most difficult part of this process. Fortunately there are many good templates to start with in the form of the built-in JMeter components.

7.7 Summary

Tool: JMeter
Purpose: Stress testing of Web applications
Version covered: 2.0.1
Home page: http://jakarta.apache.org/jmeter/
License: The Apache Software License, Version 2.0
Further Reading:

- http://jakarta.apache.org/jmeter/extending/index.html—More details on adding custom components to JMeter.
- *Java Performance and Scalability, Volume 1: Server-Side Programming Techniques,* by Dov Bulka, Addison-Wesley, 2000. Provides a wealth of information on how to optimize Java code.

CHAPTER 8

Simplifying Bean Development with BeanUtils

The preceding chapters dealt with tools that are external to the program being developed. These tools are meant to simplify the development of a program and verification of the program's correctness. We now turn to tools that are incorporated into programs being developed. These tools solve common problems and reduce the quantity and complexity of code that must be written.

One very common problem is the issue of hierarchical data. This problem takes many forms, such as a network of nested beans, an XML document, or several tables in a database with one-to-many or many-to-many relationships. In all these cases the common feature is that one object may have many connections to other objects, which may themselves have many connections, and so on. In data structure terms all these hierarchies can be represented as trees.

The general techniques for dealing with trees are well known. However, the APIs for traversing and manipulating such trees may vary significantly depending on the underlying implementation.

This chapter looks at the first of two tools that make working with trees much easier. This tool is called BeanUtils, and it works with JavaBeans only. This is not a very limiting restriction because tools exist that convert many other kinds of hierarchical data into beans.

Another way of thinking about BeanUtils is that it greatly simplifies the process of writing code that does reflection. In classic tool fashion, BeanUtils provides a number of ready-to-use methods that handle common reflection problems, which can save a developer hours of writing code.

8.1 Introduction to BeanUtils

Beans and hierarchies of beans are ubiquitous throughout Java development. On the client side the hierarchy of frames, panels, buttons, and other widgets may be represented as a tree of Swing beans. On the server side a user's Web session will likely consist of a tree of beans that may hold anything from game scores to items in a shopping cart.

One of the primary factors that makes beans so useful is their dynamic nature. Through the use of the **reflection APIs** that are part of the Java core library any program can create and manipulate beans without any advance knowledge of the implementing class. Although these introspection techniques are powerful, they can also be difficult to use. Something relatively simple such as finding and retrieving a property may take several lines of code. Such code will often appear several times throughout a program with slight modifications based on the particular situation.

BeanUtils provides a higher-level API that is both simpler and more powerful than the standard API. Typically pages full of reflection code can be replaced by a single call to BeanUtils. To see this in action it will be useful to consider a typical application such as a program that maintains information about a CD collection. Listing 8.1 shows a bean representing a musical artist.

Listing 8.1 A bean representing a musical artist

```
package com.awl.toolbook.chapter08;

import java.util.HashMap;
import java.util.ArrayList;
import java.io.Serializable;

public class Artist implements Serializable {
    public Artist() {}

    private String name;
    public String getName() {return name;}
    public void setName(String name) {this.name = name;}
    private HashMap albums = new HashMap();
    public int getNumAlbums() {return albums.size();}
```

```
public Album getAlbum(String name) {
    return (Album) albums.get(name);
}

public void setAlbum(String name,Album a) {
    // find this album in the ordered list
    int index = -1;
    for(int i=0;i<orderedAlbums.size();i++) {
        if(getOrderedAlbum(i).getName() == name) {
            index = i;
        }
    }

    if(index == -1) {
        orderedAlbums.add(a);
    } else {
        orderedAlbums.set(index,a);
    }

    albums.put(name,a);
}

private ArrayList orderedAlbums = new ArrayList();

public Album getOrderedAlbum(int i) {
    return (Album) orderedAlbums.get(i);
}

public void setOrderedAlbum(int i,Album a) {
    if(i == orderedAlbums.size()) {
        orderedAlbums.add(a);
    } else {
        orderedAlbums.set(i,a);
    }

    albums.put(a.getName(),a);
}
```

Listing 8.1 A bean representing a musical artist *(continued)*

```
    private HashMap annotations = new HashMap();
    public String getAnnotation(String name) {
        return annotations.get(name).toString();
    }

    public void setAnnotation(String name, String val) {
        annotations.put(name,val);
    }
}
```

Along with the bean from Listing 8.1 will be a set of beans representing information about the other elements of a collection. Listing 8.2 shows the outline of these beans. The full implementation follows the patterns from Listing 8.1 and may be found on the companion CD-ROM.

Listing 8.2 Outline of the CD beans

```
public class Collection {
    private HashMap artists;
}

private class Album {
    private String name;
    private HashMap annotations;
    private int releaseYear;
    private ArrayList tracks;
}

private class Track {
    private HashMap annotations;
    private String name;
    private double time;
}
```

Conceptually a collection contains a number of artists, each artist contains a number of albums, and each album contains a number of tracks. Each of these entities has particular data fields intrinsic to it, such as the name of an artist or the length of a track. In addition, it is possible to add annotations to any entity. Such an annotation might mark a track or album as a live recording or indicate a genre for an artist or album. Finally, note that there are two ways to obtain an album from an artist; either by the name of the album or by the order in which it was released. Code in the `setOrderedAlbum()` and `setAlbum()` methods ensures that this data remains synchronized.

8.2 Simple Properties

The heart of BeanUtils is a class called `PropertyUtils`, which provides a variety of static methods for getting and setting properties. The simplest usage gets a property such as a single string, integer, or object. For example, the call to get the name of an artist is

```
PropertyUtils.getSimpleProperty(artist, "name");
```

It is just as easy to set an artist's name

```
PropertyUtils.setSimpleProperty(artist, "name",
                                "the new name");
```

8.3 Indexed Properties

In addition to simple properties, `PropertyUtils` has methods for dealing with **indexed properties.** Conceptually an indexed property may be thought of as an array, although more literally the requirement is that the `get` method must take an integer argument, and the `set` method must take an integer argument along with the new value. One way to get an artist's first album is fairly obvious

```
PropertyUtils.getIndexedProperty(artist, "orderedAlbum", 0);
```

`PropertyUtils` offers an even more convenient means to accomplish the same task. `getIndexedProperty()` can take a single argument with a special syntax that specifies both the name of the property and the index. This is designated by enclosing the index in brackets, just as would be done in Java code.

```
PropertyUtils.getIndexedProperty(artist, "orderedAlbum[0]");
```

The number here must be a literal; it cannot be a reference to a variable or another property.

There are also set methods that correspond to both forms of the get method:

```
Album firstAlbum = new Album();
...
PropertyUtils.setIndexedProperty(artist, "orderedAlbum",
                                 0, firstAlbum);
PropertyUtils.setIndexedProperty(artist, "orderedAlbum[0]",
                                 firstAlbum);
```

There is no intrinsic notion of the size of an indexed property, although many such properties are implemented as arrays that do have a size. Therefore, the behavior of these methods when asked to get or set a value beyond the number of available elements is entirely dependent on how the bean implements the get and set methods. If those methods throw an `ArrayIndexOutOfBoundsException`, then so will the `PropertyUtil` methods.

There are tradeoffs to be made when deciding how to implement indexed properties. Often it is desirable to grow a set of elements by simply setting a new value. When an artist comes out with a second album, it is convenient to be able to write

```
PropertyUtils.setIndexedProperty(artist, "orderedAlbum[1]",
                                 newAlbum);
```

and have this automatically expand the underlying storage as needed. This is the way the beans in Listings 8.1 and 8.2 work. Indexed properties are stored in `ArrayLists`. If the provided index is one greater than the current size when performing a set, the element will be added instead of modified. This behavior is not strictly in keeping with the JavaBean specification, which states that the only way to change the size of an indexed property is to call a set method that replaces the current array with a new one. Developers need to weigh for themselves the pros and cons of convenience versus strict adherence to the specifications.

8.4 Mapped Properties

In the JavaBeans specification properties can only be simple or indexed by a number. BeanUtils adds a new ability for properties to be indexed by strings, as in a `Map`. Such properties are called **mapped properties.** These closely parallel indexed properties, except that the get and set methods take strings instead of integers. The following line could be used to retrieve the annotation, indicating whether a track is live:

```
PropertyUtils.getMappedProperty(track, "annotations" "live");
```

Mapped properties can be accessed with a shorthand syntax similar to that used for indexed properties. For mapped properties the key appears within parentheses.

```
PropertyUtils.getMappedProperty(track, "annotations(live)");
```

8.5 Nested Properties

Often the value of a bean property is itself a bean; indeed this is what makes trees of beans possible. It is always possible to traverse such a structure by repeatedly calling the appropriate set methods. For example, the name of an artist's first album could be obtained with

```
Album album =
    (Album) PropertyUtils.getIndexedProperty(artist,
                  "orderedAlbums[0]");
String name =
    (String) PropertyUtils.getSimpleProperty(album, name);
```

Clearly this requires several of lines of code along with a lot of casting. Once again, BeanUtils provides an easier way by introducing the concept of **nested properties.** If an expression such as "track[2]" or "albums(Wishfire)" would result in a bean, a property of that bean can be specified by appending a dot followed by the name of the property.

```
PropertyUtils.getNestedProperty(artist,
                              "orderedAlbums[0].name");
```

Note that this still resembles Java syntax, although it pretends that all the members are public and hides the fact that under the covers get and set methods are being called. Properties can be set using the same syntax.

Finally, there are two methods of `PropertyUtils` that are so useful that they practically subsume all the other methods discussed. These are `getProperty()` and `setProperty()`. These allow an arbitrary sequence of simple, indexed, mapped, and nested properties to be specified by a single string. For example, to get the name of the first track on "Sever" by This Ascension:

```
PropertyUtils.getProperty(collection,
"artist(This Ascension).orderedAlbums[0].tracks[0].name");
```

There is also a set method, which could be used to mark the first track of an album as a live recording as

```
PropertyUtils.setProperty(collection,
   "artists(VNV Nation).albums(Honor 2003)." +
   "track[1].annotations(live)",
Boolean.TRUE);
```

The first argument string is broken into two pieces to make it fit the printed page, but this also illustrates an important point. Because the argument is just a string, it is easy to dynamically build and traverse paths. For example, the following code could be used to get the name of the first tracks on all albums by Sunshine Blind:

```
Integer count =
  (Integer)
      PropertyUtils.getProperty(
          collection,
          "artist(Sunshine Blind).numAlbums");


for int(i=0;i<count.intValue();i++) {
  System.out.println(PropertyUtils.getProperty(collection,
    "artist(Sunshine Blind).album[" +
    i +
    "].track[0].name");
}
```

Given how powerful the general `getProperty()` and `setProperty()` methods are, it is natural at this point to wonder why anyone would ever use the more specific, limited methods discussed earlier in this chapter. The answer has to do with error conditions. If any of the elements in a long expression does not exist, an exception will be thrown and it may be difficult to find the exact point at which the failure occurred and recover appropriately. There are lots of reasons such an expression might fail: The name of a simple property might have been mistyped, or an indexed property might not have as many elements as expected, or a mapped property might be missing the given key. In light of these possibilities it sometimes makes sense to traverse a tree step by step.

8.6 Converters

All the calls to the set methods of `PropertyUtils` in the preceding sections passed in objects that matched the type expected by the underlying set method in the bean. For example, when setting `album.name` a string was provided, and when setting `artist.orderedAlbums[0]` an instance of `Album` was given. The situation is somewhat more complicated when setting something that is not an object, such as the year an album was released. The temptation would be to call `setSimpleProperty()` with an `int` as the second argument, but the method only accepts objects. This means that the `int` would normally need to be boxed in an `Integer`

```
PropertyUtils.setSimpleProperty(album, releaseYear,
                                new Integer(2003));
```

The low-level reflection API automatically handles any needed conversion from objects to primitive types when setting properties and from primitive types to objects when getting properties.

BeanUtils takes this idea several steps further by introducing **converters.** Converters are classes that can automatically convert from one type to another based on the type that is needed and the type that is provided. In particular this makes it possible to set int and `Integer` values from a `String`, as in

```
PropertyUtils.setSimpleProperty(album,releaseYear,"2003");
```

Converters are also available that convert to `Double`, `Boolean`, and so on. There are even converters that can translate from strings to arrays. An array may be represented as a sequence of elements separated by commas or white space and for clarity may also be delineated by braces—for example, "{1,8,45,2}" could be used as the value for a property comprising an array of integers.

The ability to use strings without worrying about the underlying type is very handy because most user input arrives in the form of a string. This is true for applications that run from the command line, GUIs, the Web, and so on.

8.7 Adding New Converters

Just as it is often useful to be able to treat strings as integers or arrays, there are many situations where it would be convenient to use a string to represent an arbitrary data type. BeanUtils makes this possible by allowing developers to extend the set of converters. A custom converter is a class with a `convert()` method that takes an object and returns an object of the desired type. Converters are registered with the system by providing the class name along with the condition under which it should be invoked. Because BeanUtils will use the provided class name to figure out what to do with objects, only one converter can be specified for any given class. However, it is possible to register one converter to handle multiple different classes.

When adding tracks to a new album, it would be useful to be able to simply pass in a string representing the name and optionally the length, rather than having to explicitly construct new `Track` objects. One possible representation would be to use brackets at the end of the name to hold the length. With this facility the tracks of a new album could be defined as

```
String baseName =
"artist(Faith and the Muse)." +
:album(The Burning Season).track";

PropertyUtils.setProperty(collection,
                          baseName+"[0]",
                          "Bait and Switch[204]");

PropertyUtils.setProperty(collection,
                          baseName+"[1]",
                          "Sredni Vashtar[215]");
```

Listing 8.3 shows the converter that will accomplish this.

Listing 8.3 A custom converter for tracks

```
package com.awl.toolbook.chapter08;

import org.apache.commons.beanutils.Converter;
import org.apache.commons.beanutils.ConversionException;

public class TrackConverter implements Converter {
    public Object convert(Class type, Object val)
        throws ConversionException
    {
        String value;

        try {
            value = (String) val;
        } catch (ClassCastException e) {
            throw new ConversionException(
                        "Unable to convert a " +
                        val.getClass()        +
                        " to a Track");
        }
```

```
        Track track   = new Track();
        int seconds   = 0;

        int pos1      = value.indexOf('[');
        int pos2      = value.indexOf(']');

        if(pos1 != -1 && pos2 != -1) {
            try {
                seconds = Integer.parseInt(
                              value.substring(pos1+1,pos2));
            } catch (NumberFormatException e) {
                throw new
                    ConversionException("Malformed time");
            }
            value = value.substring(0,pos1);
        }

        track.setName(value);
        track.setTime(seconds);

        return track;
    }
}
```

The bulk of Listing 8.3 is concerned with munging the provided string in order to extract the necessary information. This will be the case for most converters.

The first argument to `convert()` is a class that represents the type that should be returned. This allows one converter to handle multiple types. The second argument is the object to be converted. While this will often be a string, there may be cases where it is useful to convert from another type. When converting to a `Date` it might be useful to accept both a string such as "10/15/2003" and a `Long` representing the number of seconds since January 1, 1970.

Once the converter has been defined, it is added to the system through a simple call to a static method:

```
org.apache.commons.beanutils.ConvertUtils.register(
     new com.awl.toolbook.chapter08.TrackConverter(),
     com.awl.toolbook.chapter08.Track);
```

This tells BeanUtils that whenever it needs a `Track` and has an instance of a different class, it should call `TrackConverter` to perform the conversion.

It is tempting to place this call in a `static` block within the `TrackConverter` class, but this is a catch-22, as the static block will not be executed until the class is loaded, and the class will not be loaded until it is first registered. Consequently registration must take place somewhere else, probably in the startup code for the application.

8.8 Dynamic Beans

BeanUtils can manage collections of arbitrary name/value pairs of data through the use of mapped properties. This approaches the idea of a dynamic bean with properties that may be defined on the fly. A `Map`- based bean falls short of this idea in a couple of ways. First, there is no check on the names. If a bean should have a property called "muse" and someone mistypes the name as "moose" in a set command, the result will be the creation of the "moose" property instead of an error. The second shortcoming of `Map`- based beans is that there is no check or conversion of types. A track could be given a `live` annotation by setting the value to `Boolean.TRUE`. If another line of code attempted to set the value to the string `"true,"` there would be be neither an error nor an automatic conversion to a `Boolean`. This could cause problems down the line if code is expecting `live` annotations to be of a particular type.

While both these defects could be fixed by using a genuine bean, such an approach also has difficulties. Notably, a new class must be written and compiled, and if it is changed, the application may need to be restarted.

BeanUtils bridges the gap between Java beans and mapped beans with objects called **DynaBeans.** DynaBeans are instances of a **DynaClass,** which contain DynaProperties. A DynaProperty has both a name and a type, eliminating most of the defects of mapped beans.

A new DynaClass can be created by defining its name and set of properties. The following code could be used to define a set of annotations for tracks that can indicate whether a track is live, the name of a guest vocalist if present, and an array of other artists who have covered the song:

```
DynaProperty[] props = new DynaProperty[] {
    new DynaProperty("live", Boolean.class),
    new DynaProperty("guestVocalist", String.class),
    new DynaProperty("coveredBy", Artist[].class),
};

DynaClass trackAnnotation =
  new BasicDynaClass("TrackAnnotation", null, props);
```

The `BasicDynaClass` is constructed with a name and an array of properties. The second argument, which is `null` in the preceding example, is a class that will serve as the implementation. A `null` value means the default implementation will be used, which is `BasicDynaBean`.

Once the class has been defined, an instance can be constructed with

```
DynaBean annotation = trackAnnotation.newInstance();
```

Clearly this means that the `annotation` property in the `Track` class should be defined as a `DynaBean` instead of a `HashMap`. However, the definition and construction of the `DynaBean` should not be done in `Track` because this would defeat the whole point of making it dynamic. Instead, any program that uses `Track` should set up the annotations as appropriate.

Although there are methods in DynaBean to get and set properties, the intended use is to allow `PropertyUtils` to do all the work. All the `PropertyUtils` methods act on DynaBeans in exactly the same way they act on regular JavaBeans. For example,

```
PropertyUtils.getProperty(track,
                          "annotation.coveredBy[0].name");
```

will return the name of the first artist to cover the song, and

```
PropertyUtils.setProperty(track,
                          "annotation.live",
                          "true");
```

will mark the track as live, correctly calling a converter to translate from the string "true" to `Boolean.TRUE`.

8.9 Enhancing DynaBeans

The `BasicDynaClass` and `BasicDynaBean` classes have certain limitations. DynaBeans may not have methods, and there is no provision for a dynamic bean to extend another the way Java classes can. It is also not possible to dynamically add new properties.

Despite these restrictions, dynamic beans can be very useful in certain applications. Notably, dynamic beans work extremely well with databases. It is often extremely convenient to represent the result of a query as an array of beans that have a property for each column. This can be done statically for beans representing tables, but it is very common for a query to return fields from multiple tables. It would not make sense to define a separate Java class for each query that might be executed throughout a program. Nor does a `Map` provide an adequate solution, because type information is important in database applications. DynaBeans fit the bill perfectly.

In cases where some additional functionality is needed it is possible to create custom dynamic beans. This can be done by writing classes that extend `BasicDynaBean` and `BasicDynaClass`, or by creating classes that implement the `DynaBean` or `DynaClass` interfaces. One possible use for this would be to equip a DynaBean with a property that is defined remotely or that continuously updates. This can be done by extending `BasicDynaBean` with regular bean properties, as in

```
public class DateDynaBean extends BasicDynaBean {
    public Date getDate() {return new Date();}

    public Object get(String name) {
        if(name.equals("date")) {
            return getDate();
        }
        return super.get(name);
    }
}
```

To use this class it is just necessary to specify `DateDynaBean.class` as the second argument when creating the `DynaClass`. Any DynaBeans thus defined will automatically have the `date` property.

8.10 Summary

Tool: BeanUtils
Purpose: Simplify bean access and enhance bean functionality
Version covered: 1.6.1
Home page: http://jakarta.apache.org/commons/beanutils/
License: The Apache Software License, Version 1.1
Further Reading:

- The JavaBeans specification: http://java.sun.com/products/javabeans/
- *Data Structures and Algorithm Analysis in Java,* by Mark Allen Weiss, Addison-Wesley, 2000—A comprehensive book on data structures, including a chapter on trees.

CHAPTER 9

Traversing Hierarchical Data with JXPath

Chapter 8 presented BeanUtils, a toolkit that offers a very Java-like syntax for traversing trees of Java objects. There is a similar but more powerful expression language that was developed to traverse XML called **XPath.** XPath was developed by the World Wide Web consortium and is not intrinsically tied to Java. JXPath is a Java implementation of this specification that is capable of applying the power of XPath to XML and other kinds of hierarchical data.

This chapter assumes some familiarity with XML. Readers who are not yet acquainted with XML can start with some of the suggestions for further reading listed at the end of this chapter.

9.1 Introduction to XPath

To facilitate the study of XPath it will help to create an XML version of the CD collection used in Chapter 8. The first step in creating this XML model is to define a DTD (Document Type Definition) indicating the entities within the collections and the rules relating to them. This DTD is shown in Listing 9.1.

Listing 9.1 The Document Type Definition

```
<!ELEMENT artist (album*)>
<!ATTLIST artist name CDATA #REQUIRED>
```

Listing 9.1 The Document Type Definition *(continued)*

```
<!ELEMENT album (track*)>
<!ATTLIST album name CDATA #REQUIRED>
<!ATTLIST album year CDATA #REQUIRED>

<!ELEMENT track (#PCDATA)>
```

An XML document with CD data is shown in Listing 9.2.

Listing 9.2 CD data in XML

```
<?xml version='1.0' encoding='iso-8859-1'>
<!DOCTYPE artist SYSTEM "cd.dtd">

<collection>
  <artist name="The Cr\"üxshadows">
    <album name="Telemetry of a Fallen Angel" year="1996">
      <track>Descension</track>
      <track>Monsters</track>
      <track>Jackal-Head</track>
    </album>
    <album name="The Mystery of the Whisper" year="1999">
      <track>Isis & Osiris (Life/Death)</track>
      <track>Cruelty</track>
      <track>Leave me Alone</track>
    </album>
    <album name="Wishfire" year="2002">
      <track>Before the Fire</track>
      <track>Return (Coming Home)</track>
      <track>Binary</track>
    </album>
  </artist>
</collection>
```

As expected, this XML is structurally very similar to the beans used in Chapter 8, and it deals with the same kinds of entities.

At the simplest level XPath resembles the syntax used by BeanUtils, except the separator is a slash (/) instead of a dot (.).

Errors to Watch For

Indexes in XPath start counting from 1 instead of from 0. This isn't really a bug, since that is the defined behavior. However, it is something to keep in mind while using JXPath.

Therefore, the XPath expression to find the second track on the first album by the first artist would be

```
/collection/artist[1].album[1].track[2]
```

Note that the expression also starts with a leading slash.

XPath and BeanUtils diverge beyond the simple mechanism used to select a specific element. One powerful feature of XPath is the ability to specify only part of an expression. Such a partial expression is a shorthand for all possible completions, so if the last set of brackets in the previous example were omitted

```
/collection/artist[1]/album[1]/track
```

then the expression would specify all the tracks on the album. This could also be done in BeanUtils, assuming there is a `getTrack()` method that returns the whole array.

The next step is something that simply cannot be done in BeanUtils. It is possible to leave off intermediate array specifiers, so an expression like

```
/collection/artist[1]/album/track
```

would return all tracks on all albums by the first artist. Such indexed and nonindexed elements can be freely mixed.

```
/collection/artist/album/track[2]
```

would return the second track on every album. Entire portions of a path can even be omitted by using two slashes, as in

```
//track
```

which would return all tracks on all albums by all artists.

Attributes can be specified by prefacing the name with an at sign (@). The expression to retrieve the name of the first artist would be

```
/collection/artist[1]/@name
```

This parallels the ability in BeanUtils to get the value of a simple property, but note the distinction in how such properties are treated. In beans, and therefore in BeanUtils syntax, a bean property may be either simple or nested. In XML simple properties are stored as attributes or `CData` subnodes, whereas compound data are always stored as subnodes. The syntax to obtain a simple property stored as an attribute must differ from the syntax used to obtain compound data stored as a node. Attributes are referenced with a dot (.) or specified with an at sign (@). Subnodes are accessed with a slash (/).

Although XPath does not provide for mapped properties, it does have something even more powerful: the ability to specify the value of an attribute to restrict the set of returned data. Such a specification appears in brackets, as in

```
//album[@name='Wishfire']/track
```

which would return all tracks from all albums named "Wishfire," of which there happens to be only one.

The set of values can be restricted based on fairly complex expressions. Expressions can check for equality and greater-than or less-than relations between an attribute and a constant, or between two attributes. Boolean operators can be used to combine expressions. There are also a number of functionlike entities that can be used, such as

```
/artist[position() < 3]
```

which would return the first two artists.

There is much more that could be said about XPath, but this will be sufficient for the remainder of this book.

9.2 Using JXPath

JXPath is quite easy to set up and use. Listing 9.3 shows a small program that takes the URL of an XML document as its first argument and an XPath expression as its second, and prints the matching elements.

Listing 9.3 Using JXPath

```
package com.awl.toolbook.chapter09;

import org.apache.commons.jxpath.*;
import org.apache.commons.jxpath.xml.DocumentContainer;
import java.net.*;
import java.util.Iterator;

class JXPathDemo {
    public static void main(String argv[]) throws Exception {
        URL url = new URL(argv[0]);

        JXPathContext context =
            JXPathContext.newContext(
                              new DocumentContainer(url));

        Iterator it =
            context.iterate(argv[1]);

        while(it.hasNext()) {
            System.out.println("Next item: " + it.next());
        }
    }
}
```

Here are some sample results using the XML document from Listing 9.1 and a variety of XPath expressions:

```
java com.awl.toolbook.chapter09.JXPathDemo
     file:collection.xml
     /collection

Next item: Descension
      Monsters
      Jackal-Head
    Isis and Osiris (Life/Death)
      Cruelty
      Leave me Alone
    Before the Fire
      Return (Coming Home)
      Binary
```

Note that when an XPath result is a compound node JXPath will convert the result into a simple string containing all the data in indented form.

```
java com.awl.toolbook.chapter09.JXPathDemo
     file:collection.xml
     /collection/artist[1]/@name

Next item: The Cruxshadows
```

In this case JXPath is asked for a specific piece of data, which is returned as a string.

```
java com.awl.toolbook.chapter09.JXPathDemo
     file:collection.xml
     "/collection/artist/album[@name = 'Wishfire']/track"

Next item: Before the Fire
Next item: Return (Coming Home)
Next item: Binary
```

This example shows the use of a constraint on the name.

Beans can be traversed with JXPath almost as easily as with BeanUtils. There is only one additional step; before a path can be traversed, a context must be created that will hold the entire tree. A `Collection` bean from Chapter 8 could be set up for traversal with

```
JXPathContext context =
    JXPathContext.newContext(collection);
```

It is almost as easy to set up a context for an XML document. Listing 9.4 shows a skeleton of the necessary code

Listing 9.4 Traversing an XML document

```
import org.apache.commons.jxpath.*;
import org.apache.commons.jxpath.xml.DocumentContainer;
import java.net.*;

...

URL url = getClass().getResource("collection.xml");

JXPathContext context =
    JXPathContext.newContext(new DocumentContainer(url));
```

In Listing 9.4 the `JXPathContext` is constructed from a wrapper around the XML document, called a `DocumentContainer`. There are many ways to construct such a `DocumentContainer`; the easiest is to build it from a URL, as is done here. The `getResource()` method will find the named file in the CLASSPATH and return it as a URL, but a URL could also be provided directly. There are no restrictions on the form of these URLs; local files can be accessed though `file:` URLs and remote data can be accessed through `http:` or `ftp:` URLs.

It is also possible to combine XML and beans. A class might contain multiple CD collections that are stored in XML, as in Listing 9.5.

Listing 9.5 Combining beans and XML

```
import org.apache.commons.jxpath.*;
import org.apache.commons.jxpath.xml.DocumentContainer;
import java.net.*;

class MultiCollection {
    private JXPathContext firstCollection = null;
    public JXPathContext getFirstCollection() {
        return firstCollection;
    }

    private JXPathContext secondCollection = null;
    public JXPathContext getSecondCollection() {
        return secondCollection;
    }

    public MultiCollection() {
        URL url = getClass().
                    getResource("collection1.xml");

        firstCollection =
            JXPathContext.newContext(
                new DocumentContainer(url));

        url = getClass().getResource("collection2.xml");
```

Listing 9.5 Combining beans and XML *(continued)*

```
        secondCollection =
            JXPathContext.newContext(
                new DocumentContainer(url));
    }
}
```

Given a bean such as that in Listing 9.5, a JXPath expression could start with one of the bean properties and proceed from there through the XML properties, as in

```
/firstCollection/artist[1].album[1].name
```

The methods for traversing a context are the same regardless of how the context was established. Single values, whether simple or compound, are obtained with the `getValue()` method. Obtaining the name of the first track on "Wishfire" would be done with

```
String name =
    (String) context.getValue(
              "/album[@name='Wishfire'].track[1].name");
```

Similarly, the whole album could be obtained using "/album[@name='Wishfire']" as the expression. Note that in the case of the bean-based tree this will return an `Album` object, but in the case of the XML-based tree, the result will be an internal object representing an XML node, which is not likely to be immediately useful.

Expressions that would result in multiple values are obtained using the `iterate()` method, which returns an `Iterator`, and may then be used in the standard way. The following prints all album names:

```
Iterator albums =
    context.iterate("/context/artist[1]/album/@name");

while(albums.hasNext()) {
    System.out.println(albums.next());
}
```

Note that the expression ends in "@name," indicating that the name, which is a string, should be obtained from each album. The albums may be beans or XML nodes, depending on where the data came from. In general it is good practice for programs to deal only with data at the leaves. Leaf data is likely to be of known types, whereas the intermediate objects may be XML representations, beans, or other containers.

Restricted values work as expected—for example

```
Iterator liveAlbums =
    context.iterate("//album/annotation[@live='true']");
```

would allow a program to loop over all live albums. Note that this will work whether `annotation` is a `Hashmap` or a BeanUtils `DynaBean`, as described in Chapter 8. This is possible because JXPath has special code for handling DynaBeans.

9.3 Setting Values

JXPath can also be used to set values, change the structure of an existing tree, or even create a new tree. Setting a simple value works as expected:

```
context.setValue(
    "//collection/artist[1]/album[1]/@yearReleased",
    "1996");
```

This example also illustrates that JXPath has converters, although unlike BeanUtils the set of converts cannot be extended. However, converters for the primitive types—integer, float, boolean, and strings—are provided, which should cover most common situations.

Compound objects can also be set in a single operation:

```
Album a = new Album();
context.setValue("//collection/artist[1]/album[1]", a);
```

However, such an operation only makes sense when dealing with a bean-based context. Attempting to set a node to a bean in an XML context will result in the object being converted to a string before being set, so a subsequent call to `getValue()` will return something like `Album@121b59a`. It will also be impossible to add further structure or attributes to such a node.

9.4 Creating New Structures

Adding new structure to an existing tree is somewhat more complicated. For JXPath to add a new node, such as `//collection/artist[2]`, it would need to figure out the type of the new node, which will be `Artist` in the case of bean-based context and a class representing a node for an XML context. JXPath would also need to know how to construct this object and how to attach it to the parent. Whereas in some cases it might be possible to determine this information through advanced introspection, such a procedure would likely be error prone and incomplete. Instead JXPath places the burden of providing this information on the developer. This is done by writing a **factory.**

In the most general sense, a factory is a class that builds instances of other classes based on certain criteria. This concept is relevant and important independently of JXPath or even Java, and constitutes one of the major **design patterns,** general ways of thinking about programming.

Within JXPath a factory is a class that knows how to create a new node and connect it to the parent. Each context can be assigned only a single factory, so that factory must be able to handle all combinations of parents and subnodes that it may be asked to handle. It also means that the factory for a bean-based context will be very different from that for a XML context. A factory for the CD beans is presented in Listing 9.6.

Listing 9.6 A factory for the CD beans

```
package com.awl.toolbook.chapter09;

import org.apache.commons.jxpath.*;
import org.apache.commons.jxpath.xml.DocumentContainer;
import com.awl.toolbook.chapter08.*;

public class CDFactory extends AbstractFactory {
    public boolean createObject(
                    JXPathContext context,
                    Pointer pointer,
                    Object parent,
                    String name,
                    int index)
    {
        if(parent instanceof Collection) {
            Collection col = (Collection) parent;

            if(name.equals("artist")) {
              Artist a = new Artist();
```

```
                try {
                    col.setArtist(index,a);
                } catch (ArrayIndexOutOfBoundsException e) {
                    return false;
                }
            }

            return true;
        } else if(parent instanceof Artist) {
            Artist artist = (Artist) parent;

            if(name.equals("album")) {
                Album a = new Album();

                try {
                    artist.setOrderedAlbum(index,a);
                } catch (ArrayIndexOutOfBoundsException e) {
                    return false;
                }
            }

            return true;
        }

        return false;
    }
}
```

In most common usage all factories will closely follow Listing 9.6. There will always be a `createObject()` method, which is required by the interface. Within this method will be several clauses that check the type of the node to which the new structure is being added. Within each of these clauses will be several subclauses that check the name of the new node to create. These subclauses will act on this name, construct the appropriate object, and then set it in the parent as a basic or indexed property as appropriate.

Note that it is possible for the set to fail—for example, if the artist array has one element and JXPath is asked to create `artist[5]`. The set will also fail if it is asked to create a node with an unknown name or a node that does not belong to the parent. In case of any kind of failure the factory returns `false`, which will result in an exception.

Once a factory has been defined and installed, it can be used by making calls to `createPath()`. This is a distinct method from `setValue()` to ensure there is no confusion between creating new structure and modifying existing values.

```
context.setFactory(new CDFactory());

context.createPath("/collection/artist[2]");
context.setValue("/collection/artist[2].name"
                 "Apoptygma Berzerk");
```

Note that after the `artist[2]` node has been created the `name` can be set without creating an additional path. This is because as soon as a new `Artist` has been created the creation of the name is implied, because name is just a field within Artist.

9.4.1 Extending JXPath

There are many kinds of hierarchical data besides beans and XML. JXPath makes it relatively painless to create new contexts that will allow other kinds of data to be accessed through XPath expressions.

The core of a new context are custom classes that extend the abstract classes `NodePointer` and `NodeIterator`. The developer must also provide a `NodePointerFactory` and register the factory with the JXPath context manager, `JXPathContextReferenceImpl`. This is the class that is responsible for building the context when `JXPathContext.newContext()` is called.

To make these ideas concrete this section will develop a new context based on file systems, which are nicely hierarchical. The context will be constructed from a `java.io.File`, which should represent a directory. Directories have certain intrinsic attributes, so the following expressions

```
/@name
/@lastModified
```

will return the name and last modified date as a string, respectively. This syntax may look a little strange, but it is perfectly consistent with everything that has been seen previously. An @ immediately following a slash refers to an attribute of the root node.

A directory also may contain subdirectories, so

```
/directory[1]
/directory[@name='java']
```

would return the first subdirectory and the subdirectory named "java."

Directories also have files so that

```
/file[1]
/directory[1]/file[2]
//file
```

refer to the first file in the directory, the second file in the first subdirectory, and all files anywhere in the current tree, respectively.

Files also have names and last modification times, which will be treated in the same way as directories. The contents of a file will be denoted by the special attribute '@contents.'

The first and easiest step is to provide a new factory that will be responsible for creating new nodes within the context. There are only three methods this class must implement: one to create a node with no parent, one to create a node with a parent, and one that specifies the order in which this factory will be invoked relative to other factories. The factory for the new file system context is shown in Listing 9.7.

Listing 9.7 The factory

```
package com.awl.toolbook.chapter09;

import org.apache.commons.jxpath.ri.model.*;
import org.apache.commons.jxpath.ri.*;
import java.util.Locale;
import java.io.*;
public class FileSystemNodePointerFactory
    implements NodePointerFactory
{
    /**
     * Get the initial node pointer.  Object should be a
     * file representing the top-level directory of
     * interest
     */
    public NodePointer createNodePointer(QName name,
                                         Object object,
                                         Locale locale)
    {
        if(object instanceof File) {
            return new FileSystemNodePointer(name,
                                             (File) object);
        }
```

Listing 9.7 The factory *(continued)*

```
        return null;
    }

    public NodePointer createNodePointer(
                          NodePointer parent,
                          QName name,
                          Object object)
    {
        if(parent instanceof FileSystemNodePointer) {
            return new FileSystemNodePointer(
                    name,
                    parent,
                    new File(parent.getName().toString(),
                             name.getName()));
        }

        return null;
    }
    public int getOrder() {
        return 80;
    }
}
```

As promised, Listing 9.7 has the three necessary methods. The node creation methods do very little; they just call the appropriate constructor for the node. Note that these methods return `null` if they are asked to process an object that is not a `File` or part of a file system tree. `newContext()` will try all available factories until one returns a non-null result.

The order in which factories are called is determined by the values returned by the `getOrder()` methods; lower numbers are called first. The general bean context returns 900 and will handle any type of object. This means that if this new file system factory returned 901, there would be no way to get the new handler. In general, the more specific types should be called earlier in the chain.

The next step is to implement the node pointer itself. This is shown in Listing 9.8.

Listing 9.8 The node

```
package com.awl.toolbook.chapter09;

import org.apache.commons.jxpath.JXPathException;
import org.apache.commons.jxpath.ri.*;
import org.apache.commons.jxpath.ri.model.*;
import org.apache.commons.jxpath.util.ValueUtils;
import org.apache.commons.jxpath.ri.compiler.*;

import java.io.File;
import java.io.FileInputStream;
import java.util.Date;
import java.util.Locale;
import java.util.ArrayList;

public class FileSystemNodePointer extends NodePointer {
    private File theFile   = null;
    private String aValue = null;
    private Object value   = null;

    public FileSystemNodePointer(QName name,File f) {
        super(null);
        this.name = name;
        theFile = f;
        value   = f;
    }

    public FileSystemNodePointer(QName name,
                                 Object parent,
                                 File f)
    {
        super((NodePointer) parent);
        theFile = f;
        value   = f;
        this.name = name;
    }
    public FileSystemNodePointer(QName name,
                                 String aValue)
```

Listing 9.8 The node *(continued)*

```
    {
        super(null);
        this.aValue = aValue;
        value       = aValue;
        attribute   = true;
        this.name   = name;
    }

    public int compareChildNodePointers(
        NodePointer pointer1,
        NodePointer pointer2)
    {
        String name1 = pointer1.getName().toString();
        String name2 = pointer2.getName().toString();

        return name1.compareTo(name2);
    }

    public Object getBaseValue() {
        return value;
    }

    public Object getImmediateNode() {
        return value;
    }

    public int getLength() {
        return 1;
    }

    private QName name;
    public QName getName() {
        return name;
    }

    public boolean isCollection() {
        return false;
    }
```

```
public boolean isLeaf() {
        return !attribute && !theFile.isDirectory();
    }

    private boolean attribute;

    public void setAttribute(boolean b) {
        attribute = b;
    }

    public boolean isAttribute() {
        return attribute;
    }

    public void setValue(Object value) {
        this.value = value;
    }

    public Object getValue() {
        return value;
    }

    public NodeIterator childIterator(NodeTest a,
                                      boolean b,
                                      NodePointer c)
    {
        if(a instanceof NodeNameTest) {
            String name =
              ((NodeNameTest) a).getNodeName().toString();

            if(name.equals("directory")) {
                return
                    new FileSystemNodeIterator(
                        getDirectories());
            } else if(name.equals("file")) {
                return
                    new FileSystemNodeIterator(getFiles());
            } else {
                return null;
            }
```

Listing 9.8 The node *(continued)*

```
        }

        return null;
    }

    public ArrayList getFiles(boolean dir) {
        File children[] = theFile.listFiles();
        ArrayList ret = new ArrayList();

        for(int i=0;i<children.length;i++) {
            if(children[i].isDirectory() == dir) {
                ret.add(children[i]);
            }
        }

        return ret;
    }

    private ArrayList getDirectories() {
        return getFiles(true);
    }

    private ArrayList getFiles() {
        return getFiles(false);
    }

    public NodeIterator attributeIterator(QName qname) {
        String name = qname.getName();

        if(name.equals("name")) {
            return new SimpleIterator(theFile.getName());
        } else if(name.equals("size")) {
            return new SimpleIterator(
                             Long.toString(theFile.length()));
        } else if(name.equals("lastModified")) {
            return
              new SimpleIterator(
              (new Date(theFile.lastModified())).
                        toString());
```

```
        } else if(name.equals("contents")) {
            if(!theFile.isDirectory()) {
                return new SimpleIterator(getContents());
            }
        }

        return null;
    }

    private String getContents() {
        try {
            byte data[]         = new byte[1024];
            StringBuffer buffy = new StringBuffer();
            FileInputStream in =
                new FileInputStream(theFile);
            int count;

            while((count = in.read(data)) > 0) {
                buffy.append(new String(data,0,count));
            }

            in.close();
            return buffy.toString();
        } catch (Exception e) {}

        return "";
    }
}
```

This class starts with constructors that set a number of internal variables. In addition to the constructors that take files, as used in the factory, there is another constructor that takes a string value. This will be used to hold attribute values, as will be made clear shortly.

`compareChildNodePointers()` is declared as abstract in the base class and so must be provided. Here a simple lexical ordering is used. There may be cases where a more complex test is needed; when comparing elements that are meant to represent dates it may be necessary to parse the strings, convert the results to `long`s and then do a numeric comparison.

getBaseValue() and getImmediateNode() implement two more abstract methods. getBaseValue() is meant to return the value at the current node, while getImmediateNode() is meant to return the node itself. For current purposes these can both be considered the same thing because the File class constitutes both a value and a node in the sense that it maintains its own set of children.

Next there are a number of simple accessors and boolean expressions, which are relatively straightforward. Most of these are also abstract in the base class and must be provided.

childIterator() is where things get interesting. This is the method that will be called whenever a subexpression is encountered, whether that subexpression indicates an entire collection such as /directories or a specific element such as /directories[2]. This implementation explicitly handles the two cases of files and directories by building an iterator with the appropriate values. The iterator code will be shown shortly.

Next are various utility methods that get an ArrayList of files or directories, as used by childIterator().

Following this is attributeIterator(), which does for attributes what childIterator() does for subnodes. Once again, each possibility is explicitly handled. Note that a different iterator class is used. Following this is getContents(), which reads the contents of the current file.

The next class is the iterator for subnodes, shown in Listing 9.9.

Listing 9.9 The iterator

```
package com.awl.toolbook.chapter09;

import org.apache.commons.jxpath.JXPathException;
import org.apache.commons.jxpath.ri.*;
import org.apache.commons.jxpath.ri.model.*;
import org.apache.commons.jxpath.util.ValueUtils;
import org.apache.commons.jxpath.ri.compiler.*;

import java.io.File;
import java.util.ArrayList;

public class FileSystemNodeIterator
    implements NodeIterator
{
    private ArrayList  files;
```

```
    public FileSystemNodeIterator(ArrayList files) {
        this.files = files;
    }

    public NodePointer getNodePointer() {
        File f = (File) files.get(position);

        return new FileSystemNodePointer(
                                    new QName(f.getName()),
                                    f);
    }

    private int position = 0;

    public int getPosition() {
        return position;
    }

    public boolean setPosition(int position) {
        if(position <= files.size()) {
            this.position = position;
            return true;
        }

        return false;
    }
}
```

This is really little more than a wrapper around an `ArrayList` of files or directories. The JXPath system will invoke `setPostion()` with a particular value when it encounters an index property. JXPath will repeatedly call `setPosition()` until it returns `false` when processing all children. This latter case can happen when user code calls `iterate()`, when every child must be scanned for a certain property such as `directory[@name='java']`, or when walking a tree recursively, as in `/directory/file`.

In the tradition of recursive tree algorithms the `getNodePointer()` method returns a new `FileSystemNodePointer()`. If that node pointer's children are accessed, it will result in the construction of a new instance of `FileSystemNodeIterator`.

A different iterator is used when dealing with attributes, shown in Listing 9.10.

Listing 9.10 The simple iterator

```
package com.awl.toolbook.chapter09;

import org.apache.commons.jxpath.JXPathException;
import org.apache.commons.jxpath.ri.model.NodeIterator;
import org.apache.commons.jxpath.ri.model.NodePointer;

public class SimpleIterator implements NodeIterator {
    private String attrib;

    public SimpleIterator(String attrib) {
        this.attrib = attrib;
    }

    public NodePointer getNodePointer() {
        return new FileSystemNodePointer(null,attrib);
    }

    public int getPosition() {return 1;}

    public boolean setPosition(int position) {
        if(position == 1) {
            return true;
        }

        return false;
    }
}
```

This is much simpler than the `FileSystemNodeIterator`, because for present purposes attributes have only a single value. When a call is made to `getNodePointer()`, it returns a new `FileSystemNodePointer` built from a string. This is the reason for the string constructor mentioned when discussing Listing 9.8. JXPath has no notion of a primitive value; everything, including attributes, is a node. Rather than create another implementation of `NodePointer` to handle single string values, `FileSystemNodePointer` is pressed into double duty. Normally this would be very bad object-oriented design, but because attributes and nodes are closely intertwined, it makes sense to put the code relating to both in the same place.

Now that all these classes have been defined, using them is as simple as registering the factory and creating the context:

```
JXPathContextReferenceImpl.addNodePointerFactory(
      new FileSystemNodePointerFactory());
JXPathContext context =
    JXPathContext.newContext(new File("/some/directory"));
```

The rest of the code from Listing 9.3 would allow a program to traverse directories using this context.

9.5 A Few Notes on Defining New Contexts

Adding a new context to JXPath can involve a significant amount of work, as can readily be seen from the preceding section. Fortunately, there are often approaches that will simplify the process.

First, it may be possible to extend or modify an existing context. In this case, it might have been reasonable to start with `BeanPointer` and related classes that handle bean-based contexts. Once again, having access to the source code can be an invaluable aid in extending the system.

Second, it may be possible to recast the problem to reuse an existing context. When considering this approach the first question to ask is whether the object in question acts like a bean. If so, then the existing JXPath bean handler can be used, and no new code needs to be written. In this case, `File` does not act enough like a bean for this to be done. The primitive values like name and modification time do behave like bean properties, but the subdirectories and files within a directory can only be obtained as an entire array, not as an indexed property.

Fortunately, there is an easy fix; it would be possible to create a bean that wraps a `File` object. Such a bean for directories is shown in Listing 9.11.

Listing 9.11 A file bean

```
package com.awl.toolbook.chapter09;

import java.io.File;
import java.util.ArrayList;

public class DirectoryBean {
    public DirectoryBean() {}

    public DirectoryBean(File f) {
        setTheFile(f);
    }
```

Listing 9.11 A file bean *(continued)*

```
private File theFile;
public File getTheFile() {return theFile;}
public void setTheFile(File theFile) {
    this.theFile = theFile;
}

public String getName() {return theFile.getName();}
public void setName(String name) {}

public long getModifiedTime() {
    return theFile.lastModified();
}
public void setModifiedTime(long modifiedTime) {}

private boolean arraysBuilt = false;
private void buildArrays() {
    if(arraysBuilt) return;
    File children[] = theFile.listFiles();

    subdirs = new ArrayList();
    files   = new ArrayList();

    for(int i=0;i<children.length;i++) {
        if(children[i].isDirectory()) {
          subdirs.add(new DirectoryBean(children[i]));
        } else {
            files.add(new FileBean(children[i]));
        }
    }
}

private ArrayList subdirs;
public File getDirectory(int i) {
    buildArrays();
    return (File) subdirs.get(i);
}
public void setDirectory(int i,File f) {}
```

```
        private ArrayList files;
        public File getFile(int i) {
            buildArrays();
            return (File) files.get(i);
        }
        public void setFile(int i,File f) {}

    }
```

Note that the subdirectories and files are not obtained until they are needed. If `buildArrays()` were called in the constructor, the entire directory tree would be read into memory when the root node was constructed, which could be very wasteful if it turned out that only a small part were needed.

The corresponding `FileBean` is similar, except it omits the `getFile()` and `getDirectory()` methods and adds `getContents()`.

Much of the problem-specific code that appeared in the custom file system context also appears in these beans, although in slightly different forms. In particular, this is the code that gets primitive values like the name, along with code that traverses a directory and gets contents from a file. What is missing is all the code that deals with the intricacies of the JXPath system. As such, wrapping the problem in a bean and using existing JXPath tools is clearly an easier solution and should be used whenever possible.

9.6 Summary

Tool: JXPath
Purpose: Traverse arbitrary collection with the XPath syntax
Version covered: 1.1
Home page: http://jakarta.apache.org/commons/jxpath/
License: The Apache Software License, Version 1.1
Further Reading:

- A tutorial on DTDs: http://www.xmlfiles.com/dtd/.
- The JXPath specification: http://www.w3.org/TR/xpath.
- A well-written tutorial on XPath: http://www.zvon.org/xxl/XPathTutorial/General/examples.html.
- *Java Design Patterns: A Tutorial,* by James W. Cooper, Addison-Wesley, 2000.

CHAPTER 10

Database Tools

Databases are important in a wide range of Java applications. It would not be overstating the case to point out that many Java applications are essentially sophisticated front-ends for databases. For example, an online commerce site allows users to browse the database of products, and purchasing an item may consist of moving an entry from an inventory table to tables that manage shipping orders.

The introduction of JDBC as part of the Java core libraries has greatly contributed to simplifying the task of creating database-aware programs. It is almost always possible to make things even easier, and this chapter discusses three tools that interact with JDBC to provide a wealth of new benefits. It is assumed that the reader has some familiarity with JDBC and SQL, although some features of each will be introduced as needed.

10.1 Hsqldb

Before looking at any other database tools, it would make sense to start with a database! There are many available, including several excellent ones that are open source. Of particular interest is a database called hsqldb.

Hsqldb can be used like any other database; it can be run as a server that will process requests received over a socket and send back resulting data. There is nothing particularly special about this functionality, although hsqldb does it well and it is much easier to set up than other databases.

What makes hsqldb especially useful is that it is written in Java and may be run **in-process.** This means that instead of making a socket connection to a separate process, any program that embeds hsqldb can execute SQL commands locally. This is often much faster and may provide other advantages.

There are two in-process modes: in-memory and stand-alone. In-memory means that data is kept only in memory and will not be stored when the program terminates. This can be useful in applets and other applications that may not be able to access the file system. Stand-alone mode will store data to disk, and it is this mode that will be of the most interest in the following sections.

Using hsqldb through JDBC works like any other database, even for in-process usage.

```
Class.forName("org.hsqldb.jdbcDriver");

Connection db = DriverManager.getConnection(
                    "jdbc:hsqldb:toolbook",
                    "sa","");

Statement st = db.createStatement();
ResultSet rs = st.executeQuery("select * from artist");
...etc...
```

Hsqldb also comes with a GUI tool for interactively issuing queries, called the database manager. The manager may be started from the command line as

```
java -cp hsqldb.jar org.hsqldb.util.DatabaseManager
```

assuming hsqldb.jar is in the current directory. It is also possible to place this jar file in the CLASSPATH.

When the manager is first started the user will be prompted for the database to use along with other connection parameters. This dialog is shown in Figure 10.1.

Once this information is provided, the manager will connect to the database if a remote database has been specified. If the database is local, it will be opened, or it will be created if it does not already exist. In either case, the user will then be presented with the main manager window, shown in Figure 10.2.

In this view, a "cd" table is being defined in the query window. Another table that holds artist information has already been defined, and the properties of this table can be examined by clicking on its name in the right-hand window.

When a query is executed, the results are displayed in the lower left window, as illustrated in Figure 10.3

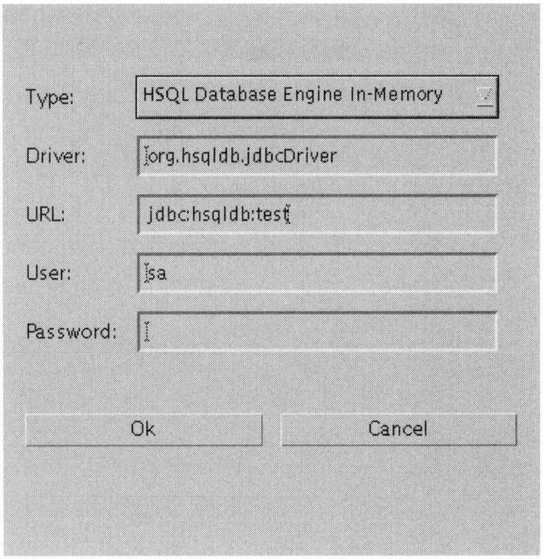

Figure 10.1. Choosing a database in hsqldb manager.

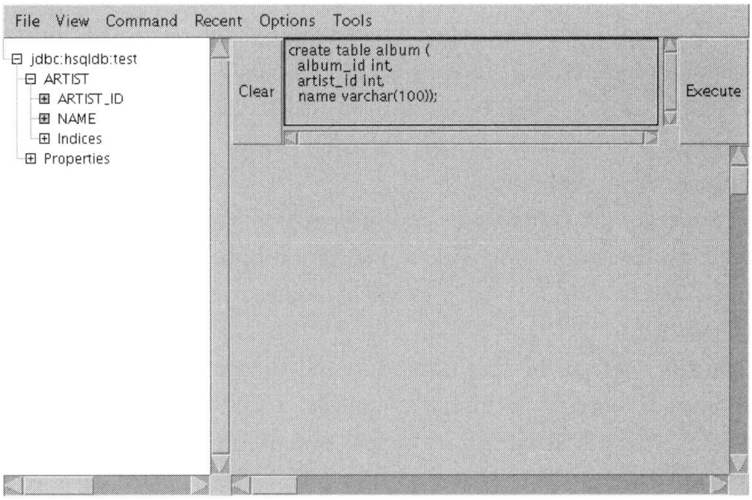

Figure 10.2. The main hsqldb manager window.

In addition to this `DatabaseManager`, there is another version that uses Swing, which provides the same functionality but in a prettier package. It may be invoked by substituting `DatabaseManagerSwing` for `DatabaseManager`. There is also a simple query tool called, appropriately enough, `QueryTool`, which allows queries to be imported from files.

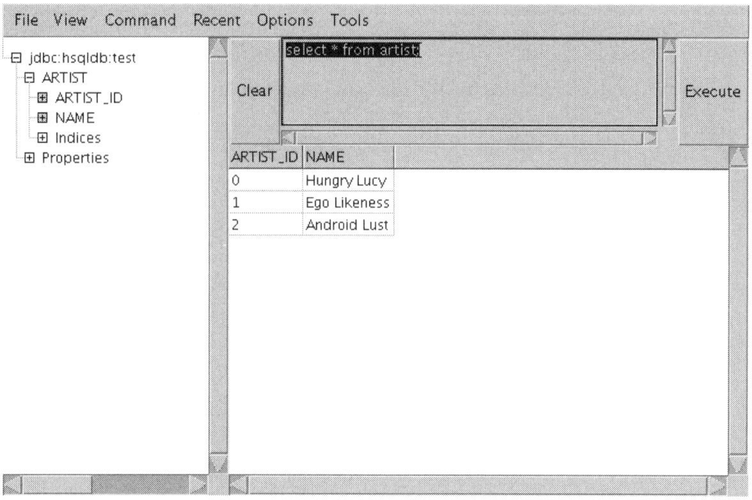

Figure 10.3. The results of a query.

In stand-alone mode, all data is stored in three files, and these files will be created automatically when the database is first opened. For a database named "foo" these files will be called "foo.properties," "foo.script," and "foo.data." Under certain conditions, to be discussed, there will also be a fourth file called "foo.backup." Note that these files are created per-database, not per-tables. Foo.script will contain the definitions and data for all tables within foo.

The properties file contains general information such as the version of hsqldb that created the database, along with configuration options. For example, there is a "read-only" property that if set to `true` will cause any attempt to modify the database to result in an error.

The data file contains the data in a compressed, binary format. For small databases, such as those used throughout this book, there is no need for this file. However, tables that are too large to be held in memory can be created with the `create cached table` command instead of the usual `create table`. Such cached tables will be held in the data file.

The backup file contains a zipped version of the data file.

Finally, the script file contains all the SQL commands that have modified the database in a plain-text form. This means it is possible to complete recreate the current state of a database by reissuing all the commands in this file.

The fact that the hsqldb's native storage mechanism is a plain file with SQL commands is extremely useful in a number of ways. First, it makes it very easy to set up a database; rather than using the database manager to interactively create every table or using a JDBC-based program to run some setup script, the SQL can be directly inserted into the script file with any common editor.

Second, having the entire state of the database represented in such a simple format makes it very easy to write unit tests that verify database operations. Conceptually this can be done by creating the initial state of the database in a `state1.script` file and the desired final state in `state2.script`. The test would then consist of the following steps:

1. Copy state1.script to db.script.
2. Open jdbc:hsqldb:db as the database.
3. Perform the actions to be tested.
4. Close the database.
5. Compare the contents of db.script to state2.script.

The test will have succeeded if the final files match. Note that this approach works in conjunction with HTTPUnit testing as well as JUnit. The standard HTTPUnit tests can ensure that the user received the correct page data, and testing hsqldb files can ensure that at the end of the transaction all the back-end processing has run successfully.

10.1.1 Extending Hsqldb

It is possible to extend hsqldb in two ways, not counting modifying the source to handle custom features. First, the set of functions can be extended by calling out to any static method. Listing 10.1 shows two such functions: one that checks whether one string ends with another and one that computes the factorial of an integer.

Listing 10.1 Some functions callable from hsqldb

```
package com.awl.toolbook.chapter10;

public class SampleFunctions {
    public static boolean endsWith(String a, String b) {
        return a.endsWith(b);
    }

    public static int factorial(int n) {
        int result = 1;
        for(int i=2;i<n;i++) {
```

Listing 10.1 Some functions callable from hsqldb *(continued)*

```
                result = result * i;
            }
            return result;
        }
    }
```

Assuming this class is properly installed in the CLASSPATH, hsqldb can invoke its methods directly. Consider the following table:

```
create table test_table (
    a_number       int,
    a_string       varchar(20),
    another_string varchar(30)
);
```

The following command would compute the factorial of every number in the `a_number` field:

```
select "com.awl.toolbook.chapter10.factorial"(a_number)
from test_table;
```

Note the name of the function is enclosed in double quotes. This command is somewhat verbose, so an alias could be used to shorten it.

```
CREATE ALIAS FACTORIAL FOR
"com.awl.toolbook.chapter10.SampleFunctions.factorial";

CREATE ALIAS ENDS_WITH FOR
"com.awl.toolbook.chapter10.SampleFunctions.endsWith";

select FACTORIAL(a_number) from test_table;
```

Custom functions can also be used in `where` clauses.

```
select * from test_table
where ENDS_WITH(a_string,another_string);
```

The arguments to such a function can be column names, constants, or the result of other expressions:

```
select * from test_table
where ENDS_WITH(a_string,'ly');
```

Functions can even be used in `insert` and `update` statements.

```
insert into test_table(a_string,a_number)
values('factorial of 10,'FACTORIAL(10));
```

Hsqldb allows the set of types to be extended, as well as the set of functions. This is done through use of the `object` type. Columns of this type can be created just as any other type:

```
create table object_collection (
    object_id   int,
    object_name varchar(20),
    the_object  object
);
```

Internally what is stored is a serialized version of the object, represented as a string of hexadecimal digits. Thus, it is not possible to insert values into such a column directly. If a program is using hsqldb via JDBC, the program can serialize the object and convert the result to a string in the proper format. However, there is a better option: Use static methods in the class being stored to handle the conversions between the object and its representation.

This concept can be used to add **large objects** to hsqldb. Large objects are entities that are too large to store directly in a database, such as entire documents, spreadsheets, or images. Instead, the database will maintain a reference to an external filename that holds the data, and functions will be provided to move data to and from this external file. Large objects are often divided into two categories: those that maintain binary data called **blobs** (for "binary large objects") and those that hold character data, or **clobs.** This implementation will not make that distinction and so will go by the more generic name "blob." An auxiliary field will store an optional content type that can be used to make the contents as character data.

The basic fields needed for the `Blob` class are a filename and the content type. Static methods will also be provided to create new blobs, get the contents of a blob, and so on. The result is shown in Listing 10.2.

Listing 10.2 An implementation of large objects, with supporting functions

```
package com.awl.toolbook.chapter10;

import java.io.*;

public class Blob implements Serializable {
    private String fileName;

    private String contentType;
    public String getContentType() {return contentType;}
    public void setContentType(String contentType) {
        this.contentType = contentType;
    }

    public Blob() {}

    public void newFileName() {
        try {
            fileName =
            File.createTempFile("blob","dat").toString();
        } catch (Exception e) {
            fileName = "tmpfile";
        }
    }

    public void delete() {
        File f = new File(fileName);
        f.delete();
    }

    public void setContents(String contents) {
        try {
            FileOutputStream out =
                new FileOutputStream(fileName);
            out.write(contents.getBytes());
            out.close();
        } catch (Exception e) {}
    }
```

```
public String getContents() {
    return readFile(fileName);
}

public static String
    makeBlobStringFromContents(String contents)
{
    return toHexString(makeBlobFromContents(contents));
}

public static Blob makeBlobFromContents(
                              String contents)
{
    Blob b = new Blob();
    b.newFileName();
    b.setContents(contents);
    b.setContentType("application/octet-stream");
    return b;
}

public static String
    makeBlobStringFromFile(String fileName)
{
    return toHexString(makeBlobFromFile(fileName));
}


public static Blob makeBlobFromFile(String fileName) {
    Blob b = makeBlobFromContents(
                  readFile(fileName));

    int pos = fileName.lastIndexOf('.');
    if(pos != -1) {
        String ext = fileName.substring(pos+1);
        if("gif".equals(ext)) {
            b.setContentType("image/gif");
        } else if("mp3".equals(ext)) {
            b.setContentType("audio/mp3");
        }
```

Listing 10.2 An implementation of large objects, with supporting functions *(continued)*

```
        }

        return b;
    }

    public static String getContents(Blob b) {
        return b.getContents();
    }

    private static final char hexDigits[] =
        {'0','1','2','3','4','5','6','7',
         '8','9','A','B','C','D','E','F'};


    public static String toHexString(Blob b) {
        byte data[] = b.getContents().getBytes();

        StringBuffer buffy = new StringBuffer();

        for(int i=0;i<data.length;i++) {
            buffy.append(hexDigits[data[i] / 16]);
            buffy.append(hexDigits[data[i] % 16]);
        }

        return buffy.toString();
    }

    private static String readFile(String fileName) {
        StringBuffer buffy = new StringBuffer();

        try {
            File f               = new File(fileName);
            FileInputStream in = new FileInputStream(f);
            byte data[]          = new byte[2048];
            int count;

            while((count = in.read(data)) > 0) {
```

```
                buffy.append(new String(data,0,count));
            }

            in.close();
        } catch (Exception e) {}

        return buffy.toString();
    }
}
```

The instance methods are all straightforward. The constructor does nothing, but it is provided to meet the serialization requirements. `newFileName()` allocates a new filename. Note that this will create the file in the default temporary directory, which is not the best place to save data that is meant to persist over long periods. A more complete implementation would specify a permanent home for such objects. `getContents()` and `setContents()` read and write to the file, respectively, and `delete()` deletes the file, as expected.

The static methods are more interesting, if not more complicated. There are two methods that create a new blob and two related methods that create a new blob and return its serialized representation. The method that does the serialization, `toHexString()`, uses the common technique of using a `ByteArrayOutputStream` to construct an `ObjectStream`.

The `makeBlobFromFile()` method attempts to use the file extension to determine the content type. Only a few options are provided for demonstration purposes, but it would be easy enough to extend this mechanism. An alternate method could also be provided that would let the user specify the type directly.

With the help of these static methods it is quite easy to use the `Blob` class from hsqldb.

```
CREATE ALIAS MAKE_BLOB_FROM_FILE FOR
"com.awl.toolbook.chapter10.Blob.makeBlobFromFile";

CREATE ALIAS GET_BLOB_CONTENTS FOR
"com.awl.toolbook.chapter10.Blob.getContents";

insert into object_collection
values(1,'A cute kitten',
       MAKE_BLOB_FROM_FILE('/images/kitten.gif'));
```

```
select GET_BLOB_CONTENTS(object)
from object_collection where
object_name='Hamlet (full text)';
```

One important thing to note is that objects have no way of knowing when they have been deleted. Following the command

```
delete * from object_collection
```

all the files comprising the blobs will still be taking up space on the disk. The solution to this problem is to use a **trigger.** A trigger is a feature of most high-end databases that is also supported by hsqldb. Triggers provide a way to specify that an action should be performed either before or after an insert, update, or delete command is processed. In this case the action takes the form of a Java class that implements the `org.hsqldb.Trigger` interface. This interface has one method, `fire()`, which is invoked with the name of the trigger, the name of the table, and the row of data that is about to be, or has just been, effected. Listing 10.3 shows a trigger that cleans up a blob.

Listing 10.3 A trigger to clean up blobs

```
package com.awl.toolbook.chapter10;

public class BlobDeleteTrigger {
    public void fire(String triggerName,
                     String tableName,
                     Object[] row)
    {
        ((Blob) row[3]).delete();
    }
}
```

This is quite straightforward; the `fire()` method simply runs through the row, deleting any blobs it finds.

This trigger could be installed with the following statement:

```
CREATE TRIGGER delete_blob_data
AFTER DELETE ON object_collection
CALL "com.awl.toolbook.chapter10.BlobDeleteTrigger"
```

This will ensure that all resources used by a blob are cleaned up as needed.

Note that extending types and methods within hsqldb can be a useful and powerful technique, but it may make it difficult to port code to another database. While some other databases supports similar functionality, the way they do so is likely to be very different.

Note also that the blob code presented here is not meant to be production-ready. There is no protection from a user deleting a blob from a disk without updating the database, nor is there sufficient protection of higher levels of code from other error conditions.

10.2 Pooling Connections with DBCP

Database operations are typically pretty fast, with the notable exception of establishing the initial connection. This is because there are many steps to establishing such a connection, including setting up the raw network connection, sending and verifying user authentication information, and so on.

In-process hsqldb usage avoids this overhead by not using a connection at all, but at the cost of restricting the database to a single process. For databases that must be used simultaneously by a number of people or programs, a server is necessary, and hence so is the need to make the connection. For desktop applications this penalty is not too severe because it is paid only once when the application first starts up. However, for Web applications a connection to the database must often be opened for every request, and the time needed to do so may noticeably impact the responsiveness of the site to the end user.

The solution to this problem is a technique called **pooling.** The idea of pooling predates JDBC and even the Web; it is applicable whenever a program will need many instances of some expensive resource. The general idea is to allocate as many instances of the resource as are likely to be needed early in the program's life cycle. These instances are placed in a pool. When one instance is needed, it is removed from the pool, and when the instance has served its purpose, it is returned to the pool, ready for the next use.

In the case of databases, the issue of establishing a connection can be reconsidered as the time needed to obtain a `Connection` object from the `DriverManager`. A number of `Connections` could therefore be obtained early and handed out as needed.

To illustrate these concepts further, Listing 10.4 demonstrates a simple pooling class.

Listing 10.4 A simple connection pool

```
package com.awl.toolbook.chapter10;

import java.sql.*;

public class SimplePool {
    private static int NUM_CONNECTIONS=20;

    private Connection connections[];
    private boolean inUse[];

    public SimplePool(String dbclass,String url) {
        connections = new Connection[NUM_CONNECTIONS];
        inUse       = new boolean[NUM_CONNECTIONS];

        try {
            Class.forName(dbclass).newInstance();

            for(int i=0;i<NUM_CONNECTIONS;i++) {
                connections[i] =
                    DriverManager.getConnection(url);
                inUse[i]       = false;
            }
        } catch (Exception e) {
            System.err.println("Unable to build pool: " +
                               e);
        }
    }

    public synchronized Connection getConnection() {
        for(int i=0;i<NUM_CONNECTIONS;i++) {
            if(!inUse[i]) {
                inUse[i] = true;
                return connections[i];
            }
        }

        return null;
    }
```

```
    public synchronized void releaseConnection(
                                     Connection c)
    {
        for(int i=0;i<NUM_CONNECTIONS;i++) {
            if(connections[i].equals(c)) {
                inUse[i] = false;
                return;
            }
        }
    }
}
```

Although Listing 10.4 shows how simple it is to create a basic pooling system, it also has a number of obvious shortcomings. Any class that needs a connection must be aware of the simple pool class. It would be far preferable if a standard JDBC or JNDI (Java Naming and Directory Interface) call could be used to obtain a connection. Calling classes must check for a `null` return value from `getConnection()` and react accordingly, perhaps by sleeping for some time and then trying again. It would be preferable for the pooling class to handle this contingency automatically. Finally, if code that is using a connection unexpectedly exits with an exception, or the developer forgets to release the connection back to the pool, then at some point the system will simply run out, and the whole program must be restarted. This could be fixed by automatically reclaiming connections after a suitable period.

Clearly writing a simple pool is easy, and writing a complete pooling solution is very difficult. At this point it should come as no surprise that an excellent open source pool is available from the Jakarta project. This tool is called DBCP (Database Connection Pool) and is based on a more general pooling tool from Jakarta called, appropriately enough, Pool. In what follows, only DBCP will be discussed directly, but references to Pool will be made as appropriate.

There are two ways to set up a connection pool; programmatically or through a configuration file. The configuration file approach is generally simpler, whereas the programmatic approach has the advantage that specific properties of the pool can be changed dynamically as needed. The programmatic approach also better illustrates what is happening behind the scenes, so it will be presented first.

The first step is to create the pool object. The Pool package provides several polling classes; `GenericObjectPool` is the most general. Rather than being initialized with a set of objects to hold in the pool, `GenericObjectPool` will use a factory to create instances as needed. This avoids a large overhead at startup and may avoid creating instances that are never used. Keep in mind that maintaining lots of connections may be a burden on the database server, so it makes sense to try to create as few as needed.

There are lots of options available when creating a pool. A maximum number of instances can be specified, as well as the behavior when this maximum is exceeded. When there are no instances available, a request to the pool can either cause the pool to call the factory to create a new instance,[1] or the call can hang until an instance is available, or it can fail and throw a `NoSuchElementException`.

A pool can also be told to **evict** objects that have been idle for a specified period of time. There are also parameters that control the minimum time after which an object may be eligible for eviction and the maximum number of idle objects that are allowed to be in the pool before some are considered for eviction.

The pool can also test objects to ensure that they are valid and can forcibly evict any objects that have "gone bad." There are many reasons why a connection may go bad; for example, some database servers may shut down connections due to inactivity. Pool can run these validity tests when an object is handed out, when an object is returned to the pool, or periodically.

Fine-tuning all these parameters may take some effort and experimentation, and the correct values will depend heavily on the details of the application. In a typical Web application each use of the database is likely to be short-lived; often just a few queries are needed to render a page. In this case the number of objects in the pool will closely parallel the number of simultaneous users of the site. Some allowance must be made for peak times when the number of users may jump significantly. Ideally users should never have to wait for a response, which would seem to imply that the pool should be allowed to grow as needed. However, after a certain point this would slow down performance for everyone, so a better solution may be to allow the pool to fail, resulting in a notice to the user that the site is busy and he or she should come back later. The issue of turning away users beyond a certain threshold was also addressed in the "How to Test" section in Chapter 7, and indeed JMeter could be used to ensure that Pool is behaving properly with an application.

If a single application server is accessing a single database, there is no great rush to release idle connections, although they should be released eventually. However, if there are multiple instances of the application running simultaneously, and they all access a central database, then idle connections should be released sooner so the other application servers can use them if needed.

Again, getting this all correct may take time. A tool like JMeter can be a great asset here by making it easy to test the performance implications of various pool configurations.

---

[1] As noted in the Pool documentation, this essentially makes the specified maximum meaningless.

There are constructors available that set various combinations of parameters, or they can be set (and changed) through accessors after the pool is constructed. The only parameter that the pool absolutely requires is the factory; one is usually provided in the constructor. In the following examples the factory is provided to the pool in a later step, so building the pool is as simple as

```
ObjectPool thePool = new GenericObjectPool();
```

The next step is to create the factory. This proceeds in two parts. The first is to create a factory that will return a new `Connection` or `DataSource`, which can be done with

```
ConnectionFactory connFactory =
new DriverManagerConnectionFactory("jdbc:hsqldb:....",
                                   "sa",
                                   "");
```

or `new DataSourceConnectionFactory()` with the same arguments. Here the factory is told to use a server instance of hsqld because it makes no sense to pool connections to the in-process version.

`connFactory` could now be used to obtain new connections, essentially taking over `DriverManager`'s job

```
Connection c = connFactory.createConnection();
Statement s  = c.createStatement(...);
...
c.close();
```

However, there is no reason to make such a call directly as this would provide none of the needed pooling functionality. Therefore, the second step of creating the factory is to build a poolable factory from the connection factory.

```
PoolableConnectionFactory poolFactory =
    new PoolableConnectionFactory(
        connFactory,
        thePool,
        null,
        null,
        false,
        true);
```

The first and second arguments to the constructor are the base connection factory and the pool, respectively. The third argument is another factory that may be used to pool prepared statements. This will be discussed in more detail shortly. The fourth argument is a string representing a validation query. If this is not `null`, it will enable the testing mechanism of the underlying pool. The final two arguments are booleans indicating whether connections should be read-only and whether changes should be committed automatically. Auto commit should be set to `false` if an application will be doing any sort of complex transaction processing.

Recall that `thePool` needs a factory, which was not provided when the pool was initially constructed. This is handled by the `poolFactory` constructor, which will register the factory with `thePool` by calling `thePool.setFactory(this)`. Developers uncomfortable with this kind of side effect can explicitly call this method, although beyond clarity there is no real motivation to do so.

This factory could in principle be invoked directly by calling `makeObject()`, which returns a poolable object that wraps the underlying connection. However, this is not the intended usage, and for all practical purposes the factory should be managed only by the pool.

The final step is to register the pool and associate it with a name. This is done through a class called `PoolingDriver`, which acts as an intermediary between the pool API and JDBC.

```
PoolingDriver driver = new PoolingDriver();
driver.registerPool("toolbook",thePool);
```

This will register the URL "jdbc:apache:commons:dbcp:toolbook" with JDBC. Subsequently when the `DriverManager` is asked for a connection with this name, it will come from the pool. The pool may fulfill this request by returning an idle connection if one is available or going to the factory if one is not. It is now almost trivially easy to use a connection from the pool:

```
Connection conn =
DriverManager.getConnection(
    "jdbc:apache:commons:dbcp:toolbook");
Statement s = conn.createStatement("select * from artist");
... execute the statement, get result set, etc ...
conn.close();
```

It was stated previously that the creation of the pool could be done through a configuration file, in addition to programmatically. Before examining this configuration file, note that most of the programmatic steps could be done in a single statement, although this statement would be horribly long and complex. Most of the constructed objects are used only as arguments in a subsequent constructors, so it would be possible to do without a lot of the intermediate variables. For example, rather than pass `connFactory` as the second argument when constructing the `PoolableConnectionFactory` it would have been possible to use the call to the constructor.

Once the code had been reduced to a series of nested constructors, introspection could be used to map an XML expression to the arguments. This is the idea behind Pool's configuration files, which describe an object tree as an XML tree giving constructor information at each node. The XML document that exactly recreates the previous pool built up programmatically is shown in Listing 10.5.

Listing 10.5 The configuration file

```
<object
  class="org.apache.commons.dbcp.PoolableConnectionFactory"
  xmlns="http://apache.org/xml/xmlns/jakarta/commons/jocl">

  <!-- The ConnectionFactory -->
  <object class=
   "org.apache.commons.dbcp.DriverManagerConnectionFactory">
    <!-- The raw JDBC url for each connection -->
    <string value="jdbc:some:connect:string"/>

    <!-- The username -->
    <string value="sa"/>

    <!-- The password -->
    <string value=""/>
  </object>

  <!-- Second arg for PoolableConnectionFactory:   -->
  <!-- the ObjectPool                              -->
  <object
     class="org.apache.commons.pool.impl.GenericObjectPool">
    <!-- The ObjectFactory: none  -->
    <object class="org.apache.commons.pool.PoolableObjectFactory"
                null="true"/>
  </object>
  <!-- end of the second arg for PoolableConnectionFactory -->
```

Listing 10.5 The configuration file *(continued)*

```
    <!-- Third argument for PoolableConnectionFactory: -->
    <!-- the KeyedObjectPoolFactory                    -->
    <object
     class="org.apache.commons.pool.StackKeyedObjectPoolFactory"
     null="true"/>
    </object>

    <!-- Fourth argument for PoolableConnectionFactory: -->
    <!-- Query to use for validation                    -->
    <string null="true"/>

    <!-- Fifth argument for PoolableConnectionFactory: -->
    <!-- default read only                             -->
    <boolean value="false"/>

    <!-- Sixth argument for PoolableConnectionFactory: -->
    <!-- default auto commit -->
    <boolean value="true"/>
  </object>
```

Note that most of the objects encountered when building the pool by hand are present in Listing 10.5. Note, too, that the nested-constructor approach Pool uses for its configuration explains the slightly odd behavior of the `PoolableConnectionFactory` with respect to taking the pool as an argument rather than doing the more natural thing and requiring that the factory be constructed first and then passed to the pool's constructor.

Assuming this file is installed in one of the directories in the CLASSPATH as "config/toolbook.jocl," a database connection could be obtained with

```
Connection conn =
DriverManager.getConnection(
    "jdbc:apache:commons:dbcp:/config/toolbook.jocl");
```

Finally, it was mentioned that statements could be cached along with connections. This may be worth doing depending on how the database client code handles statements and how statements are constructed by the application. If the database client code simply transmits queries in plain text to the backend, and the application only sends static queries, then there is nothing to be gained by pooling statements. On the other hand, if the client code does heavy parsing and preprocessing of queries, which will often be the case when using `PreparedStatements`, then pooling can be a significant time saver. Pooling statements is clearly different from pooling connections because all connections are identical, but when a particular statement is needed, no other will do. Therefore, a different kind of pool is needed.

Statements can be pooled easily, by passing

```
new StackKeyedObjectPoolFactory()
```

as the third argument in the constructor for `PoolableConnectionFactory`; everything else is handled automatically. The "keyed" in the name refers to the fact that each entry in the pool is identified by a key, which is what allows the system to retrieve a particular statement from the pool when it is needed.

10.3 Mapping Databases to Objects with OJB

Using a pool can make a program or Web site run much faster, but it does nothing to make development any easier. As useful and powerful as JDBC is, the fact remains that there is a mismatch between databases and Java. Databases and JDBC deal with entities like rows and columns and metadata, whereas Java programs deal with classes and objects. If databases could store objects, then the task of making JDBC calls could be reduced to calling accessors in objects, which is much simpler and more familiar. This would also make it possible to use tools like BeanUtils and JXPath to traverse information from databases.

There are some databases, called **object databases** that allow objects to be stored directly. However, these have never been as successful as relational databases, so what is needed is some way to bridge the gap between databases and objects. Such a tool is called an **object-relational mapping tool,** and Apache provides an excellent one called OJB.

There are several steps to using OJB. First, the classes and underlying database must be defined. Then OJB must be configured to properly connect tables and classes. This is accomplished through a number of XML files. Finally, OJB provides a series of APIs that allow objects to be retrieved, stored, modified, and deleted. Each of these steps will be examined in turn.

10.3.1 Defining the Database and Objects

Before using OJB some thought must be given to what information will live in objects, what information will live in the database, and how the two sets of data will be related. In almost all situations the "obvious" connection is the right one; there will be one bean class for each table, and within those beans there will be one property for each database column.

For primitive data types there is an obvious parallel between bean properties and database columns. For example, the basic fields of the `Artist` bean from Chapter 8 could be mapped to a table with the following definition:

```
create table artist (
   artist_id  int,
   name       varchar(100),

   unique (artist_id),
   primary key (artist_id)
);
```

The designation of `artist_id` as unique ensures that no two artists have the same ID. The designation as a primary key allows certain optimizations. In particular, in hsqldb this will automatically create an **index,** an internal data structure that can be used to rapidly find data without having to scan through all rows. Not all databases will automatically create such an index; those that don't should also be issued the following command:

```
create index index_artist_id
on artist(artist_id);
```

Marking the primary key and creating the index are not necessary to use OJB because OJB is capable of treating a field as a primary key even if it is not marked as such in the database. However, it is good standard practice to mark primary keys and create indexes where appropriate because doing so often leads to dramatic improvements in database performance.

So far no mention has been made of compound data, such as the list of albums available for each artist. There are numerous ways in which such relationships may be defined in the database. The two most common are called **one-to-many relationships** and **many-to-many relationships.**

In one-to-many relationships one row or item of data is connected to many others, such as one artist with many albums. These are defined with a reference to the parent table in the child, so the definition for the album table would include a reference to the artist table

```
create table album (
    album_id int,
    artist_id int,
```

```
    year_released int,
    name varchar(200)

    unique (album_id),
    primary key (album_id),
    foreign key (artist_id) references artist(artist_id)
);

create index index_album_artist_id
on album(artist_id);
```

Once again the primary key, album_id is indicated and marked as unique. In addition the artist_id is marked as a **foreign key,** meaning that any value assigned to this field must have a corresponding entry in the artist table. Such a reference ensures **referential integrity,** meaning the database will always be in a consistent state. In this case, this makes it impossible to create an album owned by a nonexistent artist. This also means an attempt to delete an artist will fail if that artist has any albums because it would leave the album entries without a parent.

An index has also been created for the artist_id field in the album table. This will enable queries that retrieve albums by artist_id to run very rapidly.

The inclusion of the artist_id field in the album table, aided by the foreign key declaration, establishes the one-to-many relationship on the database side. On the bean side it would be natural to want the Artist bean to have an array or List of Albums, just as in Chapter 8. The good news is that this is exactly how OJB handles such relationships. The details will be discussed shortly.

In addition, it may be useful to introduce inverse relationships, also called **back pointers** in the beans. Although all previous examples started with an Artist and from there accessed the list of Albums and then Tracks, in a full-fledged application there may be instances where an Album would be obtained first, perhaps by searching for a particular album name. From the album the user might want to get the name of the artist, which in BeanShell notation would be expressed as album.artist.name.

This information is already present in the database in the form of the artist_id in the album table. On the bean side this means it is possible to get an Artist by calling getArtistId() and using the returned ID to ask OJB for the corresponding Artist bean. To make things more convenient, it is worth adding an Artist property to the Album bean and letting OJB populate this property automatically. Note that this is a **one-to-one relationship,** because each album has only one artist. Therefore, the Album bean will have only a single Artist rather than an array.

The definitions of the `track` table and `Track` bean follow the same pattern and so will not be shown here. They can be found on the companion CD-ROM.

Many-to-many relationships are somewhat more complicated than one-to-many. To see this, consider how the database would be extended to track live shows. A logical approach would be to create a new `venue` table with information such as the name and address of the venue. An artist may have appeared at many venues, and one venue will have hosted many artists, so there is a many-to-many relationship. This information could be stored by placing an `artist_id` in the venue table and a `venue_id` in the artist table. This would be terribly inefficient, however, because every time an artist played a new venue, a new entry would need to be made in the `artist` table identical to the previous entry except for the `venue_id`. Similar redundancy would arise every time a venue hosted a new artist. So instead of storing the relationship information in the tables a third table, called a **join table,** will be introduced. This table will hold a `venue_id` and `artist_id`, and as an added bonus a `date` indicating when the event took place (or will take place, in the more useful case of an upcoming show).

```
create table venue (
    venue_id int,
    address1 varchar(50),
    address2 varchar(50),
    city     varchar(20),
    state_province varchar(10),
    country        varchar(10),

    unique (venue_id),
    primary key (venue_id)
);

create table live_show (
    venue_id int,
    artist_id int,
    event_date datetime,

    foreign key (venue_id) references venue(venue_id),
    foreign key (artist_id) references artist(artist_id)
);
```

```
create index show_artist_id
on live_show(artist_id);

create index show_venue_id
on live_show(venue_id);
```

On the bean side, many-to-many relationships may be represented in two ways. The first would be to act as if each table had a reference to the other and give each bean an array of the other bean. Alternately each bean could have an array of the bean representing the join table. The former approach is slightly more convenient; BeanUtils could represent all venues an artist had performed at as `artist.venue`, whereas using the join table a program would need to manually walk over the set of `artist.live_show` and call `getVenue()` on each. On the other hand, skipping the join table makes it more difficult to get auxiliary information like the date.

Although both approaches will be discussed there is a solution that maintains both the convenience of a direct connection and availability of all data. The solution is simple: Use JXPath instead of BeanUtils! Using JXPath the names of venues at which an artist had performed would be represented as `/artist//venue/@name` and the dates of those performances would be `/artist/liveShow/@date`. This illustrates how different open-source tools can be combined in different ways to achieve different effects and in turn how the use of a particular tool can influence how another tool may be configured.

This concludes everything that needs to be said regarding the beans and underlying tables. The next step is to configure OJB to correctly map between the two.

To summarize the ideas discussed in this section, Listing 10.6 shows the code for the `Artist` bean, which differs in some small but significant ways from the version in Chapter 8.

Listing 10.6 The artist bean

```
package com.awl.toolbook.chapter10;

import java.util.HashMap;
import java.util.List;
import java.util.ArrayList;
import java.io.Serializable;

public class Artist
    extends PersistentObject
    implements Serializable
```

Listing 10.6 The artist bean *(continued)*

```
{
    public Artist() {super();}

    private int artistId;
    public int getArtistId() {return artistId;}
    public void setArtistId(int artistId) {
        this.artistId = artistId;}

    private String name;
    public String getName() {return name;}
    public void setName(String name) {this.name = name;}

    private List albums = new ArrayList();
    public List getAlbums() {return albums;}
    public void setAlbums(List albums) {
        this.albums = albums;
    }

    public Album getAlbum(int i) {
        return (Album) albums.get(i);
    }

    public void setAlbum(int i,Album a) {
        if(i == albums.size()) {
            albums.add(a);
        } else {
            albums.set(i,a);
        }
    }

    private List venues = new ArrayList();
    public List getVenues() {return venues;}
    public void setVenues(List venues) {
        this.venues = venues;
    }

    public Venue getVenue(int i) {
        return (Venue) venues.get(i);
```

```
    }

    public void setVenue(int i,Venue a) {
        if(i == venues.size()) {
            venues.add(a);
        } else {
            venues.set(i,a);
        }
    }


    private List liveShows = new ArrayList();
    public List getLiveShows() {return liveShows;}
    public void setLiveShows(List liveShows) {
        this.liveShows = liveShows;
    }

    public LiveShow getLiveShow(int i) {
        return (LiveShow) liveShows.get(i);
    }

    public void setLiveShow(int i,LiveShow a) {
        if(i == liveShows.size()) {
            liveShows.add(a);
        } else {
            liveShows.set(i,a);
        }
    }
}
```

For the moment disregard the extended class, `PersistentObject`; its purpose will be made clear shortly. The simple fields, `artistId` and `name`, remain the same standard bean properties they have always been. The compound data, `albums`, still has indexed accessors that take an integer argument, and similar `venues` and `liveShows` properties have been added. However, the type of these fields have been changed from `ArrayList` to `List`, and accessors that get and set the whole `List` in one call have been added. These changes are needed to accommodate OJB, which stores collections in an internal class that implements the `List` interface, and passes such collections to the parent objects in a single call.

It is worth pointing out that it is not strictly necessary to provide bean-style accessors; OJB is capable of using introspection to get and set fields that are declared `public` without going through the accessors. Typically using the accessors is more efficient, in addition to making it possible to use the class in other applications or contexts that require adherence to bean conventions, such as BeanUtils and JXPath.

10.3.2 Defining the Object-Relational Mapping

OJB is configured through a number of files. The first, `OJB.properties`, controls all aspects of the system at the highest level but does not deal directly with any mapping information.

OJB is highly configurable, and most of the classes that compose it are defined as interfaces or factories, making it easy to swap in custom implementations. For example, at some point between objects and the database OJB must generate SQL, and it uses a class called `SqlGeneratorDefaultImpl` to do so based on the beans to be retrieved and various constraints. The generated SQL should work well with most databases, but some may offer features that are not expressible in standard SQL. If this is the case, the SQL generator can be swapped for a custom one that knows about these features just by changing the `SqlGeneratorClass=` line in `OJB.properties`. Such enhancements are beyond the scope of the book, and OJB comes with a default set of definitions that will work quite well for a wide range of applications and environments.

Much of the rest of `OJB.properties` is concerned with logging. OJB can be configured to report information about the SQL that has been generated, the results that have been returned, various internal activities, and a great deal more. All this configuration and logging happens through the Apache log4j APIs, which is discussed in Chapter 11.

Of the remaining properties, only a few are of immediate interest:

```
repositoryFile=repository.xml
maxIdle=-1
maxWait=2000
timeBetweenEvictionRunsMillis=-1
minEvictableIdleTimeMillis=1000000
whenExhaustedAction=0
```

The `repositoryFile` specifies the name of the XML file through which the mapping is defined. The other properties should look familiar because they define settings that were used in DBCP. This is no coincidence; OJB uses DBCP internally to cache connections. Thus, using OJB includes all the benefits of pooling for free.

The repository.xml file contains all the information about the database and the mapping between tables and beans. There is a lot of information here, so for clarity the repository is typically split into three pieces, and repository.xml serves only to group these pieces together. A typical repository is shown in Listing 10.7.

Listing 10.7 The repository definition

```
<?xml version="1.0" encoding="UTF-8"?>

<!DOCTYPE descriptor-repository SYSTEM "repository.dtd" [
<!ENTITY database SYSTEM "repository_database.xml">
<!ENTITY internal SYSTEM "repository_internal.xml">
<!ENTITY user SYSTEM "repository_user.xml">
]>

<descriptor-repository version="1.0"
  isolation-level="read-uncommitted">
    &database;

    &internal;

    &user;
</descriptor-repository>
```

This specifies a DTD for the file and each piece; indicates that the database entity should come from the repository_database.xml file, and similarly for the other pieces; and then includes all three entities. There is nothing special about either the entity or filenames, but the ones just used are descriptive and used in example programs that comes with OJB.

The repository_database.xml file contains information relevant to the database connection, and it is shown in Listing 10.8. Recall that OJB.properties contains configuration information for DBCP but none of the underlying database information.

Listing 10.8 The database definition

```
<jdbc-connection-descriptor
    jcd-alias="default"
    default-connection="true"
    platform="Hsqldb"
    jdbc-level="2.0"
```

Listing 10.8 The database definition *(continued)*

```
    driver="org.hsqldb.jdbcDriver"
    protocol="jdbc"
    subprotocol="hsqldb"
    dbalias="test"
    username="sa"
    password=""
    eager-release="false"
    batch-mode="false"
    useAutoCommit="1"
    ignoreAutoCommitExceptions="false"
    >

    <connection-pool
        maxActive="21"
        validationQuery="" />

    <sequence-manager
        className="org.apache.ojb.broker.util.sequence.
                   SequenceManagerHighLowImpl">
        <attribute attribute-name="grabSize"
                   attribute-value="20"/>
        <attribute attribute-name="autoNaming"
                   attribute-value="true"/>
        <attribute attribute-name="globalSequenceId"
                   attribute-value="false"/>
        <attribute attribute-name="globalSequenceStart"
                   attribute-value="10000"/>
    </sequence-manager>
</jdbc-connection-descriptor>
```

The parent `jdbc-connection-descriptor` node contains all the JDBC configuration information. The alias value of `default` is special. It is possible to associate different kinds of objects with different databases; when an object is not specifically associated with a database, it will map to the default.

Within the `jdbc-connection-descriptor` is a `connection-pool` node; values here will override those in `OJB.properties` on a per-database basis.

Finally, there are various definitions relating to the `sequence-manager`, which can manage the allocation of new primary keys when objects are created. Note that the class name is broken over two lines to make it fit the printed page.

The `repository_internal.xml` file contains a number of mappings used internally by OJB that should not be changed. Most are even marked by comments that loudly proclaim "do not edit." These mappings refer to tables that must be created in the database, which are used to store information such as which objects are locked and information relating to primary keys. OJB can use another Jakarta project called **Torque** to create these definitions, but it is even easier to just append the relevant `create table` commands to the database creation script containing user tables. These commands are included on the companion CD-ROM, as "ojbinternal.sql" in the "chapter10" directory.

All the interesting mappings between tables and objects happens in `repository_user.xml`. This file consists of a series of nodes associating objects to tables, and within these nodes are nodes mapping fields to columns. An entry mapping the primitive fields of the `artist` and `album` tables is shown in Listing 10.9.

Listing 10.9 Mapping simple fields

```
<!-- Artist definition -->
<class-descriptor
  class="com.awl.toolbook.chapter11.Artist"
  table="ARTIST">

   <field-descriptor
      name="artistId"
      column="ARTIST_ID"
      jdbc-type="INTEGER"
      primarykey="true"
      autoincrement="true"
   />

   <field-descriptor
      name="name"
      column="NAME"
      jdbc-type="VARCHAR"
   />
</class-descriptor>

<!-- Album definition -->
<class-descriptor
  class="com.awl.toolbook.chapter11.Album"
  table="ALBUM">
```

Listing 10.9 Mapping simple fields *(continued)*

```
    <field-descriptor
        name="albumId"
        column="ALBUM_ID"
        jdbc-type="INTEGER"
        primarykey="true"
        autoincrement="true"
    />

    <field-descriptor
        name="name"
        column="NAME"
        jdbc-type="VARCHAR"
    />

    <field-descriptor
        name="yearReleased"
        column="YEAR_RELEASED"
        jdbc-type="INTEGER"
    />

</class-descriptor>
```

Each `class-descriptor` node specifies the `table` and the implementing `class`. Each `field-descriptor` associates a `column` in the table with the `name` of a field in the class. The `jdbc-type` is also provided. There is no need to specify the type of the bean field because it can be obtained through introspection.

The `field-descriptor` entries for `artistId` and `albumId` are marked as primary keys and configured to auto-increment. The auto-incrementing functionality ties into the `sequence-manager` noted in the `repository_database.xml` file in Listing 10.8 and will be discussed in the section on using OJB.

The definition in Listing 10.9 is valid as it stands and could be used to create new artists and albums or to retrieve artist and album data by name or id. The next step is to add descriptors for the one-to-many and many-to-many relationships. Such relationships are called **collections** in the xml files.

To define a collection OJB must know the name of the field in the parent class that will hold the children, the name of the class representing each child, and how the relationship is stored in the database. This information is packaged into a `collection-descriptor` node, which resides at the same level as the field-descriptor nodes within the class-descriptor. Adding the album information is done with the following descriptor:

```
<collection-descriptor
   name="albums"
   element-class-ref="com.awl.toolbook.chapter10.Album"
   orderby="year_released"
   sort="ASC"
   auto-retrieve="true"
   auto-update="true"
   auto-delete="true"
>
   <inverse-foreignkey field-ref="artistId"/>
</collection-descriptor>
```

The name refers to the name of the property in the bean. The element-class-ref indicates the class attribute of the class-descriptor, which describes the child class and table. The orderby and sort attributes are not necessary, but generally it will make sense to build the collection in some order. In this case, these two attributes specify that the collection should be arranged in the order in which albums were released, with the first album at the start. Finally, the role of the three auto- attributes will be discussed in the section on the OJB APIs.

The inverse-foreignkey indicates how to build the query by specifying both the name of the field in the child table and the name of the property in the current table to use as a value. Note that the **Java** version of the name is used, not the SQL name.

For the albums belonging to the artist whose artist_id is 1, this will result in the following query:

```
select * from album where artist_id=1
order by year_released asc;
```

For each row returned by this query a new Album will be constructed. Its fields will be set according to the rules in the class-descriptor, and a List will be constructed internally by OJB containing all such objects. Then the setAlbums() method of the parent Artist will be called with this List.

There are two ways to handle many-to-many relationships. In one, the connection between the first table and the join table is treated as a one-to-many relationship, and the connection between the join table and the second table is treated as one-to-one.

This is exemplified by the relationship between the `artist` and `live_show` tables. One `artist` may have many `live_shows`, and it is possible to obtain the `venue` from the `live_show`. The first step in defining these mappings is defining the descriptors for the `venue` and `live_show` tables, which is shown in Listing 10.10.

Listing 10.10 The venue and live show descriptors

```
<class-descriptor
  class="com.awl.toolbook.chapter11.Venue"
  table="VENUE">

   <field-descriptor
      name="venueId"
      column="VENUE_ID"
      jdbc-type="INTEGER"
      primarykey="true"
      autoincrement="true"
   />

   <field-descriptor
      name="address1"
      column="ADDRESS1"
      jdbc-type="VARCHAR"
   />
</class-descriptor>

<!-- Live Show definition -->
<class-descriptor
  class="com.awl.toolbook.chapter11.LiveShow"
  table="LIVE_SHOW">

   <field-descriptor
      name="artistId"
      column="ARTIST_ID"
      jdbc-type="INTEGER"
   />

   <field-descriptor
      name="venueId"
```

```
        column="VENUE_ID"
        jdbc-type="INTEGER"
    />

    <field-descriptor
        name="eventDate"
        column="EVENT_DATE"
        jdbc-type="DATETIME"
    />

    <!-- 1-1 references to objects -->
    <reference-descriptor
        name="venue"
        class-ref="com.awl.toolbook.chapter11.Venue"
    >
        <foreignkey field-ref="venueId"/>
    </reference-descriptor>

    <reference-descriptor
        name="artist"
        class-ref="com.awl.toolbook.chapter11.Artist"
    >
        <foreignkey field-ref="artistId"/>
    </reference-descriptor>
</class-descriptor>
```

The descriptor for `venue` is straightforward, containing only primitive fields (not all of which are shown in the interests of space). It would be easy enough to add `liveShows` and `artists` references, from which it would be possible to get lists of all shows that had taken place at a particular location. These fields could be added to `Venue` in almost exactly the same way they are added to `Artist`; the details are left as an exercise for the reader.

The descriptor for `liveShow` has three primitive values: `artistId`, `venueId`, and `eventDate`. There are also two one-to-one mappings to obtain the `Artist` and `Venue`. These are defined with `reference-descriptor` nodes, which are similar to `collection-descriptors`, with the obvious difference that they only expect a single result.

With these two definitions it is a simple matter to add the list of `liveShows` to the `artist` descriptor:

```
<collection-descriptor
   name="liveShows"
   element-class-ref="com.awl.toolbook.chapter10.LiveShow"
   orderby="eventDate"
   auto-retrieve="true"
   auto-update="true"
   auto-delete="true"
   sort="ASC"
>
   <inverse-foreignkey field-ref="artistId"/>
</collection-descriptor>
```

This looks and functions exactly like the list of `Albums`.

OJB also make it possible to bypass the join table entirely and go straight from an `Artist` to the list of `Venues`. This is done through a variation of the `collection-descriptor` that contains information about the intermediary join table and the foreign key connections to each table.

```
<collection-descriptor
   name="venues"
   element-class-ref="com.awl.toolbook.chapter10.Venue"
   auto-retrieve="true"
   auto-update="true"
   auto-delete="true"
   indirection-table="LIVE_SHOW"
>
   <fk-pointing-to-this-class column="ARTIST_ID"/>
   <fk-pointing-to-element-class column="VENUE_ID"/>
</collection-descriptor>
```

The `indirection-table` names the table, the `fk-pointing-to-this-class` indicates the field of the current table and by implication the property of the current class, and `fk-pointing-to-element-class` does the same for the elements of the collection, which is specified to be `Venue` by the `element-class-ref`. For the artist with `artistId` 1, this will result in the following query:

```
select venue.*
from venue,live_show
```

```
where venue.venue_id=live_show.venue_id
and   venue.artist_id=1
```

That completes coverage of the mapping features of OJB. There is more that can be done with this mapping, but between basic fields and one-to-one, one-to-many, and the two mechanisms for many-to-many relationships, the information provided previously should suffice for the great majority of purposes.

A final word on developing with OJB: Writing beans and database definitions are typically reasonably straightforward activities, although both can have their subtleties. It should therefore not be surprising that often the most difficult part of starting an OJB-based program is getting the mapping file right. OJB is fairly good about reporting errors. A typo in a class or field name usually results in an error that describes the situations and reports the incorrect value. An error in the bean, such as the lack of a `List` for collections, results in an error that the collection could not be set and again provides the name of the collection in question. Problems in SQL, such as a nonexistent table or column, are reported as they come from the underlying database.

However, there are cases where error messages are less helpful, such as certain introspection errors that result in mysterious null pointer exceptions. It may help when isolating these kinds of errors to remove `field-descriptors` one at a time until the problematic one is identified and then reviewing all the database and bean code related to that field.

There may also be instances where the generated SQL is valid but does not do what is needed, in which case no error may be generated, but the results will be incorrect. Although the documentation states that all the generated SQL can be viewed by setting the appropriate log level, at the time of this writing this did not work, and there appears to be no way to view the executed SQL. Some JDBC drivers, such as MySQL provide their own mechanism for debugging SQL, which may help. If not, the best that can be done is to study the mapping file very closely and manually try to construct the SQL as OJB will. Or it would be possible to fix the SQL generator or provide an extended version that does log correctly. Another triumph for open source: When something doesn't work as desired, the in-house developers can fix it immediately.[2] There is no need to complain to a company that may not fix the problem until its next release, if ever.

[2] Of course, if any such fix is done, the code should be sent to the OJB maintainers so they can make it available to all other users.

10.4 Using OJB

The APIs to OJB are quite straightforward, and it is very easy to use them to create, update, and retrieve data. Everything goes through a PersistenceBroker, which is responsible for transparently managing all the mapping details. Obtaining a PersistenceBroker is done through a factory:

```
import org.apache.ojb.broker.PersistenceBroker;
import org.apache.ojb.broker.PersistenceBrokerFactory;

...

PersistenceBroker broker = null;

try {
    broker =
      PersistenceBrokerFactory.defaultPersistenceBroker();
} catch (Throwable t) {
    t.printStackTrace();
}
```

It is possible to define several PersistenceBrokers, perhaps each pointing at a different database. Recall that the default database was defined in repository_database.xml; this is the database that will be used by the default broker.

Once a broker has been obtained, storing a new instance of any defined object is pleasantly simple:

```
Artist newArtist = new Artist();
newArtist.setName("Imagica");

try {
    broker.beginTransaction();
    broker.store(newArtist);
    broker.commitTransaction();
} catch (PersistenceBrokerException e) {
    broker.abortTransaction();
    System.out.println("Unable to save: " + e);
}
```

The object is created and values are set, just as with any bean. To save the object to the database a transaction is started, and the `store()` method is used to write the object data to the database according to the mapping. The transaction is then committed. If anything goes wrong, the transaction can be rolled back.

Deleting an object is just as easy: Simply call `broker.delete()` instead of `store()`.

Note that the `albumId` was not set before being stored. Because OJB knows that `albumId` is the primary key and auto increment has been set to "true" in the mapping file, OJB will automatically allocate a new primary key when it detects that `albumId` is `null`. This is done by the `sequence-manager` defined in `OJB.properties`. The default implementation stores the next available primary keys in a table called `OJB_HL_SEQ`, which is one of the internal tables mapped in `repository-internal.xml`.

Many databases provide their own mechanism for automatically allocating primary keys, but these often vary widely between different databases. Putting all the primary key logic in the application, as with OJB, makes it very easy to move from one database to another. With OJB developers can use hsqldb, and the application can be deployed on Oracle without having to change a single line of application code or configuration data. However, this means that if any other application that will be writing to the database—including commands entered by hand through an interpreter—must also update the `OJB_HL_SEQ` table. Failure to do so may lead to conflicts as OJB tries to allocate a new primary key that has already been assigned.

If OJB detects that all the object's primary keys are present when it is saved, then it will perform an update instead of an insert. This is valid because the only ways in which an object can have a primary key are by already having one in the database or by being assigned one by OJB prior to initially being saved. In either case, it means that the object must already exist, so any save operation must be updating data. This makes it very easy for a band to change its name—for example, the artist in the previous example:

```
artist.setName("The Birthday Massacre");
...
broker.store(artist);
...
```

It is reasonable to expect that when storing or updating an object all the primitive fields would be saved, and this is indeed the case. It is less clear what OJB will do with collections. This behavior is controlled by the `auto-update` attribute of the collection-descriptor noted in passing in the section on "repository-user." When this attribute is set to true, OJB will traverse the collection and automatically save any objects. This means the following code will work as expected:

```
Artist artist = new Artist();
artist.setName("");

Album first = new Album();
first.setName("");
first.setYearReleased();

Album second = new Album("");
second.setName("");
second.setYearReleased();

... save the artist ...
```

OJB will save artist, which will entail allocating a new artistId. After the record has been written to the database, OJB will examine all the collections and then attempt to save each album. When doing so it will notice that each needs a primary key and so will allocate new albumIds. It will also know that artistId in Album is a foreign key and will assign it with the artistId that was handed out as the new primary key to artist. OJB will then save the albums, having ensured that all the database constraints have been satisfied.

The auto-delete attribute works similarly. When this is set to true, deleting an object will cause objects in that objects collections to be deleted first. Typically this makes sense: If an artist is being removed from the database, all that artist's albums should be removed as well. In fact, by declaring a foreign-key relationship in the database definition, this constraint will be enforced; any attempt to delete an artist who still has albums will fail with an error. Setting auto-delete and auto-update to true thus ensures that the semantics of the object is identical to the semantics of the database as defined in the schema, in addition to mapping the hierarchical structures.

10.5 Retrieving Data

Retrieving data is also done through the proxy, via objects called **queries.** In the simplest form a query specifies only the class to retrieve, which is equivalent to specifying the table to select from

```
Query query = new QueryByCriteria(Artist.class, null);
Iterator iter = broker.getIteratorByQuery(query);

while (iter.hasNext()) {
    Artist artist = (Artist) iter.next();
    System.out.println("Artist: " + artist.getName());

    Album first = artist.getAlbum(0);
    System.out.println(
        "First album: " + album.getName() +
        " released in " + album.getYearReleased());
}
```

The second argument in the constructor for `QueryByCriteria` is additional constraints, which will be discussed shortly. With this argument `null` the query is equivalent to

```
select * from artist;
```

It is important to note that the albums are available immediately, so there is no need to run any additional queries by hand. This behavior is specified by setting `auto-retrieve="true"` in the mapping file. This means that after the initial query to get the artists, for *each* artist an additional query will be executed consisting of

```
select * from album where artist_id=...;
```

where the ellipses are replaced by the relevant `artistId`. The resulting `Album` objects will then be constructed, and each of their tracks will then be similarly obtained. Building the whole tree as soon as each root object is loaded is called **eager evaluation.**

There are both pros and cons to eager evaluation. Loading all the data at once means that the minimum number of queries will be needed. In this case a single query loads all the albums for each artist, so the total number of queries is one plus the number of artists. In common usage, where only a single artist is loaded, this number reduces to two. Obviously many more queries would be needed if each album were loaded one at a time. Eager evaluation also means that all the data will be available in memory, and so the tree can be traversed quickly and efficiently.

On the other hand, eager evaluation means a lot of work will need to be done up front, leading to an initial delay when an artist is first loaded. If the tree is very large, lots of memory will be consumed right away. Both of these penalties may not be worth paying if only a small amount of data is needed by the application. For example, if a program only needs to know the year of an artist's debut, there is no need to load any album but the first and no need to load any of the track data.

It is also possible to configure OJB to use what is called **lazy evaluation,** where data is only retrieved as it is needed. This is discussed in a later section. For the moment, all collections will be loaded eagerly.

Eager evaluation raises a potentially dangerous issue that must be considered. Recall from the section on mapping that a backpointer was placed in the `Album` table containing the `Artist`. Due to eager evaluation, this means that as soon as the `Album` is loaded, OJB will attempt to resolve all the relationships, including the `Artist`. But it has already been stated that as soon as an `Artist` is loaded, OJB will fill in all of that artist's `Albums`. Will this lead to an infinite loop, forever alternating between loading the `Artist` and the `Albums` until memory is exhausted or something similarly horrible happens? The answer, happily, is a resounding "No!"

OJB contains some very sophisticated caching that allows it to realize when it goes to load the `Artist` for the second time that it has already obtained that data and will reuse it when setting the `Artist` in the `Album`. This means all the backpointers will literally *be* backpointers, containing not only the same data but the same object. Or, more formally, this ensures that if `artist` has been loaded by OJB, then

```
artist == album.getAlbum(0).getArtist()
```

will evaluate to `true`.

10.6 More Sophisticated Queries

It is relatively uncommon for an application to need all data of a given type from the database. It is far more common to request data satisfying certain criteria, and OJB provides several ways to do this.

The simplest is to specify the equivalent of an SQL `where` clause through objects called **criteria.** For example, a `Criteria` object could be used to retrieve an artist with a particular name as follows:

```
Criteria criteria = new Criteria();
citeria.addEqualTo("name","VNV Nation");
Query query = new QueryByCriteria(Artist.class, criteria);
```

The first argument to `addEqualTo()` specifies the name of a field in the class. There is an equivalent method called `addColumnEqualTo()` that takes the name of the database column. The second argument is an `Object`, which will be treated properly for the underlying type. Once the query has been constructed, it may be passed to the broker to get an iterator over the results, or if only a single result is expected, `getObjectByQuery()` may be used.

There are many methods in the `Criteria` class that add different kinds of constraints, including equality, less-than and greater-than, `in` and `like` expressions, and so on. Each call to such a method adds another constraint to the `where` clause that OJB will ultimately construct. For example, the following will construct a query to find all albums released in the 1980s with the word "Black" in the title:

```
Criteria criteria = new Criteria();
citeria.addBetween("yearReleased",
                   new Integer(1980),
                   new Integer(1989));
criteria.addLike("name","%Black%");
Query query = new QueryByCriteria(Album.class, criteria);
```

and the resulting query will look like

```
select * from album
where name like '%black%'
and yearReleased between 1980 and 1989
```

For queries that contain only constraints on equality it is often easier to use `QueryByIdentity`[3] instead of `QueryByCriteria`. `QueryByIdentity` takes an object as an argument and builds quality constraints from all the `non-null` fields in that object. For example, here is another way to find an artist by name:

```
Artist artist = new Artist();
artist.setName("Faith and Disease");
Query qry = new QueryByIdentity(artist);
```

Note the class to retrieve is implied by the object.

Both `QueryByIdentity` and `QueryByCriteria` allow searching only by criteria on one table. The first argument to all the add methods in `Criteria` must be a column or field in the table specified by the first argument to the constructor for

[3]As of this writing, attempting to use `QueryByIdentity` throws a `ClassCastException` deep in the OJB code. This will likely be fixed in a subsequent version.

QueryByIdentity. Clearly QueryByIdentity deals with only one table and its fields. More general queries requiring several tables can be issued through the QueryBySQL class, which takes the name of a class to build, along with arbitrary SQL. For example, to find all the albums that have a track named "Standing"

```
Query query =
  new QueryBySQL(Album.class,
                 "select album.* from album,track " +
                 "where track.name='Standing' "     +
                 "and track.album_id=album.album_id");
```

Note that the selected fields must all come from one table, and OJB will use metadata to match column names to property names in the class. Apart from that, there are no restrictions on the query; it may contain multiple tables, inner selects, outer joins, and so on.

10.7 Lazy Evaluation

As mentioned previously, based on the setting of auto-load in the mapping file, collections and objects can be loaded either eagerly or lazily. Eager evaluation makes it easy to write application code because the code can always assume that cascaded data will be present. However, eager evaluation may load a lot more data than the application uses, impacting both performance and memory usage.

There are two different ways in which evaluation of a collection may be lazy: at the collection level or at the object level. Laziness at the collection level means that a stub List will be provided when the parent object is first loaded. The methods in this List will load the data if necessary before performing the usual List action. For example, the first time get() or iterate() is called, the List will first run the necessary query and populate itself. This means the same total number of queries will be executed, as in eager evaluation, but they will be delayed until needed. On the other hand, this means that as soon as any element of the List is accessed, all elements will be read into memory.

Object-based laziness implies that when the parent object is loaded a List is prepared with stubs for each of the children, and each individual child is loaded as it is accessed. This may mean many more queries will be executed—one for the parent, one to find out how many children there are, and one for each child. The benefit is that only the data that is used by the program will be loaded.

One approach to collection-level lazy evaluation would be to manually load collections, either in the application code or in the bean. Album data could be handled in the `Artist` bean with code like the following:

```
private Collection albums = null;

public Collection getAlbums() {
    if(albums != null) return albums;
    Album a = new Album();
    a.setArtistId(getArtistId());
    Query qry = new QueryByIdentity(a);
    PersistenceBroker broker =
        PersistenceBrokerFactory.defaultPersistenceBroker();
    albums = broker.getCollectionByQuery(query);

    return albums;
}
```

Note the use of the new broker method `getCollectionByQuery()`. This would need some effort to make it produce a `List`, properly handle exceptions, and other such details.

While this approach would certainly work, it is far from ideal because it makes the job of writing persistable beans much more difficult. Even if most of the work in the preceding method were abstracted into a method in a base class, it inexorably ties the beans to the persistence model, which is undesirable.

The most salient feature of the preceding code snippet is the the conditional right at the top. The implication of this test is that the data will be loaded the first time it is needed, when the `albums` are first requested. This test can be moved from the bean into the `Collection` class, which is what OJB does. To enable this kind of lazy evaluation, it is just necessary to add `proxy="true"` to the `collection-descriptor`, as in

```
<collection-descriptor
        name="albums"
        element-class-ref="com.awl.toolbook.chapter10.Album"
        orderby="year_released"
        sort="ASC"
        proxy="true"
>
    <inverse-foreignkey field-ref="artistId"/>
</collection-descriptor>
```

Note that `auto-update` and `auto-delete` have been removed. It is possible to leave these features enabled, but note that doing so will cause the entire collection to be read from the database when a save or delete operation occurs.

Object-level lazy evaluation is somewhat more difficult. What is needed is a means for OJB to automatically detect that an object is being used without requiring the user to add any code. Note that, to be as lazy as possible, simply accessing `albums.get(3)` should not cause the third album to be read. This should only happen when member data is used, as in `albums.get(3).getName()` or `artist.getAlbum(3).getYearReleased()`.

This is asking rather a lot of OJB because the calls to the `Album` methods do not invoke OJB at all. One way OJB could intercept the calls to these methods is to use a **proxy,** a class that sits between OJB and the `Artist` bean, which provides the same methods and performs the special handling required by lazy collections. An outline of such a class is shown here.

```
public class AlbumProxy {
    private Album theAlbum = null;

    public int getYearReleased() {
        if(theAlbum == null) {
            loadAlbum();
        }
        return theAlbum.getYearReleased();
    }
}
```

The `loadAlbum()` method would do essentially the same thing as the `getAlbums()` from the previous example. Any calls to a broker that result in an `Album` being generated would instead return an `AlbumProxy`.

So far this solution looks even worse than putting the code in the `getAlbum()` method. The same code must be written, plus more, and all application code must be changed to use `AlbumProxy` instead of `Album`. A little of this burden could be avoided by using an interface that defines the `Album` methods and having both `Album` and `AlbumProxy` implement this interface. At least then application code could use one type name consistently.

Now a remarkable feature of Java enters the picture. As of JDK 1.3 it is possible for a class to declare that it implements an interface at runtime. This feature is relatively unknown. Readers who have not previously encountered it may wish to read more details in Appendix A.

The practical upshot of this feature is that once the interface has been defined, no more code needs to be written! OJB can declare that a generalized proxy implements the interface. This general proxy will then intercept all method calls and will automatically load collections that have not yet been loaded.

This feature is enabled in the descriptor for the class rather than any collection that may use the class. It will therefore impact all references to the class, whether in collections, backpointers, or anywhere else. A typical definition is as follows:

```
<class-descriptor
  class="com.awl.toolbook.chapter10.Album"
  proxy="dynamic"
  table="Album"
>

  <!-- field definitions, as before -->
</class-descriptor>
```

10.8 Related Tools

Although it is often easiest to define the tables, beans, and mapping file at the same time, there are a number of tools available that will aid in the creation of some of these from the information contained in the others. Of particular note are the following four tools that are designed to generate classes and a mapping file from an existing database:

- reverse-db, included with OJB
- rdbs2j, a tool developed separately from OJB and available from http://sourceforge.net/projects/rdbs2j
- reverse-db2, an update of reverse-db
- the Impart plugin for Eclipse, available from http://www.impart.ch/download.htm

Unfortunately, at the time of this writing none of these tools work. reverse-db cannot read table information from either hsqldb or mysql, although it may work with other databases. rdbs2j is in a beta release, but all the program text is in German (the program itself may work perfectly well for those who can read the menu items and dialogs). reverse-db2 seems to be an early effort, with no functionality implemented yet beyond the ability to explore the database.

The fourth option, the Eclipse plugin from Impart, worked with Eclipse 2.1.5 but does not work with 3.0.0. This will likely be fixed in the near future as 3.0.0 matures. For the time being, the following section describes usage of this plugin with 2.1.5.

Installation is a simple matter of unzipping the downloaded file in the Eclipse "plugins" directory and then restarting Eclipse.

This plugin requires a configuration file called "ImpartOJBGenerator.properties" to be placed in the home directory under Unix variants or `C:\Documents and Settings\login_name` under Windows. This file contains the typical set of database connection information as well as mappings for JDBC types. See the readme file that accompanies the plugin for more details.

The new features that this plug adds to Eclipse are accessible from the "Window" menu. Select "Show view" then "Other..." and the pop-up shown in Figure 10.4 will be displayed.

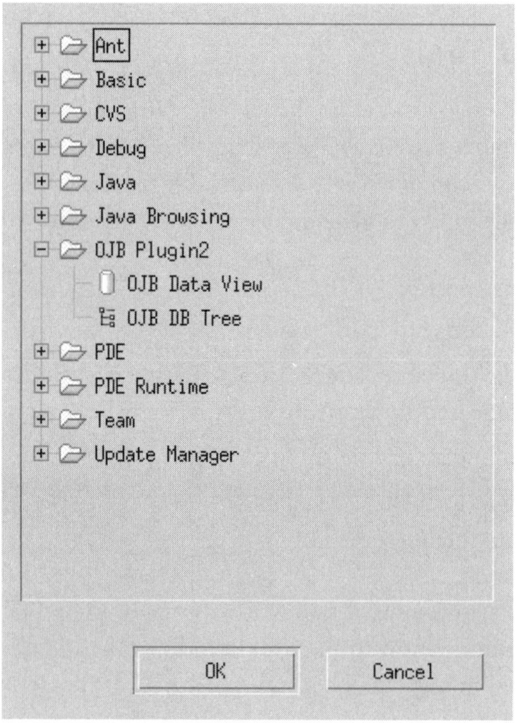

Figure 10.4. The Eclipse other view selector.

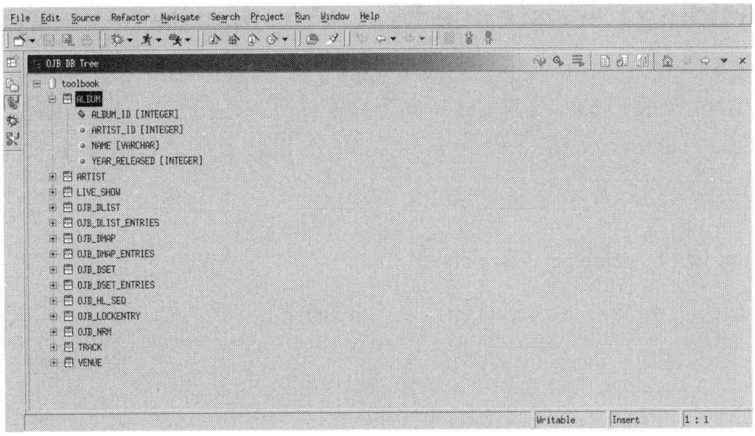

Figure 10.5. The OJB DB Tree view.

Selecting the "OJB DB Tree" will bring up a database browser window. By default this Window will occupy the space usually taken by the console or task list seen in previous Eclipse screenshots. In Figure 10.5 this window has been expanded to become the main window, and the `ALBUM` table has been expanded. All the tables that begin with the prefix `OJB_` are the internal OJB tables mentioned in the discussion of the "repository_internal.xml" mapping file.

There are three icons on the right of the window toolbar. The first will reload the table data from the database. The second will generate Java files for all selected tables. The third will generate both "repository_database.xml" and "repository_user.xml" mapping files. It is important when generating such a file to ensure that the OJB internal tables are not selected because the generated mappings will conflict with those in "repository_internal.xml."

The generated code and mapping files have some slight differences from those that have been used in this chapter. The convention used until now is that underscores in names of tables and fields are omitted and the following letter capitalized in the corresponding class and property names. Impart leaves names as they appear in the database, capitalizing only the first letter.

Impart is able to detect primary keys, and these will be correctly marked in the mapping file. Impart is not able to detect foreign key relationships, so no collections will be placed in the generated class files or mapping files. These will need to be added by hand. Even with these shortcomings, Impart is a useful tool that can save a great deal of tedious typing.

10.9 Hiding Persistence from Applications

Because the `PersistenceBroker` is obtained through a static call to a factory, it is possible to put code that loads and saves beans within the beans themselves. In fact, due to the generality of the API, it is possible to hide all the OJB code in a simple base class, as shown in Listing 10.11.

Listing 10.11 A base persistent object

```
package com.awl.toolbook.chapter10;

import java.util.ArrayList;
import java.util.Iterator;

import org.apache.commons.beanutils.PropertyUtils;

import org.apache.ojb.broker.PersistenceBroker;
import org.apache.ojb.broker.PersistenceBrokerFactory;
import org.apache.ojb.broker.PersistenceBrokerException;
import org.apache.ojb.broker.query.*;

public class PersistentObject {
    private PersistenceBroker broker_ = null;

    public PersistentObject() {
        try {
            broker_ =
            PersistenceBrokerFactory.
                defaultPersistenceBroker();
        } catch (Throwable t) {
            t.printStackTrace();
        }
    }

    public boolean getSave() {return true;}
    public void setSave(boolean b) {
        save();
    }
```

```
public void save() {
    try {
        broker_.beginTransaction();
        broker_.store(this);
        broker_.commitTransaction();
    } catch (PersistenceBrokerException e) {
        broker_.abortTransaction();
        System.out.println("Unable to save: " + e);
    }
}

public void delete() {
    try {
        broker_.beginTransaction();
        broker_.delete(this);
        broker_.commitTransaction();
    } catch (PersistenceBrokerException e) {
        broker_.abortTransaction();
        System.out.print("Unable to delete: ");
        System.out.println(e);
    }
}


public ArrayList getMatching() {
    ArrayList ret = new ArrayList();

    try {
        broker_.beginTransaction();
        String cname = getClass().toString();
        int pos      = cname.lastIndexOf('.');
        cname        = cname.substring(pos+1);
        cname   = cname.substring(0,1).toLowerCase() +
                  cname.substring(1) + "Id";

        String value = null;

        try {
```

Listing 10.11 A base persistent object *(continued)*

```
                value =
    PropertyUtils.getSimpleProperty(this,cname).toString();
            } catch (Exception e) {
                e.printStackTrace(System.err);
            }

            Criteria criteria = new Criteria();
            criteria.addEqualTo(cname,value);

            Query qry = new QueryByCriteria(getClass(),
                                            criteria);
            Iterator iter =
                broker_.getIteratorByQuery(qry);

            while (iter.hasNext()) {
                ret.add(iter.next());
            }

            broker_.commitTransaction();
        } catch (PersistenceBrokerException e) {
            broker_.abortTransaction();
            System.out.print("Unable to save: ");
            System.out.println(e);
        }

        return ret;
    }
}
```

Any class that extends `PersistentObject`, such as `Artist` in Listing 10.6, can simply call `save()` to save itself to the database, and application code will not need to worry about obtaining brokers or the details of inserts versus updates. The `setSave()` and `getMaching()` methods will be useful in cases where the only interface between external code and these data beans are through bean properties. One example of this situation is beans used from within JavaServer Pages, as discussed in Chapter 19.

The somewhat convoluted code in `getMatching()` is meant to determine the primary key of the current object and set the criteria appropriately. It assumes that the name of the id field is the name of the class, with the first letter lowercased and "Id" appended to the name. It uses `PropertyUtils`, discussed in Chapter 8, to get the id. If `QueryByIdentity` worked, this would be unnecessary, but this just goes to show that sometimes it is necessary to work around bugs, even in open source projects.

10.10 Beyond This Book

There is more that could be said about all three of the tools discussed in this chapter, although the material presented will go a great deal toward the creation of any application, Web-based or otherwise.

Hsqldb can be run in server mode and can even be tunneled through HTTP for use behind firewalls. In this mode, combined with cached tables hsqldb makes a very respectable database server for small applications or groups. At the other end of the scale, hsqldb is small and light enough that it can be run on many PDAs that support Java, making it possible to carry a full-featured database in one's pocket. Hsqldb also supports an impressive subset of the SQL standards, and readers are encouraged to check out the details at the hsqldb Web site. Beyond the standards, it is possible to extend the built-in types and functions through custom Java classes. See the class mappings in the script file for an introduction to how this works.

DBCP and Pool both have numerous other configuration options for allocating and reclaiming objects. It is also easy to pool things other than collections. There are also some interesting possibilities in persistent stores, where the pool itself is maintained in a database.

Finally, OJB is a very large, complex suite, and it was only possible to scratch the surface of its features here. A particularly important point is that OJB supports two industry standards for persistent objects. The first is ODMG (Object Data Management Group), which is a comprehensive, general, language-neutral specification for persistent objects. The second is JDO (Java Data Objects), a specification based on ODMG and refined through the Java Community Process.

10.11 Summary

Tool: Hsqldb
Purpose: Lightweight, pure-Java database
Version covered: 1.7.2 Release candidate 6c
Home page: http://hsqldb.sourceforge.net/
License: Custom license requiring copywrite notices be maintained

Tool: DBCP
Purpose: Caches database connections
Version covered: 1.2.1
Home page: http://jakarta.apache.org/commons/dbcp/
License: The Apache Software License, Version 2.0

Tool: OJB
Purpose: Object-relational mapping
Version covered: 1.0 rc 7
Home page: http://db.apache.org/ojb/
License: The Apache Software License, Version 2.0
Further Reading:

- The ODMG home page: http://www.odmg.org/.
- More information on JDO: http://java.sun.com/products/jdo/.
- *JDBC API Tutorial and Reference,* Third Edition, by Maydene Fisher et al. Addison-Wesley, 2003.

CHAPTER 11

Logging

There are many times where it is useful or even necessary to peer inside a program and observe what it is doing. The most complete way to do this is with a debugger, such as the one included in Eclipse. This is not always a possible or practical solution for many reasons, not the least of which is that there is no way to run a production system in a debugger. Therefore, it must become the program's task to report on its internal state. In the most general sense this task is called **logging.**

An obvious and much-used technique to log information is to liberally sprinkle `println()` statements throughout a program. However, this approach quickly proves to be insufficient for many reasons.

Printing all log messages ignores the fact that there are many kinds of logging that may be needed. A program should certainly report errors such as uncaught exceptions to the developers. A program may also need to issue warnings about potentially troublesome conditions. There may also be general information that developers or administrators are interested in, such as who is using the system or how it is being used. Finally, during development detailed information such as the values of variables or which branch of a conditional has been taken may be of interest. This gives rise to the notion of a **log level.**

Printing log messages directly also lacks configurability. When there are many developers working on a large project, each will likely be interested in only a small subset of log messages, typically those from code for which he or she is responsible. If all log messages are generated though print statements, there is no way to disable some messages and enable others at run time. There is thus a need for **runtime log configuration.**

It is also possible that different kinds or sets of messages should be sent to different places. At the very least it may be desirable for errors to be sent to `System.err` with everything else going to `System.out`. More generally, information about who is using a system might need to go to one file so management can judge the success of a site, whereas warnings and errors should go to a file that is sent to developers. This means that a logging system should support **configurable log destinations.**

This chapter examines two complete logging systems: the one built into J2SE 1.4 and log4j from Apache. Both of these systems provide facilities for all three requirements just discussed, although each has strengths and weaknesses that may make it better suited for particular situations.

11.1 The Java.util.logging Package

As of J2SE 1.4 logging facilities are provided as part of the standard Java libraries. Many of the ideas behind this package seem to have been inspired by log4j, which preceded 1.4 by over a year. Some of the features of log4j were omitted, leading to an API that is easier to use. Because this package is included in the Java standard, there is no need to download or distribute any additional jar files. However, many people believe that too many features were omitted from `java.util.logging` and that log4j is still a preferable solution.

In J2SE 1.4 all logging is done through a `Logger` object. A static method in `Logger` maps names to particular instances, and different instances can be given different properties. Therefore, a logging operation begins by obtaining the appropriate logger by name.

```
Logger logger =
    Logger.getLogger("com.awl.toolbook.chapter11.sample");
```

The only points to note about logger names are that they must be valid Java identifiers and that they are hierarchical. This latter point means that logging properties can be assigned to the logger named `com.awl.toolbook`, and by default the logger used above will inherit these properties.

One obvious approach to naming is for each class in the project to have its own logger, and the name of the logger to match the full name of the class. Loggers are thread-safe, which means multiple instances of a class can all use the same logger without worrying about interfering with each other. This means that each class's logger can be obtained statically

```
import java.util.logging.*;

public class Sample {
    private static Logger logger =
        Logger.getLogger(Sample.class.getName());
}
```

Using this approach makes it easy to configure logging on a package-by-package level, with a logger at the top of the hierarchy having default values. The logger for each subpackage can override values and can be enabled or disabled as needed.

This is a valid and often useful approach, but it is certainly not the only one. Multiple classes throughout several packages might comprise a single logical unit, and in such a case the name of that unit might be used as the logger name. For example, a project designed along model/view/controller lines might have a logger named `view` and subloggers representing different kinds of views such as `view.jsp`, `view.jsp.taglib`, `view.swing`, and so on.

It is also possible for one class to play several different roles, in which case one class may need to obtain several `Logger` instances.

11.1.1 Logging Messages

Logging a message once a logger has been obtained is a simple matter. The simplest log method is called `log()`, and it takes a log level and a message to be logged. Levels are represented by `final static` values in the `Level` class, so the call to log some general information would look like

```
logger.log(Level.INFO,"New user logged in");
```

As a convenience `Logger` also provides methods that reflect the predefined log levels, so the preceding call could be replaced by `logger.info("New user")`. There are also versions of these methods that accept an exception as an additional argument.

The following log levels are defined in `Level`:

- NONE
- SEVERE
- WARNING
- INFO

- CONFIG
- FINE
- FINER
- FINEST
- ALL

Levels have an implied order that is maintained by static integer values assigned to each. Loggers also have an associated log level; when a message is logged, the logger checks whether the level of the message is less than its own level. If so, the message is discarded.

Because logger levels can be configured at run time, this makes it easy to filter messages. During development a logger might be set to the `FINEST` level so that all debug messages will be logged. When the system is put in production, the level might be changed to `WARNING` so that only serious and potentially serious problems will be reported.

Each of the predefined levels has a corresponding set of methods in `Logger`; there are methods called `severe()` and `fine()` and so on. The special value `NONE` means that no messages should be logged, and `ALL` means that every message should be logged. `FINE`, `FINER`, and `FINEST` are meant to represent different levels of debugging output, although the precise meaning is left to the developer. One possibility is that each method call could be logged at the `FINE` level, leaving `FINER` and `FINEST` to represent different amounts of detail as to what methods are doing.

It is possible to create new log levels by subclassing `Level` and adding new constants. Care must be taken not to conflict with values of the predefined levels, and for that reason and others, creating new levels is not recommended.

11.1.2 How Logging Is Handled

Once a message has been logged with a call to `log()` or a related method, several things happen. First, a new instance of `LogRecord` is created and populated with values including the message, log level, and the exception if one is provided. The `LogRecord` is also given the current time and the names of the class and method from where the logging call occurred. These last two pieces of data are inferred automatically by the logging system and may not always be accurate. For example, during dynamic optimization hotspot may change the way in which methods are called. When exact values are needed, there is an alternate set of log methods that allows them to be specified.

It is also possible for client code to create and log LogRecord objects manually, with code such as

```
LogRecord record = new LogRecord();
record.setLevel(Level.FINE);
record.setMessage("Test code entered");
record.setSourceClassName("com.awl.toolbook.chapter11.Test");
record.setSourceMethodName("manualLogRecord");
record.setThreadID(Thread.currentThread().hashCode());

logger.log(record);
```

Regardless of how the record is created, the logger passes the record to one or more Handler objects. The set of handlers to invoke are associated with the named logger, so it is possible to define different sets of handlers for different packages or parts of the system.

It is the Handler objects that make the LogRecords available to end users. There are predefined handlers that write log messages to System.out, System.err, or files. There are also handlers that hold log messages in memory where they can be programmatically examined. There are even handlers that send log messages through a socket. It is also possible to define new handlers that perform custom actions such as storing log events in a database or sending them to a system administrator's pager. This later handler could be tied to SEVERE events such as the system experiencing a critical failure in order to provide an immediate alert.

Many of the preceding handlers use classes called Formatters to process the LogRecord data into a human-readable or machine-readable format. Two formatters are provided: SimpleFormatter, which writes a short, easy to read summary such as

```
Aug 9, 2003 4:03:35 PM com.awl.toolbook.chapter11.Sample
INFO: New user logged in
```

and XMLFormatter, which creates an XML structure

```
<?xml version="1.0" encoding="ISO-8859-1" standalone="no"?>
<!DOCTYPE log SYSTEM "logger.dtd">
<log>
<record>
  <date>2003-08-09T16:13:23</date>
  <millis>1060460003493</millis>
  <sequence>1</sequence>
  <logger>com.awl.toolbook.chapter11.manual</logger>
```

```
    <level>INFO</level>
    <class>com.awl.toolbook.chapter11.LogSample</class>
    <method>manual</method>
    <thread>10</thread>
    <message>New user logged in</message>
  </record>
  </log>
```

Sometimes assigning a level to a logger is insufficient, such as cases where it is desirable to send error messages and debugging messages to different files. If a logger is configured at the WARNING level, the debug messages will be ignored, but if the logger is set to the FINEST level, all messages will be sent to the handlers, and both kinds of messages will end up jumbled together in both of the target files. One way around this would be to use two different loggers with different names and different levels, but this means that extra logging code must be added to the application.

For this reason, handlers also have associated levels. If a handler's level is set to WARNING, it will only log events at the WARNING and SEVERE levels. Note, however, that if the logger's level is set to NONE, then the log records will not be sent to the handlers at all.

11.1.3 Filtering

Some situations require more fine-grained control over logging than can be provided by a level. For example, a handler designed to page an administrator with error messages might only need to run after normal business hours. Therefore, the Java logging API provides a general mechanism by which handlers and loggers can determine whether to log particular messages. These are called **filters.** A filter is a class with a method called isLoggable() that is passed the LogRecord before the logger or handler handles it. The isLoggable() method returns a boolean indicating whether the record should be processed. Listing 11.1 shows a simple filter that recreates the existing level-based test by checking whether the LogRecord is at an appropriate level.

Listing 11.1 A simple filter

```
package com.awl.toolbook.chapter11;

import java.util.logging.*;
```

```
public class LevelFilter implements Filter {
    private Level minLevel = Level.FINEST;

    public LevelFilter() {}

    public LevelFilter(Level minLevel) {
        this.minLevel = minLevel;
    }

    public boolean isLoggable(LogRecord record) {
      return
      minLevel.intValue() >= record.getLevel().intValue();
    }
}
```

This class could be used as follows:

```
handler.setFilter(new LevelFilter(Level.WARNING));
```

There is no limit to what can be done in the `isLoggable()` method. A filter could do different things based on the time of day, the exact format of the message, the presence or absence of a `Throwable` with the log message, and so on. It is even possible to alter fields in the `LogRecord`, although this is not recommended.

Note that each logger and handler may have at most one filter each; there is no `addFilter()` method. However, it is possible to create a "master filter" that itself contains many other filters that will be checked in turn. It is difficult to imagine a filtering situation that would need such complex logic, but the facility is there if needed.

11.1.4 Configuring Logging through the API

To review: Loggers are named; each logger has a level and a set of handlers; and some handlers use formatters to prepare output. All of these steps can be controlled programmatically, as illustrated in following example:

```
public void manual() throws Exception {
    Logger logger      =
        Logger.getLogger(
            "com.awl.toolbook.chapter11.manual");
    FileHandler handler = new FileHandler("logdata.xml");
    handler.setFormatter(new XMLFormatter());
```

```
        logger.addHandler(handler);
        logger.setLevel(Level.ALL);

        logger.info("New user logged in");
    }
```

This example creates a new `FileHandler` that is configured to send its data to `logdata.xml` and to format the data with a `FileHandler`. The handler is then added to the `Logger` obtained in the first line, and that `Logger`'s level is set to `ALL`. Then an info-level log message is generated. It is not surprising that after this example is run, `logdata.xml` will contain a message much like the XML sample just shown. What may be surprising is that a message formated by the `SimpleFormatter` is also sent to the console. This is because the new handler is added to the logger, and the default root logger already has the console handler.

Due to the hierarchical nature of logger, if another logger is constructed with a name beneath the previous one in the hierarchy, it will have the same properties. After executing

```
    Logger logger2 =
        Logger.getLogger(
            "com.awl.toolbook.chapter11.manual.sublogger");
    logger2.info("Hello");
```

the "Hello" message will end up in the same `logdata.xml` file. However, `logger2` is a distinct `Logger` instance, so if its level or set of handlers were altered programmatically, the changes would not automatically propagate up to `logger`.

While an entire hierarchy could be defined in this way, it is clearly tedious, and hard-coding such configuration within a program is never a good idea. It is much more common and efficient to use a configuration file.

11.1.5 Using Configuration Files

Logging is configured through a set of name/value pairs rather than through XML. This makes configuration very simple but implies some limitations, as will be seen shortly.

Typically configuration starts by setting properties for the root logger, the one at the top of the hierarchy. As all loggers are descendants of the root, setting properties for the root logger effectively sets defaults for the entire logging system. The root logger is named "" (the empty string), which can make relevant definitions look a little strange such as the level definition in the following example, which begins with a dot:

```
handlers = java.util.logging.ConsoleHandler,\
java.util.logging.FileHandler
.level = ALL
```

This will log all messages to both the console and a default file, using simple formatting. When the system is placed in production, the value of ALL might be changed to WARNING. Note that the level here is associated with the root logger, not the individual handlers that the logger is using.

Each handler can also be given a level and formatter, and some handlers have additional properties that can be set:

```
java.util.logging.ConsoleHandler.level = INFO
java.util.logging.ConsoleHandler.formatter = \
    java.util.logging.SimpleFormatter

java.util.logging.FileHandler.level = FINEST
java.util.logging.FileHandler.pattern = debuglog.xml
java.util.logging.FileHandler.formatter = \
    java.util.logging.XMLFormatter
```

these lines indicate that log messages at the information and higher levels should be sent to the console and that all debugging and higher messages should be saved to a file. The file is configured to use the XMLFormatter and to save its output in debuglog.xml The reason the file name property is called "pattern" instead of "name" is that it accepts a number of special characters that will be resolved by the logging system to form the file name. For example "%h" indicates the current user's home directory, and "%t" represents the system location for temporary files (typically/tmp on Unix and C:\temp for Windows).

It is possible to create an arbitrary number of additional loggers, each with its own level:

```
com.awl.toolbook.level = NONE
com.awl.toolbook.chapter12.level = INFO
com.awl.toolbook.chapter11.sample.level = ALL
```

This turns off logging for the book, enables information messages for most of the Chapter 11 examples, but it allows all messages for the "sample" logger within Chapter 11.

While each logger may have its own level, the `handlers` property is global, as are the attributes of each handler. This means there is no way to send the output for chapter 11 code to a separate file or to send it only to the console. There are a few workarounds for this, but they all involve doing some manipulation in Java code. This would split the configuration between two places, which in turn makes it more difficult to maintain. Log4j has a more flexible configuration system, as will be seen in the next section.

The logging system may be told to use a particular configuration file by specifying it on the command line:

```
java  \
  -Djava.util.logging.config.file=logconfig.properties \
  classToRun
```

11.1.6 Creating New Handlers

Handlers are defined by an abstract class, so creating a new handler is just a matter of extending this class and providing implementations of the abstract methods.

A handler that might be useful is one that saves log messages to a database. This is not particularly useful for debugging messages or even for errors and warnings, but it may be very useful for informative messages about how a system is being used. Therefore, this kind of handler might be used in conjunction with a custom filter that only passes through messages at the `INFO` level, instead of `INFO` and above.

Conceptually writing a log message to a database using straight JDBC calls would not be difficult, but there is an even easier possibility. Because the `LogRecord` class largely adheres to the bean-naming convention, records can be saved to a database directly using OJB, as discussed in Chapter 10. To do this, a table definition and mapping will be needed. The table simply has fields for the properties of interest:

```
create table log (
    millis      int,
    message     varchar(200),
    class_name  varchar(80),
    method_name varchar(20)
);
```

Likewise the mapping is straightforward:

```
<class-descriptor
  class="java.util.logging.LogRecord"
  table="LOG">

   <field-descriptor
      name="millis"
      column="ATIST_ID"
      jdbc-type="INTEGER"
   />

   <field-descriptor
      name="name"
      column="NAME"
      jdbc-type="VARCHAR"
   />

   <field-descriptor
      name="name"
      column="NAME"
      jdbc-type="VARCHAR"
   />

   <field-descriptor
      name="name"
      column="NAME"
      jdbc-type="VARCHAR"
   />
</class-descriptor>
```

These definitions do not include all of the fields in `LogRecord`. Some fields are not useful in a database context. Other fields, like the log level, are useful but are not directly obtainable from `LogRecord`. This is because `getLevel()` returns a `Level` object, not an integer or other type that can be mapped to a JDBC type. Similarly, the time in `LogRecord` is stored in milliseconds, whereas JDBC needs a `Timestamp`.

With these definitions properly installed, the handler itself is fairly simple and is shown in Listing 11.2.

Listing 11.2 A handler that logs to a database

```
package com.awl.toolbook.chapter11;

import org.apache.ojb.broker.PersistenceBroker;
import org.apache.ojb.broker.PersistenceBrokerFactory;
import org.apache.ojb.broker.PersistenceBrokerException;

import java.util.logging.*;

class OJBHandler extends Handler {
    private PersistenceBroker broker_ = null;
    private Logger logger =
        Logger.getLogger("com.awl.toolbook.db");

    public OJBHandler() {
        try {
            broker_ =
            PersistenceBrokerFactory.
                defaultPersistenceBroker();
        } catch (Throwable t) {
            t.printStackTrace();
        }
    }

    public void publish(LogRecord record) {
        if(!isLoggable(record)) {
            return;
        }

        try {
            broker_.beginTransaction();
            broker_.store(record);
            broker_.commitTransaction();
        } catch (PersistenceBrokerException e) {
            broker_.abortTransaction();
            logger.severe("Unable to log to database");
            logger.log(record);
        }
    }
```

```
    public void flush() {}

    public void close() {}
}
```

The `flush()` and `close()` methods are declared abstract in the base class and so must be provided. They are meant to store all accumulated log messages and close the connection to the log repository, respectively.

All the action takes place in the `publish()` method. First, the `isLoggable()` method, which is defined in the base class, is called. This ensures that the level of the record is appropriate and that any installed filters will be checked. Then the record is stored using the standard OJB calls. It is almost as simple as that, but there is a serious danger lurking in this code.

This handler uses the logging system to report on problems it may encounter when writing to the database. In itself there is nothing wrong with a handler or other logging-related class using the logging API. In this case if the logger being used happens to be configured to use the `OJBHandler`, an infinite loop will occur. If the database write fails, then a log message will be generated, which will result in an attempt to write a record to the database, which will fail, and so on endlessly. There are a number of ways around this problem. The easiest is to call `System.err.println()` instead of using the log system. Alternately the logger could be manually configured within the constructor to ensure that it is only using safe handlers. Code could also be added to `publish()` to ignore messages from `OJBHandler` or a check that the level is `INFO` could be done in `publish()` instead of relying on it being configured in `isLoggable()`.

Incidentally, note that the name of the logger is `com.awl.toolbook.db`, which does not exactly reflect the package name but instead suggests that all database-related activity will be logged to the same place.

There is a more subtle problem than the infinite loop lurking in Listing 11.2, which is that database access tends to be slow. Logging should be so fast that the addition of logging statements will have no noticeable effect on a program.

One fix to this problem would be to save log messages to the database asynchronously. In this model `publish()` would save the `LogRecord` to a `Vector` or `ArrayList` and a separate thread would periodically save all of the accumulated records to the database.

11.1.7 More on Formatting

The Java logging package has sophisticated, if somewhat convoluted, facilities for internationalizing log messages. The process relies on the Java platform's built-in internationalization features.

The process of internationzalizing logging messages starts by associating the name of a `ResourceBundle` with a logger. In Java code this can be done by providing the name as a second argument to `getLogger()`.

```
Logger logger =
    Logger.getLogger("com.awl.toolbook.chapter11.sample",
                     "logMessages");
```

Regrettably this information cannot be specified in the configuration file, so in normal use the resource bundle name must be specified in every call to `getLogger()`. Since resource bundle names are inherited hierarchically, the impact of this can be minimized by attaching a resource bundle to the root logger in initialization code:

```
Logger.getLogger("","logMessages");
```

The resource bundle should contain every message that the program will log, and there should be a version of the bundle for every locale that will be supported. By associating the bundle name with the root logger a single file would contain all of a program's messages. If this file is too large or unwieldy, it may make sense to split it into several bundles, but the cost is that now the program will need to keep track of different bundle names when calling `getLogger()`.

A typical file for English-speaking countries would be called `logMessage_en.properties` and would contain lines such as

```
startMessage=Started successfully
infoMessage=New user {0} entered at {1,date} {1,time}
errorMessage1=Unable to save data: {0}
errorMessage2=Something terrible happened
```

while a file for German-speaking countries would be called `logMessages_de.properties` and would contain

```
startMessage=richtig begonnen
infoMessage=Neues Benutzer{0} kam bei {1,date} {1,time}
errorMessage1=Nicht imstande, Daten zu speichern: {0}
errorMessage2=Schreckliches etwas ist geschehen
```

Each entry is a string suitable for use with `MessageFormat` from the `java.text` package.

With such a resource bundle in place logging calls will no longer pass a message to be logged but rather the name of a key within the bundle to use for formatting plus an array of objects, which will be used as parameters. For the preceding definitions, any of the following calls might be used in the program:

```
logger.log(Level.INFO,"startMessage",new Object[] {});

logger.log(Level.INFO,"infoMessage",
                      new Object[] {username, new Date()});

logger.log(Level.WARNING,"errorMessage1",
           new Object[] {theException});

logger.log(Level.SEVER,"startMessage",new Object[] {});
```

11.2 Log4j

Log4j is a logging system originally developed by IBM and later turned over to the Jakarta project. It has a great deal of similarity to the Java Logging API, which is not surprising because Java Logging was greatly influenced by Log4j, although the APIs were simplified and streamlined. Consequently, the built-in API is somewhat simpler to use but also somewhat less powerful.

11.2.1 Using Log4j

At first glance, the log4j APIs closely resemble those for Java logging. Both use a class called `Logger` as their entry point, and loggers in log4j also have a hierarchical relationship. Both APIs also have `Level` classes, along with static instances used to indicate the levels of messages and set the level of loggers. The levels in log4j are called `DEBUG`, `INFO`, `WARN`, `ERROR`, and `FATAL`.

Loggers in log4j also have convenience methods named after the various log levels. Apart from some slight naming differences, the following log4j code

```
Logger logger1 = Logger.getLogger("com.awl.toolbook");
Logger logger2 =
    Logger.getLogger("com.awl.toolbook.chapter11");

logger2.setLevel(Level.WARN);

logger1.debug("Hello");
logger1.log(Level.WARN,"something is amiss");
logger2.warn("Something is amiss");
```

exactly resembles the corresponding Java logging code.

Beyond this, the two APIs start to diverge. Log4j uses `Appenders` instead of `Handlers` and `Layouts` instead of `Formats`. Despite these name differences, programmatically configuring log4j is very similar to configuring Java logging, as shown in Listing 11.3

Listing 11.3 Programmatically configuring log4j

```
package com.awl.toolbook.chapter11;

import org.apache.log4j.*;

public class L4JManual {
    public static void main(String argv[]) {
        Logger theLogger =
            Logger.getLogger(L4JManual.class.getName());

        FileAppender appender = new FileAppender();
        appender.setFile("manual.log");

        Layout layout =
            new PatternLayout("[%p] %d{HH:mm} - %m\n");

        appender.setLayout(layout);
        appender.activateOptions();

        theLogger.addAppender(appender);

        theLogger.setLevel(Level.INFO);
        theLogger.info("Hello");
    }
}
```

The only elements that stand out in this example are the call to `activateOptions()` and the pattern used in the `Layout.activateOptions()` is used to turn on the appender. It is needed because there are typically many parameters that must be set to configure an appender, each of which must be done through a separate call. The appender has no way to know when the final parameter has been set, and any attempt to open the log repository before all parameters have been set may result in an error or the wrong action being taken.

The pattern provides many options to specify how log messages will be stored. See the documentation for `PatternLayout` for full details on the available options. These are some particularly useful options:

- %p indicates the priority level of the message.
- %m is the message provided in the code.
- %d is the date and time. Following %d with braces and an inner pattern indicates how the date and time should be formatted, following the rules for the `DateFormat` class in `java.text`.
- %l turns into information about the calling class, method, and line. The documentation for log4j indicates that obtaining this information can be extremely slow and so should be not be used except when speed is not an issue.

After running Listing 11.3, the "manual.log" file will contain

```
[INFO] 13:21 - Hello
```

Log4j supports filters similar to those used in the Java logging API, with some important differences. The first is that it is possible to associate multiple filters with an appender, and these filters will each be checked in order. Consequently, filters may return three values instead of a boolean. These values are `DENY`, meaning the log message will be discarded without consulting any other filters; `ACCEPT`, meaning the log message will be recorded without consulting the other filters; and `NEUTRAL`, meaning the rest of the filters will be consulted. If the last filter returns `NEUTRAL`, the message will be recorded.

11.2.2 Configuring Log4j

One of the biggest differences between log4j and Java logging is in the configuration files; log4j configuration files are much more flexible. The most immediate difference is that lines that specify a level for a logger may also specify the set of appenders to which that logger will send records. The following lines

```
log4j.rootLogger=WARN, appender1, appender2
log4j.logger.com.awl.toolbook=DEBUG, appender1
```

specify that the root logger and all its descendants should log at the `WARN` level and send their output to appenders called `appender1` and `appender2`. The logger called `com.awl.toolbook` and all its descendants should log at the `DEBUG` level and send their output to `appender1` only.

Each appender is defined on a separate set of lines:

```
log4j.appender.appender1=org.apache.log4j.FileAppender
log4j.appender.appender1.File=debug.log
log4j.appender.appender1.layout=\
org.apache.log4j.PatternLayout
log4j.appender.appender1.layout.ConversionPattern=\
[%p] %d{HH:mm:ss} - %m (%l)

log4j.appender.appender2=org.apache.log4j.ConsoleAppender
log4j.appender.appender2.layout=org.apache.log4j.PatternLayout
log4j.appender.appender2.layout.ConversionPattern=\
[%p] %d{HH:mm} - %m
```

The first set of lines specifies that `appender1` should send output to the file called `debug.log`, using `PatternLayout` to do the formatting. Likewise, the second set of lines indicates that `appender2` should send output to the console with a specified pattern.

Although the properties file format is a little easier to read for very simple log files, the preferred format for log4j is XML.[1] The XML syntax groups attributes together in a cleaner way and clarifies the distinction between log levels and appenders. These attributes appear undifferentiated on one line in the property file. The XML equivalent of the above configuration would contain the following:

```
<?xml version="1.0" encoding="UTF-8" ?>
<!DOCTYPE log4j:configuration SYSTEM "log4j.dtd">

<log4j:configuration
    xmlns:log4j='http://jakarta.apache.org/log4j/'>

  <appender name="appender1"
            class="org.apache.log4j.FileAppender">
    <param name="File" value="temp"/>
    <layout class="org.apache.log4j.PatternLayout">
      <param name="ConversionPattern"
            value="[%p] %d{HH:mm:ss} - %m (%l)"/>
```

[1]Indeed, the properties file format is deprecated and may be removed in a future release.

```
      </layout>
    </appender>

    <appender name="appender2"
              class="org.apache.log4j.ConsoleAppender">
      <layout class="org.apache.log4j.PatternLayout">
        <param name="ConversionPattern"
               value="[%p] %d{HH:mm} - %m"/>
      </layout>
    </appender>


    <category name="com.awl.toolbook">
      <priority value="warn" />
      <appender-ref ref="appender1"/>
    </category>

    <root>
      <priority value ="debug"/>
      <appender-ref ref="appender1"/>
      <appender-ref ref="appender2"/>
    </root>
  </log4j:configuration>
```

The term "category" in this file really means "logger." This is a holdover from an early version of the API.

Another advantage to the XML format is that it allows the definition of filters, which cannot be done through a property file. For example, the `StringMatchFilter` examines log messages and can either `DENY` or `ACCEPT`, based on whether the string is found. To allow only messages about new users to be logged, the following configuration would be used:

```
<appender name="appender2"
          class="org.apache.log4j.ConsoleAppender">
  <layout class="org.apache.log4j.PatternLayout">
    <param name="ConversionPattern"
           value="[%p] %d{HH:mm} - %m\n"/>
  </layout>

  <filter class="org.apache.log4j.varia.StringMatchFilter">
    <param name="StringToMatch" value="new user"/>
```

```
    <param name="AcceptOnMatch" value="true"/>
  </filter>
</appender>
```

Log4j obtains its configuration file differently than Java logging. Log4j will search the CLASSPATH for a files called `log4j.properties` and `log4j.xml` and will use the first one it finds. This means that no information needs to be provided explicitly on the command line, and hence configuration files can be shipped as part of a Web application without requiring any special treatment when the application is installed.

11.2.3 The Log4j Appenders

Log4j comes with a rich set of appenders beyond the basic `ConsoleAppender` and `FileAppender` already encountered. The set discussed following is not exhaustive but does represent the variety of available options.

RollingFileAppender

This is an extension of the `FileAppender` that **rolls** the logs. Rolling consists of maintaining a set of log files, with names like "log.1" through "log.4." When a certain criteria has been met, such as size of the file reaching a specified maximum, "log.3" would be renamed to "log.4"; "log.2" would be renamed to "log.3"; and so on. "log.4" would be discarded, and a new current log file would be started.

The extra attributes needed to configure a `RollingFileAppender` are the number of backup log files to maintain, and the size a file should reach before being rolled. These may be specified in either the property-based or XML-based configuration file—for example,

```
<appender name="appender1"
          class="org.apache.log4j.RollingFileAppender">
  <param name="File" value="log"/>
  <param name="maxBackupIndex" value="4"/>
  <param name="maxFileSize" value="10KB"/>
  <layout class="org.apache.log4j.PatternLayout">
    <param name="ConversionPattern"
          value="[%p] %d{HH:mm:ss} - %m (%l)\n"/>
  </layout>
</appender>
```

Note that the file size is specified as the combination of a number—in this case, 10—and a unit—in this case, kilobytes. This means that the log will be rolled when the file exceeds 10240 bytes in length. A similar property, `maximumFileSize`, can be used with a number in bytes.

DailyRollingFileAppender

This is a variation of the `RollingFileAppender` that rolls files based on time instead of file size. Therefore, in the configuration a parameter indicating the times at which logs should be rolled must be provided. This parameter is called `datePattern`.

The syntax used to specify times comes from the `SimpleDateFormat` class. Conceptually, this is used by continuously formatting the current time, using the specified pattern. If the resulting string is different than the last time this was done, then the log is rolled. So the pattern "YYYY" would result in the logs being rolled once a year at midnight on January 1. "YYYY-MM" would result in the logs being rolled at midnight on the first of each month. "YYYY-MM-dd" would cause the logs to roll once a day, and so on.

The pattern is also used to name the rolled files. Using the pattern, "YYYY-MM-dd" would result in files with names like "log.2003-01-01," "log.2003-01-02," and so on. Note that this means there is no limit to the number of log files that will be maintained.

Although a pattern like "YYYY/MM" would roll on the same schedule as "YYYY-MM," the slash in the former pattern would be interpreted as a directory when the log is rolled. This may or may not be what is desired, but it does mean that some care must be taken when choosing patterns.

SocketAppender

This appender sends log records to a socket in a binary format that is not meant to be human-readable. The other end of the socket is supposed to be server running a `SocketNode`, a class that receives log records and handles them according to the configuration on the **server** end. That means that one client could send records to many servers, and each server could log a different subset of events or format them differently. This provides a mechanism for an application to report on its status and activities to several different people at once, while avoiding the need for all of those people to have access to any particular set of files.

For example, the marketing department might have a log server that filters out everything except reports on how the system is being used. The administrators might have another server that reports any `SEVERE` messages about system problems. The developers might have yet another server that captures debugging information.

The appender on the client side needs the name of a server and the port to which to connect.

```
<appender name="appender1"
          class="org.apache.log4j.net.SocketAppender">
  <param name="remoteHost" value="log_host"/>
  <param name="port" value="8099"/>
</appender>
```

Note that no format is provided because all formatting is done on the server. Note also that only a single host and port are specified. If logging information should be sent to many servers, each will need its own appender.

There is nothing special about configuration on the server side, and any set of appenders can be used. The logger that is invoked on the server side will be the one with the same name as that which wrote to the `SocketAppender` on the client. That is, if the logger writing to `appender1` in the preceding example were named `foo.bar`, then the server would also look for a logger called `foo.bar`. As always, if there is no such logger on the server, it will use the properties associated with `foo` if any are specified and the root logger otherwise.

It is quite easy to create a basic log server because the `SocketNode` does most of the work. All the application code needs to do is set up the basic server functionality. A very basic server is shown in Listing 11.4.

Listing 11.4 A simple log server

```
package com.awl.toolbook.chapter11;

import java.net.Socket;
import java.net.ServerSocket;

import org.apache.log4j.*;
import org.apache.log4j.net.*;
import org.apache.log4j.spi.LoggerRepository;

public class LogServer {
    public static void main(String argv[])
        throws Exception
    {
        int port = Integer.parseInt(argv[0]);
        ServerSocket serverSocket = new ServerSocket(port);
```

```
        LoggerRepository theRepository =
                         LogManager.getLoggerRepository();

        while(true) {
            Socket socket = serverSocket.accept();

            SocketNode handler =
                new SocketNode(socket,theRepository);

            Thread t = new Thread(handler);
            t.start();
        }
    }
}
```

As usual, all the configuration on the server side will happen through the `log4j.properties` or `log4j.xml` files.

The `SocketAppender` only supports TCP (Transmission Control Protocol) sockets, which ensures that if the server is running, all packets will eventually reach it. Developers needing or desiring UDP (User Datagram Protocol) sockets need to write their own implementation.

TelnetAppender

This appender provides some of the same functionality as the `SocketAppender` but works in almost the exact opposite way. Whereas the `SocketAppender` acts as a client and reports log records to a remote server, the `TelnetAppender` acts as a server to which clients can connect to see log messages. Records are sent to clients in a format that is specified by a `Layout`. The protocol is simple, which means the standard `telnet` program can be used to connect, but it also means that each client cannot do its own filtering and will display all the records that the server chooses to send.

The only parameter needed is the port on which to listen for clients. With the following connection in place

```
<appender name="appender1"
          class="org.apache.log4j.RollingFileAppender">
  <param name="port" value="8099"/>
  <layout class="org.apache.log4j.PatternLayout">
    <param name="ConversionPattern"
          value="[%p] %d{HH:mm:ss} - %m (%l)\n"/>
  </layout>
</appender>
```

a client could view log events with

```
telnet localhost 8099
```

The `TelnetAppender` places no restrictions on who may connect or how many connections may be present. Both of these represent potential security concerns. Typically, this appender would only be used during development in environments where the file system and standard output are not readily available. If the TelnetAppender is to be used in production, then at the very least any application using this appender should be behind a firewall so that random users on the Internet cannot peek in on internal log messages. However, even allowing everyone in a company or department to see log information may be too insecure. If this is the case, it would be possible to extend `TelnetAppender` to require some sort of authentication. Because log messages are transmitted in plain text, there is also some danger that a third party may eavesdrop on log reports. This could be corrected by extending `TelnetAppender` to use SSL (Secure Sockets Layer), although doing so is well beyond the scope of this book.

SMTPAppender

This appender sends a formatted e-mail to a specified recipient. This is particularly useful for `ERROR` and `FATAL` message, even more so when combined with a service that forwards e-mail to a pager.

The configuration needed for this appender includes an address from which e-mail will be sent, the address to which e-mail will be sent, and the name of a computer with an SMTP (Simple Mail Transfer Protocol) server. This is typically the same computer that is used as the "outgoing mail server" in a mail client such as outlook. For example, using this configuration

```
<appender name="appender1"
          class="org.apache.log4j.net.SMTPAppender">

  <param name="SMTPHost" value="localhost"/>
  <param name="from" value="logger@awl.com"/>
  <param name="to"   value="developer@awl.com"/>
  <param name="subject" value="Log message from log4j"/>

  <layout class="org.apache.log4j.PatternLayout">
    <param name="ConversionPattern"
          value="[%p] %d{HH:mm:ss} - %m (%l)\n"/>
  </layout>
</appender>
```

and the following code

```
Logger l = Logger.getLogger("com.awl.toolbook.sample");

l.debug("This is a debug message");
l.error("Yikes, this is an error message!!");
```

will result in the following e-mail being sent:

```
From: logger@awl.com
To: developer@awl.com
Subject: Log message from log4j
Date: Sat, 16 Aug 2003 17:54:16 -0400 (EDT)

[DEBUG] 17:54:15 - This is a debug message
(com.awl.toolbook.chapter11.L4JExample.main
 (L4JExample.java:11))

[ERROR] 17:54:15 - Yikes, this is an error message!!
(com.awl.toolbook.chapter11.L4JExample.main
 (L4JExample.java:12))
```

Notice that this one e-mail contains both messages. By default the `SMTPAppender` will buffer log messages until a `ERROR` or `FATAL` message is logged, at which point all buffered messages will be sent. An additional parameter called `bufferSize` can be used to control how many log records are kept in the buffer and hence sent with the e-mail. Typically, it is useful to see a few of the messages leading up to an error to help diagnose the problem.

The `SMTPAppender` requires the Java Mail API and the JavaBeans Activation Framework. Both are available from http://java.sun.com/products/javamail/.

NTEventLogAppender

This appender is used to log events to the system log on Windows NT-based systems. This cannot be done in pure Java and requires the use of native code, but log4j provides this in the form of `NTEventLogAppender.dll`. This dll must be placed in a directory that is somewhere in the PATH.

SyslogAppender

This appender is used to send log records to a Unix system logging daemon. The parameters needed are the host where the daemon is running and the "facility" to log to. See Unix manual for syslog, syslogd, and syslog.conf for more information on Unix logging.

Unlike system logging on NT, system logging on Unix requires no special native library. This is because Unix logging is based on standard sockets.

JDBCAppender

As the name implies, this appender can be used to write log records to a database. The parameters are the usual those for database activity: the name of the driver class, database URL, username, and password. In addition, a pattern is used to generate the SQL that will be executed. The syntax of this attribute is the same as that used for the `PatternLayout`. A typical log table might be defined as follows:

```
create table log (
    level char(5),
    timestamp datetime,
    message   varchar(100)
)
```

With this `log` table, the configuration would be

```
<appender name="appender1"
          class="org.apache.log4j.jdbc.JDBCAppender">

  <param name="user"     value="sa"/>
  <param name="password" value=""/>
  <param name="driver"   value="org.hsqldb.jdbcDriver"/>
  <param name="URL" value="jdbc:hsqldb:jspbook:toolbook"/>
  <param name="sql"
      value="insert into log
             values('%p', '%d{YYYY-MM-dd HH:mm}', '%m')"/>
</appender>
```

Note the use of single quotes in the expression and the use of the date pattern to render the timestamp in the standard SQL `datetime` format. Also note that if the message contains a single quote, the resulting SQL expression will be invalid.

Finally, the documentation for log4j states that the current incarnation of the `JDBCAppender` may change radically in the near future. It is expected that equivalent functionality will be provided, although the configuration may need to change.

AsyncAppender

The `AsyncAppender` is unlike all the other appenders seen so far in that it does not itself write log information to any destination. Instead, the `AsyncAppender` wraps another appender in a separate thread so all logging is handled asynchronously. This can be useful in conjunction with any of the appenders that may take some time to perform their actions, such as the `JDBCAppender` and the `SMTPAppender`.

The only parameter to the `AsyncAppender` is a reference to the name of another appender:

```
<appender name="appender2"
          class="org.apache.log4j.AsyncAppender">
    <appender-ref ref="appender1"/>
</appender>
```

Any logger may write to either `appender1` or `appender2`; the latter will work asynchronously.

Note that the `AsyncAppender` can only be configured through XML-style configuration files because there is no notion of an `appender-ref` in the property files.

11.2.4 Extending Log4j

Log4j comes with a very complete set of appenders, as can be seen from the previous section. In the very rare instance where none of the provided appenders meets a particular need, it is easy enough to create new appenders. Most of the hard work is encapsulated in a class called `AppenderSkeleton`. All that a developer needs to do is provide implementations for a few abstract methods.

To illustrate how this is done, Listing 11.5 shows an appender that sends formatted log messages to an external program. This could be used to invoke an existing application that pops up an alert window on an administrators screen such as "net send" on Windows or "xmessage" under Unix.

This appender will need two parameters. The first is the program name that must be fully qualified if the program is not in the PATH. The second is a flag indicating whether the program should be started once for each log message or if it should be started once and then fed each log message as it comes in.

Listing 11.5 An appender that sends log messages to a program

```
package com.awl.toolbook.chapter11;

import java.io.InputStream;
import java.io.OutputStream;

import org.apache.log4j.*;
import org.apache.log4j.spi.LoggingEvent;


public class ExecAppender extends AppenderSkeleton {
    public ExecAppender() {}

    private String programName = null;
    public String getProgramName() {return programName;}
    public void setProgramName(String programName) {
        this.programName = programName;
    }

    private boolean openEachTime = false;
    public boolean getOpenEachTime() {return openEachTime;}
    public void setOpenEachTime(boolean openEachTime) {
        this.openEachTime = openEachTime;
    }

    private Process process;
    private InputStream instream;
    private OutputStream outstream;

    public void activateOptions() {
        if(programName == null) {
            errorHandler.error(
              "No program specified for appender named [" +
              name + "].");

            return;
        }
```

```
        if(!openEachTime) {
            openProgram();
        }
    }

    public void append(LoggingEvent event) {
        event.getThreadName();
        event.getNDC();
        event.getLocationInformation();

        if(openEachTime) {
            openProgram();
        }

        String formatted = layout.format(event);

        try {
            outstream.write(formatted.getBytes());
            outstream.flush();
        } catch (Exception e) {
            errorHandler.error(
                "Unable to write log event to " +
                programName + ": " + e);
        }

        int count;

        try {
            while((count = instream.available()) > 0) {
                byte data[] = new byte[count];
                instream.read(data);
            }
        } catch (Exception e) {
            errorHandler.error(
                "Unable to consume input from " +
                programName + ": " + e);
        }
```

Listing 11.5 An appender that sends log messages to a program *(continued)*

```
        if(openEachTime) {
            closeProgram();
        }
    }

    public boolean requiresLayout() {
        return true;
    }

    public void close() {
        if(!openEachTime) {
            closeProgram();
        }

    }

    private void openProgram() {
        try {
            Runtime r = Runtime.getRuntime();
            process   = r.exec(programName);
            instream  = process.getInputStream();
            outstream = process.getOutputStream();
        } catch (Throwable t) {
            errorHandler.error("Unable to exec " +
                               programName +
                               ": " + t);
        }
    }

    private void closeProgram() {
        try {
            instream.close();
            outstream.close();
            process.destroy();
        } catch (Exception e) {
        }
    }
}
```

The program starts with an empty constructor, which is needed by the log4j configurator. Then there are two beanlike properties for the `programName` and the `openEachTime` flag. No special code is needed for these properties to be set from standard configuration files; this is handled by introspection in the configurator.

The `activateOptions()` method does not have to be provided because there is a do-nothing implementation in the base class. `activateOptions()` is a useful place to ensure that attributes are set up properly, as is done here. Note the use of the `errorHandler`, which is essentially a special instance of a logger. This can be used to report errors from within the logging system itself, avoiding the kind of potential infinite loop that was encountered when writing a handler for Java logging.

The real action happens in `append()`, which is an abstract method that must be provided. This method starts by calling methods in the `event` that fill it in with auxiliary values that may or may not be needed. Then the program is opened if necessary. Next the event is formatted using a `layout` that is defined in the base class, and the formatted string is sent to the program. Anything printed by the program is read in and discarded. This has nothing to do with logging per se, but failure to do this might cause the program to block.

The `requiresLayout()` method is used by the configurator to determine whether a layout object must be provided. Here, `true` is returned, so if no layout is provided in the configuration file, an error will occur when log4j first starts up.

`close()` is another abstract method that must be implemented. It is used to clean up any resources allocated by the appender, which in this case means closing the program if it is still open.

The code ends with methods that invoke and shut down the program.

Configuring this appender is done just like any other appender seen so far:

```
<appender name="appender1"
          class="com.awl.toolbook.chapter11.ExecAppender">
  <param name="programName"  value="alert.sh"/>
  <param name="openEachTime" value="true"/>
  <layout class="org.apache.log4j.PatternLayout">
    <param name="ConversionPattern"
          value="[%p] %d{HH:mm:ss} - %m (%l)\n"/>
  </layout>
</appender>
```

One thing that must be pointed out is that `ExecAppender` sends log messages to the external program through the program's input. Some programs need to take their arguments on the command line. While it would be easy enough in principal to modify `ExecAppender` to handle these cases, another option is to use a wrapper script. For example "alert.sh" used in the preceding example invokes xmessage as follows:

```
#!/bin/sh

read message
xmessage $message &
```

A similar short VB script program could be used to invoke net send on Windows.

11.3 Beyond This Book

The information presented in this chapter will go a long way toward meeting any logging need with either log4j or Java logging. There are a few APIs that were not covered, such as creating new formatters or layouts, but these are pretty simple. When there is a need to create custom logging classes, there is a distinct advantage to log4j because the source code can serve as a basis for new code or just a means to learn how things work.

Beyond the tools, there is an art to adding logging to a program. A program can potentially generate a great deal of information, and it is easy for the important data to be lost amidst a sea of logging messages. The ability to name loggers and enable only those that are generating relevant messages can be of immense help.

Within code logging statements can either serve as additional documentation, or they can obscure what a program is doing. As with many other tools, developers and teams will discover what works for them through experience.

It is also important to note that code within logging statements will be executed whether or not logging is enabled. For example,

```
logger.log(Level.INFO,"Pi to 300 digits is: " +
                     computePi(300));
```

will compute the value of pi even if logging at the warning level is disabled. This will significantly slow down the program. The lesson is that a program should not perform complex calculations just to log the result; information to be logged and the arguments to logging methods should be very light, fast, and simple. Static strings are best, and appending strings or calls to get properties from beans are not bad. Beyond that, some attention must be given to the value of the reported information versus the impact on the program.

11.4 Summary

Tool: Java Logging
Purpose: Logging
Version covered: J2SE 1,4
Home page: N/A, part of Java
License: Sun's
Tool: log4j
Purpose: Logging
Version covered: 1.2.8
Home page: http://logging.apache.org/log4j/docs/index.html
License: The Apache Software License, Version 2.0
Further Reading:

- An introduction to internationalization: http://java.sun.com/docs/books/tutorial/i18n/.

CHAPTER 12

Configuring Program Options

Modern Java applications are typically quite flexible. Much of this flexibility takes the form of options and parameters that can be given to a program when it first starts up. In a typical example, a program may need to be told which of several related tasks it should perform and will need to be given information relevant to that task. This in turn means that the program must be able to process this information in order to know what to do. Some options, such as the major task to perform, are internal switches. Other options require a value, such as the URL of a database. Still others may require multiple options, such as a list of files to be processed.

Closely related to this issue is that a well-written program can tell its users about options. There is no substitute for good documentation, but it can be very convenient for the program itself to be able to remind the user of the names of the options.

Many of the tools already encountered have their own ways of doing such configuration. Ant has build files, OJB has mapping files, Java logging has property files, log4j uses XML-based configuration, and so on. This chapter will look at two general tools—Jakarta CLI and Jakarta Digester—both of which remove a lot of the tedious work that can be involved in processing configuration data.

12.1 Jakarta CLI

In these days of Gnome and OS X and Windows XP it sometimes seems like the command-line interface (CLI) is all but dead. In reality there will always be situations in which a CLI is more appropriate than a GUI (graphical user interface). Consider Ant, for example. It is certainly possible to integrate it into a GUI like that provided by Eclipse, but doing so of necessity restricts the set of options and variations in how Ant can be invoked. As complex as CLIs may appear, a GUI that exposes all the options of a sophisticated program could involve dozens of nested windows and panels and tabs, to the point where it becomes too complex to use—or at least to use effectively. As noted author Neal Stephenson said, "The command-line interface opens a much more direct and explicit channel from user to machine than the GUI."[1]

CLIs are generally easier to develop than GUIs, but there is still work to be done to parse the command-line arguments, set options based on them, and notify the user of what the options are. Jakarta CLI consists of a number of classes that do most of this work.

The best way to understand what CLI does is to see it in action. To do so a program roughly equivalent to Unix's "cat" or DOS's "type" will be developed. This program will read and display one or more files. Optionally a line number may be prepended to each line, and the format of these numbers may be specified. In addition, an output file can be specified, and all data will be written to that file. By convention many programs respond to an option of "-h" by printing a help message; the cat program will adhere to this convention.

The first thing the program needs to do is specify the set of options that are available. There are many ways to do this; the simplest is to create an `Options` object and repeatedly call `addOptions()` on this object. `addOptions()` takes three arguments: a single character for the option, a boolean flag indicating whether the option has any arguments, and a string describing the option. For the cat program, this code would consist of

```
Options options = new Options();

options.addOption("n", false,
              "Display line number before each line");
options.addOption("h", false,
              "Display help message and exit");
options.addOption("f", true,
              "Format for line numbers (default '###:')");
options.addOption("o", true,
          "Name of output file (default standard output)");
```

[1]"In the Beginning was the Command Line," available free from http://www.cryptonomicon.com/beginning.html.

Parsing a set of provided arguments against a set of options is handled by a parser class that takes the options and arguments and returns a `CommandLine` object. There are a few parser classes; the simplest is called `BasicParser`, and it is appropriate for the options that have been just defined.

```
CommandLineParser parser = new BasicParser();
CommandLine cmd = parser.parse(options,args);
```

Once the command line has been parsed, it can be queried for the presence of arguments and options:

```
boolean showNumbers = cmd.hasOption("n");
if(cmd.hasOption("f")) {
    format = cmd.getOptionValue("f");
}
```

In addition to the named options there is an arbitrary number of "unnamed" filenames that appear at the end of the command. These may be obtained as a `List` or an array.

```
List filenames = cmd.getArgList();
```

All the parsers provided with CLI use Unix-styling options, meaning they expect options to be prefixed with a single dash ('-'). If DOS-style arguments are desired with switches indicated by slashes (as in the DOS command "format /s"), a new class could be written implementing the `CommandLineParser` interface. Because the source is available, it would be very easy to modify the `Parser` class, which provides the base for all parsers.

According to the rules of the `BasicParser` the special argument "——" will cause the parser to treat all following arguments as part of the `argList`. This can be used when there is a file whose name starts with a dash; either of the following commands would cause an error because there is no such option as "q":

```
java com.awl.toolbook.chapter12.Cat -q file1 file2
```

```
java com.awl.toolbook.chapter12.Cat file1 file2 -q
```

However, the following will work and will look for files called "file1," "file2," and "-q."

```
java com.awl.toolbook.chapter06.Cat -- file1 file2 -q
```

After seeing the "——" the parser will know not to look for any further switches, so `-q` will be treated as a filename.

Finally, there is a utility called `HelpFormatter` that generates a help message from the `Options` and sends it to `System.out`.

```
HelpFormatter formatter = new HelpFormatter();
formatter.printHelp("cat", options);
```

would generate

```
usage: cat
 -f    Format for line numbers (default '###:')
 -h    Display help message and exit
 -n    Display line number before each line
 -o    Name of output file (default standard output)
```

The "usage" line displays only the command name because that is all `HelpFormatter` displays by default. The `Options` object will need to be told the name of the file argument and how the arguments can be used before this can be fixed. This will be remedied shortly, but first Listing 12.1 shows the Cat program in its entirety.

Listing 12.1 A complete program that uses CLI

```
package com.awl.toolbook.chapter12;

import java.text.DecimalFormat;
import java.io.*;
import java.util.List;
import java.util.Iterator;

import org.apache.commons.cli.*;

public class Cat {
    private static Options makeOptions() {
        Options options = new Options();

        options.addOption("n", false,
                "Display line number before each line");
        options.addOption("h", false,
                "Display help message and exit");
        options.addOption("f", true,
                "Format for line numbers (default '###:')");
        options.addOption("o", true,
```

```
                "Name of output file " +
                "(default standard output)");

        options.addOption(OptionBuilder.hasArg()
           .withDescription("This is a sample option")
           .withType(new Integer(12))
           .create("a"));

        return options;
    }

    public static void usage(Options options) {
        HelpFormatter formatter = new HelpFormatter();
        formatter.printHelp("cat", options, true);
    }

    private static void handleFile(String name,
                                   boolean showNumbers,
                                   DecimalFormat format,
                                   PrintWriter out)
    {
        BufferedReader in = null;
        int count         = 0;
        String line;

        try {
            in = new BufferedReader(
                    new FileReader(name));
        } catch (Exception e){
            System.err.println("Unable to open " + name);
            return;
        }

        try {
            while((line = in.readLine()) != null) {
                if(showNumbers) {
                    out.print(format.format(count));
                    count++;
                }
```

Listing 12.1 A complete program that uses CLI *(continued)*

```
                out.println(line);
            }
        } catch (Exception e) {
            System.err.println("Error reading " + name);
        }

        try {
            in.close();
        } catch (Exception e) {}
    }

    public static void main(String args[]) {
        // Variables with default values
        boolean showNumbers  = false;
        PrintWriter out      = new PrintWriter(System.out);
        DecimalFormat format = new DecimalFormat("###: ");

        // Options and related objects
        Options options = makeOptions();
        CommandLineParser parser = new BasicParser();
        CommandLine cmd = null;

        // Parse the arguments, if there's an error
        // report usage
        try {
            cmd = parser.parse(options,args);
        } catch (ParseException e) {
            System.err.println(e.getMessage());
            usage(options);
            System.exit(-1);
        }

        // If the user has asked for help, display it
        // and exit
        if(cmd.hasOption("h")) {
            usage(options);
            System.exit(-1);
        }
```

```
        // Process other arguments
        showNumbers = cmd.hasOption("n");
        if(cmd.hasOption("f")) {
            format =
                new DecimalFormat(cmd.getOptionValue("f"));
        }

        if(cmd.hasOption("o")) {
            String outName = cmd.getOptionValue("o");

            try {
                out = new PrintWriter(
                          new FileWriter(outName));
            } catch (Exception e) {
                System.err.println("Unable to open " +
                                   outName);
                System.exit(-1);
            }
        }

        List files = cmd.getArgList();
        Iterator i = files.iterator();
        while(i.hasNext()) {
            handleFile((String) i.next(),
                       showNumbers,
                       format,
                       out);
        }

        try {
            out.close();
        } catch (Exception e) {}

        System.exit(0);
    }
}
```

The options-handling portions of Listing 12.1 work just as described previously. The `Options` object is created; a `SimpleParser` is used to generate a `CommandLine`; and the `CommandLine` is checked for each option, which can then be handled in a simple manner. A `HelpFormatter` is also used to print usage information, which will happen when the user asks for help or enters an invalid command.

The features of CLI examined so far can create options and indicate which need arguments, but there is much more that a program may need. First, a program may need to indicate which options are mandatory. This is important both in presenting help messages and in parsing the command line. Second, an option may need to take an arbitrary number of values instead of exactly one. Finally, it is useful in help messages to be able to name arguments.

These abilities are all present in CLI, although they are slightly harder to use. Instead of having dozens of different constructors in `Option` for various combinations of information that an option may need, a class called `OptionBuilder` is used.

The `OptionBuilder` class uses a design pattern called, not surprisingly, the **builder** pattern, which has some features in common with the factory pattern discussed in Section 9.2.

The general idea is that, like factories, a builder is capable of creating a new object. In this case, `OptionBuilder` has two methods that create `Options`, one that takes a character for the name and one that takes a string.

```
Option a = OptionBuilder.create('a');
Option longname = OptionBuilder.create("longname");
```

Unlike factories, builders have a number of static attributes that may be enabled. The attributes will effect the next object to be built and will be reset afterward. To indicate that an option has a description and to provide it with a name, the following code could be used:

```
OptionBuilder.hasArg();
OptionBuilder.withDescription("This is a sample option");
Option a = OptionBuilder.create('a');
```

When creating options with lots of configuration attributes, such code could clearly become very verbose and ugly. To avoid such ugliness, the builder methods that set attributes return the builder itself. This means that the calls to these methods can be chained as follows:

```
Option a = OptionBuilder.hasArg()
           .withDescription("This is a sample option")
           .create("a");
```

This code may look a little strange, but it is perfectly valid Java. It has not even been reformatted for print; Java syntax allows arbitrary whitespace around "." separators. Recall that Java evaluates most expressions left to right, so `OptionBuilder.hasArg()` returns the static `OptionBuilder` with the `arg` attribute set, then the `withDescription()` method is invoked on that, and so on.

There are many attributes available to the builder. Here are some of the more useful ones:

- `hasArg()` Indicates the option must have exactly one argument
- `hasArgs()` Indicates the option can have any number of arguments but must have at least one
- `hasOptionalArg()` Indicates an option has an optional argument—that is, it may be followed by zero or one argument
- `hasOptionalArgs()` Indicates an option has optional arguments—that is, it may be followed by zero or more arguments
- `isRequired()` Indicates the option is required
- `withArgName()` Specifies the name of the argument
- `withDescription()` Provides a description from the option for displaying in help text
- `withLongOpt()` Provides an alternate long form of the option name

Keep in mind that these options will affect both the way arguments are parsed and the text of help messages. Optional entities, whether options or arguments, will appear within brackets in help menus. Exceptions will be thrown when nonoptional entities are omitted from commands.

To see these new abilities in action, the options for the `Cat` program will be modified. The format will become an optional argument to the 'n' option, and long names will be added to every option. In addition, a "filter chain" will be introduced. This is a list of one or more programs; the content of each file will be sent to the first program, the output from that program will be sent to the second program, and so on. This functionality is better handled by the shell, but it is included here as an excuse to demonstrate multiple arguments. Finally, the set of input files will be changed from the unused tail options to a new named option. This will make it easier to require that at least one file is provided. Providing no files, however, should not necessarily be considered an error. Error conditions are generally reserved for cases where a program cannot continue. In this case the program will operate perfectly well and will produce no output, which is the correct behavior.

The code to generate the options now becomes

```
Options options = new Options();

options.addOption(
  OptionBuilder
   .withLongOpt("help")
   .create('h'));

options.addOption(
  OptionBuilder
   .withDescription("Show line numbers")
   .hasOptionalArg()
   .withLongOpt("linenumbers")
   .withArgName("format")
   .create('n'));

options.addOption(
  OptionBuilder
   .withDescription("Write output to a file")
   .hasArg()
   .withLongOpt("output")
   .withArgName("file")
   .create('o'));

options.addOption(
  OptionBuilder
   .withDescription("Filter output through programs")
   .hasArg()
   .withLongOpt("filterchain")
   .withArgName("programs")
   .create('f'));

options.addOption(
  OptionBuilder
   .withDescription("Input files")
   .hasArgs()
   .isRequired()
   .withLongOpt("inputfiles")
```

```
        .withArgName("files")
        .create('i'));
```

All of the preceding options use the OptionBuilder, but it is common to mix OptionBuilder calls with the previous style that passed names directly to addOption(). The latter is still appropriate for optional options that have only a short name.

With the new definitions a HelpFormatter would produce the following output:

```
usage: cat
 -f,--filterchain <programs>    Filter output through programs
 -h,--help                      Print help and exit
 -i,--inputfiles <files>        Input files
 -n,--linenumbers <format>      Show line numbers
 -o,--output <file>             Write output to a file
```

There is an alternate version of printHelp() that will add more information on the "usage" line by showing a short synopsis of the options. Adding true as a third argument will produce

```
usage: cat -i files [-n format] [-o file] [-h] [-f programs]
```

This provides a handy at-a-glimpse view of the options; it is clear which options are required, and naming the arguments gives some clue as to what they do, although obviously the description provides more information.

However, information is still missing from this description. The fact that "files" and "programs" are plural indicates that these options may take multiple arguments, but it does not do so very clearly. The standard syntax for an option that can take any number of arguments is with a nested list, like so

```
-i [file [file2 [file3] ...]]
```

Similarly an option that can take one or more options would be represented as

```
-i file [file2 [file3] ...]
```

In other words, each additional optional argument is a new level of "optionalness" and hence is enclosed in a nested set of brackets.

At present CLI has no way to automatically build such an expression, although in theory it has enough information about each option to do so. The escape hatch for such situations is to turn off automatic rendering of options in the usage line and provide the entire usage string as the first argument.

```
HelpFormatter formatter = new HelpFormatter();
formatter.printHelp(
   "cat -i file [file2 [file3] ...] " +
      "[-o file] " +
      "[-h]"       +
      "[-f program1 [program2 [program3]]]",
   options);
```

Using CLI as just described makes it easy to write programs that accept simple, dynamic configuration options at run time. There are situations, however, where this may not be sufficient, and a more general configuration mechanism is needed. This is where Digester comes in.

12.2 Jakarta Digester

It is appropriate to handle some types of configuration on the command line. However, more complex configuration, or configuration that is likely to remain static over multiple invocations of a program, needs a more permanent mechanism. A natural way to store such configuration is in files, and a powerful format for storing configurations is XML. XML allows configuration well beyond the simple name/value or name/sets of values pairs of a command line and can express special cases such as ordered arguments, nested arguments, and so on.

This is one of the motivations behind Jakarta Digester, although Digester is much more than just a configuration tool. Digester provides the ability to map XML expressions to Java objects in much the same way that OJB provides the ability to map from a database to Java objects. This can be used in any situation where it helps to have a representation of an object tree that can be edited, transmitted using standard protocols like HTTP or SMTP, and so on. Configuration is certainly one such situation.

Digester is built around three concepts: an **object stack, element matching patterns,** and **processing rules.**

The object stack is what it sounds like: a stack of objects that have been built or are in the process of being built. There are API calls available to examine and manipulate this stack. In simple usage these APIs are not necessary, and the stack can be treated as an internal data structure.

Element matching patterns are expressions that are matched against the input XML. The syntax used is a subset of XPath (see Chapter 9). An expression like "a/b" will match any nodes called "b" whose parent is a node called "a." The pattern "*/c" will match nodes called "c" regardless of their parent or how deep in the hierarchy they are.

Processing rules specify what to do when a node matching a pattern is encountered. There is a general mechanism for this that will be explored later, but a number of built-in rules are provided. Here are some:

- `ObjectCreateRule` creates an object of a type associated with the node name, and places it on the stack.
- `SetPropertiesRule` matches attribute names with properties in the object on top of the stack and calls corresponding `set` methods.
- `SetNextRule` passes the object on top of the stack to a specified method in the next-to-the-top object on the stack.

As a simple example, consider again a CD application, this time limited to artists and albums. An XML representation of a portion of a collection might look like this:

```
<?xml version='1.0'?>

<!-- Internal definition of DTD -->
<!DOCTYPE collection [
  <!ELEMENT collection (artist*)>
  <!ELEMENT artist (album*)>
  <!ATTLIST artist name CDATA #REQUIRED>
  <!ELEMENT album EMPTY>
  <!ATTLIST album name CDATA #REQUIRED year CDATA #REQUIRED> ]>

<!-- Content -->
<collection>
  <artist name="Claire Voyant">
    <album name="Time and the Maiden" year="2001"/>
    <album name="Love Is Blind" year="2002"/>
  </artist>

  <artist name="Siddal">
    <album name="The Crossing" year="1996"/>
    <album name="Mystery and the Sea" year="1997"/>
  </artist>
</collection>
```

On the Java side, simple beans could be used to hold this data, and they are shown in Listings 12.2, 12.3, and 12.4.

Listing 12.2 The collection bean

```
package com.awl.toolbook.chapter12;

import java.util.ArrayList;

public class CDCollection {
    private ArrayList artists = new ArrayList();
    public void addArtist(Artist a) {
        artists.add(a);
    }
}
```

Listing 12.3 The artist bean

```
package com.awl.toolbook.chapter12;

import java.util.ArrayList;

public class Artist {
    private String name;
    public String getName() {return name;}
    public void setName(String name) {this.name = name;}

    private ArrayList albums = new ArrayList();
    public void addAlbum(Album a) {
        albums.add(a);
    }
}
```

Listing 12.4 the album bean

```
package com.awl.toolbook.chapter12;

public class Album {
    private String name;
    public String getName() {return name;}
    public void setName(String name) {this.name = name;}
```

```
        private int yearReleased;
        public int getYearReleased() {return yearReleased;}
        public void setYearReleased(int yearReleased) {
            this.yearReleased = yearReleased;
        }
    }
```

The digester code that will map the XML to the beans is somewhat verbose, although underneath the verbosity it is quite simple. The first step is to obtain a `Digester` and set any desired features.

```
    Digester digester = new Digester();
    digester.setValidating(true);
```

This tells the `Digester` to validate the XML against the DTD. This is not strictly necessary, but it is strongly encouraged because hard-to-find errors may result in the absence of validation.[2] The reason will become clear shortly.

Next it is necessary to identify the XML patterns that will trigger actions. Since the XML is simple, so are the patterns. The `collection` node should clearly cause the creation of a `CDCollection` object, the code to do this is

```
    digester.addObjectCreate(
        "/collection",
        "com.awl.toolbook.chapter12.CDCollection");
```

Errors to Watch For

Digester objects maintain a lot of internal state, and consequently it is recommended that each instance be used to parse only one XML document and never reused. Instances of rules may be reused safely.

[2]The implication of this is that a DTD must be provided. In the example it is included within the document itself, which is convenient but means that the DTD must be repeated in each collection. An alternative would be to place the DTD in a separate file and reference it from the XML with <!DOCTYPE artist System "Cd.dtd">. In that case, some care must be take to ensure that Digester can locate the DTD.

Likewise an `artist` node should trigger the creation of an `Artist` bean:

```
digester.addObjectCreate(
    "/collection/artist",
    "com.awl.toolbook.chapter12.Artist");
```

In this case it is not enough to create the object, the attributes must also be set. This is specified with

```
digester.addSetProperties("/collection/artist");
```

Note that this means the digester will have two rules for the "/collection/artist" pattern. This illustrates an important point: that an arbitrary number of rules can be associated with any pattern, and they will be evaluated in order. In this case it means that the object will be created and then the properties will be set, which makes sense. This handling of multiple rules holds whenever multiple patterns would match the same node, even if the patterns are not identical. That is, the call to `AddObjectCreate()` could use the "/collection/artist" pattern, and `addSetProperties()` could use "*/artist," and everything would still work as expected.

After the object has been created and populated, it must be associated with the parent `CDCollection` node.

```
digester.addSetNext(
    "/collection/artist",
    "addArtist");
```

This means that the `addArtist()` method below the current object in the stack will be invoked. This assumes that the object is an instance of `CDCollection`, but according to the rules that have been established and the structure of the XML, this must be the case. This is why validation against the DTD is so important; without it a well-formed but invalid document could result in some other object being on the stack below the `Artist`, and attempting to call `addArtist()` would result in an introspection error.

The rules for handling `album` nodes is very similar to that for `artist` nodes:

```
digester.addObjectCreate(
    "/collection/album",
    "com.awl.toolbook.chapter12.Album");
digester.addSetProperties("/collection/album");
digester.addSetNext(
    "/collection/album",
    "addAlbum");
```

So far one important point has been glossed over. It was stated previously that `setNextRule()` removes the current object from the stack. If this is the case, then it seems that after handling an `Artist` node, the object remaining on the stack would be the `CDCollection`, so the attempt to call `setAlbum()` for the inner `album` node would fail. This problem is avoided because rules can be fired either at the start or end of a node. This, however, is not specified in the configuration code but managed internally by each rule. This will become clearer in the section on creating new rules.

One final point: Recall that OJB from Chapter 10 maps between beans and database tables. In conjunction with Digester this provides the ability to move XML into database tables. All that is needed is a way to turn beans into XML, and it would become possible to move almost effortlessly among beans, XML, and databases. While it is possible to write a general bean-to-XML translator, it is also easy enough to handle this in the beans themselves. For example, the `CDCOllection` could add the following method:

```
public String toXML() {
    StringBuffer buffy = new StringBuffer();
    buffy.append("<collection>");
    for(int i=0;i<artists.size();i++) {
        buffy.append(((Artist) artists(i)).toXML());
    }
    buffy.append("</collection>");
    return buffy.toString();
}
```

Next, consider a more general version of the `Cat` program. A useful extension would be the ability to read from a variety of sources including files, programs, and URLs. The output filter introduced in the previous section could also be enhanced so that arguments to programs could be provided along with the program names. It would also be useful to send the final output to a number of destinations instead of just the standard output or a single file. A sample configuration file for this super-enhanced cat is shown in Listing 12.5.

Listing 12.5 A sample cat configuration

```
<cat-config>
  <inputs>
    <file name="file1.txt"/>
    <program name="pagegen">
      <arg value="-pagetype"/>
```

Listing 12.5 A sample cat configuration *(continued)*

```
      <arg value="2"/>
    </program>
    <file name="file2.txt"/>
  </inputs>

  <filters>
    <class
      className="com.awl.toolbook.chapter12.LineNumberFilter">
      <arg name="format" value="000: "/>
    </class>

    <program name="grep">
      <arg value="-v"/>
      <arg value="monkey"/>
    </program>
  </filters>

  <outputs>
    <console/>
    <file name="output.txt"/>
  </outputs>
</cat-config>
```

This indicates that the contents of "file1.txt," the output of running "pagegen-pagetype 2," and the contents of the URL "http://www.slashdot.org" should all be obtained. The combined text from all these inputs should be fed through a line number filter, which will prepend a line number using the format "000: " to each line, and then through the "grep" program,[3] which will remove all lines containing the word "monkey." Finally, the result will be printed to the console and saved in a file called "output.txt."

Some of the advantages to using XML as a configuration language are immediately obvious from this example. The hierarchical nature of XML makes it clear when an expression is meant as a value for a program or class rather than as an argument to `Cat` itself. XML also makes it very clear what each element is: a class, a program, an argument to a program, and so on. Storing this configuration in a file also has

[3]grep is a standard Unix utility that can select or remove lines from files in a wide variety of ways. It is available for Windows from http://www.interlog.com/~tcharron/grep.html, among other places.

immediate benefits such as the ability to store a set of such files, each of which performs a specialized task, such as mailing a selection of Web pages to a user.

Another advantage of configuration through XML is that it allows for better object-oriented design in the program. In the input section a `file` node will result in an object that can read a file, and the result of a `program` node will result in an object that can get the output of as program. These objects can both implement an interface that will be called `Readable`. The master program will then have a list of `Readables` and will not need to worry about where or how each object is obtaining its data. Contrast this to command line-based configuration, where the master program must make decisions on the code to invoke based string values.

Listing 12.6 shows the `Readable` interface.

Listing 12.6 The Readable interface

```
package com.awl.toolbook.chapter12;

public interface Readable {
    public String[] read();
}
```

This is simple enough; as might be expected, it provides a method that returns an array of strings. There will also be corresponding interfaces called `Filter` and `Writable` that support methods with signatures `String[] filter(String[])` and `void write(String[])`, respectively.

Because the code for reading and writing will be the same regardless of the source or destination, it makes sense to put all this code in a common base class. This code is shown in Listing 12.7.

Listing 12.7 IO Utilities

```
package com.awl.toolbook.chapter12;

import java.io.*;
import java.util.ArrayList;

public class IOUtils {
    public String[] doRead(InputStream in) {
        try {
            return doRead(
                           new BufferedReader(
                               new InputStreamReader(in)));
```

Listing 12.7 IO Utilities *(continued)*

```
        } catch (Exception e) {}

        return new String[0];
    }

    public String[] doRead(Reader in) {
        try {
            return doRead(new BufferedReader(in));
        } catch (Exception e) {}

        return new String[0];
    }

    public String[] doRead(BufferedReader in)
        throws IOException
    {
        ArrayList ret = new ArrayList();
        String line;

        while((line = in.readLine()) != null) {
            ret.add(line);
            System.out.println("I like goonlin? " + line);
        }

        System.out.println("Tree?");
        String ret1[] = new String[ret.size()];
        for(int i=0;i<ret.size();i++) {
            ret1[i] = (String) ret.get(i);
        }

        System.out.println(ret1.length);
        return ret1;
    }


    public void doWrite(OutputStream out, String lines[])
        throws IOException
```

```
    {
        doWrite(new PrintWriter(
                        new OutputStreamWriter(out)),
                lines);
    }

    public void doWrite(Writer out, String lines[])
        throws IOException
    {
        doWrite(new PrintWriter(out),lines);
    }

    public void doWrite(PrintWriter out, String lines[])
        throws IOException
    {
        for(int i=0;i<lines.length;i++) {
            out.println(lines[i]);
        }
    }
}
```

There is nothing very special here either—just a variety of methods that obtain a `PrintWriter` or `BufferedReader` from other IO types and uses them accordingly.

From here writing the particular classes is easy, and the class for handling files is shown in Listing 12.8.

Listing 12.8 The file handler

```
package com.awl.toolbook.chapter12;

import java.io.FileReader;
import java.io.FileWriter;

public class FileHandler
    extends IOUtils
    implements Readable, Writeable
{

    public FileHandler() {}
```

Listing 12.8 The file handler *(continued)*

```
    private String name;
    public String getName() {return name;}
    public void setName(String name) {
        this.name = name;
    }

    public String[] read() {
        String ret[] = new String[0];

        try {
            FileReader in = new FileReader(name);
            ret = doRead(in);
            in.close();
        } catch (Exception e) {
            System.err.println("Error reading: " + name);
            e.printStackTrace(System.err);
        }

        return ret;
    }

    public void write(String lines[]) {
        try {
            FileWriter out = new FileWriter(name);
            doWrite(out,lines);
            out.close();
        } catch (Exception e) {
            System.err.println("Error writing: " + name);
            e.printStackTrace(System.err);
        }
    }
}
```

Note that this class implements both `Readable` and `Writeable`, which will make it suitable for use in both the `input` and `output` sections.

The `ProgramHandler` is similar, except that it supports the `Readable`, `Writeable`, and `Filter` interfaces. The code that invokes and talks to the external program is identical to that used in Listing 11.5 and so will not be repeated here. The only difference of note is that `ProgramHandler` has a list of `Argument` objects and an `AddArgument()` method that adds an instance to the list. The `Argument` class is shown in Listing 12.9.

Listing 12.9 The argument class

```
package com.awl.toolbook.chapter12;

public class Argument {
    private String name;
    public String getName() {return name;}
    public void setName(String name) {this.name = name;}

    private String value;
    public String getValue() {return value;}
    public void setValue(String value) {
        this.value = value;
    }
}
```

`Argument` has both a `name` and `value` because it will be needed for another purpose. However, `ProgramHandler` only uses the `value`. In this context `Argument` is something of a waste, as it is nothing more than a wrapper around a string. However, there is no better solution immediately available. It is tempting to make an `AddObjectCreate()` rule that creates a `String` when it sees "*/program/arg," but the problem is that `String` has no set methods, so there is no way to assign the `value` though a `setProperties` rule. This will be addressed shortly by a custom rule.

There are three ways to handle the `class` node in filters. The first and easiest is to use a variation of the `objectCreateRule`, which gets the name of the class from an attribute instead of using the class name provided when the rule is added. This would be done with

```
addObjectCreate("cat-config/filters/program",
    "com.awl.toolbook.chapter12.StubFilter",
    className);
```

where there is a property that automatically set the `className` variable from the XML attribute, and `StubFilter` is a filter that does nothing and is provided only because the API requires the name of a valid class as the second argument. Digester uses the class named in the second argument when the attribute is not present in the XML.

There is a slight problem with this approach. Filters may need additional arguments, such as the line number filter, which takes an optional `format` parameter. For these to be attributes they would have to be listed in the DTD, and there is no way to list every possible attribute. Therefore, parameters of filter classes must be nested objects. But there is no rule that uses a nested object to set a property in the parent. This means every filter would need to provide an `add()` method that accepts an `Argument` and use the name and value in that `Argument` to set its own properties. This is less than ideal because classes should not need to include special code to accommodate any particular configuration tool.

The second option is to use another custom rule, which will be presented shortly. The third alternative is to use a proxy class. In this approach the proxy class will be created by Digester, and the name of the real class of interest will be passed as an attribute, the same as has been done with other classes up to this point. The proxy class will use this information to construct an instance of this class, and the proxy class's `filter()` method will just call `filter()` on the instance it has constructed. Properties for the inner class will be handled like any other nested attributes, with an `setNext` rule. In this way, all the special code to handle configuration is kept in one class, and particular filters can be written without regard to how they will be invoked.

The proxy class will need to provide a method that the `nextRule` will invoke, and this method will need to set a property in the constructed instance. Fortunately, there is a tool that makes this easy: BeanUtils from Chapter 8. The code for the proxy class is shown in Listing 12.10.

Listing 12.10 A generalized filter

```
package com.awl.toolbook.chapter12;

import org.apache.commons.beanutils.PropertyUtils;

public class ClassFilter implements Filter {
    Filter theFilter = null;

    private String className;
    public String getClassName() {return className;}
    public void setClassName(String className) {
        try {
            Class c = Class.forName(className);

            theFilter = (Filter) c.newInstance();
```

```
        } catch (Exception e) {
            System.err.println("Unable to instantiate " + className);
            e.printStackTrace(System.err);
        }
    }

    public void addArgument(Argument arg) {
        try {
            PropertyUtils.setSimpleProperty(
                            theFilter,
                            arg.getName(),
                            arg.getValue());
        } catch (Exception e) {}
    }

    public String[] filter(String lines[]) {
        return theFilter.filter(lines);
    }
}
```

`setClassName()` will be called by Digester as the result of a `setProperties` rule. `setProperty()` will be called with `Argument` objects as a result of a `setNext` rule.

Now that all the component classes have been written the latest version of `Cat` needs to set up Digester and then perform the requested actions. The result is shown in Listing 12.11.

Listing 12.11 Digester-based cat

```
package com.awl.toolbook.chapter12;

import java.io.File;
import java.io.IOException;

import java.net.URL;
import java.util.ArrayList;

import org.xml.sax.SAXException;
import org.apache.commons.digester.*;
```

Listing 12.11 Digester-based cat *(continued)*

```
public class Cat3 {
    /* Input patterns */
    private final static String inputFile =
        "cat-config/inputs/file";

    private final static String inputProgram =
        "cat-config/inputs/program";

    private final static String inputURL =
        "cat-config/inputs/url";

    /* Filter patterns */
    private final static String filterProgram =
        "cat-config/filters/program";

    private final static String filterClass =
        "cat-config/filters/class";

    private final static String filterClassArg =
        "*/filters/class/arg";

    /* Output patterns */
    private final static String outputFile =
        "cat-config/outputs/file";

    private final static String outputConsole =
        "cat-config/outputs/console";


    /* Special pattern for all programs */
    private final static String programArg =
        "*/program/arg";


    /*** Names of classes  ***/
    private final static String fileHandler =
        "com.awl.toolbook.chapter12.FileHandler";
```

```
private final static String programHandler =
    "com.awl.toolbook.chapter12.ProgramHandler";

private final static String classHandler =
    "com.awl.toolbook.chapter12.ClassFilter";

private final static String URLHandler =
    "com.awl.toolbook.chapter12.URLHandler";

private final static String argObject =
    "com.awl.toolbook.chapter12.Argument";

/*** Names of methods ***/
private final static String addInput    = "addInput";
private final static String addFilter   = "addFilter";
private final static String addOutput   = "addOutput";
private final static String addArgument =
    "addArgument";

public Cat3() {}

public static Cat3 config(String fileName)
    throws IOException, SAXException
{
    Digester digester = new Digester();
    URL url = null;

    try {
        url = new URL("cat-config.dtd");
    } catch (Exception e) {}

    // digester.push(this);
    digester.addObjectCreate("cat-config", Cat3.class);

    // File input
    digester.addObjectCreate(inputFile, fileHandler);
    digester.addSetProperties(inputFile);
    digester.addSetNext(inputFile,addInput);
```

Listing 12.11 Digester-based cat *(continued)*

```
// Program input
digester.addObjectCreate(inputProgram,
                         programHandler);
digester.addSetProperties(inputProgram);
digester.addSetNext(inputProgram,addInput);

// URL input
digester.addObjectCreate(inputURL,URLHandler);
digester.addSetProperties(inputURL);
digester.addSetNext(inputURL,addInput);

// Program filter
digester.addObjectCreate(filterProgram,
                         programHandler);
digester.addSetProperties(filterProgram);
digester.addSetNext(filterProgram,addFilter);

// Class filter
digester.addObjectCreate(filterClass,classHandler);
digester.addSetProperties(filterClass);
digester.addSetNext(filterClass,addFilter);

// Class filter arguments
digester.addObjectCreate(filterClassArg,argObject);
digester.addSetProperties(filterClassArg);
digester.addSetNext(filterClassArg,addArgument);


// File output
digester.addObjectCreate(outputFile,fileHandler);
digester.addSetProperties(outputFile);
digester.addSetNext(outputFile,addOutput);


// Program arguments
digester.addObjectCreate(programArg,argObject);
digester.addSetProperties(programArg);
```

```
        digester.addSetNext(programArg,addArgument);

        File input = new File(fileName);
        Cat3 cat = (Cat3) digester.parse(input);
        return cat;
    }

    private ArrayList inputs = new ArrayList();
    public void addInput(Readable r) {
        System.out.println(this);
        System.out.println("arr: " + r);
        inputs.add(r);
    }

    private ArrayList filters = new ArrayList();
    public void addFilter(Filter f) {
        filters.add(f);
    }

    private ArrayList outputs = new ArrayList();
    public void addOutput(Writeable w) {
        outputs.add(w);
    }

    public void process() {
        String lines[] = new String[0];

        for(int i=0;i<inputs.size();i++) {
            Readable r = (Readable) inputs.get(i);
            lines      = mergeArray(lines,r.read());
        }

        for(int i=0;i<filters.size();i++) {
            Filter f = (Filter) filters.get(i);
            lines    = f.filter(lines);

            System.out.println("M: " + f.getClass());
            System.out.println("M: " + lines.length);
```

Listing 12.11 Digester-based cat *(continued)*

```
        }

        for(int i=0;i<outputs.size();i++) {
            Writeable w = (Writeable) outputs.get(i);
            w.write(lines);
        }
    }

    private String[] mergeArray(String arr1[],
                                String arr2[])
    {
        if(arr1 == null) {
            return arr2;
        }

        String ret[] = new String[arr1.length +
                                  arr2.length];
        System.arraycopy(arr1,0,ret,0,arr1.length);
        System.arraycopy(arr2,0,ret,arr1.length,
                         arr2.length);
        return ret;
    }

    public static void main(String argv[]) throws Exception {
        Cat3 cat = Cat3.config(argv[0]);
        System.out.println(cat);
        cat.process();
    }
}
```

There are lots of rules to set up here, so the initialization code is fairly verbose, although each piece is simple enough. Most pieces consist of three rules: one to create the object, one to set its properties, and one to add it to its parent. Because programs can be used as inputs, filters, and outputs, the rule to handle program arguments is set globally, using "*/program/arg".

Note how simple the `process()` method is. Because each class is well encapsulated, and because Digester takes care of all the hard work of constructing objects and building the tree, the job of using the objects is reduced to a few simple loops. This is characteristic of Digester-based applications.

12.2.1 Custom Handlers

Using some clever tricks, like the wrapper in Listing 12.9 and the proxy in Listing 12.10, it is possible to do almost everything one might need with the provided Digester rules. However, there are instances where it may be more convenient or general to use custom rules rather than special classes. There may also be unusual circumstances that demand special rules. Naturally Digester makes it possible to implement such custom rules and use them as easily as the built-in rules.

Creating a custom rule is as simple as extending the `Rule` class, overriding one or more **lifecycle methods.** These methods are as follows:

- `begin()`, which is called when the pattern is first encountered. All the attributes from the matched node are passed as a parameter.
- `body()`, which is called when nested CDATA is encountered.
- `end()`, which is called when the closing tag is encountered. Any nested XML nodes will have already been processed.
- `finish()`, which is called after the closing tag has been parsed. This is provided as a way for rules to clean up any data or resources they may have allocated.

Within these methods code will have access to the `digester` instance from which the rule is being used and can use this `digester` to examine and manipulate the stack, as illustrated in Listing 12.12.

Listing 12.12 A rule that sets program arguments

```
package com.awl.toolbook.chapter12;

import org.apache.commons.beanutils.BeanUtils;
import org.apache.commons.digester.Rule;
import org.xml.sax.Attributes;

public class SetProgramArgRule extends Rule {
    public void begin(String namespace,
                      String name,
                      Attributes attributes)
        throws Exception
```

Listing 12.12 A rule that sets program arguments *(continued)*

```
    {
        // Find the value attribute
        // (should be the only one)
        String valueAttribute = null;

        for (int i=0; i<attributes.getLength(); i++) {
            String aName = attributes.getLocalName(i);

            if ("value".equals(aName)) {
                valueAttribute = attributes.getValue(i);
            }
        }

        if(valueAttribute == null) {
            return;
        }

        // Get the object on top of the stack,
        // which should be a ProgramHandler

        Object top          = digester.peek();
        ProgramHandler h = (ProgramHandler) top;

        h.addArgument(valueAttribute);
    }
}
```

This is as simple as it looks. The sax API is used to examine the attributes until a `value` is found. Then the top object on the stack is obtained with `peek()`, and the argument is set with a call to `addArgument()`.

To use this rule, just replace the existing rules for program arguments with

```
digester.addRule(programArg,new SetProgramArgRule());
```

where programArg is a variable containing the appropriate pattern. Note there is only one rule here; in particular there is no `objectCreate` or `setNext` rules used because no object is created to hold the program argument.

It is almost as easy to set an arbitrary property in a parent object as it is to set a program argument. Recall that special handling was needed for the class handler because the object created may have arbitrary parameters that need to be set, and the DTD cannot possibly specify them all. To set properties from nested nodes instead of attributes, it is just necessary to obtain the name and value from the nested node, then get the object from the stack, and use BeanUtils to do the setting. This is shown in Listing 12.13.

Listing 12.13 A rule that sets arbitrary properties

```
package com.awl.toolbook.chapter12;

import org.apache.commons.beanutils.BeanUtils;
import org.apache.commons.beanutils.PropertyUtils;
import org.apache.commons.digester.Rule;
import org.xml.sax.Attributes;

public class SetObjectPropertyRule extends Rule {
    public void begin(String namespace,
                      String name,
                      Attributes attributes)
        throws Exception
    {
        // Find the name and value attributes
        String nameAttribute  = null;
        String valueAttribute = null;

        for (int i=0; i<attributes.getLength(); i++) {
            String aName = attributes.getLocalName(i);

            if ("value".equals(aName)) {
                valueAttribute = attributes.getValue(i);
            } else if ("name".equals(aName)) {
                nameAttribute = attributes.getValue(i);
            }
        }

        if(nameAttribute == null || valueAttribute == null) {
            return;
        }
```

Listing 12.13 A rule that sets arbitrary properties *(continued)*

```
        // Get the object on top of the stack,
        // which should be a ProgramHandler

        Object top = digester.peek();

        PropertyUtils.setProperty(top,
                                  nameAttribute,
                                  valueAttribute);
    }
}
```

The configuration to use this new rule is also simple: Just replace the rules with

```
digester.addRule("/cat-config/filters/class/arg"
                 new SetObjectPropertyRule());
```

There is just one issue now remaining: how to construct an instance of the desired class instead of the proxy class that was used previously. This can be accomplished through an alternate version of the `ObjectCreate` rule that looks for an optional attribute and, if found, will use it as the name of the class to construct instead of the provided class name. In this case the rule would be added with

```
digester.addObjectCreate(
            "/cat-config/filters/class",
            "com.awl.toolbook.chapter12.ClassFilter",
            "classname");
```

With these two rules in place, the syntax of the configuration file can remain unchanged.

12.3 Beyond This Book

There are many other ways to configure a program. Configuration information can be stored in property files, which is suitable for settings consisting of name/value pairs. Configuration information can also be stored in a database. This approach could be used in conjunction with OJB to create objects that have already been properly configured, much as Digester does from the XML description. It would even be possible to combine the two approaches by creating a `loadFromDatabase` rule that populates a configuration object from a database based on a primary key.

In the final analysis configuration is a very important aspect of any large program but should not comprise a significant portion of the code or consume much developer time. Using either of the tools discussed in this chapter allows developers to quickly move past configuration and into the more interesting parts of a project.

12.4 Summary

Tool: CLI
Purpose: Command-line-based configuration
Version covered: 1.0
Home page: http://jakarta.apache.org/commons/dbcp/
License: The Apache Software License, Version 2.0

Tool: Digester
Purpose: XML-based configuration
Version covered: 1.5
Home page: http://jakarta.apache.org/commons/digester/
License: The Apache Software License, Version 2.0

Further Reading:

- More information and discussion on the builder pattern: http://c2.com/cgi-bin/wiki?BuilderPattern.

CHAPTER 13

Working with Text 1: Regular Expressions

The tools presented in the preceding few chapters have dealt with structured data, data organized into rows in a database or trees in the form of beans or XML. This chapter and Chapter 14 address tools for working with an important type of **unstructured** data: raw text.

Text appears within applications in a variety of forms and contexts. Text may exist within a larger structured context, such as a name, address, or description field in a database. Text may also live in large collections with minimal structure, such as a e-mail folders or hierarchies of directories of memos or reports. Applications may need to perform similar tasks in all these cases: determine whether a particular piece of text matches some requirement, find all text elements that match a set of requirements, and transform text according to some rule.

One of the most common tasks relating to text is to impose structure on a block of otherwise unstructured text. Conceptually this consists of defining a structure, determining whether text can be made to align with the structure and if so identifying the parts of the text that match up with parts of the structure. This can be used to identify whether text meets structural requirements, to pull text apart according to specified rules, and to transform text according to similar rules. This chapter examines three tools that provide these capabilities.

13.1 Regular Expressions

Before looking at the tools themselves it is necessary to describe how the structure will be specified. There are many ways of defining a structure, including XML DTDs, which may be thought of as a set of rules that a block of text must obey to be considered well formed.

One common tool used to define structure is called **regular expressions** or **regexs,** or sometimes **regexps** for short. Regular expressions comprise a language for specifying patterns of text. This is not a full-fledged language like Java; regexps are both simpler and less powerful,[1] but they turn out to be powerful enough for a wide variety of applications. In addition, the simplicity of regular expressions makes it possible for them to be implemented very efficiently. In what follows a regular expression will be called a **pattern,** and the text to be tested will be called the **input.**

Before describing the regular expression syntax in detail, a few preliminary words on how regexps are evaluated are in order. Patterns are matched left to right, and in general any pattern can be evaluated by examining each character of the input only once. Regular expressions have no notion of memory in the general sense. At each step of processing a regular expression knows only what action to take based on the next character. This means regular expressions cannot be used to describe structures such as palindromes, strings that read the same backward as forward. This is because to check for palindromes it would be necessary to either remember what had been seen in the first half of the string when evaluating the second half or to move back and forth across the string to compare characters at each end. Basic regular expressions cannot even check for things like the presence of every vowel in any order. This would require the regexp to remember which vowels it had already seen as it moved through the string.

Keeping these rules in mind, here are the basic elements of regular expressions:

- Single characters match themselves. The pattern 'a' matches the input "a," the pattern 'q' matches "q," and the unicode character '\u00FC' matches "ü." However, 'a' would not match "apple" even though "apple" contains the letter 'a.'[2]

---

[1]The notion of the "power" of a language has a precise definition in computer science. Although it is beyond the scope of this book, full languages like Java are equivalent to an abstract computing model called "turing machines," whereas regular expression are equivalent to another model called "finite state machines" or "finite automata."

[2]The regular expression packages in many languages, such as Perl, do allow substrings or subpatterns to match against the entire input, so "a" would match "apple," as would "le." However, the usual formal definition of regular expressions agrees with the rule given in stating that single characters only match themselves. Except where otherwise noted, the regular expression libraries considered in the chapter use the formal definition.

- It follows immediately from the left-to-right processing rule that strings of characters match the corresponding literal strings, so the pattern "apple" matches the input "apple" and "Cr\u00FCxshadows" matches "Crüxshadows." "Hello" will not match "Hello, world."
- A single dot '.' matches any single character, so the pattern '.' will match "a" or "b" or "ö" or so on. By the left-to-right rule this means that the pattern "c.t" will match "cat," "cot," "cut," or even "czt". The pattern ".." will match any two characters, "e.." will match any three characters beginning with 'e,' and so on. Note that this is not quite the same thing as saying "all three-letter words" because "e.." will also match strings with spaces such as "e t".
- An asterisk following a pattern means that the immediately preceding pattern may be repeated zero or more times. The pattern "a*" will match any number of instances of the letter 'a' including "" (the empty string), "aa," "aaaaa," and so on.
- Following a dot with an asterisk means any single character will match any number of times, which is the same thing as matching any input. ".*" will match anything at all; "a.*" will match any input beginning with 'a'; ".*ly" will match any input ending in "ly," and ".*qq.*" will match any input that contains "qq" anywhere within it. Note that this is equivalent to checking whether a input contains "qq," which is also equivalent to checking that `string.indexOf("qq") != -1`.
- A plus sign ('+') in a pattern indicates that the preceding pattern must match one or more times. The pattern "a+" will match the strings "a" and "aaa" but not the empty string. Note that if p represents a pattern, then "p+" is equivalent to "pp*".
- A question mark ('?') indicates that the preceding pattern must match exactly zero or once. "z?" matches the strings "z" and "".
- A pattern may be followed by a number or pair of numbers enclosed in braces ({}) to specify the number of times, or a range of times, a pattern should occur. ".{4}" matches all inputs of four characters and is equivalent to "....". "a{2,}" will match all inputs consisting of the character 'a' at least twice, which is equivalent to the pattern "aaa*". The pattern "a{2,4}" will match inputs with at least two but no more than four occurrences of the letter 'a' (that is, "aa," "aaa," and "aaaa"). This rule can be considered a generalization of the previous two.
- Patterns consisting of lists of characters enclosed in brackets ([ ]) match any of the enclosed characters. The pattern "[ab]" matches the strings "a" and "b".

"[ab]*" matches inputs with any combination of 'a's and 'b's, such as "a," "b," "aabb," "baabaab," and so on.

- As a shortcut, ranges of characters can be expressed with a dash, so "[d-g]" means the same thing as "[defg]". Ranges can be listed sequentially, "[a-dx-z]" means the same thing as "[abcdxyz]". Note that this is *not* the same as "[a-d][x-z]," which matches two-character inputs such as "az" and "dx". This means that "[a-zA-Z]{3}" matches all three-letter words.
- Starting a range or set of characters with a caret (^) negates the list. "[^a]" matches any character except 'a'; "[^a-d]" matches any character except 'a,' 'b,' 'c,' or 'd.'
- A caret outside brackets means the start of a line and so should only appear at the beginning of a pattern. Likewise a dollar sign ($) represents the end of a line.
- A vertical bar (|) separating two patterns matches if the input matches the pattern on the left or the right. "a | b" means the same as "[ab]," which is not that interesting. "a | zz" matches either a single 'a' or two 'z's.
- So far there has been a slight ambiguity in the regular expression syntax; "abc{3}" could mean either "abcabcabc" or "abccc." Pattern modifiers effect only the immediately preceding pattern, so "abc{3}" is equivalent to "abccc." To make a modifier affect a string of characters the characters must be enclosed in parentheses, so "(abc){3}" matches "abcabcabc." Any pattern can be enclosed in parentheses in order to apply a modifier to it. "(a[bc]){3}" matches strings consisting of three iterations of the pattern "a[bc]," such as "ababab," "acabab," and so on.

There are other options, and all three of the regular expression packages that will be discussed add their own twists. The syntax covered is enough for common use and allows many interesting possibilities. Here are a few:

- `.*q[^u].*` finds all words containing a 'q' that is not followed by a 'u.'
- `.*z.*x.*|.*x.*z.*` finds all words with both a 'z' and an 'x'. Note the use of an "or" pattern to represent the two cases, the 'z' before the 'x' and the 'x' before the 'z'. In principle this same approach could be used to find words where every vowel appears once, but because there are 120 ways to order five vowels, this is impractical.
- `^([aeiou][^aeiou]*){11}$` matches all words that start with a vowel and contain eleven vowels. `[aeiou][^aeiou]*` matches a vowel followed by any number of nonvowels, and the `{11}` modifier repeats this eleven times.

13.2 ORO Regular Expressions

Once regular expressions are understood, the APIs for using them are straightforward. Prior to JDK 1.4 there was no regular expression facilities included with Java, and many third-party packages arose to fill the gap. One of the most comprehensive and widely used is the ORO package, originally from ORO, Inc. and later donated to the Jakarta project.

ORO handles many kinds of regular expressions, most of which follow the conventions of various Unix utilities including Awk and the "globbing" patterns used by various shells. The most sophisticated regular expressions provided by ORO work like those in version 5 of the Perl language. These patterns may be considered an extension to the regular expressions discussed in the pervious section and will be the ones used throughout this book.

Regular expressions are a language, and like most other languages they can be evaluated faster if they are compiled prior to being used. `Pattern` represents a compiled expression, and classes implementing the `Compiler` interface are used to build a `Pattern` from the string representation of a pattern.[3]

```
import org.apache.oro.text.regex.*

Perl5Compiler compiler = new Perl5Compiler();
Pattern p = compiler.compile("^a[^az]z$");
```

the object returned in this case is a `Perl5Pattern`, which implements the `Pattern` interface. In general, when declaring variables it is better to use the more generic type, which in this case means declaring `p` to be a `Pattern` instead of a `Perl5Pattern`. This allows the compiler to ensure that `p` is used in such a way that a different kind of pattern could be easily substituted if the need ever arises.

A number of flags that change the behavior of patterns can be specified when the pattern is compiled. A full list is available in the Java docs for the `Perl5Compiler` class, but two particularly useful ones are `CASE_INSENSITIVE_MASK`, which causes inputs to match regardless of case, and `SINGLELINE_MASK`, which allows patterns to span multiple lines.

```
Perl5Compiler compiler = new Perl5Compiler();
Pattern p = compiler.compile("Hello.*world",
                Perl5Compiler.CASE_INSENSITIVE_MASK |
                Perl5Compiler.SINGLELINE_MASK);
```

[3]Regular expressions are not compiled into Java byte codes but into an internal representation of a finite state machine.

Once a pattern has been compiled, it is usually used as an argument to a PatternMatcher along with the input to be checked.

```
Perl5Matcher m = new Perl5Matcher();
if(m.matches("Hello, you great big world",p)) {
    System.out.println("It matches");
}
```

In addition to determining whether a string matches a pattern it is also possible to determine whether a string contains a pattern with the contains() method. Note that asking whether an input contains a pattern p is equivalent to asking whether it matches the pattern .*p.*.

Following a call to matches() or contains() more information on the match is available through a MatchResult object.

```
if(m.contains(input,pattern)) {
    MatchResult r = m.getMatch();
    System.out.println("The portion that matches is: " +
                       r.toString());
    System.out.println("The matching portion begins at " +
                       r.begin(0));
    System.out.println("The matching portion ends at " +
                       r.end(0));
}
```

The meaning of the 0s used as arguments to begin() and end() will be made clear shortly.

It is possible for an input to contain multiple instances of a pattern. The methods that have just been used can be used to access each match in turn, but an auxiliary class is needed to hold information such as how far into the input the parser has reached. This auxiliary class is PatternMatcherInput, and it is constructed from the input to be checked. Subsequent calls to contains() will determine whether the pattern is matched again starting at a point beyond where the previous match was found. This makes it easy to iterate over all matches.

```
Perl5Compiler compiler = new Perl5Compiler();
Pattern pattern = compiler.compile(thePattern);
PatternMatcherInput input = new PatternMatcherInput(theInput);
Perl5Matcher m = new Perl5Matcher();
```

```
while(m.contains(input,pattern)) {
    MatchResult r = m.getMatch();
    System.out.println("The portion that matches is: " +
                       r.toString());
}
```

13.2.1 Subpatterns

Following a match it is often useful to determine which characters of the input correspond to a specific portion of the pattern. For example, the pattern "Hello, [A-Z][a-z]*" could be used to match against the first line of a letter. The name of the person being addressed will always correspond to the portion of the pattern consisting of an uppercase letter and an arbitrary number of lowercase letters. The ability to extract this information would make it easy to obtain the name for further processing.

A mechanism called **subpatterns** is available to do this. This consists of surrounding the portion or portions of interest of the pattern with parentheses, such as "Hello, ([A-Z][a-z]*)." At first, this may seem confusing because parentheses were also used to group subpatterns together, so a modifier such as "*" or "+" could act on all of them. There is no ambiguity, however, because parentheses followed by a modifier means a grouping, whereas parentheses followed by anything else means a subpattern. The two can even be combined: "aa((ba)*)" matches strings starting with two 'a's and followed by an arbitrary number of occurrences of "ba," capturing those occurrences as a subpattern.

After matching against a pattern containing subpatterns, the `MatchResult` object will have information about each submatch. Specifically, the `begin()` and `end()` methods will be able to identify the start and end of each submatch, and a method called `group()` will return the entire submatched string. Group zero is taken to be the entire pattern, which is why zero was used as an argument in previous uses of `begin()` and `end()`. The first submatch is then group one, the second is group two, and so on.

```
Perl5Compiler compiler = new Perl5Compiler();
Pattern pattern =
    compiler.compile("Hello ([A-Z][a-z]*)");
PatternMatcherInput input =
    new PatternMatcherInput("Hello Leela, how are you?");
Perl5Matcher m = new Perl5Matcher();
```

```
if(m.contains(input,pattern)) {
    MatchResult r = m.getMatch();
    System.out.println("The complete match is: " +
                       r.group(0));

    System.out.println("The letter was addressed to " +
                       r.group(1));
}
```

As a more realistic example, consider the task of parsing XML. An XML tag consists of an opening angle bracket, followed by a word, followed by an arbitrary number of name/value pairs, and a closing angle bracket. Then there may be a body, which for simplicity will be assumed to have no nested tags. Finally, there is a closing tag.

The opening tag without attributes may be represented by the pattern `<\w+>`. This introduces a new convenience available with Perl5 patterns. The string `\w` represents any character that may appear within a word; it is equivalent to "[a-zA-Z0-9]." Similarly, `\W` represents any nonword character including punctuation and white space.

The attributes are represented by the complex-looking pattern `(\W*\w+=\w+)*`. This means "any number of iterations of any amount of white space, followed by a word, followed by an equals sign, followed by another word."

The body portion is refreshingly simple, `[^<]*` meaning any number of characters except an opening bracket.

There is also a simple pattern that will match the closing tag `<\w+>`. This will match any closing tag, not just the one for the tag that is currently being parsed. Using generic regular expressions, this is the best that could be hoped for because, as noted previously, regular expressions have no memory and so cannot remember what the opening tag was when they come to the closing tag. However, Perl5 regular expressions can do better because they can include **back references.** A back reference in a pattern matches the exact sequence of characters contained in a subpattern and are denoted by a slash followed by a number indicating which subpattern to use. Therefore, the pattern `([a-z]*)\1` will match any string that repeats twice, such as "tartar."

Therefore, the pattern for closing brackets will be `<\1>`, and writing a simple XML parser is now a matter of wrapping each portion of the pattern in parentheses and proceeding as previously:

```
Perl5Compiler compiler = new Perl5Compiler();

Pattern pattern =
    compiler.compile(
```

```
        "<(\\w*)(\\W*\\w*=\"\\w*\")*>([^<]*)</\\1>",
        Perl5Compiler.MULTILINE_MASK);

PatternMatcherInput input =
    new PatternMatcherInput("<h1 color=\"red\">Hello!</h1>");

Perl5Matcher m = new Perl5Matcher();

if(m.contains(input,pattern)) {
    MatchResult r = m.getMatch();
    System.out.println("Opening tag: " + r.group(1));
    System.out.println("Attributes: " + r.group(2));
    System.out.println("Body: " + r.group(3));
}
```

Note that `MULTILINE_MASK` is set, allowing the XML expression to span multiple lines. With this flag set, `\W` will match newline characters. Also note that every backslash in the regular expression needs to be preceded by an additional backslash in order to satisfy the rules for Java strings. Consequently the expression is rather complicated, but it can be understood by considering each small piece individually.

13.2.2 Greediness and Reluctance

At this point is is natural to wonder if the restriction that the body must contain only text without nested tags could be removed. Because the pattern guarantees that the closing tag will match the opening tag, it would seem that arbitrary XML, such as

```
<tag1>
  some text
  <tag2>other text</tag2>
</tag1>
```

would match correctly. While the pattern works correctly in this case, it will not work in general. Consider the XML

```
<tag1>
  some text
  <tag2>other text</tag2>
</tag1>
<tag1>Yet more text</tag1>
```

Modifiers such as "*" and "+" are **greedy,** meaning they will consume as much of the pattern as possible without causing the match to fail. In the preceding example the closing pattern could match either of the </tag1> tags, and greediness will cause it to pick the second. This means the body will be parsed as

```
some text<tag2>other text</tag2></tag1><tag1>Yet more text
```

which is not correct.

Modifiers can be made **reluctant** by following them with a question mark, causing them to match the minimum number of occurrences of the pattern. Given the input "aaaabbbb" the pattern `(a+)([ab]*)` will set group one to "aaaa" and group two to "bbbb." The pattern `(a+?)([ab]*)` would cause group one to be "a" and group two to be "aaabbbb."

In the XML example a reluctant pattern could be used for the body that fixes the case of two tags appearing consecutively. This introduces a new problem with nested tags, the input

```
<tag1>
  some text
  <tag1>Yet more text</tag1>
</tag1>
```

matched with a reluctant pattern would determine that the body is

```
some text<tag1>Yet more text
```

which is incorrect. The regrettable conclusion is that regular expressions are not quite powerful enough to parse full XML, more sophisticated techniques must be used.

13.2.3 Substitutions

Another common programming task involves replacing the portion of an input that matches a pattern with new text. For example, consider a story about some blueberries, a bluebird, and Bluebeard the pirate, and imagine that for some unknown reason the author wished to change it to blackberries, a blackbird, and Blackbeard. It would not be correct to just change all occurrences of "blue" to "black" as this would also inadvertently change "the sky was very blue" to "the sky was very black." What is needed is some way to capture strings matching the pattern "blue[a-z]+" and only change the "blue" part.

This could be done with the APIs already discussed by finding the start and end of the appropriate subpatterns and manually splicing in the new text. This is such a common situation that a special `substitute()` method has been provided in the `Util` class. This method uses a `Perl5Substitution`, which implements the more general `Substitution` interface and contains the text to substitute. Within the substitution, numbers preceded by dollar signs refer to group numbers: $1 means group 1, and so on.

```
String text = "Bluebeard the pirate and his bluebird " +
              "ate blueberries " +
              "beneath this sky so blue.";

Perl5Compiler c = new Perl5Compiler();

Pattern pattern =
    c.compile("blue([a-z]+)",
              Perl5Compiler.CASE_INSENSITIVE_MASK);

Perl5Matcher m = new Perl5Matcher();

Substitution s =
    new Perl5Substitution("black$1");

String newText =
    Util.substitute(m,pattern,s,text,Util.SUBSTITUTE_ALL);

System.out.println(newText);
```

would result in "Blackbeard the pirate and his blackbird ate blackberries beneath this sky so blue." Note that the `CASE_INSENSITIVE_MASK` flag still causes the occurrence starting with a capital B to match, but the substitution has no way to determine that the first letter of "black" should be correspondingly capitalized. This could be remedied by using the pattern `([bB])lue([a-z]+)` and the replacement string `$1lack$2`.

13.3 Jakarta Regexp

Although ORO is quite comprehensive, it is not the only available regular expression package. It is not even the only one available from Jakarta! Another tool called Regexp was donated to the Jakarta project before ORO, and it is still available on the principles that different people have different needs, and choice is always a good thing.

Regexp's regular expression syntax is largely similar to OROs. All the standard features introduced in the first section of this chapter are supported, as are backreferenceces and greedy/reluctant modifiers.

Regexp also supports patterns representing sets of characters as defined in the POSIX standard for regular expressions.[4] These include "[:alpha:]" for any alphabetic characters; "[:alnum:]" for alphanumerics; "[:space:]" for whitespace, and others.

One distinguishing feature of Regexp is that it offers a more streamlined API than ORO. The class encapsulating a regular expression is called `RE`, and its constructor does the compilation automatically.

```
import org.apache.regexp.*;

RE pattern = new RE("([A-Z])([a-z ]*)");
```

There are a set of flags that can be passed in as the second argument that effect how matches are done, including `MATCH_CASEINDEPENDENT`, which makes matching case-independent, and `MATCH_SINGLELINE`, which causes all input to be treated as a single line.

```
RE pattern = new RE("[a-z]*",RE.MATCH_CASEINDEPENDENT);
```

is equivalent to a pattern of "[a-zA-Z]*" (which is also equivalent to "[:alpha:]*").

An instance of `RE` can be used to check for a match directly.

```
if(pattern.match("Hello world")) {
    System.out.println("It matches!");
}
```

Following a successful call to `match()`, any subpatterns will be available. `RE` calls these **parens,** and as with ORO the zeroth paren is the entire matching pattern. For example, using `([A-Z])([a-z ]*)` as the pattern and `Hello, world` as the input `pattern.getParen(0)` would return `Hello, world`, and `pattern.getParen(2)` would return `ello world`.

The `match()` method works like Perl5's pattern matching (see footnote 2) and hence will consider there to be a match if the pattern matches a substring of the input. However, there is no method that directly corresponds to the `match()` method in ORO. The equivalent effect can be achieved by adding a caret before the pattern,

[4]POSIX is a standard developed by The Portable Application Standards Committee, which is meant to ensure a level of interoperability between applications, APIs, and operating systems.

which matches the start of the input, and a dollar sign at the end, which matches the end of the input.

Regexp also provides a number of utility methods that simplify common tasks. First, there is a method to split an input into pieces delineated by occurrences of a pattern.

```
RE pattern = new RE("[:digit:]+");
String pieces[] = pattern.split("octopus8thing726moose000");
for (int i=0;i<pieces.length;i++) {
    System.out.println(pieces[i]);
}
```

will print "octopus," "thing," and "moose." Note that if `[:digit:]*` were used instead, each individual letter would be printed because any two of the letters are separated by at least zero digits.

Second, Regexp provides a substitution facility much like OROs.

```
RE pattern = new RE("([^l])oose");
System.out.println(
    pattern.subst("The moose and goose are on the loose",
                  "$1eese",
                  RE.REPLACE_ALL |
                  RE.REPLACE_BACKREFERENCES));
```

prints "The meese and geese are on the loose," which is correct outputs despite the fact that the plural of "moose" is not "meese."

Errors to Watch For

At the time of this writing substitutions with backreferences do not work, and an exception is thrown as a result of the `subst()` method.

13.4 The JDK1.4 Pattern Matching Classes

Finally, it is worth mentioning that as of JDK1.4 regular expression facilities are available as part of the standard Java libraries by way of the `java.util.regex` package. This package provides yet another API, which some developers may prefer.

The regular expressions used by this package are nearly equivalent to those used in other packages. POSIX sets are specified with braces instead of brackets and preceded by `\p`—for example, `\p{Lower}` for all lowercase letters. Subgroups (called **capturing patterns**) and backreferences are also supported.

The fundamental regex class is `Pattern`, and it contains a static method that does the necessary compilation:

```
import java.util.regex.*;

Pattern p = Pattern.compile("m([aeiou])\\1se");
```

Once a pattern has been compiled, it is typically used to obtain another object called a `Matcher`, which will be used for subsequent activities.

```
Matcher m = p.matcher("moose");
```

Note that a `Matcher` matches against a particular input; if there are several inputs that must be checked against a pattern, a new `Matcher` must be obtained for each.

The most obvious thing a `Matcher` can do is determine whether the pattern matches the input.

```
System.out.println(m.matches());
```

will print `true` for the preceding input and pattern used. Note again that this does a complete match, not a check for containment, and so would return `false` for the input "here is a moose."

The `Pattern` class has a shortcut if all that is needed is to check one input against one pattern.

```
Pattern.matches(pattern,input);
```

is exactly equivalent to

```
Pattern.compile(pattern).matcher(input).matches()
```

The bulk of the methods in `Matcher` deal with the case where a pattern occurs several times in an input. Normal usage is to obtain sequential occurrences of a match with `find()` and then use either the `group()` method or `begin()` and `end()` methods to locate the substring that matched.

```
String input = "The moose and goose are on the loose";
Pattern p    = Pattern.compile(".oose");
Matcher m    = p.matcher();

while(m.find()) {
    System.out.println(input.substring(m.start(),m.end()));
}
```

prints, as expected, `moose`, `goose`, and `loose`. Printing `m.group()` would have exactly the same result.

There is also an easy way to do the converse: find all strings outside matching regions. This can be done directly through the `Pattern` without using a `Matcher` by using the `split()` method, as with Regexp:

```
String input = "The moose and goose are on the loose";
Pattern p    = Pattern.compile(".oose");
String strings[] = p.split(input);

for(int i=0;i<strings.length;i++) {
    System.out.println(strings[i]);
}
```

prints the strings `The`, `and` and `are on the`. This can be thought of as a regex-enhanced version of the `StringTokenizer` class.

There is no way in the JDK1.4 regexp API to determine which part of a matching group is contained in a subpattern. It is possible to do substitutions based on subpatterns, which is provided by the `replaceAll()` and `replaceFirst()` methods in `Matcher`. These calls take a string that should replace the matching group, and within that string numbers preceded by a dollar sign refer to the contents of a subpattern, just as with the other packages discussed. Given the pattern "(a*)b(c*)," the input string "aaabcc," and the replacement string "$1 – $2," the result would be "aaa – cc."

13.4.1 Two Longer Examples

Most variations of Unix come equipped with an incredibly useful utility called "grep"[5] that searches through files for lines matching a given regular expression. There are many options to grep, including the ability to print only the names of matching files

[5] The name *grep* comes from the sequence of commands "g/regular expression/p," which is a command in the "ed" editor that goes to a line matching a regular expression, then prints that line.

or the matching lines, with or without line numbers. Grep can also be case sensitive or insensitive. It is possible to implement grep in Java using any of the tools discussed in this chapter. Listing 13.1 is such an implementation, using the built-in Java API, although it does not handle all of grep's features. In addition, the regular expression syntax provided by JDK1.4 more closely matches the syntax used by an extended version of grep called egrep, so egrep has been used as the name of the class.

Listing 13.1 A Java implementation of egrep

```
package com.awl.toolbook.chapter13;

import java.util.List;
import java.util.regex.*;
import java.util.Iterator;
import java.io.BufferedReader;
import java.io.FileReader;

import org.apache.commons.cli.*;

public class Egrep {
    // Output options
    private boolean showFilename = true;
    private boolean showLineNum  = false;
    private boolean showLine     = true;

    // Match options
    private boolean showMatching = true;
    private boolean ignoreCase   = false;

    private Pattern thePattern = null;
    private int count          = 0;

    private static Options makeOptions() {
        Options options = new Options();

        options.addOption(OptionBuilder
         .withDescription(
             "print line number with output lines")
         .withLongOpt("line-number")
         .create('n'));
```

```
        options.addOption(OptionBuilder
         .withDescription("ignore case distinctions")
         .withLongOpt("ignore-case")
         .create('i'));

        options.addOption(OptionBuilder
         .withDescription(
             "print the filename for each match")
         .withLongOpt("with-filename")
         .create('H'));

        options.addOption(OptionBuilder
         .withDescription("suppress the prefixing " +
                          "filename on output")
         .withLongOpt("no-filename")
         .create('h'));

        options.addOption(OptionBuilder
         .withDescription("select non-matching lines")
         .withLongOpt("invert-match")
         .create('v'));

        options.addOption(OptionBuilder
         .withDescription(
             "only print FILE names containing " +
                          "matches")
         .withLongOpt("files-with-matches")
         .create('l'));

        options.addOption(OptionBuilder
         .withDescription(
             "only print FILE names containing " +
                          "no match")
         .withLongOpt("files-without-match")
         .create('L'));

        return options;
    }
```

Listing 13.1 A Java implementation of egrep *(continued)*

```
public static void usage(Options options) {
    HelpFormatter formatter = new HelpFormatter();
    formatter.printHelp(
        "egrep [OPTION] ... PATTERN [FILE] ...",
        options,
        true);
}

private void handleFile(String name) {
    BufferedReader in = null;
    String line;

    try {
        in = new BufferedReader(
                 new FileReader(name));
    } catch (Exception e){
        System.err.println("Unable to open " + name);
        return;
    }

    try {
        boolean done = false;

        while(!done && (line = in.readLine()) != null)
        {
            Matcher m = thePattern.matcher(line);

            if(m.find()) {
                output(line,name,count);
                done = !showLine && !showLineNum;
            }
            count++;
        }
    } catch (Exception e) {
        System.err.println("Error reading " + name);
    }
```

```
        try {
            in.close();
        } catch (Exception e) {}
    }

    private void output(String fname,String line,int num) {
        if(showFilename) {
            System.out.print(fname);
        }

        if(showLineNum) {
            System.out.print(':');
            System.out.print(count);
        }

        if(showLine) {
            System.out.print(‘:');
            System.out.print(line);
        }

        System.out.println();
    }

    public static void main(String args[]) {
        Egrep e = new Egrep(args);
        e.processArgs(args);
    }

    public Egrep() {}

    public Egrep(String args[]) {
        processArgs(args);
    }

    public void processArgs(String args[]) {
        CommandLine cmd = null;
        Options options = makeOptions();
        CommandLineParser parser = new BasicParser();
```

Listing 13.1 A Java implementation of egrep *(continued)*

```
// Parse the arguments, if there's an error
// report usage
try {
    cmd = parser.parse(options,args);
} catch (ParseException e) {
    System.err.println(e.getMessage());
    usage(options);
    System.exit(-1);
}

ignoreCase   = cmd.hasOption('i');
showFilename = cmd.hasOption('f');
showLineNum  = cmd.hasOption('n');
showMatching = !cmd.hasOption('v');

if(cmd.hasOption('l')) {
    showFilename = true;
    showLine     = false;
    showLineNum  = false;
    showMatching = true;
}

if(cmd.hasOption('L')) {
    showFilename = true;
    showLine     = false;
    showLineNum  = false;
    showMatching = false;
}


List others = cmd.getArgList();
Iterator it = others.iterator();

// The first other arg should be the pattern
// if it is not present, abort
if(!it.hasNext()) {
    usage(options);
    System.exit(-1);
}
```

```
            if(ignoreCase) {
                thePattern = Pattern.compile(
                                  it.next().toString(),
                                  Pattern.CASE_INSENSITIVE);
            } else {
                thePattern = Pattern.compile(
                                  it.next().toString());

            }

            Iterator files = others.iterator();
            while(files.hasNext()) {
                handleFile(files.next().toString());
            }

            System.exit(0);
        }
    }
```

The numerous options are handled by the Jakarta CLI package, introduced in Chapter 12. After parsing the options the first remaining argument is taken to be the pattern, and the remaining arguments are file names. Each file is processed a line at a time, looking for matches, When one is found, the `output()` method displays it according to the options. If the user has elected to display only the file name, processing of the file stops after the first match is found; otherwise it continues.

One mildly entertaining way to waste a couple of minutes during a lengthy compilation is to make up regular expressions and find English words that match it. This can be done by running Egrep over a comprehensive dictionary containing one word per line. Such a dictionary is provided with the Unix utility ispell, and it is also included on the companion CD-ROM for those without access to this utility. An example earlier in this chapter was designed to find all words with both an 'x' and a 'z'; this could be determined with

```
java com.awl.toolbook.chapter13.Egrep 'z.*x|x.*z' words
```

It is also possible to use `Egrep` to find all words that contain each vowel exactly once. It was mentioned earlier that this cannot be done with a single regular expression because it would require state to be maintained. A way around this problem is to invoke `Egrep` multiple times—once to select all words that have exactly one 'a,' once to select from that list words that have exactly one 'e,' and so on. It is slightly more efficient to extract the letters containing 'u' first because 'u' is much less common in

English than 'e' or 'e.' The whole command would be

```
java com.awl.toolbook.chapter14.Egrep '^[^a]*a[^u]*$' \
                                       words | \
java com.awl.toolbook.chapter14.Egrep '^[^e]*e[^o]*$' | \
java com.awl.toolbook.chapter14.Egrep '^[^i]*i[^i]*$' | \
java com.awl.toolbook.chapter14.Egrep '^[^o]*o[^a]*$' | \
java com.awl.toolbook.chapter14.Egrep '^[^u]*u[^e]*$'
```

There are more matches than one might expect, 1556, although many of these are not in common use.

Another possible use of regexps is in conjunction with databases. SQL has a simple expression language that can be used with the `like` keyword. The only pattern in standard SQL is `%`, which means the same thing as the regular expression ".*", so

```
select * from table where name like '%a'
```

would select all rows where the value of `name` contains an 'a.'

It would be useful to be able to select data based on more sophisticated criteria. While this isn't possible in every database, it is easy with hsqldb, covered in Chapter 10. Recall from that chapter that hsqldb can invoke any static Java method as a stored procedure. So by creating the following class

```
public class RegexpLike {
    public static boolean like(String pattern,
                               String value)
    {
        Perl5Compiler compiler = new Perl5Compiler();
        Pattern p = compiler.compile(pattern);
        Perl5Matcher m = new Perl5Matcher();
        return m.matches(value,p);
    }
}
```

regular expressions could be used in SQL as easily as

```
create alias RE_LIKE
    "com.awl.toolbook.chapter14.RegexpLike.like";

select * from table where RE_LIKE('[bB]lue.*',name);
```

While this will work, it will be very inefficient. Using the `matches()` method will cause the pattern to be recompiled every time, which in this case means once for every row. A hashtable could be used to get around this problem by mapping the string representation of a regular expression to the compiled form. This will solve the performance problem but at the cost of introducing potential space issues as the number of stored patterns increases. To fix this, a thread could be used that periodically clears out the old pattern. A version of a `RegexpLike` with these enhancements is shown in Listing 13.2

Listing 13.2 An efficient implementation of RegexpLike

```
package com.awl.toolbook.chapter13;

import java.util.Hashtable;
import java.util.Iterator;

import org.apache.oro.text.regex.*;

public class RegexpLike implements Runnable {
    private static Hashtable regexps = new Hashtable();
    private static Hashtable times   = new Hashtable();
    private static Thread runner     = null;

    public static boolean like(String pattern,
                               String value)
    {
        if(runner == null) {
            runner = new Thread(new RegexpLike());
            runner.start();
        }

        Pattern p = (Pattern) regexps.get(pattern);

        if(p == null) {
            Perl5Compiler compiler = new Perl5Compiler();

            try {
                p = compiler.compile(pattern);

                regexps.put(pattern,p);
                times.put(pattern,
                    new Long(System.currentTimeMillis()));
            } catch (Exception e) {}
        }
```

Listing 13.2 An efficient implementation of RegexpLike *(continued)*

```
        if(p != null) {
            Perl5Matcher m = new Perl5Matcher();
            return m.matches(value,p);
        }

        return false;
    }

    private static Long fiveMinutes =
        new Long(1000*60*5);

    public void run() {
        while(true) {
            try {Thread.sleep(fiveMinutes.longValue());}
            catch (Exception e) {}

            Long now =
                new Long(System.currentTimeMillis());

            Iterator i = regexps.entrySet().iterator();

            while(i.hasNext()) {
                Object o = i.next();
                Long l   = (Long) times.get(o);

                if(fiveMinutes.longValue() <
                   (now.longValue() - l.longValue()))
                {
                    regexps.remove(o);
                    times.remove(o);
                }
            }
        }
    }
}
```

The `like()` method starts an auxiliary thread if it is not already running. It then looks for the pattern in the `regexps` hashtable, and if not found it creates the pattern and a timestamp. Once every five minutes, the auxiliary thread cleans out all patterns that were created more than five minutes ago.

13.5 Beyond This Book

Although all of the tools discussed provide roughly equivalent capabilities, they all do so in slightly different ways. Try all three and decide which best fits your requirements and personal taste. Once one has been chosen, it is best to stick with it; it would be greatly inefficient for different members of a team to use different packages.

Regardless of the tool used, it is worth taking some time to learn the theory behind regular expressions, finite state machines, and similar formalism from computer science. Besides being a fascinating topic in its own right, it will help developers learn how to think about problems in new ways and use relevant tools more efficiently.

13.6 Summary

Tool: ORO
Purpose: Regular expressions
Version covered: 2.0.8
Home page: http://jakarta.apache.org/oro/
License: The Apache Software License, Version 1.1

Tool: Jakarta regexp
Purpose: Regular expressions
Version covered: 1.3
Home page: http://jakarta.apache.org/regexp/
License: The Apache Software License, Version 1.1

Tool: Java regexp
Purpose: Regular expressions
Version covered: 1.4.1
Home page: N/A, included with Java

Further Reading:

- *Introduction to Automata Theory, Languages, and Computation*, 2/e, by John E. Hopcroft, Rajeev Motwani, and Jeffrey D. Ullman, Addison-Wesley, 2001—Contains lots of information about regular expressions and finite state machines.
- The POSIX standards committee: http://www.pasc.org/.

CHAPTER 14

Working with Text 2: Searching

Chapter 13 discussed one common approach to working with text, defining a structure through a language called regular expressions and checking an input against this structure. One application of this approach is finding portions of text from a collection that meet a certain precisely defined criteria.

A very common related problem is finding documents from within a large collection that meet a less precisely defined requirement—for example, finding all Web pages that discuss JavaServer Pages or finding all e-mails from John Smith. This is called a **text search** or **free text search** to enforce the idea that the desired text is "free" to appear anywhere in the documents.

Text searches could be tackled by the tools discussed in Chapter 13. The `Egrep` tool could be used to examine a set of Web pages for the pattern "JavaServer\W*pages" or e-mails for the pattern "John\W*Smith." This approach is so inefficient as to be worthless for anything beyond a small set of documents. First, the full power of regular expressions is wasted on simple patterns consisting of two static strings. Second, every character of every document has be be examined to determine which ones contain the patterns. This is a tremendously slow operation by computer standards.

A better approach in this case would be to construct an **index** containing every significant word or phrase that appears in every document, along with a reference indicating which documents contain each word. There are a great deal of issues with this approach: determining what constitutes "significant," arranging the index itself for efficiency, and so on. These problems have been extensively studied by both companies and academic computer scientists, and although general approaches are well-understood, implementations of these approaches have tended to be proprietary, expensive, or both.

All that changed with the introduction of Lucene, accurately described on its home page as "a high-performance, full-featured text search engine written entirely in Java." Lucene is able to create indices based on unstructured text and structured fields that may exist within or outside documents. Lucene also supports a query language and APIs to search through the indices in sophisticated ways. Finally, it is possible to extend Lucene to work with arbitrary document types including XML, HTML, and indeed any file type for which a parser can be written.

14.1 Creating Indices

Indices are concerned with two things: the objects being indexed and the object that will extract useful data from each of these objects. Objects to be indexed are generically called **documents** and are encapsulated by the `Document` class. Classes that extract data from documents are called **analyzers.**

Documents are collections of **fields** implemented as instances of the `Field` class. A field consists of a name and a value. The value may be free text or a static string. Any field may be stored in the index, and any field may be indexed for searching. These are independent decisions; it is possible to have a field that is indexed and not stored, or stored and not indexed.

Indexed fields may be searched—for example, the `Document` representing a Web page might have a searchable field for the page body and another for the title. It would then be possible to search for pages where the title contains "lucene" and the body contains "create index."

Stored fields are available as the result of a search. The Web page `Document` might have a stored field for the URL so that after a search, the location of the page is readily available. Note that the title might be stored, but the body probably would not be because doing so would make the index huge. Thus, even though it is would be possible to search for bodies containing given text, to display that body, it would be necessary to access the file via the stored URL.

The `Field` class contains a number of static methods that create fields of various types. `UnIndexed()` creates a field that is stored but not indexed. There are a few variations of the `Text()` method, including one that creates a stored and indexed static string and one that takes a `Reader` and creates a field that will be indexed based on the data read but will not be stored. A number of these variations are used in Listing 14.1, which shows a class that constructs `Document` instances suitable for storing information about files. The `Document` class is `final`; otherwise Listing 14.1 would likely extend it.

Listing 14.1 A simple container for File information

```
package com.awl.toolbook.chapter14;

import java.io.*;
import org.apache.lucene.document.*;

public class FileDocument {
    public static Document makeDocument(File f)
        throws IOException
    {
        Document d = new Document();

        // Stored and indexed
        d.add(Field.Text("path", f.getPath()));

        // Stored and indexed
        d.add(Field.Keyword("lastModified",
                            DateField.timeToString(
                                f.lastModified())));

        // Stored, not indexed
        d.add(Field.UnIndexed("length",
                              Long.toString(f.length())));

        // Indexed, not stored
        d.add(Field.Text("contents",
                         new FileReader(f)));

        return d;
    }
}
```

The `path` and `lastModified` fields are stored and indexed. The `DateField.timeToString()` method converts a date into a form that can be lexigraphically ordered, ensuring that searches on date fields are meaningful.

An analyzer's job is to convert the fields in a document into streams of **tokens.** A token may be thought of as a single word, although in general the issue is more complex. When indexing XML or HTML documents, for example, under some circumstances it might be useful to include tag names, under other circumstances it might not. Likewise, attribute values might be useful to index, but attribute names are less likely to be of use.

Tokenizing can be a complex process. When processing a binary format like Microsoft Word, a great many "words" will actually be sequences of control characters representing formatting information that should not be indexed. To properly index such a document, the tokenizer would need to be able to pull the text out from among the formatting and control information. There is a Jakarta tool called POI that is working toward this capability, and it will be discussed in Chapter 15. Future versions of Lucene will likely come with a tokenizer and analyzer that work with POI.

At the API level all an `Analyzer` must do is provide a `tokenStream()` method that takes as arguments the name of a field and a `Reader` from which the data will be obtained. This method should return an instance of a class that extends `TokenStream`. This class must provide a `next()` method that will return the next token, or `null` when there are no more tokens available. Lucene provides a `StandardTokenizer` that uses rules common to many European languages to split a stream into words.

Along with the `StandardTokenizer` there is a provided `StandardAnalyzer` class, which will be more than sufficient for a great many applications. In addition to using the words obtained from `StandardTokenizer`, `StandardAnalyzer` also discards **stop words,** common English words like "a" and "the" that are not useful for searching.[1]

The `TokenStream` and `Analyzer` are two of the three classes that are needed in order to create indices. The third class is `IndexWriter`, which is provided as part of Lucene and does not need to be extended. `IndexWriter` is initialized with the name of the index to create, an analyzer, and a flag indicating whether a new index should be created or an existing one should be opened for appending.

Listing 14.2 shows a program that will create an index from a collection of files and directories specified on the command line.

Listing 14.2 A simple program to index files

```
package com.awl.toolbook.chapter14;

import java.io.File;
import java.io.IOException;
```

[1]Readers familiar with how compilers work may note interesting parallels between the lexing and parsing phases, and tokenziers and analyzers. In both there is a first a step that determines what the symbols are and a second that determines what they mean.

```
import org.apache.lucene.analysis.standard.*;
import org.apache.lucene.analysis.Analyzer;
import org.apache.lucene.index.IndexWriter;


public class SimpleIndex {
    public static void main(String[] args)
        throws Exception
    {
        SimpleIndex indx = new SimpleIndex();

        for(int i=0;i<args.length;i++) {
            indx.addToIndex(new File(args[i]));
        }

        indx.close();
    }

    private int count   = 0;
    private IndexWriter indexWriter = null;

    public SimpleIndex()
        throws Exception
    {
        Analyzer analyzer = new StandardAnalyzer();

        File f = new File("index");
        if(f.exists()) {
            indexWriter = new IndexWriter("index",
                                          analyzer,
                                          true);
        } else {
            indexWriter = new IndexWriter("index",
                                          analyzer,
                                          false);
        }
    }

    public void close() throws IOException {
        System.out.println("");
```

Listing 14.2 A simple program to index files *(continued)*

```
        System.out.println("Indexed " + count +
                           " documents");
        indexWriter.optimize();
        indexWriter.close();
    }

    public void addToIndex(File f)
        throws Exception
    {
        if(f.isDirectory()) {
            String[] files = f.list();

            for(int i=0;i<files.length;i++) {
                addToIndex(new File(f, files[i]));
            }
        } else {
            indexWriter.addDocument(
                FileDocument.makeDocument(f));
            count++;
            if(count % 100 == 0) {
                System.out.print(count + "...");
            }
        }
    }
}
```

`main()` simply creates an instance of `SimpleIndex` and passes each of the arguments to `addIndex`. The name used to create the index—`index` in this case—names a directory, and several files will be created in this directory. The constructor for `SimpleIndex` checks whether there is already an index contained in the `index` directory. If so, it opens the index for appending; if not, it creates a new index.

The single most important line in the program is the call to

```
indexWriter.addDocument(FileDocument.createDocument())
```

First, a new `Document` is created, and the various fields are initialized. When this is passed to `indexWriter`, each of the fields will be examined. Fields that are not indexed will be written into the index verbatim. Those fields that are indexed will be passed to the `BasicAnalyzer`, which will use `BasicTokenStream` to split the field into tokens, each of which will be added to the index.

After all the documents have been processed, the index is optimized and closed, making it ready for use.

14.2 Using Indices

Searching is handled by an instance of the `IndexSearcher` class, which is constructed with the name of the index to use. To prepare a program to use the index constructed in the preceding section, it would just be necessary to do the following:

```
Searcher searcher = new IndexSearcher("index");
```

Details about the search to perform are encapsulated in objects that extend the base `Query` class. There are numerous ways to obtain such a `Query`, which will be examined shortly.

Assuming a `Query` has been obtained, performing the search and processing the results are straightforward. The `Query` is passed to the `IndexSearcher`, which returns a `Hits` object. This object provides methods to obtain the number of matching documents and the documents themselves. Methods are also available to obtain a **score,** a number representing how well each document matches the given query. The documents obtained from the `IndexSearcher` are closely related to the documents that were originally given to the `indexWriter.addDocument()` method, except that nonstored fields are not available. These ideas are illustrated in the following code snippet:

```
Hits hits = searcher.search(query);
int len   = hits.length();

System.out.println("Found " + len + " documents");

for(int i = 0; i < len; i++) {
    Document doc = hits.doc(i);
    System.out.println(i + ". " +
                       doc.get("path") +
                       " (" + hits.score(i) + ") " +
                       "Length:" + doc.get("length") +
                       " Modified:" + doc.get("lastModified"))
}
```

Queries may be constructed programmatically or through a user-friendly query language that can be parsed into a query. The programmatic method will be presented first.

The most basic kind of query searches for the occurrence of a word in a field. This is done through use of an auxiliary class called a `Term`. For example, to search for all documents whose contents contain the word "jakarta"

```
Term term   = new Term("contents","jakarta");
Query query = new TermQuery(term);
```

Closely related to `TermQuery` is `PhraseQuery`, which looks for a sequence of terms in order. The following will search for the phrase "lucene makes searching easy" in file contents:

```
Query query = new PhraseQuery();
query.add(new Term("contents","lucene"));
query.add(new Term("contents","makes"));
query.add(new Term("contents","searching"));
query.add(new Term("contents","easy"));
```

Note that each call to `add()` appends the `Term` to the end. Also note that this is *not* equivalent to

```
Query query =
    new TermQuery(
        new Term("contents","lucene makes searching easy"));
```

This is because the `BasicTokenStream` splits contents into individual words, and it is these words that are indexed. While it is certainly possible to create a tokenizer that splits fields into sentences or larger units, this was not done in the example, and therefore there is no single token that contains the entire phrase. Consequently, a search on the whole phrase with a single `TermQuery` will return zero results.

There is also a `WildcardQuery` that can search for terms with a limited regular expression syntax. A question mark in a term represents a single letter, and an asterisk represents any number of letters.

```
Query query = new WildcardQuery(
                  new Term("contents","?oose"));
```

will find all documents containing any of "moose," "goose," and so on. Similarly,

```
Query query = new WildcardQuery(
                  new Term("contents","m*se"));
```

will find documents with "moose," "muse," and so on. Note that this only matches single tokens, so documents containing "my nose" will not match.

There is also a `FuzzyQuery` that matches words that are "somewhat like" the given term. The exact algorithm by which this is done is beyond the scope of this book, but the intent is to catch common misspellings. The best way to get a feel for how this works is to try it by experimenting with the code provided in this chapter.

Finally, there is a `RangeQuery` that matches all terms in a given range. This may be used on text fields, as well as dates.

```
Query query = new RangeQuery(
                  new Term("contents","oa"),
                  new Term("contents","oz"),
                  true);
```

will match all documents that contain any word starting with the letter "o." The first argument in the constructor is the lower bound, the second is the upper bound, and the last is a flag indicating whether the search should be inclusive. Note that this is equivalent to `WildCardQuery("o*")`.

```
Query query = new RangeQuery(
                  new Term("lastUpdated","20020301"),
                  new Term("lastUpdate","20020331"),
                  true);
```

will match documents that were last modified in March of 2002.

Each of these is an **atomic** query meaning it places a single restriction on a single field. Atomic queries may be combined into `BooleanQueries` to express more complex searches such as documents containing two terms or documents created in a certain time range that do not contain a certain term.

A `BooleanQuery` is initially created empty:

```
BooleanQuery bq = new BooleanQuery();
```

Any query may be made part of a `BooleanQuery` by calling the `add()` method. This method takes three arguments: the query, a flag indicating whether the query must match a document in order for the document to be included in the results of the search, and another flag indicating whether then query must *not* match in order for the document to be included in the results. Adding two required queries, as in

```
nested.add(new TermQuery("contents","java"),
           true,
           false);
```

```
nested.add(new TermQuery("contents","linux"),
           true,
           false);
```

means that returned documents must contain both "java" and "linux." All queries added with the required flag set to `true` are therefore logically connected by boolean `AND`.

Adding a query with the "forbidden" flag set to true will remove matching documents. Adding the following lines to the preceding ones

```
bq.add(new RangeQuery(
           new Term("lastUpdated","20020601"),
           new Term("lastUpdate","20020631"),
           true),
       false,
       true);
```

will result in the retrieval of documents containing "java" and "linux" except those created in June 2002. Queries added in this way are thus logically connected by boolean `AND NOT` operators.

Clearly a condition cannot be both required and forbidden, and so it is an error to set both flags to `true`. However, a condition can be neither required nor forbidden, in which case it is optional. If all the queries added to a `BooleanQuery` have neither flag set, then at least one query must match for a document to be included in the results. Such queries are therefore connected by boolean `OR`.

```
nested.add(new PhraseQuery("contents","java search tool"),
           false,
           false);

nested.add(new TermQuery("contents","lucene"),
           false,
           false);
```

will find documents containing either the phrase "java search tool," the word "lucene," or both.

Any query can be added into a `BooleanQuery`, including other `BooleanQueries`. This allows complex logical expressions to be constructed, as in

```
BooleanQuery bq = new BooleanQuery();

bq.add(new TermQuery("contents","java"),
       true,
       false);

bq.add(new RangeQuery(
           new Term("lastUpdated","20021201"),
           new Term("lastUpdate","20021231"),
           true);

BooleanQuery nested = new BooleanQuery();

nested.add(new TermQuery("contents","linux"),
           false,
           false);

nested.add(new TermQuery("contents","windows"),
           false,
           false);

bg.add(nested,true,false);
```

which represents a search for documents that were last modified between December 1, 2002, and December 31, 2002, and that contain the word "java" along with either "linux," "windows," or both.

Programmatically building queries allows rules to be specified precisely, but it can be rather limiting. Typically search application do not hard-code the search parameters but allow the end user to enter them interactively. Writing a query as a sequence of Java statements makes it impossible to support this kind of interactivity. For that reason Lucene supports a **query language** with a simple user-friendly syntax that can be easily parsed into a query.

Term queries are represented as the name of the field to search, followed by a colon, followed by the term. For example,

```
contents:java
```

or

```
lastUpdated:20030301
```

When the search is performed on a field specified as the default, the name of the field can be omitted.

Queries with wildcards are automatically handled as `WildCardQueries`, such as `m?se` or `octo*`.

Phrase queries are indicated by quotation marks around the phrase, such as

```
title:"how to use lucene"
```

Queries can be grouped with parentheses and can be connected by logical operators `AND`, `OR`, and `NOT`.

```
java AND (linux OR windows) AND NOT title:"installing"
```

would search for documents containing "java" and either "linux" or "windows" in the default field, omitting documents with "installing" in the title.

Logical constraints can also be specified with the + and – modifiers. A + before a term, phrase, or other clause requires that term just as setting the required flag to `true`. Likewise, a - requires that a term not be present, just as setting the forbidden flag to `true`.

The preceding example is therefore equivalent to

```
+java (linux windows) -title:installing
```

Note that `linux` and `windows` have no modifiers; this is because the default operator is `OR`.

A field specifier can precede a group, so

```
title:(lucene OR search)
```

means the same as

```
(title:lucene OR title:search)
```

Fuzzy matches are indicated by a tilde (~) following the word, as in `lucene~`. Adding a number after the tilde effects the "degree" of fuzziness; `lucene~10` will match documents with words that are further from "lucene" than `lucene~4`.

Range queries are indicated with the word `TO` and enclosed in brackets, as in `modifiedDate:[20030101 TO 20030201]` or `title:[aardvark TO ant]`.

Programs can support the query language with two lines of code. A static `parse()` method in the `QueryParser` class takes care of all the hard work. This method takes a string representing the query to be parsed, the name of the default field, and an `Analyzer`, which will usually be the same one with which the index was built.

```
Analyzer analyzer = new BasicAnalyzer();
Query query = QueryParser.parse(line, "contents", analyzer);
```

The resulting query can be used as normal. Listing 14.3 shows a complete search application that takes as an argument a search expression and returns the list of matching documents.

Listing 14.3 A simple search application

```
package com.awl.toolbook.chapter14;

import org.apache.lucene.analysis.Analyzer;
import org.apache.lucene.analysis.standard.*;
import org.apache.lucene.document.Document;
import org.apache.lucene.queryParser.QueryParser;
import org.apache.lucene.search.*;

public class BasicSearch {
    public static void main(String[] args)
        throws Exception
    {
        Searcher searcher = new IndexSearcher("index");
        Analyzer analyzer = new StandardAnalyzer();
        Query query       = QueryParser.parse(args[0],
                                              "contents",
                                              analyzer);

Hits hits = searcher.search(query);
        int len   = hits.length();

System.out.println("Found " + len + " documents");

        for(int i = 0; i < len; i++) {
            Document doc = hits.doc(i);
            System.out.println(i + ". " +
                  doc.get("path") +
                  " (" + hits.score(i) + ") " +
                  "Length:" + doc.get("length") +
                  " Modified:" + doc.get("lastModified"));
        }
    }
}
```

Note that Listing 14.3 expects the entire search expression as the first argument. In most shells this will mean putting single or double quotes around compound expressions.

14.3 Indexing Web Pages

Lucene is useful for searching through many kinds of documents in addition to flat files stored on local disks. One particularly important example is searching Web pages, and a tool for indexing such pages will be developed in this section. Although this tool poses no threat to companies like Google, it is nonetheless useful for indexing a small to medium-sized intranet or Web site.

The first step in developing an index application is the `Analyzer`. In particular, the first consideration should be whether the `StandardAnalyzer` meets the needs of the project. In this case the answer is "no" because the Web index should omit tags and attributes. This means a custom `Analyzer` and custom `TokenStream` will be needed.

The analyzer is straightforward and is shown in Listing 14.4.

Listing 14.4 A simple analyzer

```
package com.awl.toolbook.chapter14;

import java.io.*;
import org.apache.lucene.analysis.Analyzer;
import org.apache.lucene.analysis.TokenStream;

public class WebAnalyzer extends Analyzer {
    public TokenStream tokenStream(String fieldName,
                                   Reader in)
    {
        char data[] = new char[2048];
        int count   = 0;
        StringBuffer buffy = new StringBuffer();

        try {
            while((count = in.read(data)) > 0) {
                buffy.append(new String(data,0,count));
            }
        } catch (Exception e) {
```

```
                System.err.println("Error reading: " + e);
            }

            return new WebTokenStream(buffy.toString());
        }
    }
```

Essentially all that Listing 14.4 does is assemble a string containing all the data and pass that string to a `WebTokenizer`. This tokenizer handles extracting text from the page, and it is shown in Listing 14.5.

Listing 14.5 A token stream that uses regexps

```
package com.awl.toolbook.chapter14;

import org.apache.lucene.analysis.TokenStream;
import org.apache.lucene.analysis.Token;
import org.apache.oro.text.regex.*;

public class WebTokenStream extends TokenStream {
    private Pattern tagPattern;
    private Pattern wordPattern;
    private PatternMatcherInput input;
    private PatternMatcherInput wordInput;
    private Perl5Matcher tagMatcher;
    private Perl5Matcher wordMatcher;

    private int baseOffset = 0;

    public WebTokenStream(String data) {
        try {
            Perl5Compiler compiler = new Perl5Compiler();
            tagPattern = compiler.compile("<[^>]*([^<]*)",
                         Perl5Compiler.SINGLELINE_MASK);

            wordPattern = compiler.compile("[\\W*]",
                         Perl5Compiler.SINGLELINE_MASK);

            input      = new PatternMatcherInput(data);
            tagMatcher = new Perl5Matcher();
```

Listing 14.5 A token stream that uses regexps *(continued)*

```
        } catch (MalformedPatternException e) {}
    }

    public Token next() {
        // Phase two - look for a word
        if(wordMatcher != null) {
            if(wordMatcher.contains(wordInput,
                                    wordPattern))
            {
                MatchResult r = wordMatcher.getMatch();
                return new Token(
                           r.toString().toLowerCase(),
                           baseOffset + r.beginOffset(0),
                           baseOffset + r.endOffset(0));
            } else {
                wordMatcher = null;
            }
        }

        // Phase one - look for blocks of words among tags
        if(tagMatcher.contains(input,tagPattern)) {
            MatchResult r = tagMatcher.getMatch();
            wordInput     =
                    new PatternMatcherInput(r.group(1));
            baseOffset    = r.beginOffset(1);
            wordMatcher   = new Perl5Matcher();
            return next();
        } else {
            return null;
        }
    }

    public void close() {}
}
```

Note the use of the ORO regular expression package, covered in Chapter 13. Here two patterns are used: `tagPattern`, which separates contiguous sequences of characters that do not contain a < from surrounding tags, and `wordPattern`, which separates sequences of word character from surrounding whitespace. Tokenizing will be a two-phase process: In the first phase each tag will be skipped, producing a block of text, and in the second that text will be split into words.

The process is implemented in the `next()` method. The `wordMatcher` is used as a flag; if it is not null, then the program is in phase two, looking for words within text. In this case the `tagMatcher` looks for the next instance of a word, and if found, a token is constructed and returned.

Note that tokens are converted to lowercase. When searches are performed, the search terms will also be converted to lowercase, which will make them effectively case-insensitive. Without this search terms would have to exactly match the case of the original text. This might be desirable in certain specific applications, but in most situations case-insensitive searches are better.

When tokens are created, they are given the position of the word in the document as well as the word itself. This information is constructed from the `baseOffset` which is the offset into the document of the sequences of words found in phase one, plus the offset of the current word within that block. In principal, this offset information could be used to pinpoint the location of terms found in a search, which in turn could be used to highlight those words when the document is shown to the end user. However, there is no API provided that exposes this functionality in a useful way. Some third-party additions to Lucene have sprung up to fill this gap. See the "Summary" section at the end of this chapter.

If `wordMatcher` does not find another word, `wordMatcher` is set to `null` and the method continues to phase one. Here the `tagMatcher` is used to find the next block of text that has no tags. If no such block is found, the method returns `null`, indicating that there are no more tokens. If a block of words is found, the `wordInput` and `wordMatcher` are set up and `next()` is called again. This will return control to the top of the method, which will once again look for a word in the current block.

The `WebTokenizer` and `WebAbnalyzer` could be used in a program like Listing 14.1 to create an index of Web pages stored in local files. It is more interesting to index pages that are out on the Internet, however. This is typically done by starting from one page and then following all links from that page to find others. Such a program is called a **spider,** because it walks across the Web. Listing 14.6 shows a simple spider. This spider starts from a specified URL and will stop when either a specified number of pages have been found or it has reached a specified depth. Depth here is defined as "the number of clicks necessary to reach the page from the starting page."

Normally, looking for links within Web pages requires some tedious programming, but we have already seen a tool that solves this problem: WebUnit, discussed in Chapter 5. While this is primarily intended to help unit test Web pages, it also happens to be an HTML parser and so can easily be adapted. Likewise, CLI from Chapter 12 can be used to handle arguments to the program such as maximum depth and number of pages, as well as generate help messages. Listing 14.6 is thus an excellent example of many toolkits working together to make programming faster and easier.

Note!

Before the code is presented, a disclaimer is necessary. Using this program on any site other than your own will likely be considered very bad behavior. Production-quality spiders as used by major search engines respect a number of established conventions to ensure they do not unduly burden remote sites. None of these features is supported in this simple example.

Listing 14.6 A Web indexer

```
package com.awl.toolbook.chapter14;

import java.util.HashMap;
import java.util.List;
import java.io.IOException;
import java.io.File;

import org.apache.lucene.document.*;
import org.apache.lucene.index.IndexWriter;
import org.apache.lucene.analysis.Analyzer;
import org.apache.commons.cli.*;
import com.meterware.httpunit.*;

public class WebIndex {
    private int maxDepth = 3;
    private int maxPages = 100;
    private int pages    = 0;
    private HashMap visitedPages = new HashMap();
    private IndexWriter indexWriter = null;

    private String[] args;
    public String[] getArgs() {return args;}
    public void setArgs(String[] args) {this.args = args;}
```

```
private static Options makeOptions() {
    Options options = new Options();

    options.addOption(OptionBuilder
     .withDescription("maximum depth to descend")
     .withLongOpt("max-depth")
     .create('d'));

    options.addOption(OptionBuilder
     .withDescription(
         "maximum number of pages to index")
     .withLongOpt("max-pages")
     .create('n'));

    return options;
}

public static void usage(Options options) {
    HelpFormatter formatter = new HelpFormatter();
    formatter.printHelp(
        "WebIndex [OPTION] url",
        options,
        true);
}


public static void main(String args[]) {
    WebIndex w = new WebIndex(args);
    w.run();
}

public WebIndex() {}

public WebIndex(String args[]) {
    setArgs(args);
}
```

Listing 14.6 A Web indexer *(continued)*

```
    public void run() {
        try {
            doRun();
        } catch (Exception e) {}
    }

    private void doRun() throws Exception {
        // Create the indexWriter
        Analyzer analyzer = new WebAnalyzer();

        File f = new File("webIndex");
        if(f.exists()) {
            indexWriter = new IndexWriter("webIndex",
                                          analyzer,
                                          true);
        } else {
            indexWriter = new IndexWriter("webIndex",
                                          analyzer,
                                          false);
        }

        // process the arguments, which will also start
        // indexing at the top page
        processArgs();

        // close and cleanup
        close();
    }


    public void close() throws IOException {
        indexWriter.optimize();
        indexWriter.close();
    }


    public void processArgs() {
        // Parse the arguments, if there's an error
        // report usage
```

```
        Options options = makeOptions();
        CommandLineParser parser = new BasicParser();
        CommandLine cmd = null;

        try {
            cmd = parser.parse(options,args);
        } catch (ParseException e) {
            System.err.println(e.getMessage());
            usage(options);
            System.exit(-1);
        }

        if(cmd.hasOption('d')) {
            maxDepth = Integer.parseInt(
                           cmd.getOptionValue('d'));
        }

        if(cmd.hasOption('n')) {
            maxPages = Integer.parseInt(
                           cmd.getOptionValue('n'));
        }

        List others = cmd.getArgList();

        try {
            indexPage(others.get(0).toString(),0);
        } catch (Exception e) {
            System.err.println("Unable to index: " + e);
        }
    }

    public void indexPage(String url, int depth)
        throws Exception
    {
        WebConversation wc = new WebConversation();
        WebRequest      req = new GetMethodWebRequest(url);
        WebResponse    resp = wc.getResponse(req);
```

Listing 14.6 A Web indexer *(continued)*

```
        visitedPages.put(url,Boolean.TRUE);
        Document doc = new Document();
        doc.add(Field.Text("title",resp.getTitle()));
        doc.add(Field.Text("url",
                           resp.getURL().toString()));

        doc.add(Field.Text(
                  "description",
                  arrayToString(
                      resp.getMetaTagContent("name",
                                             "description"))));

        doc.add(Field.UnStored(
                  "keywords",
                  arrayToString(
                      resp.getMetaTagContent("name",
                                             "keywords"))));


        doc.add(Field.UnStored("body",resp.getText()));

        indexWriter.addDocument(doc);

        if(depth < maxDepth) {
            WebLink links[] = resp.getLinks();
            int newDepth    = depth+1;

            for(int i=0;i<links.length;i++) {
                String newUrl = links[i].getURLString();
                if(visitedPages.get(newUrl) == null  &&
                   pages < maxPages)
                {
                    indexPage(newUrl,newDepth);
                    pages++;
                }
            }
        }
    }
```

```
    private String arrayToString(String in[]) {
        StringBuffer buffy = new StringBuffer();
        for(int i=0;i<in.length;i++) {
            buffy.append(in[i]);
            buffy.append(' ');
        }

        return buffy.toString();
    }
}
```

The beginning portions of Listing 14.6 are responsible for processing options. The real fun starts in the `indexPage` method, which adds a page to the index. First, an HTTPUnit `WebConversation` is used to load the page, and the results are captured in a `WebResponse`. After the page is loaded, an entry is put in the `visitedPages HashMap`. This will be used to ensure that no page is visited twice, which is a likely possibility; many pages on a site are likely to link back to the same index page, for example.

Next, a new `Document` is constructed, and fields are added to it. The title and URL are simple fields that are stored and indexed. The keyword and content metadata are also indexed if they are available. Note that the `getMetaTagContent()` returns an array of results; these are all concatenated into a single string for indexing purposes. Also note that the description is stored, but the keywords are not. Likewise, the body of the page is indexed but not stored. The `getText()` method does nothing to strip out tags from the text, but that is not a problem because it will be handled by the `WebAnalyzer`. The document is then added to the index in the standard way.

If the current depth is less than the maximum depth, then the links are obtained from the page with the `getLinks()` method. A check is done to determine whether these links are in `visitedPages`. If so, or if the total number of pages has exceeded the maximum, the link will not be processed.

The index built by `WebIndex` can be searched by a program very similar to the `BasicSearch` program from Listing 14.2. The name of the the index directory would need to be changed from `index` to `WebIndex`, and the name of the retrieved fields would also need to be modified. A better solution would be to allow the name of the index and retrieved fields to be specified on the command line.

14.4 Beyond This Book

Lucene is useful in any application that manages large quantities of text, whether this text is in local files, remote files, or even in a database. In the database case Lucene could be used to search through clobs, as discussed in Chapter 10, and this search could be exposed as a enhanced `like` method, such as the `patternLike` used in Chapter 13.

The `Document` mechanism is a flexible one and need not correspond exactly to a file, URL, or database row. A document could span several files by including a field that lists the component documents. Alternately a document could consist of a single mail message in a file containing an archive of many such messages by including fields containing the start and end lines.

General free text search is a surprisingly powerful capability, and some thought may suggest ways in which it can enhance any number of applications.

14.5 Summary

Tool: Lucene
Purpose: Free text searches
Version covered: 1.4
Home page: http://jakarta.apache.org/lucene/docs/index.html
License: The Apache Software License, Version 2.0

Further Reading:

- http://home.clara.net/markharwood/lucene/highlight.htm—An add-on tool that supports highlighting keywords based on offset information.
- http://www.iq-computing.de—Another such tool with a different approach. Note that this site is in German.

CHAPTER 15

Creating Office Documents with POI

For good or ill, Microsoft office documents have become a de facto standard, especially in the business world. There are a number of free and open source editors that can read and write Word documents, and there are free and open source spreadsheet tools available that can similarly handle files in Excel format. None of these tools is quite complete, but many come fairly close. Of particular interest is OpenOffice from http://www.openoffice.org.

Although these tools can be very useful to end users who need to read or create Office documents, Office offers other important capabilities to programmers. Specifically, Office components can be controlled and queried through visual basic and other languages. This opens up a world of possibilities. Typically company data is stored in a database, ensuring that it is centrally available and allowing for sophisticated queries. It would often be useful to import this data into Excel for presentations, specific kinds of research, or to prepare graphs and charts. Using a script, Excel could be automatically invoked, told to create a new spreadsheet and import the data from the database. The same principal works in reverse; an employee on the road might populate a spreadsheet on a laptop, and the data in that spreadsheet could be imported into the database once he or she returns to the office.

Other possibilities include using a Word document as a template and importing timely data to prepare executive summaries. All the formatting could be removed from an uploaded Word document to prepare a plain-text version that could be indexed with a tool like Lucene, covered in Chapter 14. The list goes on and on.

As useful as these capabilities are, they are limited by being available only on Windows, requiring a full installation of Office, and not being available to Java developers. This is where POI[1] comes in. POI provides 100 percent pure Java APIs to create, access, and modify Office documents.

> **Note!**
>
> A caveat is needed here: POI, like the open source Office alternatives mentioned earlier, are designed to work with Office 97 through 2000. Microsoft has recently introduced a new XML-based format for Office documents. This may make writing Office-compatible programs easier, harder, or impossible—at this point it is hard to tell. In addition, Microsoft is in the process of adding DRM—which officially stands for "digital rights management," although many free and open source software developers believe "digital restrictions management" is more apt—to the Office suite. Depending on how this is deployed, it is possible that, in combination with the DMCA (digital millennium copyright act, a U.S. law passed in 1998), it may become a federal crime in the United States to even attempt to create a program that will read such files.
>
> This is a complex legal issue, well beyond the scope of this book. However, the question of what developers and end users may do with files written by closed source programs goes right to the heart of many of the principles of open source software. Interested readers are encouraged to familiarize themselves with these issues and draw their own conclusions.

15.1 POIFS

At the base of the POI APIs is the "POI file system," or POIFS, which provides a Java implementation of the OLE 2 Compound Document Format. OLE 2 is an archive format, conceptually much like JAR files. Both provide a way of combining hierarchical data into a single file, a concept that maps naturally to a file system.

POIFS presents a compound document as a series of `DirectoryEntry` and `DocumentEntry` objects. There is a special top-level or **root** directory,

[1] POI originally stood for "Poor Obfuscation Implementation," a reference to the developers' disdain for what they perceived as the poor quality of the OLE 2 Compound Document Format that underlies all Office documents. References to this acronym have been removed from current versions of the POI site, and POI should now be considered simply a name that does not necessarily mean anything.

obtainable through the `getRoot()` method. The `DirectoryEntry` class has a `getEntries()` method that returns an `Iterator`, which can be used to walk through all the children of a directory. `DocumentEntry` objects do not have children, but an `InputStream` can be obtained to read the contents of such an entry.

Listing 15.1 illustrates these principles by displaying some or all of the entries within an archive or displaying the contents of a particular document. The first argument should be the name of a Word or Excel file. The OLE 2 format is used for many other files besides Office documents, and Listing 15.1 will happily handle these as well. Although the rest of this chapter is concerned only with Office, it may be informative to run this program on various application files to discover which are secretly OLE 2 archives and, if so, what their contents are.

The second argument to Listing 15.1 is optional; if present it should be the name of an entry in the archive. If this name refers to a `DirectoryEntry`, only elements within that directory will be displayed. If the name refers to a `DocumentEntry`, the contents of that document will be displayed.

Listing 15.1 A tool for examining POI filesystems

```
package com.awl.toolbook.chapter15;

import java.io.FileInputStream;
import java.util.Iterator;
import org.apache.poi.poifs.filesystem.*;


public class POIDump {
    public static boolean found = false;
    public static String  name  = ".";

    public static void main(String argv[])
        throws Exception
    {
        FileInputStrcam in =
            new FileInputStream(argv[0]);

        POIFSFileSystem fs =
            new POIFSFileSystem(in);

        DirectoryEntry root = fs.getRoot();
```

Listing 15.1 A tool for examining POI filesystems *(continued)*

```
        if(argv.length > 1) {
            name = argv[1];
        } else {
            found = true;
        }

        dump(root,0);
    }

    public static void dump(Entry e, int depth)
        throws Exception
    {
        String entryName  = e.getName();

        entryName = entryName.replace((char) 1,'?');
        entryName = entryName.replace((char) 5,'?');

        boolean foundHere = name.equals(entryName);

        found = found || foundHere;

        if(found) {
            for(int i=0;i<depth;i++) {
                System.out.print('.');
            }
        }

        if(e instanceof DirectoryEntry) {
            if(found) {
                System.out.println(entryName + '/');
            }

            DirectoryEntry d = (DirectoryEntry) e;

            for(Iterator i=d.getEntries();i.hasNext();) {
                Entry entry = (Entry) i.next();
                dump(entry,depth+1);
            }
```

```
            if(foundHere) {
                found = false;
            }
        } else if (e instanceof DocumentEntry) {
            if(found) {
                if(!foundHere) {
                    System.out.println(entryName);
                } else {
                    DocumentEntry doc = (DocumentEntry) e;
                    DocumentInputStream in =
                        new DocumentInputStream(doc);
                    byte data[] = new byte[2048];
                    int count   = 0;

                    while((count = in.read(data)) > 0) {
                        System.out.print(
                            new String(data,0,count));
                    }
                    System.out.println("");
                    in.close();

                    found = false;
                }
            }
        } else {
            System.out.println("Unknown: " + e.getClass());
        }
    }
}
```

The `main()` method starts everything off by opening the specified file as an `InputStream` and creating a `POIFSFileSystem` from that stream. The root directory is obtained via the `getRoot()` method and then dumped.

The `dump()` method obtains the name of the current entry. The next two lines clean the output by substituting a question mark for control characters, which are common in entry names. `foundHere` indicates whether the current entry matches the second argument to the program, and `found` indicates whether the second argument has been found anywhere yet. If the target has been found, leading dots are printed to indicate the depth of the current entry within the archive.

If the current entry is a `DirectoryEntry`, additional formatting may be done, and then all the child entries are handled recursively by passing them in turn to `dump()`.

If the current entry is a `DocumentEntry`, and if it is the one the user is looking for as indicated by `foundHere`, then a `DocumentInputStream` is obtained and used to display the contents in the usual way.

At present, a POIFS can only contain objects of type `DirectoryEntry` and `DocumentEntry`, but the documentation cautions that other types may be introduced in the future. This is why there is a final `else` in dump; should such a future enhancement be discovered, at least it can be reported.

Running Listing 15.1 on a typical Word document produces the following output:

```
Root Entry/
.WordDocument
.?SummaryInformation
.?DocumentSummaryInformation
.1Table
.ObjectPool/
.?CompObj
```

Running Listing 15.1 on an Excel file produces

```
Root Entry/
.?SummaryInformation
.?DocumentSummaryInformation
.Workbook
```

Filesystems are recursive, and so recursive algorithms like that in Listing 15.1 are often natural. They may not always be the most efficient or easiest to program, however. Consequently POIFS provides an alternate **event-driven** API that uses the Java event/listener pattern. Classes may implement the `POIFSReaderListener` interface and register themselves with a `POIFSReader`. When a class registers itself, it may also indicate the document in which it is interested. When a matching document is encountered by the `POIFSReader`, the `processPOIFSReaderEvent()` method of the `POIFSReaderListener` will be invoked with a `POIFSReaderEvent` object containing information about the document, as well as a means to get the `DocumentInputStream`. Note there is no directory event and hence no way for a listener to be informed when a directory is encountered.

The disadvantage of the event-driven API is that the set of listeners must be specified before reading begins. This means there is no way for a program to decide that a certain document may be of interest based on the presence or absence of another document or directory. On the other hand, the event-driven API is more efficient because it avoids having to load the entire filesystem into memory. The only objects loaded will be those that have been registered as of interest.

Listing 15.2 shows the event API in action.

Listing 15.2 A tool for examining POI filesystems

```
package com.awl.toolbook.chapter15;

import java.util.StringTokenizer;
import java.io.FileInputStream;

import org.apache.poi.poifs.filesystem.*;
import org.apache.poi.poifs.eventfilesystem.*;

public class EventDemo implements POIFSReaderListener {
    boolean dump = false;

    public EventDemo() {}

    public EventDemo(boolean dump) {
        this.dump = dump;
    }

    public void processPOIFSReaderEvent(
                   POIFSReaderEvent event)
    {
        if(!dump) {
            String name = event.getPath() +
                event.getName();

            name = name.replace((char) 1,'?');
            name = name.replace((char) 5,'?');

            System.out.println("Document event: " + name);
```

Listing 15.2 A tool for examining POI filesystems *(continued)*

```
        } else {
            DocumentInputStream in = event.getStream();
            byte data[] = new byte[2048];
            int count   = 0;

            try {
                while((count = in.read(data)) > 0) {
                    System.out.print(
                        new String(data,0,count));
                }
            } catch (Exception e) {}
            System.out.println("");
        }
    }

    public static void main(String args[])
        throws Exception
    {
        POIFSReader reader = new POIFSReader();

        if(args.length == 1) {
            reader.registerListener(new EventDemo());
        } else {
            POIFSReaderListener listener =
                new EventDemo(args[1].equals("true"));

            for(int i=2;i<args.length;i++) {
                if(args[i].indexOf('/') == -1) {
                    reader.registerListener(
                        listener,args[i]);
                } else {
                    StringTokenizer st =
                        new StringTokenizer(args[i],"/");
                    int count     = st.countTokens();
                    String path[] = new String[count-1];

                    for(int j=0;j<count-1;j++) {
                        path[i] = st.nextToken();
                    }
```

```
                    String name = st.nextToken();

                    reader.registerListener(
                        listener,
                        new POIFSDocumentPath(path),
                        name);
                }
            }
        }

        FileInputStream in =
            new FileInputStream(args[0]);

        reader.read(in);
        in.close();
    }
}
```

The `EventDemo` class implements the `POIFSReaderListener` and provides the necessary `processPOIFSReaderEvent()` method. This method uses the `dump` flag to determine whether to display the document's name or dump the contents.

The `main()` method creates a `POIFSReader` and then checks the program arguments. If there is only one argument, it is assumed to be the name of a file. In that case, an instance of `EventDemo` with `dump=false` is created and configured to receive all events. This is done with the call to `registerListener()` with no arguments other than the `EventDemo`.

If there are multiple arguments, the second is taken to be a boolean flag indicating whether documents should be dumped, and an `EventDemo` is created appropriately.

The remaining arguments are taken to be either the names of documents in the root directory or complete document paths with directories separated by slashes (/). The `EventDemo` is configured to listen for simple file names via the call to `registerListener()` that takes the file name as the second argument. Arguments representing full paths are broken into components by the `StringTokenizer` and used to create a `POIFSDocumentPath`. This object is then used in the final call to `registerListener()`. Running this program on the same Word document as used in the preceding example produces:

```
Document event: /?SummaryInformation
Document event: /?DocumentSummaryInformation
```

```
Document event: /WordDocument
Document event: /?CompObj
Document event: /1Table
```

Running the program with additional arguments of `false WordDocument` produces, as expected

```
Document event: /WordDocument
```

It is tempting to look at the outputs from these two programs and then attempt to run `POIdump` to retrieve the contents of the `WordDocument` entry in the hopes of extracting the text contained within the document. Such curiosity is a good trait in a developer, and the facility to view a `DocumentEntry` has been added specifically to satisfy such curiosity.

While it is true that `WordDocument` is the `DocumentEntry` that contains the text, it also contains a great deal of formatting and other information. It may or may not be possible to pick out the text from the control codes, depending on a number of factors.

This is not a deficiency in POIFS. Just as the `java.util.jar` package provides the means to extract a JPEG image from a jar archive but can not itself display the image, POIFS can extract the elements of an OLE compound document, but POIFS itself has no knowledge of what these pieces are or what they mean. This level of control must be handled by higher-level APIs, and these will be discussed shortly.

Before moving on to these higher-level APIs, there are additional features of POIFS that are worth discussing. First, APIs are provided to create new archives. These APIs work in a simple, logical way—directories are created with `createDirectory()` and documents with `createDocument()`, which uses an `InputStream` to obtain the data for the new document. The following code snippet shows how these APIs might be used:

```
POIFSFileSystem fs  = new POIFSFileSystem();
DirectoryEntry root = fs.getRoot();
InputStream data1   =
    new ByteArrayInputStream("This is data1".getBytes());
root.createDocument("data1",data1);

DirectoryEntry subdir =
    createDirectory("subdirectory");
InputStream data2   =
    new ByteArrayInputStream("This is data2".getBytes());
subdir.createDocument("data2",data2);
```

```
FileOutputStream out =
    new FileOutputStream("sample.ole");
fs.writeFilesystem(out);
```

Running `POIDump` on the result of this code would produce, as expected

```
Root Entry/
.data1
.subdirectory/
..data2
```

and running `POIDump sample.ole data2` would produce

```
This is data2
```

Like reading a POIFS, the ability to write a new file system is not immediately useful on its own. If the goal is to combine multiple files into a single file for storage or transmission, then JAR is a far better choice, because JAR files can be handled by existing zip utilities as well as the built-in `java.util.jar` package. Simply creating an OLE file whose document entries match those of an Excel spreadsheet will not result in a file that is readable by Excel. Once again, a higher-level API is needed. However, it is worth understanding the creation APIs because they are used by the higher levels.

15.2 Excel

The POI APIs for dealing with Excel files are collectively called HSSF.[2] APIs are provided to manipulate low-level Excel data structures, and much more convenient higher-level APIs for reading, writing, and modifying Excel files are also provided. All of this functionality rests on top of POIFS, and a tiny bit of knowledge of POIFS is necessary to begin an HSSF program.

The high-level APIs deal with conceptual entities that will be familiar to anyone who has used Excel. A workbook consists of many sheets, a sheet has many rows, and a row has many cells. Methods are provided to iterate through these collections, as well as address specific elements by number. This is illustrated in Listing 15.3, which displays all the data in a spreadsheet.

---

[2]HSSF originally stood for "Horrible Spreadsheet Format," but like the original acronym for POI, this has been downplayed because POI has put on a more professional face.

Listing 15.3 Using the high-level APIs

```
package com.awl.toolbook.chapter15;

import java.io.FileInputStream;
import java.util.Iterator;

import org.apache.poi.poifs.filesystem.*;
import org.apache.poi.hssf.usermodel.*;

public class ReadSpreadsheet {
    public static void main(String args[])
        throws Exception
    {
        FileInputStream in = new FileInputStream(args[0]);
        POIFSFileSystem fs = new POIFSFileSystem(in);
        HSSFWorkbook book  = new HSSFWorkbook(fs);

        int numSheets = book.getNumberOfSheets();
        for(int i=0;i<numSheets;i++) {
            HSSFSheet sheet = book.getSheetAt(i);
            System.out.println("Sheet: " + i);

            Iterator rows = sheet.rowIterator();

            while(rows.hasNext()) {
                HSSFRow row = (HSSFRow) rows.next();
                System.out.println(
                    "  Row #" + row.getRowNum());
                Iterator cells = row.cellIterator();
                while(cells.hasNext()) {
                    HSSFCell cell =
                        (HSSFCell) cells.next();

                    switch(cell.getCellType()) {
                        case HSSFCell.CELL_TYPE_BLANK:
                          System.out.println("    Blank");
                            break;
                        case HSSFCell.CELL_TYPE_FORMULA:
                            System.out.println(
```

```
                                    "    Formula: " +
                                    cell.toString());
                                break;
                            case HSSFCell.CELL_TYPE_NUMERIC:
                                System.out.println(
                                  "    Number: " +
                                  cell.getNumericCellValue());
                                break;
                            case HSSFCell.CELL_TYPE_STRING:
                                System.out.println(
                                    "    String: " +
                                    cell.getStringCellValue());
                                break;
                            default:
                                System.out.println(
                                "Unknown or unhandled type");
                                break;
                        }
                    }
                }
            }
        }
    }
```

At the lowest level, most of the classes comprising HSSF exactly parallel data structures specified in BIFF8, the underlying format of Excel data as specified in the *Microsoft Excel 97 Developer's Kit,* published by Microsoft Press (currently out of print). These data structures are called **records.** They are defined in the `org.apache.poi.hssf.record` package and subpackages. The base class for all of these is called `Record`, and there are 125 different subclasses of `Record` listed in the HSSF Javadocs.[3]

There is certainly not space in this book to document all of these subclasses, and in any case, many will be encountered only infrequently. Here are a few of the most common records.

[3]Only 98 of these classes are included in the most recent jar files. The remaining classes are probably not yet implemented.

- BOFRecord represents the beginning of any of several types of object within a spreadsheet. This has a type field indicating the type of object that may be TYPE_WORKBOOK, TYPE_VB_MODULE, TYPE_WORKSHEET, TYPE_CHART, TYPE_EXCEL_4_MACRO, or TYPE_WORKSPACE_FILE. The most important of these are TYPE_WORKBOOK, which contains the entire data portion of a spreadsheet, and TYPE_WORKSHEET, which indicates the start of a particular sheet.
- BoundSheetRecord defines a sheet within a workbook. This contains the name of the sheet and internal information about where in the document the data for the sheet lives.
- EOFRecord indicates the end of an object whose start was indicates with a BOFRecord. Objects are nested; a EOFRecord will always match the most recently encountered BOFRecord.
- RowRecord contains information about a particular row, including formatting data.
- SSTRecord contains a table of strings and other constants used within a sheet.
- BlankRecord contains information about a blank cell. This includes the row and column number of the cell as well as formatting information such as font, font size, and vertical and horizontal alignments. This same information is available for any Record that contains cell data, including the next four items.
- LabelSSTRecord contains an index into the table provided by the SSTRecord.
- LabelRecord is a read-only string used as a label. LabelSSTRecord is more common and more useful.
- NumberRecord contains a numeric value in a cell.
- FormulaRecord contains a formula within a cell. Formulae are stored in an internal compiled format, but the toString() method can usually convert this back into an expression that would be entered by a user.

Although it is possible to read an Excel spreadsheet directly by using these record objects, it is much more convenient to use the provided event-driven API. This is done by providing a class that implements the HSSFListener interface. This interface requires a processRecord() method that takes a Record as an argument. One or more of these listeners are added to a HSSFRequest, specifying the events in which they are interested. An instance of HSSFEventFactory is responsible for parsing the underlying data and invoking the appropriate listeners. The event API is demonstrated in Listing 15.4.

Listing 15.4 A program that dumps Excel records

```
package com.awl.toolbook.chapter15;

import java.io.*;

import org.apache.poi.poifs.filesystem.*;

import org.apache.poi.hssf.record.*;
import org.apache.poi.hssf.record.aggregates.*;
import org.apache.poi.hssf.eventusermodel.*;

public class SimpleReader implements HSSFListener {
    public void processRecord(Record record) {
        System.out.println("Found record " +
                           record.getClass().getName());
        System.out.println(record.toString());
    }

    public static void main(String[] args)
        throws Exception
    {
        FileInputStream in = new FileInputStream(args[0]);
        POIFSFileSystem fs = new POIFSFileSystem(in);
        InputStream workbook =
            fs.createDocumentInputStream("Workbook");

        HSSFEventFactory factory = new HSSFEventFactory();
        HSSFRequest req = new HSSFRequest();

        // Listen for all events with this class
        req.addListenerForAllRecords(new SimpleReader());

        factory.processEvents(req, workbook);

        in.close();
        workbook.close();
    }
}
```

	A	B	C	D	E	F	G
1	Code produced by team A				Code produced by team B		
2	Name	Classes	Lines		Name	Classes	Lines
3	Aardvark, Arthur	9	302		Bat, Beatrice	11	375
4	MacDude, Dude	6	276		Dingus, Dirkly	2	2
5	Octopus, Ophelia	8	256		Walrus, Wally	6	400
6							
7	Total	23	834			19	777
8	Average	7.67	278			6.33	259

Figure 15.1. A sample spreadsheet.

The `main()` method uses `createDocumentInputStream()`, discussed in the section on POIFS, to obtain the `Document` containing the spreadsheet data. The rest of the method directly follows the preceding discussion.

Figure 15.1 shows a simple spreadsheet tracking developing for two teams. The total and average columns are all given by formulas. When `SimpleReader` is run on this spreadsheet, it produces a surprising 210 records, and the information dumped in the `toString()` representation of these records comprises 3074 lines.

The next issue that must be addressed is how to handle different record types in the `processRecord()` method. The `Record` base class defines a `sid`, a numeric ID that uniquely identifies each subclass. Each subclass also has a corresponding static `sid`. Therefore, if a method accepts an argument of type `Record`, it can determine whether the argument is really of a particular subtype—say, `BOFRecord`—by checking

```
if(record.getSid() == BOFRecord.sid) {
    System.out.println("It is a BOFRecord");
}
```

Readers who have programmed in C may recognize this pattern as C-style `structs` and `unions`. Indeed, the Microsoft specifications define these structures in C terms, and the POI team has translated these into Java in the cleanest and most straightforward way possible. This means that typical code to handle `Record` objects also resembles C code:

```
switch (record.getSid()) {
    case RowRecord.sid:
        RowRecord rowrec = (RowRecord) record;
        ... handle the row record ...
        break;
```

```
        case NumberRecord.sid:
            NumberRecord numrec = (NumberRecord) record;
            ... handle the number record ...
            break;

        ... other cases ...
    }
```

Clearly, this is not very Java-like. An alternative would be to avoid the `sid` and work with classes directly, as in

```
    try {
        RowRecord rowrec = (RowRecord) record;
        ... handle the row record ...
        return;
    } catch (ClassCastException e) {}

    try {
        NumberRecord numrec = (NumberRecord) record;
        ... handle the number record ...
        return;
    } catch (ClassCastException e) {}
```

While this example looks more like standard Java, it is grossly inefficient because code may have to go through 124 attempted casts before getting to the right one.

In addition to these deficiencies, both approaches have the disadvantage of creating very long methods in which it may be difficult to find and isolate the clause that deals with a particular subclass of `Record`.

Provided with this book is a class called `HSSFDispatcher`[4] that attempts to remedy some of these problems. This class implements the `HSSFListener` interface and provides an implementation of `processRecord()` that uses a `switch` statement with a `case` for every `sid` in the 98 available records. Each clause of these `cases` casts the `Record` to the appropriate subtype and then passes it to a method whose name is the name of the subclass, prepended by the word "handle." All of these methods simply pass the `Record` to a method called `handleDefaultRecord()`,

[4]The `HSSFDispatcher` class is automatically generated by a bash script called `makeDispatcher.sh`, which is also included on the CD-ROM.

which does nothing. If the record passed to `processRecord()` does not match any known type, which may happen if later versions of POI added new record types, then the record is passed to `handleUnknownRecord()`, which also does nothing. A small portion of `HSSFDispatcher` is shown below:

```
package com.awl.toolbook.chapter16;

import org.apache.poi.hssf.record.*;
import org.apache.poi.hssf.record.aggregates.*;
import org.apache.poi.hssf.eventusermodel.HSSFListener;

public class HSSFDispatcher
    implements HSSFListener
{
    public void processRecord(Record record) {
        switch (record.getSid()) {
            case AreaFormatRecord.sid:
                handleAreaFormatRecord(
                    (AreaFormatRecord) record);
                break;
            case AreaRecord.sid:
                handleAreaRecord((AreaRecord) record);
                break;
            ... every other SID ...
            default:
                handleUnknownRecord(record);
                break;
        }
    }

    public void handleAreaFormatRecord(
                   AreaFormatRecord record)
    {
        handleDefaultRecord(record);
    }

    public void handleAreaRecord(AreaRecord record) {
        handleDefaultRecord(record);
    }
```

```
    ... Every other method ...

    public void handleDefaultRecord(Record record) {}
    public void handleUnknownRecord(Record record) {}
}
```

Programs wishing to use HSSF can extend `HSSFDispatcher` and override those methods that handle records of interest. `handleDefaultRecord()` can be overridden to catch any remaining records. This approach in used in Listing 15.5.

Listing 15.5 Using the dispatcher

```
package com.awl.toolbook.chapter15;

import java.io.*;

import org.apache.poi.poifs.filesystem.*;

import org.apache.poi.hssf.record.*;
import org.apache.poi.hssf.record.aggregates.*;
import org.apache.poi.hssf.eventusermodel.*;

public class ExcelReader
    extends HSSFDispatcher
{
    private SSTRecord sstrec = null;


    public void handleBOFRecord(BOFRecord bof) {
        if (bof.getType() == bof.TYPE_WORKBOOK) {
            System.out.println("Workbook found");
        } else if (bof.getType() == bof.TYPE_WORKSHEET) {
            System.out.println("Sheet reference found");
        }
    }

    public void handleSSTRecord(SSTRecord record) {
        sstrec = record;
    }
```

Listing 15.5 Using the dispatcher *(continued)*

```
public void handleMergeCellsRecord(
                MergeCellsRecord mcr)
{
    for(int i=0;i<mcr.getNumAreas();i++) {
        MergeCellsRecord.MergedRegion region =
            mcr.getAreaAt(i);
        System.out.println("Merged region, from (" +
                           region.row_from + "," +
                           region.col_from + ") to (" +
                           region.row_to + "," +
                           region.col_to + ")");
    }
}

public void handleBoundSheetRecord(
                BoundSheetRecord bsr)
{
    System.out.println("Found sheet named: " +
                       bsr.getSheetname());
}

public void handleRowRecord(RowRecord rowrec) {
    System.out.println("Row found, first column at "
                       + rowrec.getFirstCol() +
                       " last column at " +
                       rowrec.getLastCol());
}


public void handleNumberRecord(NumberRecord numrec) {
    System.out.println("(" + numrec.getRow() + "," +
                       numrec.getColumn() + "): " +
                       "number=" +
                       numrec.getValue());
}

public void handleFormulaRecord(FormulaRecord frec) {
    System.out.println("(" + frec.getRow() + "," +
```

```
                         frec.getColumn() + "): " +
                         "forumla=" +
                         frec.toString());
}

public void handleLabelSSTRecord(LabelSSTRecord lrec) {
    System.out.println("(" + lrec.getRow() + "," +
                         lrec.getColumn() + "): " +
                         "string=" +
                         sstrec.getString(
                             lrec.getSSTIndex()));
}


public void handleBlankRecord(BlankRecord blank) {
    System.out.println("(" + blank.getRow() + "," +
                         blank.getColumn() + "): blank");
}

public void handleDefaultRecord(Record rec) {
    if(rec instanceof CellValueRecordInterface) {
        System.out.println("Unhandled record type: " +
                             rec.getClass().getName());
    }
}

public void handleUnknownRecord(Record rec) {
    System.out.println("Unknown record type: " +
                         rec.getClass().getName());

}

public static void main(String[] args)
    throws Exception
{
    FileInputStream in = new FileInputStream(args[0]);
    POIFSFileSystem fs = new POIFSFileSystem(in);
    InputStream workbook =
        fs.createDocumentInputStream("Workbook");
```

Listing 15.5 Using the dispatcher *(continued)*

```
        HSSFEventFactory factory = new HSSFEventFactory();
        HSSFRequest req = new HSSFRequest();

        // Listen for all events with this class
        req.addListenerForAllRecords(new ExcelReader());

        factory.processEvents(req, workbook);

        in.close();
        workbook.close();
    }
}
```

Here is a partial list of the output from Listing 15.5:

```
Workbook found
Found sheet named: Sheet1
Found sheet named: Sheet2
Found sheet named: Sheet3
Sheet reference found
Row found, first column at 0 last column at 7
Row found, first column at 0 last column at 7
...
(0,0): string=Code produced by team A
(0,1): blank
(0,2): blank
(0,4): string=Code produced by team B
(0,5): blank
(0,6): blank
(1,0): string=Name
(1,1): string=Classes
(1,2): string=Lines
...
(4,0): string=Octopus, Ophelia
(4,1): number=8.0
(4,2): number=256.0
...
(6,0): string=Total
```

```
(6,3): blank
(6,4): blank
(7,0): string=Average
(7,3): blank
(7,4): blank
Merged region, from (0,0) to (0,2)
Merged region, from (0,4) to (0,6)
```

Note that no output is generated for the formula cells. This would appear to be a bug in the current version of POI as of the time of this writing. The expected value would be a `FormulaRecord`.

The implementation of `handleDefaultRecord()` will print out any record that implements `CellValueRecordInterface`, which is implemented by all records that contain values for cells. As nothing results from this method, it is clear that the formula cells are not being represented by an unexpected type of cell value. The `handleUnknownRecord()` method ensures that the formulas are not showing up as some unexpected type, thus confirming that they are currently being ignored by POI.

The `MergeCellsRecord` contains information about the groups of cells used for the banners. The handler for this record is included to illustrate the diversity in how particular types of information are stored. In particular, note that a single `MergeCellsRecord` contains information about all the groups throughout the sheet; there is not a different record for each group. Developers writing applications that need to respond to formatting will need to read the javadocs for many of the `Record` classes. Of course, a large category of applications will only be interested in data cells.

15.3 Creating Spreadsheets

The API to create spreadsheets is somewhat different from the one that reads spreadsheets. In some sense the creation API is a higher level API because it deals with conceptual entities such as cells and fonts instead of underlying implementation entities such as `Records`. The general technique for creating a spreadsheet is as follows:

1. Create a new `HSSFWorkbook` object.
2. Use the workbook object to obtain a new `HSSFSheet`.
3. Use the sheet object to obtain a new `HSSFRow`.
4. Use the row object to obtain a new `HSSFCell`.
5. Populate the cell's value and optionally its formatting.

Step 5 can be repeated to create multiple cells in a row, step 4 can be repeated to create multiple rows in a sheet, and so on. Listing 15.6 shows these ideas in action.

Listing 15.6 Creating a simple spreadsheet

```
package com.awl.toolbook.chapter15;

import java.io.FileOutputStream;
import org.apache.poi.hssf.usermodel.*;


public class MakeSpreadsheet {
    public static void main(String args[])
        throws Exception
    {
        FileOutputStream out =
            new FileOutputStream("sample.xls");
        HSSFWorkbook book = new HSSFWorkbook();
        HSSFSheet sheet = book.createSheet("Sheet 1");

        HSSFRow row   = null;
        HSSFCell cell = null;

        // Create the first row, with some headers
        row  = sheet.createRow((short) 0);

        cell = row.createCell((short) 0);
        cell.setCellValue("Name");

        cell = row.createCell((short) 1);
        cell.setCellValue("Value");

        // Create the second row with some values
        row  = sheet.createRow((short) 1);

        cell = row.createCell((short) 0);
        cell.setCellValue("A");

        cell = row.createCell((short) 1);
        cell.setCellValue(88.8);
```

```
            // Create the third row with some values
            row  = sheet.createRow((short) 2);

            cell = row.createCell((short) 0);
            cell.setCellValue("B");

            cell = row.createCell((short) 1);
            cell.setCellValue(67.90);

            // Create the fourth row with a total
            row  = sheet.createRow((short) 3);

            cell = row.createCell((short) 0);
            cell.setCellValue("Total");

            // Not yet implemented
            // cell = row.createCell((short) 1);
            // cell.setCellFormula("b2 + b3");

            // Save and close
            book.write(out);
            out.close();
        }
    }
```

This is a bit tedious but straightforward and effective. After running Listing 15.6, `sample.xls` will contain the spreadsheet shown in Figure 15.2

It is of interest to note that when SimpleReader from Listing 15.4 is run on this spreadsheet, 100 records are reported. This dramatically illustrates the fact that records are a lower-level structure than cells, and it highlights the advantages of using

	A	B
1	Name	Value
2	A	88.8
3	B	67.9
4	Total	

Figure 15.2. The spreadsheet created by Listing 15.6.

a cell-based API for creating new spreadsheets. It must also be noted that Listing 15.2 reports a RecordFormatException after reading the last EOFRecord, possibly indicating some skew between the underlying reading and writing code.

15.3.1 Formatting

All of the formatting features available through Excel are also available through the APIs, although using them often requires a lot of code. Most formatting is done through the creation of HSSFCellStyle instances that contain information about fonts, colors, borders, and so on. These are then assigned to cells.

For example, to make the "name" and "value" labels created by Listing 15.6 bold, blue, 16 points, and centered both vertically and horizontally, the style would first be created with the following code:

```
HSSFCellStyle style = book.createCellStyle();
HSSFFont font       = book.createFont();

font.setFontHeightInPoints((short) 16);
font.setColor(HSSFColor.BLUE.index);
font.setBoldweight(HSSFFont.BOLDWEIGHT_BOLD);

style.setFont(font);
style.setAlignment(style.ALIGN_CENTER);
style.setVerticalAlignment(style.VERTICAL_CENTER);
```

Both labels would then be set to use this style with

```
cell.setCellStyle(style);
```

In addition, to accommodate the larger font, the row should be made taller. This can be done with an operation on the row that takes a size in a unit called "twips," equivalent to 1/20th of a point.

```
row.setHeight((short) 0x249);
```

It is also possible to add borders, although once again the process is somewhat tedious. To enclose the whole region, the "name" cell needs borders at the top and left, and the "value" cell needs borders at the top and right. This means they can no longer use the same HSSFCellStyle, even though their styles are otherwise identical. Likewise, the "A" and "B" cells need borders only on the left and the numbers only on the right. The bottom cells need borders on the left and bottom, and right and bottom, respectively. This means different HSSFCellStyles must be created. Borders are

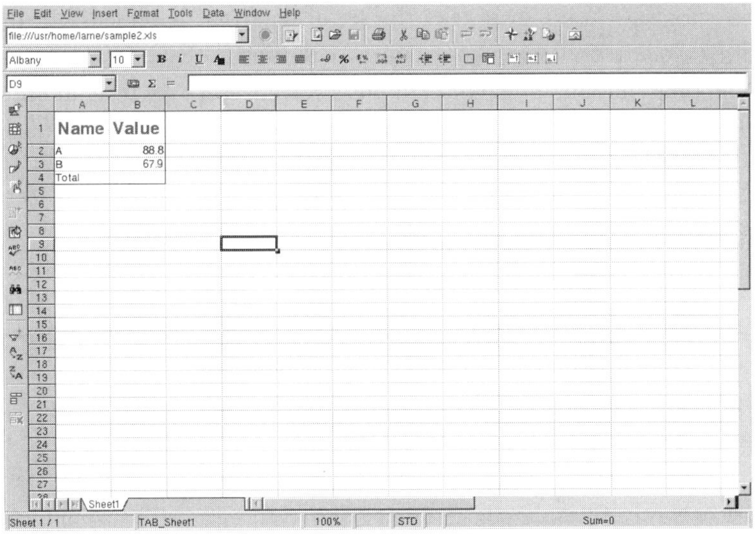

Figure 15.3. The spreadsheet with some formatting.

added to styles with various `setBorder()` methods; for example, the following specifies the borders for the "name" cell:

```
style.setBorderLeft(style.BORDER_THICK);
style.setBorderTop(style.BORDER_THICK);
```

With these additions to Listing 15.6 the generated spreadsheet will resemble Figure 15.3.

15.4 Templating

Doing formatting from within code can require a great deal of effort, as the preceding section illustrated. A better solution would be to take the formatting from an existing spreadsheet and have the program populate any necessary data. This idea is called **templating.** An end user can create a template from within Excel, adding a few special values that the program will use to determine how data should be formatted. When this template is processed, all formatting will be copied from the rows and cells with these special values, and data will be provided from an external source.

The most useful place from which data could be drawn is a database, and the easiest way to access a database is through OJB, the object-relational mapping tool discussed in Chapter 10. To use OJB the user must specify a class to populate. The program will allow the name of this class to be specified on either the command line or in the first cell of the first row of the template sheet.

A user may also want to restrict the set of data that is pulled into the sheet. This will be done by allowing constraints in the form of name/value pairs to be specified on the command line. For example, a spreadsheet may contain information about a CD collection, populated from the tables used in examples in Chapter 10. Specifying

```
com.awl.toolbook.chapter10.Artist
```

as the class name will populate the sheet with information about all artists, and adding `name="Unto Ashes"` on the command line will restrict the data retrieved to just that artist, his or her albums, the tracks on those albums, and so on.

Next, syntax is needed to allow users to indicate how retrieved data should be placed in the spreadsheet. The convention will be that a string preceded and followed by two octothorps (#) will be considered a **token**[5] and will be taken to be the name of a property of the object. So using the `Artist` bean `##name##` would refer to the artist's name.

Using this scheme, `##albums##` would refer to the whole array of albums. Although this doesn't make sense as the value for a single cell, it makes perfect sense as a collection over which to repeat a set of rows. To clarify the scope of such iterations, start and end markers must be used and must be placed in the first column of rows. In this case these markers will be `##BEGIN:albums##` and `##END:albums##`. Every row between the rows with these markers will be repeated once for each album. Within that scope tokens will refer to the current album, so `##name##` will refer to the album name, not the artist name. In addition, within this region `##tracks##` will be available to iterate over the set of tracks. A sample template is shown in Figure 15.4.

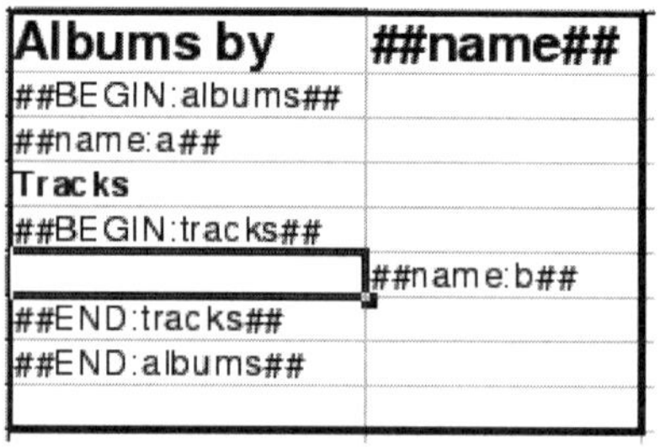

Albums by
##name##
##BEGIN:albums##
##name:a##
Tracks
##BEGIN:tracks##
##name:b##
##END:tracks##
##END:albums##

Figure 15.4. A spreadsheet template.

[5]This convention follows one that was used at CapitalThinking and is due to Raphael Thiney.

Errors to Watch For

As of this writing there is a bug in POI that makes it throw a `NullPointerException` if two cells have identical string values. This is obviously a problem for the template, where artists, albums, and tracks all have a field that would be addressed as `##name##`. As a workaround for this bug, a colon and arbitrary string may be appended to a name, such as `##name:a##`. The colon and whatever follows it will be ignored.

Because the template engine is large, it will presented over several Listings. Listing 15.7 shows the prelude, including the all-important imports.

Listing 15.7 Imports

```
package com.awl.toolbook.chapter15;

import java.io.FileInputStream;
import java.io.FileOutputStream;
import java.util.List;
import java.util.Iterator;
import java.beans.Beans;

// BeanUtils
import org.apache.commons.beanutils.PropertyUtils;

// POI
import org.apache.poi.poifs.filesystem.*;
import org.apache.poi.hssf.usermodel.*;

// OJB
import org.apache.ojb.broker.PersistenceBroker;
import org.apache.ojb.broker.PersistenceBrokerFactory;
import org.apache.ojb.broker.query.Criteria;
import org.apache.ojb.broker.query.Query;
import org.apache.ojb.broker.query.QueryByIdentity;
import org.apache.ojb.broker.query.QueryByCriteria;

// CLI
import org.apache.commons.cli.*;
```

Listing 15.7 Imports *(continued)*

```
// Log4J
import org.apache.log4j.*;

public class TemplateProcessor {
    private Logger logger =
        Logger.getLogger(
         "com.awl.toolbook.chapter15.TemplateProcessor");
```

As mentioned, POI will be used to handle the spreadsheet manipulation, and OJB will be used to talk to the database. Because OJB presents data as an object tree, a means to retrieve individual fields from these objects is needed. BeanUtils from Chapter 8 provides this functionality exactly. In addition, CLI will be used as in previous chapters to handle command-line arguments and help messages. Finally, this program will handle many complex situations, so it's a good idea to log its progress so log4j is also imported. The first thing this class will do when constructed is get a logger for use throughout the class.

Listing 15.8 shows the option-handling code.

Listing 15.8 Option handling

```
private static Options makeOptions() {
    Options options = new Options();

    options.addOption(OptionBuilder
     .withDescription(
         "New sheet name (default=result)")
     .hasArg()
     .withArgName("sheet name")
     .withLongOpt("sheet-name")
     .create('n'));

    options.addOption(OptionBuilder
     .withDescription("Input file")
     .hasArg()
     .withArgName("input file")
     .isRequired()
     .withLongOpt("input-file")
     .create('i'));
```

```
        options.addOption(OptionBuilder
         .withDescription(
             "Output file (default=output.xls)")
         .hasArg()
         .withArgName("output file")
         .withLongOpt("output-file")
         .create('o'));

        options.addOption(OptionBuilder
         .withDescription("name of db class")
         .hasArg()
         .withArgName("class name")
         .withLongOpt("class-name")
         .create('c'));

        options.addOption(OptionBuilder
            .withArgName("property=value")
            .hasArg()
            .withValueSeparator()
            .withDescription(
                "Set a constraint in the DB object")
            .create("D"));

        return options;
    }

    public static void usage(Options options) {
        HelpFormatter formatter = new HelpFormatter();
        formatter.printHelp(
            "TemplateProcessor",
            options,
            true);
    }

    private String inputFileName;
    public String getInputFileName() {
        return inputFileName;
    }
```

Listing 15.8 Option handling *(continued)*

```
public void setInputFileName(String inputFileName) {
    this.inputFileName = inputFileName;
}

private String outputFileName = "output.xls";
public String getOutputFileName() {
    return outputFileName;
}
public void setOutputFileName(String outputFileName) {
    this.outputFileName = outputFileName;
}

private String sheetName = "result";
public String getSheetName() {return sheetName;}
public void setSheetName(String sheetName) {
    this.sheetName = sheetName;
}

private String className = null;
public String getClassName() {return className;}
public void setClassName(String className) {
    this.className = className;
}

private String[] constraints = new String[0];
public String[] getConstraints() {return constraints;}
public void setConstraints(String[] constraints) {
    this.constraints = constraints;
}

public void processArgs(Options options,String args[])
    throws Exception
{
    CommandLineParser parser = new BasicParser();
    CommandLine cmd = null;
```

```
    try {
            cmd = parser.parse(options,args);
    } catch (Exception e) {
        logger.error("Unable to parse command line",e);
        throw e;
    }

    if(cmd.hasOption('n')) {
        String val = cmd.getOptionValue('n');
        logger.info("Set sheet name from args: " +
                    val);
        setSheetName(val);
    }

    if(cmd.hasOption('c')) {
        String val = cmd.getOptionValue('c');
        logger.info("Set class name from args: " +
                    val);
        setClassName(val);
    }

    if(cmd.hasOption('o')) {
        String val = cmd.getOptionValue('o');
        logger.info("Set output file from args: " +
                    val);
        setOutputFileName(val);
    }

    if(cmd.hasOption('i')) {
        String val = cmd.getOptionValue('i');
        logger.info("Set input file from args: " +
                    val);
        setInputFileName(val);
    }

    if(cmd.hasOption('D')) {
        setConstraints(cmd.getOptionValues('D'));
    }
}
```

Listing 15.8 follows patterns established previously. `makeOptions()` creates an `Options` object, and `usage()` uses this object to display a help message to the user. Next there are a number of properties that will be set from the command line. These are exposed as bean properties to make it easier for other programs to invoke `TemplateProcessor`. `processArgs()` processes the arguments and builds a `CommandLine`. Options are also logged.

Next, Listing 15.9 shows `main()` and other top-level processing.

Listing 15.9 Top-level processing

```
public TemplateProcessor() {}

public static void main(String args[])
    throws Exception
{
    Options options = makeOptions();
    TemplateProcessor t = new TemplateProcessor();

    try {
        t.processArgs(options,args);
    } catch (ParseException e) {
        usage(options);
        System.exit(-1);
    }

    t.process();
    System.exit(0);
}

public void process() throws Exception {
    logger.info("starting processing");

    FileInputStream in =
        new FileInputStream(inputFileName);
    POIFSFileSystem fs = new POIFSFileSystem(in);
    HSSFWorkbook book  = new HSSFWorkbook(fs);
    HSSFSheet sheet    = book.getSheetAt(0);
    HSSFSheet newSheet = book.createSheet(sheetName);

    short firstRow   = (short) sheet.getFirstRowNum();
    short lastRow    = (short) sheet.getLastRowNum();
```

```
    copySheetProperties(sheet,newSheet);

    if(className == null) {
        className = getDBClassName(sheet,firstRow++);
        logger.info("Got class name from sheet " +
                    className);
    }

    Iterator iter    = getDBObjectIterator();

    while(iter.hasNext()) {
        logger.info("Processing block");

        processBlock(iter.next(),
                  sheet,
                  newSheet,
                  (short) (firstRow),
                  lastRow);
    }

    FileOutputStream out =
        new FileOutputStream(outputFileName);
    book.write(out);
    out.close();
}

private String getDBClassName(HSSFSheet sheet,
                              short firstRow)
{
    HSSFRow row = sheet.getRow(firstRow);
    return getFirstCellText(row);
}

private void copySheetProperties(HSSFSheet oldSheet,
                                 HSSFSheet newSheet)
{
    logger.debug("Copying sheet properties");
```

Listing 15.9 Top-level processing *(continued)*

```
try {
    for(int i=0;
        i<oldSheet.getNumMergedRegions();
        i++)
    {
        newSheet.addMergedRegion(
            oldSheet.getMergedRegionAt(i));
        logger.debug("Copied merge region " + i);
    }
} catch (Exception e) {
    logger.warn("getNumMergedRegions threw null");
}

newSheet.setDefaultColumnWidth(
    oldSheet.getDefaultColumnWidth());

newSheet.setDefaultRowHeight(
    oldSheet.getDefaultRowHeight());

// newSheet.setHeader(oldSheet.getHeader());
// newSheet.setFooter(oldSheet.getFooter());

// Copy the column widths
HSSFRow row = oldSheet.getRow(
                    oldSheet.getFirstRowNum());

short firstCell = row.getFirstCellNum();
short lastCell  = row.getLastCellNum();

for(short cellNum=firstCell;
    cellNum<lastCell;
    cellNum++)
{
    HSSFCell cell = row.getCell(cellNum);

    if(cell == null) {
        continue;
    }
```

```
            short width = oldSheet.getColumnWidth(cellNum);

            logger.debug("Set width of field " + cellNum +
                         " to " + width);

            if(width > 100) {
                newSheet.setColumnWidth(
                               cellNum,
                               width);
            }
        }
    }
```

main() constructs a TemplateProcessor, has it evaluate the arguments, and then starts everything off by calling process().

process() opens the input file and gets the HSSFWorkbook, and from there the first sheet that will be assumed to be the template. process() also creates a new sheet, which will hold the populated template. Note that the output file will contain both the template sheet and the result. This is because a great deal of formatting and other information is stored with the workbook, and rather than copy all this into a new book, it is easier to create a new sheet that will automatically be able to use all this information.

Various properties of the template sheet are then copied into the new one. As can be seen from copySheetProperties(), these consist of such things as the merged regions and default sizes. The size of each cell is also copied, although this requires examining each cell in the first row. The header and footer are commented out in this method because they do not exist, despite being listed in the POI javadocs. Presumably they will be added in a future release.

Returning to process(), after the sheet has been set up, the set of objects is obtained with a call to getDBObjectIterator(), which will be shown following. For now just note that this method returns an iterator over a set of the class specified, matching any constraints that were specified. For each of these objects, processBlock() is called to populate a segment of the sheet. processBlock() is shown in Listing 15.10.

Listing 15.10 Processing a block

```
private void processBlock(Object obj,
                          HSSFSheet sheet,
                          HSSFSheet newSheet,
                          short firstRow,
                          short lastRow)
```

Listing 15.10 Processing a block *(continued)*

```
{
    for(short rowNum=firstRow;
        rowNum<=lastRow;
        rowNum++)
    {
        HSSFRow row = sheet.getRow(rowNum);

        if(row == null) {
            logger.warn("Row " + rowNum + " is null");
            continue;
        }

        String iterateStart = getStartFlag(row);
        boolean endMarker   = isEndMarker(row);

        if(endMarker) {
            // do nothing
        } else if(iterateStart != null) {
            logger.debug(
                "Found start of an iteration: " +
                iterateStart);

            short endRow =
                findLastIterateRow(sheet,
                                   iterateStart,
                                   rowNum,
                                   lastRow);

            logger.debug("End of iteration at " +
                         endRow);

            Object iterateObjects = null;

            try {
                iterateObjects =
                    PropertyUtils.getProperty(
                    obj,
                    iterateStart);
```

```
        logger.debug(
            "Found iteration objects");
    } catch (Exception e) {
        logger.error(
            "Unable to get iteration objects",
            e);
    }

    try {
        Object objArray[] =
            (Object[]) iterateObjects;

        for(int i=0;i<objArray.length;i++) {
            processBlock(objArray[i],
                         sheet,
                         newSheet,
                         (short) (rowNum+1),
                         (short) (endRow-1));
        }
        rowNum = (short) (endRow);
    } catch (ClassCastException e) {
        logger.info(
          "Object collection is not an array");
    }

    try {
        List objList =
            (List) iterateObjects;

        Iterator iter = objList.iterator();
        while(iter.hasNext()) {
            processBlock(iter.next(),
                         sheet,
                         newSheet,
                         (short) (rowNum+1),
                         (short) (endRow-1));
        }
        rowNum = (short) (endRow);
    } catch (ClassCastException e) {
```

Listing 15.10 Processing a block *(continued)*

```
                logger.info(
                    "Object collection is not a list");
            }



        } else {
            HSSFRow newRow =
                newSheet.createRow(nextRow++);

            processRow(obj,row,newRow);
        }
    }
}
```

`processBlock()` iterates over a set of rows from the original sheet. First, it uses `getStartFlag()` to determine whether the current row starts an iteration—that is, whether the first cell in the row looks like `##BEGIN:##`. If it is, then `iterateStart` will be set to the name of the variable over which to iterate—for example, `tracks`. Similarly, `isEndMarker()` determines whether the current row is the end of an iteration.

End markers are simply skipped, so they do not end up in the result sheet.

If the current row is a start marker, then the corresponding end row is found. Then `PropertyUtils` from BeanUtils is used to obtain the set of objects. Currently this may take the form of either an array or a `List`, and both these options are examined and handled. Note that in either case `proccessBlock` will be called recursively. Because iterations can be nested arbitrarily, this is appropriate.

If the current row is neither the start nor the end of an iteration block, then it is a normal row and is handled by `processRow()`, which is shown in Listing 15.11.

Listing 15.11 Processing a single row

```
public short nextRow=0;

private void processRow(Object obj,
                        HSSFRow row,
                        HSSFRow newRow)
{
    logger.debug("Processing a row");

    newRow.setHeight(row.getHeight());
```

```
        short firstCell = row.getFirstCellNum();
        short lastCell  = row.getLastCellNum();

        for(short cellNum=firstCell;
            cellNum<=lastCell;
            cellNum++)
        {
            HSSFCell cell = row.getCell(cellNum);

            if(cell == null)
                continue;

            HSSFCell newCell = newRow.createCell(cellNum);
            processCell(obj,cell,newCell);
        }
    }

    private void processCell(Object obj,
                             HSSFCell cell,
                             HSSFCell newCell)
    {
        logger.debug("Processing a cell");

        newCell.setCellStyle(cell.getCellStyle());

        switch(cell.getCellType()) {
            case HSSFCell.CELL_TYPE_BLANK:
                break;
            case HSSFCell.CELL_TYPE_FORMULA:
                logger.warn("Formula found");
                break;
            case HSSFCell.CELL_TYPE_NUMERIC:
                logger.debug("Copying numeric value");
                newCell.setCellValue(
                             cell.getNumericCellValue());
                break;
            case HSSFCell.CELL_TYPE_STRING:
                String val = cell.getStringCellValue();
                if(val.startsWith("##") &&
                   val.endsWith("##"))
```

Listing 15.11 Processing a single row *(continued)*

```
{
    int pos = val.indexOf(':');
    if(pos == -1) {
        pos = val.length()-2;
    }

    String prop  = val.substring(2,pos);

    logger.debug("Processing variable: " +
                 prop);

    Object value = null;

    try {
        value =
            PropertyUtils.getProperty(obj,
                                     prop);
        logger.debug("Found value: " +
                     value);
    } catch (Exception e) {
        logger.error("Unable to get value",
                     e);
        newCell.setCellValue("ERR");
    }

    if(value == null) {
        newCell.setCellValue("");
    } else if(value instanceof Number) {
        newCell.setCellValue(
          ((Number) value).doubleValue());
    } else {
        newCell.setCellValue(
            value.toString());
    }
} else {
    newCell.setCellValue(val);
}
```

```
                break;
            default:
                System.out.println(
                    "Unknown or unhandled type");
                break;
        }
    }
```

`processRow()` itself is simple; it just iterates over the set of cells by calling `processCell()`. `processCell()` determines the type of the cell and copies simple types into a new cell in the new row. If a cell contains a string, and the string looks like a token, then `PropertyUtils` is once again used to obtain the value.

That completes the major functionality of `TemplateProcessor`. Each of a set of objects is handled by `processBlock()`, which will repeatedly call `processRow()` to manage row data, which in turn will call `processCell()` to copy or populate each cell. The only remaining major piece is to to get the initial data used by `process()`, and this is shown in Listing 15.12.

Listing 15.12 Loading data

```
private Iterator getDBObjectIterator()
    throws Exception
{
    PersistenceBroker broker = null;

    try {
        broker =
            PersistenceBrokerFactory.
                defaultPersistenceBroker();
    } catch (Exception t) {
        logger.fatal("Unable to get broker");
        throw t;
    }

    Class klass = null;

    try {
        klass = getClass().
            getClassLoader().
            loadClass(className);
    } catch (Exception e) {
```

Listing 15.12 Loading data *(continued)*

```
        logger.fatal("Unable to build DB object",e);
        throw e;
    }


    Criteria criteria = new Criteria();

    for(int i=0;i<constraints.length;i++) {
        int pos       = constraints[i].indexOf('=');
        String name   = constraints[i].substring(0,pos);
        String value = constraints[i].substring(pos+1);

        logger.debug("Setting constraint " +
                     name + " to " + value);

        criteria.addEqualTo(name,value);
    }

    Query query = new QueryByCriteria(klass,
                                      criteria);

    return broker.getIteratorByQuery(query);
}
```

Listing 15.12 is where all the OJB code lives. First, a `PersistenceBroker` is obtained in the usual way. Then the specified class is loaded. Next a `Constraints` object is constructed and populated from any constraints provided on the command line. In principal it would not be hard to extend this code to handle constraints such as greater-than and less-than in addition to equality. Finally, a `QueryByCriteria` is constructed, and the `broker` uses this to obtain the matching objects.

Finally, Listing 15.13 shows a number of utility methods.

Listing 15.13 Miscellaneous utilities

```
private String getStartFlag(HSSFRow row) {
    HSSFCell cell = row.getCell((short) 0);
    if(cell == null)
        return null;
```

```
        if(cell.getCellType() == HSSFCell.CELL_TYPE_STRING)
        {
            String val = cell.getStringCellValue();
            if(val.startsWith("##BEGIN:") &&
               val.endsWith("##"))
            {
                return val.substring(8,val.length()-2);
            }
        }

        return null;
    }

    private boolean isEndMarker(HSSFRow row) {
        String text = getFirstCellText(row);

        if(text == null) {
            return false;
        }

        if(text.startsWith("##END:") &&
           text.endsWith("##"))
        {
            return true;
        }

        return false;
    }

    private String getFirstCellText(HSSFRow row) {
        HSSFCell cell = row.getCell((short) 0);

        if(cell == null)
            return null;

        if(cell.getCellType() == HSSFCell.CELL_TYPE_STRING)

        {
            return cell.getStringCellValue();
        }
```

Listing 15.13 Miscellaneous utilities *(continued)*

```
    return null;
}

private short findLastIterateRow(HSSFSheet sheet,
                                 String property,
                                 short start,
                                 short end)
{
    String lookFor = "##END:" + property + "##";

    for(short rowNum=start;rowNum<=end;rowNum++) {
        HSSFRow row = sheet.getRow(rowNum);

        if(row == null) {
            continue;
        }

        HSSFCell cell = row.getCell((short) 0);
        if(cell == null) {
            continue;
        }

        if(cell.getCellType() ==
           HSSFCell.CELL_TYPE_STRING)
        {
            String val = cell.getStringCellValue();
            if(val.equals(lookFor)) {
                return rowNum;
            }
        }
    }

    return end;
}
```

When `TemplateProcessor` is run on the sample template from Figure 15.4, the result is the spreadsheet shown in Figure 15.5.

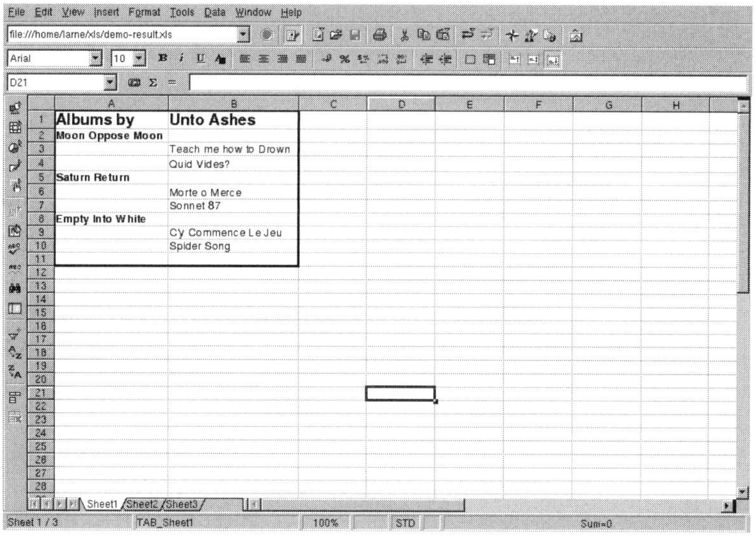

Figure 15.5. The populated spreadsheet.

Note how multiple nested blocks are handled correctly and how the formatting is preserved. Also note that by including the iterator rows within a bordered region the border correctly surrounds the appropriate resulting region.

15.5 Word

A set of APIs called HWPF is currently being developed to handle Microsoft Word documents. Like HSSF, this will be developed on top of POIFS, and it is reasonable to expect that there will be both high-level and low-level APIs. There is no timetable for a release of HWPF, but it will obviously be tremendously useful, so keep an eye on the POI Web site. Once this is available it should be a simple matter to modify `TemplateProcessor` to generate Word documents. Rather than iterating over columns it is likely such a program would iterate over blocks of text.

15.6 Beyond This Book

As mentioned at the start of this chapter, there are open source programs that allow users to edit Excel and Word documents. It is natural to wonder whether any of these can also be used programmatically. The answer is a limited yes. In particular, OpenOffice provides a set of Java APIs by which an external program can invoke functions in a running instance of OpenOffice. This means OpenOffice could be started, and a program like `TemplateProcessor` could repeatedly make calls to read and create rows and cells.

Obviously the need to have OpenOffice running places some restrictions on the usefulness of this approach, but there is an intermediate solution that reduces this overhead. OpenOffice's native format is a ZIP archive containing XML files. It is therefore possible to ask OpenOffice to convert an Excel file into its native format, and then the resulting file can be manipulated through standard ZIP and XML tools, including JXPath as discussed in Chapter 9. An advantage to this approach is that the program needs to know nothing about Excel per se and can concentrate on building XML. An additional advantage is that OpenOffice already supports Word, and it supports a greater subset of Excel than POI does, including formulas.

POI is also in the process of moving to an XML-based system. The HSSF **serializer,** the code responsible for translating to and from the binary BIFF8 representation, is moving to Apache Cocoon. Cocoon is a toolkit that enables components to be assembled into an XML pipeline. When this move is completed, it will be possible to feed an XML document to Cocoon and get an Excel file out, and vice versa. Pipeline components can also pull data from a database and inject it into XML prior to translation to Excel. Cocoon is discussed in Chapter 20.

15.7 Summary

Tool: POI
Purpose: Read and write Excel and (eventually) Word documents
Version covered: 2.5
Home page: http://jakarta.apache.org/poi/
License: The Apache Software License, Version 2.0

CHAPTER 16

Scripting

The term "scripting language" is vague and may mean different things to different people. Generally such languages are **interactive** and **interpreted** rather than compiled and are often embedded within larger applications to provide certain kinds of configuration. At first glance it may seem as if such languages have nothing to do with Java, which is compiled, noninteractive, and almost never embedded in a larger system.

One of the remarkable things about programming languages is that any sufficiently powerful language can be used to implement any other language, and indeed Java itself is largely implemented in C++. This means it is possible to implement a scripting language within Java.

To illustrate this idea and begin to demonstrate its value, consider a simple calculator such as the one in Listing 16.1.

Listing 16.1 A class with calculator methods

```
package com.awl.toolbook.chapter16;

public class Calc {
    public Calc() {}

    public int add(int a,int b) {
        return a + b;
    }
```

Listing 16.1 A class with calculator methods *(continued)*

```
    public int sub(int a,int b) {
        return a - b;
    }

    public int addSquares(int a,int b) {
        return a*a + b*b;
    }
}
```

To use this class, another class must be written with a `main()` method, which constructs an instance of `Calc` and invokes the appropriate method. If no generalization were done, one such class would need to be written for each method of `Calc`. Even then the resulting classes would be of no use for calling methods in other classes.

A better solution would be to write an interpreter for a simple language whose expressions could specify a class, a method, and the arguments to that method. For example the `addSquares()` method could be invoked as

```
com.awl.toolbook.chapter16.Calc.addSquares<3,4>
```

which would return 25.

Listing 16.2 contains a scripting engine that handles this very simple language.

Listing 16.2 A simple scripting engine

```
package com.awl.toolbook.chapter16;

import java.util.StringTokenizer;
import java.lang.reflect.Method;

import org.apache.oro.text.regex.*;

public class SimpleLang {
    public SimpleLang() {}

    public static void main(String args[])
        throws Exception
    {
        Perl5Compiler compiler = new Perl5Compiler();
        Pattern p =
```

```
        compiler.compile("^(.*)\\.([^<]*)<([^>]*)>");
    Perl5Matcher m = new Perl5Matcher();

    if(m.contains(args[0],p)) {
        MatchResult r      = m.getMatch();
        String className   = r.group(1);
        String methodName = r.group(2);
        String margs       = r.group(3);

        System.out.println(
            processExpression(className,
                              methodName,
                              margs));
    } else {
        System.err.println("Malformed expression");
    }
}

private static Object processExpression(
                        String className,
                        String methodName,
                        String args)
    throws Exception
{
    Class cls = Class.forName(className);
    Object obj = cls.newInstance();

    StringTokenizer st = new StringTokenizer(args,",");
    int numArgs          = st.countTokens();
    Integer argArray[] = new Integer[numArgs];
    Class argTypes[]    = new Class[numArgs];

    for(int i=0;i<numArgs;i++) {
        argArray[i] = new Integer(st.nextToken());
        argTypes[i] = Integer.TYPE;
    }

    Method method = cls.getDeclaredMethod(methodName,
                                          argTypes);
```

Listing 16.2 A simple scripting engine *(continued)*

```
        if(method == null) {
            throw new NoSuchMethodException();
        }

        return method.invoke(obj,argArray);
    }
}
```

The expression is provided as an argument that is broken into a class name, method name, and arguments by a regular expression, as covered in Chapter 13. It is possible to use parentheses as part of a pattern, but doing so makes the patterns rather complex because parentheses are also used to denote grouping. To avoid this complexity, angle brackets are used in the input to contain arguments.

The specified class is then loaded, and the appropriate method is obtained using features of the introspection API. The method is then invoked, and the result printed.

Although the language handled by `SimpleLang` is very rudimentary, it should be clear in principle how it could be expanded. The simple regular expression could be expanded into a full **parser** that would look for keywords such as `if` and `for`, and `processExpression()` could be expanded to handle such keywords.

Having demonstrated that a scripting language can be implemented in Java, the next logical question is whether doing so accomplishes anything. While the motivation for `SimpleLang` was admittedly rather artificial, in general, scripting languages have a great deal to offer developers. The discussion of these benefits will be deferred until later, following a closer look at a particularly powerful scripting language called BeanShell.

16.1 Running BeanShell

BeanShell started as a scripting language with a Java-like syntax, although it has recently been expanded to be completely Java-compatible. This new functionality will be discussed shortly.

BeanShell may be used in two ways: as an application or as an API. Although the language itself is the same in either case, the principles are best demonstrated in application mode.

Within application mode BeanShell may be run either within a console or in its own Swing-based window. The latter may be invoked by adding bsh.jar to the `CLASSPATH`, and running

```
java bsh.Console
```

This will bring up the window shown in Figure 16.1.

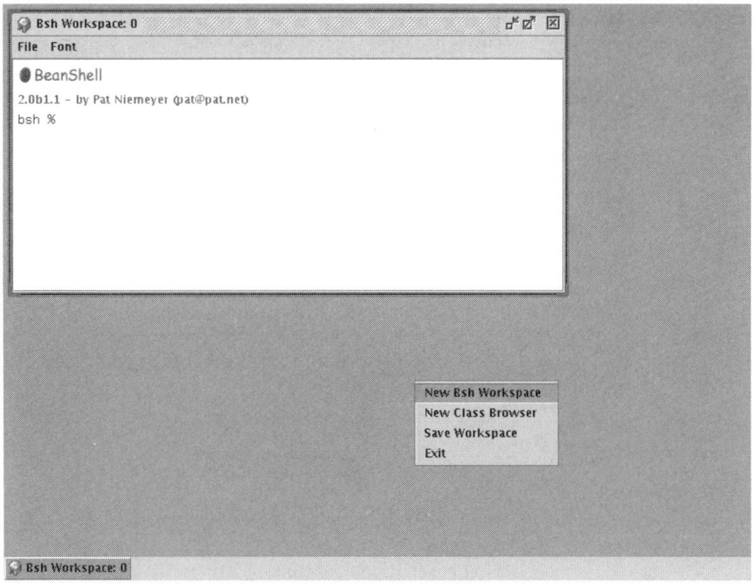

Figure 16.1. The BeanShell GUI.

Expressions may be interactively entered in the workspace. The up arrow key will scroll through previously entered expressions that can be edited or reentered by pressing "return." The menu shown in the lower right corner is raised by right-clicking on the background. From this menu another workspace may be started. Workspaces are completely independent; anything done in one will not affect any others.

The menu can also be used to bring up a class browser, much like that seen in Eclipse from Chapter 3. This view is shown in Figure 16.2.

This works in the obvious way: a hierarchy can be clicked to display a list of classes, and a class may be clicked to bring up a list of methods.

The console version of BeanShell is started as

```
java bsh.Interpreter
```

This will present a prompt much like a single workspace, except that the arrow keys will not work. The interpreter may also be given the name of a file containing BeanShell expressions and commands. It will evaluate these expressions in order and then exit.

16.2 The BeanShell Language

In the simplest use BeanShell looks a lot like Java with a few important differences. Here is a sample session with the interpreter.

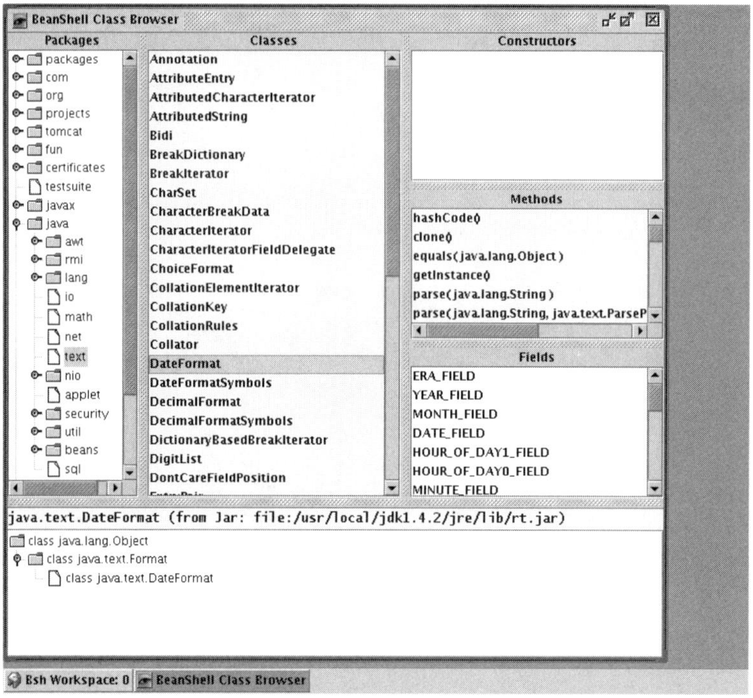

Figure 16.2. The BeanShell class browser.

```
BeanShell 2.0b1.1 - by Pat Niemeyer (pat@pat.net)
bsh % print(3+4);
7
bsh % print("Hello " + "world");
Hello world
bsh % for(i=0;i<5;i++) print("Hello: " + i);
Hello: 0
Hello: 1
Hello: 2
Hello: 3
Hello: 4
bsh % exit();
```

This example illustrates several features. Expressions must end with a semicolon, just as in Java. The + operator is also overloaded because it is in Java and works with numbers, strings, and combinations of the two. The `for` syntax is also very much like Java.

The `print` command is a built-in function in BeanShell. As will shortly be illustrated, the standard `System.out.print()` and `System.err.print()` are also available, but `print()` sends its output to the current workspace in GUI mode, whereas `System.out.print()` sends output to the console. Generally for interactive use `print()` is preferable.

Unlike in Java, variables do not need to be explicitly declared or given a type. The `i` in the `for` loop is automatically created and holds a kind of arbitrary type that may be set to any value. This behavior is further illustrated in the next example:

```
bsh % i=12;
bsh % print(i);
12
bsh % i="hello";
bsh % print(i);
hello
```

Although it is not necessary to declare variables, it is possible, and this enables BeanShell to detect type errors that might otherwise lead to strange problems in a complex program:

```
bsh % int j = 1;
bsh % j="a string";
// Error: EvalError: Variable assignment: j
: Can't assign java.lang.String to int :
at Line: 6 : in file: <unknown file> : j = "a string"
```

Note that BeanShell error messages are quite comprehensive and give the location of the error, the problem, and the full line that caused the problem.

Strings and numbers are certainly useful, but the real power of BeanShell lies in its ability to interact with and use full Java classes, as illustrated in the next example:

```
bsh % import com.awl.toolbook.chapter16.*;
bsh % c = new Calc();
bsh % print(c.addSquares(8,1+2));
73
bsh % print(c.add(2,c.add(3,4)));
9
```

This starts with an `import` statement that works just like the Java equivalent, except that `import` statements may be issued at any time. Then a `Calc` is constructed and used. Note again that the type of `c` does not need to be specified, although it could have been. This fulfills the need for which `SimpleLang` was created, and much more flexibly. Arbitrarily complex expressions can be entered and evaluated, as the last line illustrates.

16.3 Functions

BeanShell allows arbitrary code to be grouped together into functions, which are something like Java methods. Here is a simple definition and use:

```
bsh % addThree(i) {i+3;}
bsh % print(addThree(4));
7
```

Note that neither the return type nor the type of the argument needs to be specified, which is consistent with the way variables work. This allows the creation of functions that take different types of arguments; for example, it is legal to call `addThree("The number is ")`, which will return `The number is 3`. Arguments can be given types if desired. Note also that the `return` keyword is not needed, although it is allowed.

Functions can also declare variables, contain iteration, use Java classes, and anything else that can be done at the top level. For example, a function that computes the factorial of a number could be defined as follows:

```
bsh % fact(n) {
    int total = 1;
    for(int i=n;i>1;i--) {
        total = total*i;
    }
    total;
}
bsh % print(fact(4));
24
```

The scoping of variables works as expected; although `total` is returned from `fact()`, the variable itself is not defined outside the definition of `fact()`, as shown by the following error:

```
bsh % print(total);
// Error: EvalError: Undefined argument: total
: at Line: 12 : in file: <unknown file> : ( total )
```

So far, this is all very much like Java, but there is much more to BeanShell functions than meets the eye. Consider what must happen when a function like `fact()` is invoked. Because nothing is compiled, BeanShell doesn't "know" that the first thing it will do is create a variable called `total` and later a variable called `i`. Each invocation of `fact()` behaves exactly as if the user were typing the definition for the first time, so these variables are created as they are encountered in the definition of the function. This implies that each method invocation must have someplace to store variables as they are created; such a construct is called a **namespace.**

The same is true at the top level; BeanShell does not know what variables or functions will be defined during a session, so a top-level namespace is also needed. Although it would be possible to have one kind of namespace for the top level and another for function invocations, BeanShell does something much more clever and makes them **identical.** One of the implications of this is that it is possible to define functions within functions:

```
bsh % addSquares(x,y) {
     square(a) {a*a;}
     square(x) + square(y);
}
bsh % print(addSquares(2,3));
13
```

Here `square()` is only available within the body of `addSquares()`. Attempting to use it outside that scope would result in the same kind of error that arose from attempting to access `total` outside of `fact()`.

Even more amazing than the existence of multiple namespaces is the ability to access and manipulate these namespaces. In any context the special variable `this` refers to the current namespace, although in this context the namespace is more properly called a **closure.** Values within a closure can be both obtained and set with the usual Java dot notation. In any context, including the top level, `this.variable_name` and `variable_name` mean the same thing.

```
bsh % i=44;
bsh % print(this.i);
44
bsh % this.i=76;
bsh % print(i);
76
```

The real utility of `this` lies in the ability to make one namespace available from another. The easiest way to do this is to return `this` from a function call.

```
bsh % makeClosure() {
    int value = 88;
    int getValuePlusOne() {return value + 1;}
    return this;
}
```

makeClosure now returns a new closure whose values can be manipulated from the top level.

```
bsh % c1=makeClosure();
bsh % print(c1.value);
88
bsh % print(c1.getValuePlusOne());
89
bsh % c1.value = 256;
bsh % print(c1.getValuePlusOne());
257
```

The reason for the name this should now be evident: Its use enables the creation of closures that act much like objects. A function that returns such a closure acts as a constructor. This similarity is further highlighted by noting that each call to makeClosure() will create a brand new namespace, just as a call to new creates a new instance of a class.

```
bsh % c2=makeClosure();
bsh % print(c2.value);
88
bsh % print(c1.value);
256
```

Unlike classes, it is possible to add new values to a closure dynamically after it has been created:

```
bsh % c1.newValue=11;
bsh % print(c1.newValue);
11
bsh % print(c2.newValue);
// Error: EvalError: Undefined argument: c2 .newValue
: at Line: 23 : in file: <unknown file> : ( c2 .newValue )
```

It is occasionally useful to do the reverse: pass the global namespace into a function so that the function may set global values:

```
bsh % setSquare(ns,n) {
    ns.lastSquare=n*n;
}
bsh % setSquare(this,4);
bsh % print(lastSquare);
16
```

16.4 Implementing Interfaces

A remarkable feature of Java as of version 1.3 is that it is possible for a class to dynamically implement an interface at run time. This feature is relatively unknown. Readers who have not previously encountered it may wish to read more details in Appendix A.

This ability ties very nicely into scripting. A special class could intercept any method call into an interface and could pass the arguments to a scripted function. This makes it very easy to change the implementation of an interface; new code can be developed and installed on the fly without needing to recompile or restart anything.

Listing 16.3 shows a sample interface that provides methods to deal with prime numbers. There are many many algorithms for computing prime numbers and checking numbers for primality; each has different advantages and disadvantages. It therefore makes sense to declare this as an interface.

Listing 16.3 An interface with prime methods

```
package com.awl.toolbook.chapter16;

public interface PrimeInterface {
    public boolean isPrime(int n);
    public int getPrime(int n);
}
```

Prime numbers are useful in a wide variety of applications, notably cryptography. Listing 16.4 shows a more artificial example, a class with one method that returns a list of prime numbers and another method that determines whether the current day of the month is a prime.

Listing 16.4 A class that uses primes

```
package com.awl.toolbook.chapter16;

import java.util.Date;
```

Listing 16.4 A class that uses primes *(continued)*

```
public class PrimeUser {
    public PrimeUser() {}

    private PrimeInterface primer;
    public PrimeInterface getPrimer() {return primer;}
    public void setPrimer(PrimeInterface primer) {
        this.primer = primer;
    }

    public int[] getPrimes(int howMany) {
        int values[] = new int[howMany];
        for(int i=0;i<howMany;i++) {
            values[i] = primer.getPrime(i);
        }

        return values;
    }

    public boolean isDayPrime() {
        Date d = new Date();
        return primer.isPrime(d.getDay());
    }
}
```

Normally the next step would be to create one or more Java implementations of `PrimeInterface` with different characteristics and perhaps experiment with their performance. However, it is much easier to write these in BeanShell, where they can be more rapidly tweaked and tested. Implementing an interface in BeanShell looks much like anonymous classes in Java. In this case the code will consist of `new PrimeInterface() {...}` with the relevant code inside the braces. Here is one such implementation:

```
p = new PrimeInterface() {
  isPrime(n) {
    for(i=2;i<n/2;i++) {
        if(n%i == 0) {
            return false;
        }
     }
```

```
            return true;
        }

        getPrime(n) {
            primes = new int[n+1];
            primes[0] = 2;
            j = 2;
            for(i=1;i<=n;i++) {
                found = false;
                while(!found) {
                    found = true;
                    j++;
                    for(k=0;k<i && found;k++) {
                        found = ((j % primes[k]) != 0);
                    }
                    if(found) {
                        primes[i] = j;
                    }
                }
            }

            return primes[n];
        }
    }
```

The implementation of `isPrime()` simply checks all numbers between 2 and half of the given number to determine if any is a factor.[1] `getPrime()` obtains the *n*th prime iteratively by checking to see if any of the previously obtained primes is a factor of the current candidate.

It is quite easy to use this implementation in conjunction with a `PrimeUser`:

```
bsh % user=new PrimeUser();
bsh % user.setPrimer(p);
bsh % print(user.getPrimes(4));
int []: {
2,
```

[1] Even this is doing too much work. It is only necessary to check up to the square root of the number. This would be an easy optimization to make in BeanShell!

```
3,
5,
7,
}
bsh % print(user.isDayPrime());
false
```

Note that printing an array in BeanShell prints all the elements of the array automatically.

16.5 Full Java Compatibility

As of version 2.0 BeanShell is fully compatible with Java. This means that it is possible to write BeanShell code using syntax that would be accepted by Javac or jikes, which makes it very easy to move from BeanShell to Java and vice versa. This compatibly goes far beyond syntax, however; it is now possible to define new Java classes dynamically in BeanShell. Here is a sample transcript that illustrates this ability:

```
bsh % public class Demo {
    public Demo() {}

    private int total = 0;
    public int getTotal() {return total;}
    public void add(int x) {total = total+x;}
}
bsh % Demo d = new Demo();
bsh % print(d.getTotal());
0
bsh % d.add(4);
bsh % d.add(7);
bsh % print(d.getTotal());
11
```

It is also possible for a class defined in BeanShell to extend a regular Java class, as illustrated in the following example, which adds a new method to the `Calc` class from Listing 16.1:

```
bsh % public class BigCalc extends Calc {
    public BigCalc() {super();}
    public int div(int x,int y) {return x/y;}
```

```
}
bsh % c = new BigCalc();
bsh % print(c.add(10,5));
15
bsh % print(c.div(16,4));
4
```

It is also possible to freely mix Java and traditional BeanShell syntax, which makes it easy to change one method without needing to redefine the entire class:

```
bsh % getMessage() {"Hello, world";}
bsh % public class Greeter {
    public void printGreeting() {
        print(getMessage());
    }
}
bsh % Greeter g = new Greeter();
bsh % g.printGreeting();
Hello, World!
bsh % getMessage() {"Hello from BeanShell!";}
bsh % g.printGreeting();
Hello from BeanShell!
```

Note that when the definition of `getMessage()` is changed, it immediately affects instances that have already been created.

Even more amazing than the ability to define classes within BeanShell is the fact that existing Java classes will treat these exactly like normal Java classes.

Listing 16.5 shows a class that builds an array of values by calling a method in another class.

Listing 16.5 A class that builds an array of values

```
package com.awl.toolbook.chapter16;

public class ValueGenerator {
    public ValueGenerator() {}

    public int[] getValues(int start, int end) {
        int values[] = new int[end-start];
        Function f = new Function();
```

Listing 16.5 A class that builds an array of values *(continued)*

```
        for(int i=start;i<end;i++) {
            values[i-start] = f.evaluate(i);
        }

        return values;
    }
}
```

Listing 16.6 provides a simple function that squares its argument for use by Listing 16.5.

Listing 16.6 A class that computes squares

```
package com.awl.toolbook.chapter16;

public class Function {
    public Function() {}

    public int evaluate(int arg) {
        return arg*arg;
    }
}
```

BeanShell could use this class as it has used previous classes, but it is also possible to completely redefine `Function`, and instances of `ValueGenerator` will use this new definition in preference to the one in the Java file, just as if the BeanShell definition were at the front of the CLASSPATH. In the following example, `Function` is redefined to compute the cube of its argument:

```
bsh % package com.awl.toolbook.chapter16;
bsh % public class Function {
    public int evaluate(int arg) {return arg*arg*arg;}
}
bsh % import com.awl.toolbook.chapter16.*;
bsh % f = new Function();
bsh % f.evaluate(12);
bsh % print(f.evaluate(2));
8
```

```
bsh % g = new ValueGenerator();
bsh % print(g.getValues(1,4));
int []: {
1,
8,
27,
}
```

As promised, the instance of `ValueGenerator` uses the definition of `Function` given within BeanShell in preference to the Java definition.

BeanShell's ability to handle full Java syntax makes another useful trick possible. If no .class file is available when BeanShell attempts to load a class, it will process the corresponding .java file. This means that during the initial stages of a project it may not be necessary to compile anything—just write Java source as necessary and run the entire project inside BeanShell. This may significantly reduce the development overhead for certain kinds of projects.

16.6 Calling BeanShell from Java

Just as it is possible to invoke Java from BeanShell, it is possible to call out to BeanShell scripts from within Java code. The key to this is the `Interpreter` class. A program may create multiple instances of `Interpreter`; each will have its own namespace and act independently of the others.

`Interpreter` has four methods of immediate interest. `set()` sets a new value in the top-level namespace and correspondingly `get()` returns a value from this namespace. `eval()` is a catch-all method that takes a string representing any valid BeanShell expression or definition and processes it just as if it had been typed in the interactive interpreter. Finally, `source()` takes the name of a file and evaluates all the expressions in that file. These methods are all demonstrated in the next example:

```
import bsh.Interpreter;

public class Demo1 {
    public static void main(String args[]) {
        Interpreter intrp = new Interpreter();
        intrp.set("aValue", 5);
        System.out.println(intrp.get("aValue"));
```

```
        intrp.set("calc",new Calc());
        System.out.println(interp.eval("calc.add(aValue,3)"));

        interp.eval("addOne(x) {x+1;}");
        interp.eval("value2 = addOne(9)");
        System.out.println(intrp.get("value2"));

        intrp.source("sample.bsh");
        System.out.println(intrp.get("thirdValue"));
        System.out.println(interp.eval("addTwo(4)"));
    }
}
```

If sample.bsh contains the following lines

```
thirdValue = 109;
addTwo(x) {x+2;}
```

then when `Demo1` is run it will produce the following output:

```
5
8
10
109
6
```

Note in particular how the assignment of `value2`, which occurred in an `eval()`, is nonetheless available from a call to `get()`.

As a final exercise in self-reference, note that `Demo1` could be invoked from BeanShell or even created within a BeanShell session—interpreters calling interpreters ad infinitum.

16.7 Motivation for Scripting

Now that BeanShell has been examined in some detail, the advantages and possibilities offered by a scripting language should begin to be evident. Here are just a few:

Experimenting with New APIs

BeanShell provides an excellent environment for trying out new tools, such as many discussed in this book. For example, the ability to easily try different patterns and see how they match different inputs can make learning regular expressions much easier.

Rapid Testing

There is no substitute for formal automated tests like those developed in Chapter 4 using JUnit. However, BeanShell makes it possible to quickly run through several test cases that may later be folded into automated tests. BeanShell makes it easy to create an instance of the class or classes to be tested, interactively feed a number of sample arguments to the methods, and make sure the results are correct.

Rapid Development

This chapter has already covered a number of ways in which BeanShell can accelerate the development process. Interfaces can be implemented in BeanShell and loaded with a call to `source()`. If the implementation doesn't work, the source BeanShell file can be changed and the application can reload it without even needing to restart. Taking this same idea further, entire systems can be developed using BeanShell, using its ability to interpret Java code and load .java files dynamically.

What these approaches have in common is that both the compilation and restart/reload steps of Java development can be completely avoided. On a fast computer each individual compilation may not take very long, but they can add up over a day, to say nothing of how this time accumulates over the entire lifetime of a project.

So far nothing has been said about how fast programs in BeanShell run. In most cases BeanShell programs will run slower than compiled versions but often by a smaller factor than might be expected. A wide class of applications are **I/O bound,** meaning they spend most of their time waiting for data from disk or a database or a network connection. For such programs BeanShell may "feel" as fast as Java. In many cases it may turn out that BeanShell is "fast enough," and there is no need to ever move certain segments of code into Java.

In addition, for programs that run only a short time, the speed differences may be offset by the ability to retry a script repeatedly in a running BeanShell session, whereas it would be necessary to restart the Java VM and reload the classes to test the Java versions.

Configurable Behavior

Chapter 12 discussed many ways to configure an application, but all those methods rested on the same fundamental concept. All the tools in Chapter 12 treated configuration as a matter of setting variables to certain values, where the values could be either simple integers or strings, or entire class hierarchies. A program may act on these values in many ways, but any behavior that can be affected by such a value must already be programmed into the application. There is no way that setting a configuration option can extend the functionality of an application.

However, BeanShell makes such extension not only possible but easy. Consider a simple e-mail system that is designed to filter out spam. The configuration file for such a system might contain a number of regular expressions, and if a message matches any of the expressions, then it will be marked as spam and discarded. This is a good start, but recall from Chapter 13 that regular expressions do not constitute a complete language; there are certain kinds of patterns or tests that they simply cannot do. Using BeanShell, the e-mail system could be extended to take the name of scripts, and messages would be passed through these scripts. This would make it possible to perform much more sophisticated tests such as determining whether the address from which the message originated is on a list of known spammers. In addition, this would make it possible to configure the system's behavior on detecting spam; spam could be discarded, written to a database for later analysis, or automatically forwarded to a spam-tracking service.

This same extensibility could be offered by writing new classes. The system would then be configured by naming these classes in the configuration file. However, this approach places a number of additional burdens on end users; they must have the full Java development kit, they must go through their own testing cycles, they must typically write more code than would be required by BeanShell, and so on.

The notions of rapid development and easy configuration through scripting will appear throughout the remainder of this book.

Along with the many advantages offered by BeanShell are some downsides that developers should be aware of. Debugging a program that mixes Java and BeanShell may be difficult because the BeanShell code cannot be examined line by line in a debugger such as the one provided in Eclipse. The ease of replacing code may make it tempting to drop new scripts into production environments without going through proper testing and QA. There may also be security issues because BeanShell makes it somewhat easier for malicious hackers to introduce arbitrary code into a system. However, with some care and thought BeanShell can be a useful and powerful tool.

16.8 Beyond This Book

BeanShell is a complete language, and one chapter could not hope to do it justice. There is much more information available in the language manual.

Scripting has proven itself to be so powerful and useful that a Java Community Process group has been formed to formally specify the best way for scripting languages and Java to interact. This is a work in progress—just announced at Java One in 2003—but a summary of the project goals and progress can be found at http://www.judoscript.com/articles/jsr223.html.

16.9 Summary

Tool: BeanShell
Purpose: Scripting language
Version covered: 2.0
Home page: http://www.beanshell.org/
License: Available under either the Sun Public License or the LGPL

Further Reading:

- There are many other scripting languages available, ranging from simple expression processors to full implementations of such languages as Scheme and Python from within Java. A comprehensive list of such languages is available from http://grunge.cs.tu-berlin.de/tolk/vmlanguages.html.
- The design and implementation of programming languages is a fascinating subject. There is a great deal of literature available. Interested readers may wish to start with *Programming Language Processors in Java: Compilers and Interpreters,* by David Watt and Deryck Brown, Prentice-Hall, 2000.

CHAPTER 17

Tomcat

So far this book has discussed applications that facilitate the process of development and toolkits that solve common problems encountered during development. Tomcat is neither of these things; rather it is an application into which developers install their code. Tomcat provides a complete environment for this code; it handles all interactions with the outside world and provides services and APIs that abstract these interactions.

Briefly stated, Tomcat is a Web and application server, meaning its principal job is to open one or more sockets, read requests over those sockets, pass the requests to appropriate handlers, and send the responses back to the end user. This description, however, greatly understates what Tomcat does. Most significantly Tomcat provides implementations of the servlet 2.4 and JSP 2.0 specifications. This means that applications written to run within Tomcat may expect certain well-defined capabilities will be available for their use. The details of these specifications are beyond the scope of this book. Readers who are not familiar with servlets or JSP can find more information in the “Further Reading” section at the end of this chapter.

One of the fundamental ideas behind Tomcat is that of a **Web application.** A Web application is a collection of pages, code, and configuration that is treated as a unit. Normally a Web application will map to a particular URL, so URLs such as http://somesite.com/app1 and http://somesite.com/app2 will invoke different Web applications called app1 and app2, respectively. Tomcat may contain an arbitrary number of Web applications simultaneously.

Tomcat is highly flexible and configurable, and it offers many points of integration into which user code can be installed. Typically user code is installed as part of a Web application, but it is also possible to enhance the way Tomcat handles security as well as a great deal more. Tomcat is a large, complex application, and it will be impossible to cover it completely in a single chapter. The material presented here will be enough for a great deal of common use, as well as some relatively rare needs.

17.1 Starting Tomcat

Tomcat comes packaged as an archive, either zipped or tarred and gzipped.[1] Once the archive is unpacked, Tomcat can be started by going into the `tomcat` directory and running

```
bin\startup.sh
```

on Unix-based systems or

```
bin/startup.bat
```

on Windows. On either system the startup script will print a short message and exit, leaving Tomcat running in the background. The message printed at startup is the last output that Tomcat will generate. After that point all messages from Tomcat will be available in files in the `log` directory.

Once tomcat is running, the default home page can be found at http://localhost:8080, and it will resemble Figure 17.1. It is worth taking some time to explore this page; in particular there is a lot of useful information available through the provided links, and some good examples running locally can be found in the "Examples" section. For the time being, disregard the "admin" links, which will be discussed later in this chapter.

17.2 A Tour of Tomcat

Before diving into details of how Tomcat is used, it is worth taking a look at its structure. Within the directories created when the archive is uncompressed are the following subdirectories.

---

[1] A customized version of Tomcat, which includes examples from this book, is included on the companion CD-ROM. See README for more details.

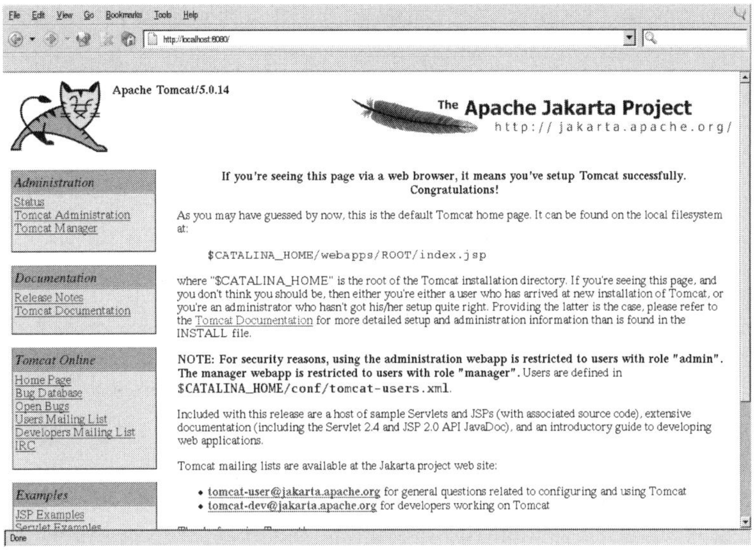

Figure 17.1. The Tomcat home page.

`bin`

This contains scripts for starting and stopping tomcat as well as some additional tools.

`conf`

This directory contains files used to configure Tomcat at the global level, although it is possible for each Web application to override many of the values provided here.

The most important file here is `server.xml`, which tells Tomcat the set of services to run when it starts up as well as what ports to listen to. This file also specifies the set of resources to make available to applications and a number of security parameters. This file will be encountered frequently throughout this chapter.

There is also a `web.xml` file in this directory, which establishes default values that may be overridden by values in each application's `web.xml`.

Two files, `catalina.policy` and `catalina.properties`, define parameters used by Tomcat as a whole. These values will almost never need to be changed, and these files may be safely ignored by all but the most advanced users.

`jk2.properties` defines a set of properties that are used when Tomcat is installed as an application server in conjunction with an external Web server such as Apache or IIS. Such usage is beyond the scope of this book, and for the remainder of this chapter it will be assumed that Tomcat is running in **stand-alone** mode, where it operates as both a Web server and application server.

There is a file called `tomcat-users.xml` that defines a set of users with special security attributes. Much more will be said about this file in the section on security following.

It is possible for one computer to have multiple names or, more formally, multiple **interfaces**. The same physical computer may be known as both www.siteone.com and www.sitetwo.org. A single instance of Tomcat may be configured to respond to both these names and may have different configuration options for each interface. These are specified in a subdirectory within `conf` called `Catalina`, and within this directory are subdirectories whose names match the names of the interfaces. When Tomcat is initially extracted, there will be a directory called `localhost` containing parameters for use when a browser from the same machine contacts Tomcat.

logs

The `logs` directory contains a number of logs created by Tomcat. The file `catalina.out` contains anything written to `System.out` and `System.err`, as well as information relevant to the server as a whole. In addition, there will be a log for each interface containing some specific information.

The `logs` directory must be writeable by the user running Tomcat. In general, it is a good idea to make all the directories within the Tomcat installation owned by this user.

common

This directory contains three subdirectories—`classes`, `lib`, and `endorsed`—which contain code used by Tomcat as a whole. The `classes` directory is effectively added to the CLASSPATH, as are any jar files in `lib` and `endorsed`. Any custom jars that may be needed throughout Tomcat, such as a JDBC driver, may be placed in these directories.

server

Like `common` this directory contains subdirectories called `classes` and `lib`. These directories contain Java classes and jars that are used by the server components within Tomcat. Note that these classes will not be available to Tomcat when it first starts up.

shared

This is another directory containing `classes` and `lib` subdirectories. The classes and jars within these directories are available to all Web applications but will not be available to the server infrastructure. Many of the tools discussed in this book, such as the ORO regular expression library and Lucene, might be placed in the `lib` directory so that all Web applications may use regular expressions and full-text searches.

webapps
This directory contains all the Web applications Tomcat is configured to run, one Web app per subdirectory. See the next section for information on the structure of these subdirectories.

work
This directory is used by Tomcat to hold servlets that it builds from jsp pages. Users will normally not need to use anything in this directory.

temp
This directory is used internally by Tomcat and may be ignored.

17.3 Creating a Web Application

A minimal Web application can be created by creating a couple of directories and a single configuration file. First, a directory within `webapps` is needed to hold the application. For the purposes of what follows a directory named `example` will be used. Within `example` a directory called `WEB-INF` is used to hold all configuration and resources for the application. The most important and only required element in `WEB-INF` is `web.xml`. A minimal version of this file could be as simple as

```
<?xml version="1.0" encoding="ISO-8859-1"?>

<!DOCTYPE web-app
 PUBLIC
 "-//Sun Microsystems, Inc.//DTD Web Application 2.3//EN"
 http://java.sun.com/dtd/web-app_2_3.dtd">

<web-app>
</web-app>
```

This is all that is needed to start creating simple content. Pages live in the top-level `example` directory, and a good place to start is with an `index.html` file such as

```
<html>
<head><title>Sample web application</title></head>
<body>
Welcome to the sample application!
</body>
</html>
```

With these files in place, Tomcat will be able to respond to a request for the page at http://localhost:8080/example/index.html. Other html and jsp pages can be added at will, along with images, mp3 files, and anything else. Although this is all that is necessary to create a minimal Web application, much more is possible with a knowledge of how Web applications are arranged.

As mentioned, the top level of the Web application is where all the content files live. It is also possible to create arbitrary subdirectories for such files, and these are accessed as URLs in the obvious way.

All the other elements of the application are in the special `WEB-INF` directory. Within this directory is the master `web.xml` configuration file, which will be examined in the next section.

Jar files may be placed in a `lib` directory within `WEB-INF`. This automatically adds these jar files to the effective CLASSPATH for the application. There are no subdirectories under lib. Code specific to the Web application may be placed in a jar file, which is then installed in `WEB-INF/lib`, or it may be placed as individual class files in `WEB-INF/classes`. This directory is added to the effective CLASSPATH, and within it code is laid out according to the usual Java rules.

It is also common to store resources, such as property files, resource bundles, serialized beans, and BeanShell scripts, in the CLASSPATH. These may therefore also be placed in jar files, which are moved to `WEB-INF/lib`, or left unarchived and placed in `WEB-INF/classes`.

Finally, by convention there is a special directory for tag library descriptors (tld) called `taglibs`. This is not enforced because the location of tld files is specified in `web.xml`, but in general it is good practice to put them all in one place. See Chapter 18 for more on tag libraries.

Once the application has been laid out according to the preceding rules, it can be packaged into a **Web application resource,** or .war, file with the following command:

```
jar -c0f ../application_name.war .
```

where `application_name` can be replaced with the chosen name for the application. In many application servers, including Tomcat, it is possible to deploy an application by simply placing the war file in the proper directory, which for Tomcat is `webapps`.

17.3.1 The web.xml File

The `web.xml` file controls everything specific to the current Web application. As with any good XML document, `web.xml` starts with a declaration, DTD reference, and root node. The top level looks like the minimal example given previously. The real meat is in the `web-app` tags and consists of the following elements in order.

An optional icon to be used by interactive configuration or maintenance applications. This can specify small (16 × 16) and large (32 × 32) images, which should live within the main directory of the Web application.

```
<icon>
  <large-icon>images/toolbook_large.jpg</large-icon>
  <small-icon>images/toolbook_small.jpg</small-icon>
</icon>
```

An optional display name, which can also be used by administration tools.

```
<display-name>JSP book examples</display-name>
```

An optional description for the benefit of people reading the `web.xml` *file or application tools.*

```
<description>
Example code from "JavaServer Pages, second edition"
</description>
```

An optional flag indicating that this Web application can be run within an application server that runs across multiple computers.

```
<distributable/>
```

Any number of context parameters consisting of a name, a value, and an optional description. These are used by a class called `servletContext` when the application starts. The details of how servlets work and utilize this information is beyond the scope of this book but will be covered in any good book on servlets.

```
<context-param>
  <param-name>defaultColor</param-name>
  <param-value>black</param-value>
  <description>Standard background color</description>
</context-param>
```

Any number of filter definitions. A filter is a special kind of servlet that handles requests before they reach the final page or servlet for which they are destined. Filters are also beyond the scope of this book.

Entries in web.xml must define the name of the filter and the implementing class and may also provide initialization parameters. In addition, an icon, a display name, and a description may be provided.

```
<filter>
  <filter-name>authFilter</filter-name>
  <display-name>Auth filter</display-name>
  <description>
    Filter that prevents unauthorized used from accessing
    special pages
  </description>
  <filter-class>
    com.awl.toolbook.ch17.AuthFilter
  </filter-class>
  <init-param>
    <param-name>protectedPages</param-name>
    <param-value>create_article.jsp</param-value>
  </init-param>
</filter>
```

Any number of filter mappings that tell the Web application which requests should be passed through each filter. It is possible to have multiple instances for any given filter. It is also possible to have multiple filters defined for any given URL. In this case a chain is constructed in the order of the filter mapping definitions.

```
<filter-mapping>
  <filter-name>authFilter</filter-name>
  <url-pattern>*.jsp</url-pattern>
</filter-mapping>
```

Any number of listeners, which are another special class defined by the servlet specification.

```
<listener>
  <listener-class>
    com.awl.toolbook.ch17.SampleListener
  </listener-class>
</listener>
```

Any number of servlet declarations specifying the name of the servlet, the implementing class, and any initialization parameters. An icon, display name, and description may also be provided. There is also additional configuration information related to security that may be provided, but such configuration is beyond the scope of this book.

```
<servlet>
  <servlet-name>action</servlet-name>
  <servlet-class>
    org.apache.struts.action.ActionServlet
  </servlet-class>
  <init-param>
    <param-name>application</param-name>
    <param-value>
      config.ApplicationResources
    </param-value>
  </init-param>
  <init-param>
    <param-name>config</param-name>
    <param-value>
      /WEB-INF/classes/config/struts-config.xml
    </param-value>
  </init-param>
</servlet>
```

Any number of servlet mappings associating a servlet name with a class of URLs. Like filters, one servlet may be configured to handle multiple sets of URLs, but unlike filters, only one servlet can handle any given URL.

```
<servlet-mapping>
  <servlet-name>action</servlet-name>
  <url-pattern>*.do</url-pattern>
</servlet-mapping>
```

An optional session config, which specifies how long in seconds sessions should last.

```
<session-config>
  <session-timeout>3600</session-timeout>
</session-config>
```

Any number of mime mappings. These associate filename extensions with mime types, which tell the browser how to handle the data. Most common types, such as text and graphics, are defined in the global `web.xml` in the top-level `conf` directory instead of with each application.

```
<mime-mapping>
  <extension>ogg</extension>
  <mime-type>audio/ogg</mime-type>
</mime-mapping>
```

An optional list of "welcome files." These specify a set of files to look for if a user tries to access a directory name. For example, it would be possible to send users going to "/directory" to "/directory/index.jsp" if that file exists or "/directory/index.html" if it doesn't, and so on.

```
<welcome-file-list>
  <welcome-file>index.jsp</welcome-file>
  <welcome-file>index.html</welcome-file>
</welcome-file-list>
```

Any number of error pages, each of which associates a page with a kind of error. Using this it is possible to send requests for a nonexistent page to one place, an application error to another, and so on.

```
<error-page>
  <error-code>404</error-code>
  <location>no_such_page.jsp</location>
</error-page>
```

Any number of tag library declarations that associate a URI as used in a JSP with a tag library descriptor (see Chapter 13).

```
<taglib>
  <taglib-uri>http://java.sun.com/jstl/core</taglib-uri>
  <taglib-location>/WEB-INF/taglibs/c.tld</taglib-location>
</taglib>
```

Any number of environment resource references. These contain an optional description plus a name and a type. See the section of resources following for more information on how these are used.

```
<resource-env-ref>
  <description>
    The database connection for user information
  </description>
  <resource-env-ref-name>
```

```
    db/UserDatabase
  </resource-env-ref-name>
  <resource-env-ref-type>
    java.sql.Connection
  </resource-env-ref-type>
</resource-env-ref>
```

Any number of environment references. Whereas environment resource references name a particular object that is shared by all Web applications, resource references refer to a factory that is invoked to obtain a new instance for the particular Web application. A flag in the definition indicates whether or not these instances are shareable.

```
<resource-ref>
  <description>Datasource for inventory</description>
  <res-ref-name>db/InventoryDatasource</res-ref-name>
  <res-type>javax.sql.DataSource</res-type>
  <res-auth>Container</res-auth>
  <res-sharing-scope>Shareable</res-sharing-scope>
</resource-ref>
```

Any number of security constraints specifying protected resources. See the section on security following for more information on how this and the next two parameters are used.

```
<security-constraint>
  <display-name>Protected pages</display-name>
  <web-resource-collection>
    <web-resource-name>Protected Area</web-resource-name>
      <url-pattern>delete.jsp</url-pattern>
      <url-pattern>*.do</url-pattern>
  </web-resource-collection>
  <auth-constraint>
    <role-name>admin</role-name>
  </auth-constraint>
</security-constraint>
```

Zero or one entries specifying how users must prove they are authorized to view protected resources.

```
<login-config>
  <auth-method>FORM</auth-method>
  <realm-name>Protected Area</realm-name>
```

```
    <form-login-config>
      <form-login-page>/login.jsp</form-login-page>
      <form-error-page>/error.jsp</form-error-page>
    </form-login-config>
  </login-config>
```

Any number of security roles used by the Web application.

```
  <security-role>
    <description>
      The role that is required to log in to this app
    </description>
    <role-name>admin</role-name>
  </security-role>
```

Finally, there are blocks of `ejb-ref` and `ejb-local-ref` entries relating to the application's use of Enterprise Java Beans.

17.4 Security

There is a lot of meaning packed into the apparently simple word "security." For the purposes of what follows it will be taken to mean the following three things:

- Ensuring that protected content can only be seen by authorized persons.
- Ensuring that the server is the one the user believes he or she is connected to.
- Ensuring that no third party between the server and client can eavesdrop on the conversation.

However, there is a great deal more involved in making a site secure than can be covered here, and administrators in charge of large sites need to consider many other aspects.

Tomcat's security is based in a few fundamental concepts. There are one or more **security roles,** each of which is designated by a name. Some typical names would be `admin` for administrators of a site, `manager` for a manager within a company, `customer` for someone who has paid for premium content, and so on. There is no restriction on the names, and new ones can be created as needed.

Web applications are protected by role, so one section of a site may be restricted to users in the `customer` role and another section restricted to users in the `premium_customer` role. Users marked as `managers` may have access to special pages that report how the site is being used, and users in the `admin` role will typically have access to the whole site.

Any individual user, identified by a user name, may have several such roles. For example, one person might be both an `admin` and a `manager`. Each user has a **credential** that proves his or her identity. Typically this is a password, but there are other possibilities, such as client certificates, covered shortly.

The full set of users, passwords, and roles is contained within a **realm.** Realm data may be stored in many different ways; this will be examined in more detail shortly.

17.4.1 Authentication

The simplest kind of security to configure is **authentication,** which requires users to prove their identity before they are allowed to view privileged content. There are many ways in which this might be accomplished, such as an electronic key or other physical security device, or biometric key such as a retinal scan. While such security measures are no longer confined to science fiction, a much more common kind of authentication is based on a username and password.

Tomcat already maintains a list of usernames and passwords within the current realm, so enabling authentication is as simple as adding some configuration to a Web application's `web.xml`. Here is a standard configuration that will protect all html and jsp files in the "example" Web application defined previously.

```
<security-constraint>
  <display-name>Protected example</display-name>
  <web-resource-collection>
    <web-resource-name>Protected Area</web-resource-name>
    <url-pattern>*.jsp</url-pattern>
    <url-pattern>*.html</url-pattern>
  </web-resource-collection>

  <auth-constraint>
    <role-name>admin</role-name>
    <role-name>example</role-name>
  </auth-constraint>
</security-constraint>

<login-config>
  <auth-method>BASIC</auth-method>
```

```
    <realm-name>Popup-based Protection</realm-name>
  </login-config>

  <security-role>
    <description>
      The administration role
    </description>
    <role-name>admin</role-name>
  </security-role>

  <security-role>
    <description>
      The example user role
    </description>
    <role-name>example</role-name>
  </security-role>
```

Within the security-constraint the web-resource-collection names all the protected content. Here jsp and html files are protected, meaning images could still be retrieved without authentication. The auth-constraint section lists the security roles that are allowed to view protected content. Here, anyone who belongs to the admin or example roles will be allowed in.

It is possible to have many such security-constraint entries with different parameters—for example, adding

```
  <security-constraint>
    <display-name>Premium content</display-name>
    <web-resource-collection>
      <url-pattern>premium/*.jsp</url-pattern>
    </web-resource-collection>

    <auth-constraint>
      <role-name>premium_customers</role-name>
    </auth-constraint>
  </security-constraint>
```

would allow only premium customers to view contents in the premium directory. Note that as it stands premium customers would not allowed to see html and jsp pages in the top-level directory. There are two remedies for this: Either premium_customer could also be added to the first security-constraint or the realm could be arranged so that all users with the premium_customer role also have the example role.

The login-config node specifies how the user should be asked for her username and password. The BASIC method invokes an http mechanism called **basic authentication,** to which most browsers will respond by presenting a pop-up dialog to the user.

Basic authentication was common in the early days of the Web, but it has since fallen out of favor. Most site designers prefer to have a page with a login form that allows the login process to fit more seamlessly with the rest of the site. Tomcat allows for this possibility as well, and it can be enabled by replacing the login-config from the previous example with the following:

```
<login-config>
  <auth-method>FORM</auth-method>
  <realm-name>Form-Based Protection</realm-name>
  <form-login-config>
    <form-login-page>/login.jsp</form-login-page>
    <form-error-page>/error.jsp</form-error-page>
  </form-login-config>
</login-config>
```

With this in place a user trying to access a protected resource will be sent to login.jsp. This page must have a form with certain properties for Tomcat to use it. Here is one such page:

```
<html>
<body>

<form method="POST" action="j_security_check">
  <table border="0">
    <tr>
      <td>User Name</td>
      <td>
        <input type="text" name="j_username" />
      </td>
    </tr>

    <tr>
      <td>Password</td>
```

```
        <td>
          <input type="password" name="j_password">
        </td>
      </tr>

      <tr>
        <td colspan="2">
          <input type="submit" value='Login'>
          <input type="reset" value='Reset'>
        </td>
       </tr>
    </table>
  </form>
  </body>
  </html>
```

The action and names of the username and password fields must be exactly as they are given here, but the rest of the page is unconstrained. Note that although this page may use images, those images must not themselves be protected. Also note that even though the security constraint indicates that all jsp files are protected, Tomcat makes exceptions for the login and error pages.

Once the user fills out and submits this form, Tomcat will check his name and password against the realm. If there is a match, the user will be allowed through to the page he initially tried to access. If not, he will be directed to error.jsp, which should explain that the login failed and provide a link back to login.jsp.

17.5 Realms

The steps described in the previous section will protect content in the example Web application, but the process is not yet complete. So far the example security role does not exist, and even if it did, there would be no users in it. To correct that, it is necessary to discuss how Tomcat manages security realms.

Configuration for realms is done in the global server.xml by use of a Realm declaration. One required attribute of this node is a className, which should name a class that implements the org.apache.catalina.Realm interface. A number of such classes are provided, and for special requirements it is also possible for users to create new ones. The subject of creating a new realm is beyond the scope of this book, although several relevant issues will be touched on later in this chapter.

17.5.1 File-Based Realm

The simplest realm, and the one that is enabled by default, is called `UserDatabaseRealm`. This realm stores users and role information in a simple XML file, which by default is located in the `conf` directory and is called `tomcat_users.xml`. Here is a sample that would allow a user to log into the example application:

```
<?xml version='1.0' encoding='utf-8'?>
<tomcat-users>
  <role rolename="example"/>
  <user
    username="exampleuser"
    password="example"
    roles="example"/>
</tomcat-users>
```

There is not much to this file; each security role in the system has a `role` entry, and each user has a `user` entry giving the name, password, and a comma-separated list of roles to which that user belongs.

Using this role requires three entries in `server.xml`. The first two define a resource containing the memory-based "database" that will hold the information from the XML file. This configuration, as taken from the default `server.xml`, is as follows:

```
<Resource
  name="UserDatabase"
  auth="Container"
  type="org.apache.catalina.UserDatabase"
  description="User database that can be updated and saved">
</Resource>

<ResourceParams name="UserDatabase">
  <parameter>
    <name>factory</name>
    <value>
      org.apache.catalina.users.MemoryUserDatabaseFactory
    </value>
  </parameter>
  <parameter>
    <name>pathname</name>
```

```
      <value>conf/tomcat-users.xml</value>
    </parameter>
  </ResourceParams>
```

The `Resource` node names the resource and specifies its type. The `ResourceParams` specify a factory class that will create instances of the resource and the name of the file to be read. See the section on resources for more information about what this all means.

The realm definition itself is straightforward:

```
<Realm
  className="org.apache.catalina.realm.UserDatabaseRealm"
  debug="0"
  resourceName="UserDatabase"/>
```

This node specifies the class that implements the `Realm` interface, turns off verbose debugging, and names the previously defined resource from where the realm will obtain its information.

17.5.2 JDBC Realm

The `UserDatabaseRealm` has the advantage that it is simple and compact, and new users may easily be added by simply editing the `tomcat-users.xml` file. However, this solution does not scale well. If there are too many users, the file will become unwieldy and difficult to maintain. In addition, Tomcat must be restarted to add new users, and only the owner of the Tomcat directories will be able to edit the file.

The solution to all these problems is to store realm information in a database, and Tomcat comes equipped with a `Realm` implementation that handles this.[2] To use this realm it is necessary to change the `Realm` definition in `server.xml` to something like the following:

```
<Realm
  className="org.apache.catalina.realm.JDBCRealm"
  debug="0"

  driverName="org.hsqldb.jdbcDriver"
  connectionURL="jdbc:hsqldb:toolbook"
```

[2]As of this writing, the database-based realm in the latest beta version of Tomcat 5 does not work. This will be fixed before Tomcat 5 is formally released, which may well happen by the time this book is printed.

```
connectionName="sa"
connectionPassword=""

userTable="users"
userNameCol="user_name"
userCredCol="user_pass"

userRoleTable="user_roles"
roleNameCol="role_name"/>
```

This definition also names the implementing class and sets the debugging level. Beyond that there is a section of standard JDBC connection information containing the driver, connection URL, username, and password to use to connect to the database.

The next three attributes specify the table within the database that contains user information and the column names within that table that hold the username and password. Here the term "cred"—short for "credential"—is used in place of "password," but in this case they mean the same thing.

The final two attributes specify a table name and column name containing role information.

Once the realm has been configured, the database must be configured to match. This can be done with the following SQL:

```
create table users (
  user_name         varchar(15) not null primary key,
  user_pass         varchar(15) not null
);

create table user_roles (
  user_name         varchar(15) not null,
  role_name         varchar(15) not null,
  primary key (user_name, role_name)
);

insert into users values('exampleuser','example');
insert into user_roles values('exampleuser','example');
```

These commands construct the tables and insert the same user and role information that was previously kept in `tomcat-users.xml`. Note that these tables may contain additional application-specific fields such as an e-mail address for each user or a description field for each role.

17.5.3 Encrypting Passwords

Both of the realms discussed will prevent an unauthorized user without a password from accessing protected content. However, the passwords themselves are rather insecure because they are stored in a human-readable format, often called **cleartext.** Anyone who can access the file used by the `UserDatabaseRealm` or the tables used by the `JDBCRealm` will have access to everyone's passwords and may log in as any user. Normally there will be security measures in place protecting system files and databases, but as a general principle even administrators or developers with access to system configuration should not be able to mimic end users.

The solution is to store passwords in an encrypted form. The idea is to use a **one-way** or **asymmetric** encryption mechanism, one that allows passwords to be encrypted easily but makes decryption computationally unfeasible. When a user is first granted a password, it is encrypted, and the encrypted version is kept in a table or `tomcat-user.xml`. When the user logs in, she provides her password to the system, and the system encrypts it, using the same algorithm that was used initially. This encrypted version is then checked against the the encrypted version in the realm, and if they match, the user is granted access. This scheme avoids the need to ever decrypt the password, and it is the way most operating systems handle login passwords.

Tomcat provides support for encrypted passwords, which may be enabled very simply. All that is needed is to add a `digest` attribute to the `Realm` node in `server.xml`. The value of this attribute should be set to one of `SHA`, `MD2`, or `MD5`, which are names of algorithms used for encryption.[3]

The only remaining task is to initially encode the passwords, and a utility is provided to do this. Three libraries must be added to the CLASSPATH: `server/lib/catalina.jar`, `common/lib/jmx.jar`, and `bin/commons-logging-api.jar`, all from the top-level Tomcat directory. Then to encrypt a password, run

```
java org.apache.catalina.realm.RealmBase \
    -a algorithm password
```

where `algorithm` should be replaced by the same name as used in the `digest` attribute, and `password` is the password to by encrypted. The encrypted version will be printed to `System.out`, and it may then be placed in the appropriate realm repository.

---

[3]At the time of this writing, MD2 was not supported.

17.6 Encryption and Server Validation

Passwords ensure that a user is who he or she claims to be, and encryption makes it difficult for unscrupulous users to use others' passwords. However, there are still several points of potential insecurity. First, the client has no guarantees that the server with which it is communicating is really who it claims to be. Second, there is the possibility that the communication between the client and the server will be intercepted by a third party. Recall that with encrypted passwords no cleartext version of the password is stored. However, the password is still transmitted from the client to the server in cleartext, so an eavesdropper may be able to capture it and, from then on, mimic the rightful owner.

Although spoofing and eavesdropping appear to be two unrelated problems, the solution to both is something called SSL, or Secure Sockets Layer. This is a feature built into all common browsers and most servers, including Tomcat. SSL is the basis for the "https" protocol, which is seen on almost every commercial Web site.

SSL is far too complex a subject to cover in depth here. Fortunately, it is possible to use SSL without fully understanding it, just as it is possible to use regular sockets without understanding the details of TCP/IP (Transmission Control Protocol/Internet Protocol).

Briefly, SSL requires the server to have a **certificate,** a digital key that contains information about that server. This certificate must be digitally signed by a **certificate authority.** Such an authority is an established company or individual who is widely trusted and whose security credentials are built into every browser. There are a few such companies; the best known and most widely used is Verisign.

When a browser connects to a server using SSL, the first thing the server does is transmit its certificate to the client. The client then verifies the certificate against its built-in list of certificate authorities. Then the client and server establish a format for encryption, and the conversation proceeds.

Note that the handling of the certificate and the encryption of the dialog are two conceptually independent processes. In principle either could happen without the other, but SSL is designed in such a way as to require both.

For many many applications, however, encryption is sufficient, and the proof of identity is unimportant. For these cases it is possible for anyone to generate a **self-signed certificate,** in which the user generates his own certificate, listing himself as the certificate authority. This is essentially useless for security; it is as if "John Smith" were to establish his identity by saying "John Smith never lies, so when I say I am John Smith, you can believe me!" However, this will allow the certificate validation portion of the SSL transaction to conclude so that the encryption phase can begin.

The Java Development Kit comes with a tool for managing all manner of digital keys, including certificates, and it has facilities for the generation of self-signed certificates. This tool is called `keytool`, and it may be found in the `bin` directory under `JAVA_HOME`.

A new self-signed certificate for use with Tomcat can be generated with the following command:

```
keytool -genkey -alias tomcat -keyalg RSA
```

The `genkey` option tells keytool to generate a new key, the `alias` option gives the new key the name `tomcat`, and `keyalg` specifies an encryption algorithm.

Keytool stores keys in **keystores,** which are binary files protected by passwords. A user may have any number of keystores; the default one is located in the home directory and is called `.keystore`.

When keytool is started, the first thing it will do is ask for the password to the keystore. The default value that is assigned to all new keystores is "changeit," a gentle reminder to select a new, more secure password. For the moment, however, this good advice will be ignored.

The rest of the interaction with keytool looks like this:

```
Enter keystore password:  changeit
What is your first and last name?
  [Unknown]:  localhost
What is the name of your organizational unit?
  [Unknown]:  examples
What is the name of your organization?
  [Unknown]:  AWL
What is the name of your City or Locality?
  [Unknown]:  New York
What is the name of your State or Province?
  [Unknown]:  New York
What is the two-letter country code for this unit?
  [Unknown]:  NY
Is CN=localhost, OU=examples, O=ExampleCo,
   L=New York, ST=New York, C=NY correct?
  [no]:  yes

Enter key password for <tomcat>
        (RETURN if same as keystore password):
```

The values marked as `unknown` indicate that no previous value has been provided. If this key were later to be edited, the values in brackets would be replaced by the values provided here. The "first and last name" field should be filled with the name of the server by which people will connect to Tomcat. "Localhost" is used here because for testing Tomcat and the Web browser will be running on the same machine. For a public site, this name should be whatever users will enter as the URL, such as "www.somesite.com."

Finally, keytool asks for a password for the new key, as distinct from the password for the keystore as a whole. In the current implementation of Tomcat these *must* be the same, so no new password was provided.

Next, the new key can be viewed by running `keytool -list`. This will once again prompt for the keytool password and print all available keys, as follows:

```
Enter keystore password:  changeit

Keystore type: jks
Keystore provider: SUN

Your keystore contains 1 entry

tomcat, Nov 29, 2003, keyEntry,
Certificate fingerprint
(MD5): 02:97:2B:04:D1:B0:9B:E7:2B:F3:80:72:1F:E0:95:99
```

Tomcat can be configured to use SSL by placing another entry in `server.xml`. To make it even easier, this entry is already present in a default Tomcat installation, although it is commented out. Turning on SSL is therefore as easy as removing the XML comment tags around the following:

```
<Connector port="8443"
  maxThreads="150" minSpareThreads="25" maxSpareThreads="75"
  enableLookups="false" disableUploadTimeout="true"
  acceptCount="100" debug="0" scheme="https" secure="true"
  clientAuth="false" sslProtocol="TLS" />
```

Most of these parameters can be safely ignored in common usage.

Once Tomcat is restarted, a browser can be directed to https://localhost:8443/. Tomcat will send its self-signed certificate, but because the browser will not recognize the certificate authority, it will pop up an alert similar to the one in Figure 17.2.

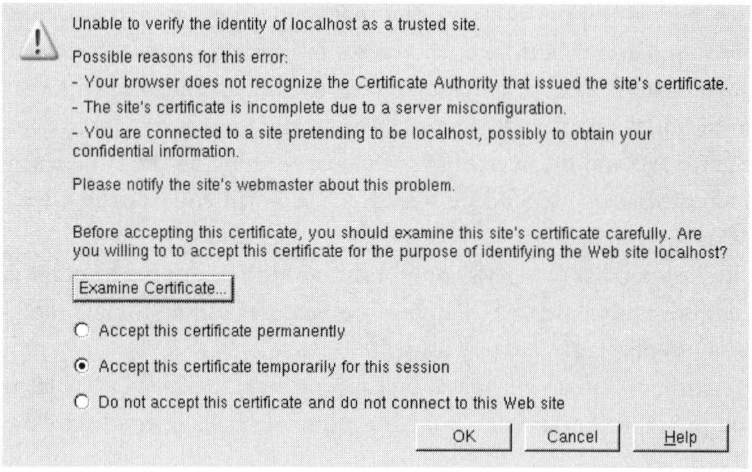

Figure 17.2. A certificate warning.

The exact form of this dialog will depend on which browser is used, but the relevant information should be equivalent. It is worth noting that if there is a mismatch between the name given to keytool and the server name in the URL, then an addition dialog will be presented warning of this mismatch. In this case no such warning is given because the name "localhost" is being used in both places.

Once the certificate is accepted, the browser may display a key icon or some other indicator that the connection is secure. Beyond that the interaction will proceed as it did before. In particular, if a user tries to access the "example" Web application, she will still need to log in, although now she can do so secure in the knowledge that her password cannot be intercepted by a malicious snooper. It is also worth noting that both BASIC and form-based authentication will continue to work under SSL.

17.7 Client Certificates

As the situation has been described so far servers may authenticate themselves to users with certificates, and users have to authenticate themselves to servers with passwords. It is natural at this point to wonder whether a browser could be given a certificate that it would use to access a server. This would certainly be useful; it would free the user from having to memorize a password as well as being potentially more secure. Such **client certificates** are possible, although they are used rarely, and their use is usually confined to corporate intranets. Tomcat provides support for client certificates, although it is one of the least-documented aspects of the system. This section will discuss how to generate and use such certificates.

Creating client certificates requires a more sophisticated set of tools than keytool can provide. There are commercial SSL toolkits that provide the needed functionality, but there is also an excellent free, open source toolkit called openssl.

Unfortunately, legal restrictions relating to cryptography make it impossible to distribute this toolkit on the companion CD-ROM. Openssl is included by default on many Linux and *BSD systems. The source code may also be found at the home site, http://www.openssl.org.

A precompiled binary for windows is available from http://www.aboveground.cx/~rjmooney/projects/misc/openssl.zip. Compiling from source on Windows is not conceptually difficult, although doing so requires the installation of the GNU C compiler and other tools, so it is not a trivial undertaking. Generally speaking it will be easier to use openssl on a Unix system to generate the certificates and then transfer the resulting files to a Windows machine.

On that note, it is worth pointing out that in situations where security is a serious concern Unix is almost always a better choice than Windows. Every operating system has its strengths; Windows includes ease of use and user friendliness, but Unix is generally much more secure.

Creation of certificates proceeds in several steps.[4] First, create three subdirectories called "ca," "client," and "server." These will hold files for the certificate authority, client certificate, and server certificate, respectively. Next, use openssl to create a new key and a request to have this key certified as a new certificate authority with the following command:

```
openssl req -new -newkey rsa:1024 -nodes -out ssl/ca/ca.csr \
-keyout ssl/ca/ca.key
```

This will start an interactive session in which information for the key will be provided, much as when keytool was used to generate self-signed certificate. Note that this is the information for the **certificate authority**'s key, not the server's. A typical session will resemble the following:

```
Generating a 1024 bit RSA private key
.................++++++

writing new private key to 'ssl/ca/ca.key'
-----
You are about to be asked to enter information that will be
incorporated into your certificate request.
```

[4]These instructions come from Christopher Williams, who posted them on the Tomcat-user mailing list. I am indebted to him for this information.

```
What you are about to enter is what is called a
Distinguished Name or a DN.

There are quite a few fields but you can leave some blank
For some fields there will be a default value,
If you enter '.', the field will be left blank.
-----
Country Name (2 letter code) [AU]:US
State or Province Name (full name) [Some-State]:New York
Locality Name (e.g., city) []:New York
Organization Name (e.g., company) [Internet Widgits Pty Ltd]:
My Certificate Authority
Organizational Unit Name (e.g., section) []:
Common Name (e.g., YOUR name) []:John Q. Developer
Email Address []:johnq@nosuchdomain.com

Please enter the following 'extra' attributes
to be sent with your certificate request
A challenge password []:
An optional company name []:
```

Next, a self-signed certificate for the certificate authority must be generated. Like any self-signed certificate this is of little value in a real security situation, but it will suffice for generating client certificates. This step is performed with the command

```
openssl x509 -trustout -signkey ssl/ca/ca.key -days 365 -req \
-in ssl/ca/ca.csr -out ssl/ca/ca.pem
```

which should print out a success message and exit.

In the next step Java must be told to trust this new certificate authority that has just been created. This is done by adding an entry for the authority in a special global keystore that Java uses internally. This is stored in a file located at `/jre/lib/security/cacerts` within `JAVA_HOME`. To perform the next step, it is necessary to have write privileges to this file. This may mean running the next command as root on a Unix system or changing the default permissions on the file. The command is

```
keytool -import -keystore $JAVA_HOME/jre/lib/security/cacerts \
-file ssl/ca/ca.pem -alias my_certificate_authority
```

This will prompt for a password, and like all keystores the default password is "changeit." Keytool will then ask for confirmation before it accepts the new key.

From this point on Java will consider "My Certificate Authority" as valid as one of the major companies such as Verisign.

Next, create a simple file that the certificate authority will use to generate serial numbers.

```
echo "02" > ssl/ca/ca.srl
```

It is now time to create a new server certificate, which is done slightly differently than before. The command is

```
keytool -genkey -alias tomcat -keyalg RSA -keysize 1024  \
-keystore ssl/server/server.ks -storetype JKS
```

Note the `keystore` option, which places the keystore in `server.ks` rather than the default `.keystore`. It is possible to use the default, but it is preferable to place this in a separate file so as not to get it mixed with any personal security keys.

Once again keystore will ask for a password and then information for the server certificate. The dialog proceeds exactly as it did when generating a self-signed certificate.

```
Enter keystore password:  changeit
What is your first and last name?
  [Unknown]:  localhost
What is the name of your organizational unit?
  [Unknown]:  My Web Site
What is the name of your organization?
  [Unknown]:  My Company
What is the name of your City or Locality?
  [Unknown]:  New York
What is the name of your State or Province?
  [Unknown]:  NY
What is the two-letter country code for this unit?
  [Unknown]:  US
Is CN=localhost, OU=My Web Site, O=My Company,
   L=New York, ST=NY, C=US correct?
  [no]:  yes

Enter key password for <tomcat>
        (RETURN if same as keystore password)
```

Next, use keytool to create a request for the server certificate to be signed by the certificate authority.

```
keytool -certreq -keyalg RSA -alias tomcat  \
-file ssl/server/server.csr -keystore ssl/server/server.ks
```

As always, a password will be required before keytool proceeds. The password is still "changeit."

Openssl can now process this request and use the certificate authority's key to sign the server certificate.

```
openssl x509 -CA ssl/ca/ca.pem -CAkey ssl/ca/ca.key \
-CAserial ssl/ca/ca.srl -req -in ssl/server/server.csr \
-out ssl/server/server.crt -days 365
```

Next, import the signed key into the keystore:

```
keytool -import -alias tomcat \
-keystore ssl/server/server.ks \
-trustcacerts -file ssl/server/server.crt
```

It is only possible to import this key because Java was told early to treat "My Certificate Authority" as a valid authority. If this had not been done, Java would refuse to import the key and would return an error reporting "Failed to establish chain from reply." The chain here refers to a "chain of trust." Although we are only dealing with two entities, the server and the certificate authority, some applications allow for a chain of relationships. For example, a key from agency A may have been signed by agency B, and B's key may have been signed by C. If C is known to be trustworthy, then by extension A's key can be trusted.

At this point the server's key has been completed and can be used just as the self-signed key was previously. The next step required for using client certificates is to import the certificate authority's certificate into the keystore:

```
keytool -import -alias my_ca \
-keystore ssl/server/server.ks -trustcacerts \
-file ssl/ca/ca.pem
```

This is needed so that Tomcat can verify the client certificates that are sent to it by a browser.

The next three steps will generate a client key. First, openssl is used to create a request:

```
openssl req -new -newkey rsa:512 -nodes \
-out ssl/client/client1.req -keyout ssl/client/client1.key
```

User and company information must be provided here, just as with the certificate authority and server certificate requests:

```
Country Name (2 letter code) [AU]:US
State or Province Name (full name) [Some-State]:New York
Locality Name (eg, city) []:NY
Organization Name (eg, company) [Internet Widgits Pty Ltd]:
My Browser
Organizational Unit Name (eg, section) []:
Common Name (eg, YOUR name) []:Jane J. Websurfer
Email Address []:jane@nosuchdomain.com

Please enter the following 'extra' attributes
to be sent with your certificate request
A challenge password []:
An optional company name []:
```

Note that a common name *must* be provided here. Although it is not documented anywhere, client certificates will not work if this field is left blank. In addition, this field will be used later as a username.

In the next step the certificate authority signs this request, making it valid:

```
openssl x509 -CA ssl/ca/ca.pem -CAkey ssl/ca/ca.key \
-CAserial ssl/ca/ca.srl -req -in ssl/client/client1.req \
-out ssl/client/client1.pem -days 365
```

Finally, all relevant information is packaged into a form suitable for loading into a browser:

```
openssl pkcs12 -export -clcerts -in ssl/client/client1.pem \
-inkey ssl/client/client1.key -out ssl/client/client1.p12 \
-name "my_client_certificate"
```

This process will complete by asking for an "export password." This can be anything.

These last three steps can be performed multiple times to generate multiple client certificates. Generally each browser or user should have his or her own.

The process of importing a client certificate into a browser will vary depending on the browser in use. Generally there will be an option under security settings to import a certificate. Select this option, and a file browser will be presented. Navigate to the `client.p12` file created in the last step and double-click on it. A dialog will then pop up asking for a password, which should be the export password. The browser may or may not need to be restarted.

The final step is to make two small configuration changes to `server.xml`. First, add `keystore=` to point to the location of the `server.ks` created previously. Second, change the `clientAuth` attribute to `true` and restart Tomcat. From that point on only browsers with a properly installed client certificate will be able to access the site; anyone else will be turned away with an error message.

17.8 Certificate-Based Authentication

Users with certificates can now go to the protected "example" Web application but will still need to log in. To make the certificate also act as a login credential, a few more changes are needed. First, the `login-config` method must be changed as follows:

```
<login-config>
  <auth-method>CLIENT-CERT</auth-method>
</login-config>
```

Next, the realm must be told to accept the user that the certificate will present. Unfortunately a major problem is encountered at this point.

In Tomcat 4 the `MemoryRealm`, which is a slight variation of the `UserDatabaseRealm`, could be configured to handle certificate-based authentication by providing the "distinguished name" of the client certificate as the username, as in

```
<user
  username="CN=Jane Q. Websurfer, O=My Browser, ST=NY, C=US"
  password=""
  roles="example"/>
```

The password is empty in this case because it is not used; the certificate itself acts as the password. In Tomcat 5, however, the equal sign (=) is no longer a valid character within an XML attribute. There is no way to circumvent this by using an escape character or other XML trick. The inescapable fact is there is no way to specify a certificate-based username in `tomcat-users.xml`. The `JDBCRealm` and others have no provision for the `CLIENT-CERT` login method at all.

If Tomcat were a closed source project, this would be a dead end. There would be no hope for certificate-based authentication short of writing to the company and asking them to fix the problem in their next release sometime next year. Fortunately, Tomcat is open source, so it is possible for industrious developers to fix the problem themselves. Now we'll look at one way to do this. In addition to enabling certificate-based authentication, this will also illustrate some of the joys—and idiosyncrasies—of working with a large open source toolkit like Tomcat.

A logical starting point is the existing implementation of `UserDatabaseRealm`. The name of this class is listed in `server.xml`, and it is easy enough to find the Java code for this class in the Tomcat source.

Although there is documentation on how realms work, it is somewhat vague as to exactly what methods will be called under different circumstances. Therefore, the first step will be to add some print statements to see how the methods are invoked. This can be done most easily by extending `UserDatabaseRealm`.

Looking at the `UserDatabaseRealm` shows three methods that look like they may be relevant: `authenticate()`, `getPassword()`, and `getPrincipal()`. The first has a good deal of code, and the other two return `null`. The extended class will implement these three methods.

The most immediately obvious possibility would be to make these methods print their arguments and then call up to the super class, as in

```
public class ModifiedUserDatabaseRealm
    extends UserDatabaseRealm
{
    public Principal authenticate(String username,
                                  String credentials)
    {
        System.out.println("authenticate() called with " +
                           "username = " + username      +
                           "credentials = " + credentials);
        return super.authenticate(username,credentials);
    }
}
```

As the inner workings of this realm are explored and fixed, it is reasonable to expect that many changes will need to be made to this code, and Tomcat will need to be restarted each time to pick up the changes. This sounds like a job for BeanShell, discussed in Chapter 16. Rather than implementing the realm methods in Java, it will be much faster to make `ModifiedUserDatabaseRealm` load and invoke BeanShell scripts, which can be quickly changed on the fly without any recompilation or restarting. The resulting version is shown in Listing 17.1.

Listing 17.1 A realm implementation that calls BeanShell

```
package com.awl.toolbook.chapter17;

import java.security.Principal;
import javax.naming.Context;

import org.apache.catalina.realm.UserDatabaseRealm;
import org.apache.catalina.UserDatabase;
import org.apache.catalina.core.StandardServer;
import org.apache.catalina.ServerFactory;

import bsh.Interpreter;

public class ModifiedUserDatabaseRealm
    extends UserDatabaseRealm
{
    public Principal authenticate(String username,
                                  String credentials)
    {
        try {
            Interpreter i = new Interpreter();
            i.source("realm.bsh");
            i.set("parent",this);
            i.set("database",database);
            i.set("username",username);
            i.set("credentials",credentials);
            return
              (Principal)
              i.eval("authenticate(username,credentials)");
        } catch (Throwable t) {
            System.out.println("Error calling BeanShell");
            t.printStackTrace(System.err);
        }

        return null;
    }
```

```
    protected String getPassword(String username) {
        try {
            Interpreter i = new Interpreter();
            i.source("realm.bsh");
            i.set("parent",this);
            i.set("database",database);
            i.set("username",username);
            return (String)
                i.eval("getPassword(username)");
        } catch (Throwable t) {
            System.out.println("Error calling BeanShell");
            t.printStackTrace(System.err);
        }

        return null;

    }


    /**
     * Return the Principal associated with the given
     * user name.
     */
    protected Principal getPrincipal(String username) {
        try {
            Interpreter i = new Interpreter();
            i.source("realm.bsh");
            i.set("parent",this);
            i.set("database",database);
            i.set("username",username);
            return (Principal)
                i.eval("getPrincipal(username)");
        } catch (Throwable t) {
            System.out.println("Error calling BeanShell");
            t.printStackTrace(System.err);
        }

        return null;
    }
}
```

Each method works essentially this way: by loading `realm.bsh`, setting some values in the global namespace, and calling a BeanShell function. The parameters to each function are set as global variables, which is the easiest way to pass them to the BeanShell functions. The `dictionary` is a class variable used by the `authenticate()`, which may also be needed in the other two methods. The `parent` variable points to the superclass of the current instance of `ModifiedUserDatabaseRealm`, which will enable the BeanShell scripts to call back into Java.

This class can then be compiled and moved to `server/classes`, which is the appropriate location for classes needed by Tomcat's server functions globally and at startup. The BeanShell jar file must also be moved into `server/lib`.

Tomcat can now be reconfigured to use this new class as its realm:

```
<Realm
  className=
    "com.awl.toolbook.chapter17.ModifiedUserDatabaseRealm"
  debug="0"
  resourceName="UserDatabase"/>
```

Tomcat can now be started, and it comes up without any complaints or error messages, indicating that there is no problem with the new realm class. Attempting to access example/index.html results in the following error in the log:

```
java.io.FileNotFoundException:
tomcat/realm.bsh (No such file or directory)
```

This is good: It means that the new realm class is trying to load the `realm.bsh` that has not yet been created. So the next step is to create the file, which is shown in Listing 17.2.

Listing 17.2 The BeanShell file with realm methods

```
import java.security.Principal;
import java.util.ArrayList;
import java.util.Iterator;

import javax.naming.Context;

import org.apache.catalina.realm.GenericPrincipal;
import org.apache.catalina.Group;
import org.apache.catalina.LifecycleException;
```

```
import org.apache.catalina.Role;
import org.apache.catalina.ServerFactory;
import org.apache.catalina.User;
import org.apache.catalina.UserDatabase;
import org.apache.catalina.core.StandardServer;
import org.apache.catalina.util.StringManager;

setAccessibility(true);

Principal authenticate(String username,
                        String credentials)
{
    System.out.println("authenticate() called");
    System.out.println("Username = " + username);
    System.out.println("Credential = " + credentials);

    return parent.authenticate(username,credentials);
}


getPassword(String username) {
    System.out.println("getPassword() called");
    System.out.println("Username = " + username);

    return (null);
}


getPrincipal(String username) {
    System.out.println("getPrincipal() called");
    System.out.println("Username = " + username);

    return (null);
}
```

All the import statements were taken directly from `UserDatabaseRealm`. Although none of these are used yet, they may be needed as development progresses. In addition, the import of `GenericPrincipal` was added because it lives in the same package as `UserDatabaseRealm` and so did not need to be imported initially.

The call to `setAccessibility(true)` allows BeanShell to access private and protected members and methods. This is needed to allow the scripts to call back into all the methods it may need.

The rest of the code is straightforward; it simply prints some diagnostic information and calls back into the parent.

This new code can be tested immediately just by clicking reload on the browser. This time the error message is replaced by the following message:

```
getPrincipal() called
Username = EMAILADDRESS=jane@nosuchdomain.com,
CN=Jane J. Websurfer, O=My Browser, L=New York, ST=New York
```

This is an excellent result; it indicates that `getPrincipal()` is the method called and that all the information from the certificate is made available to this method. It is no wonder the default implementation does not work for client-based authentication because `getPrincipal()` returns `null`.

Now that it is clear how the realm handler is invoked, it is possible to start implementing a fix. The first task will be to extract a meaningful name from the username, and CN seems like a good choice. There are many ways this information could be extracted. One obvious choice would be to use one of the regular expression packages discussed in Chapter 13. To accomplish this, jakarta-oro-2.0.7.jar must be copied into `server/lib`, and the definition of `getPrincipal()` in the BeanShell script must be changed as follows:

```
import org.apache.oro.text.regex.*;

getPrincipal(String username) {
    System.out.println("getPrincipal() called");
    System.out.println("Username = " + username);

    Perl5Compiler compiler = new Perl5Compiler();
    Pattern pattern =
        compiler.compile("CN=([^,]*)");

    PatternMatcherInput input =
        new PatternMatcherInput(username);
    Perl5Matcher m = new Perl5Matcher();

    if(m.contains(input,pattern)) {
        MatchResult r = m.getMatch();
```

```
            System.out.println("CN = " +
                               r.group(1));
        }

        return (null);
    }
```

Note the new import statement.

When the browser's reload button is pressed, an unpleasant surprise shows up in `catalina.out`: the following error message:

```
Sourced file: inline evaluation of:
"getPrincipal(username);" :
Typed variable declaration : Class:
Perl5Compiler not found in namespace
: at Line: 43 : in file: realm.bsh : Perl5Compiler
```

This is unexpected; the jar file is available, and the class was properly imported. The only possible explanation is that although Tomcat can load BeanShell itself from `server/lib`, for some reason the BeanShell interpreter is unable to access jars in that directory. The only possible fix would be to move the jar to a directory that is more widely available to Tomcat, and indeed moving the jar to `common/lib` fixes the problem. On the next reload the logs report

```
CN = Jane J. Websurfer
```

We now have a simple name that can be used to authenticate the user. Tomcat can be notified of this user by adding an entry to `tomcat-users.xml`, just as was done for users using regular password authentication.

```
<user
  username="Jane J. Websurfer"
  password="ignore"
  roles="example"/>
```

At this juncture it is worth pointing out that this format of the file is extremely sensitive. To an extent this is to be expected because all XML files require strict adherence to certain rules. The way Tomcat handles invalid files may be unexpected, however. If there is a problem with an entry—for example, if `username` were mistyped as `usrname`—Tomcat would silently and without warning discard the entry, both from the database in memory and from the file itself! A perplexed administrator trying to find out why Jane cannot log into the system might be surprised to discover her entry had mysteriously vanished.

All that remains is to modify `getPrincipal()` to find this user and return an appropriate `Principal` object. It is not immediately clear how to do this, but once again the open source nature of Tomcat comes to the rescue. The original code for `authenticate()` in `UserDatabaseRealm` also returns a principal, using information from the `dictionary` object. That code can easily be extracted and used in `getPrincipal()`, and the result is

```
getPrincipal(String username) {
    System.out.println("getPrincipal() called");
    System.out.println("Username = " + username);

    Perl5Compiler compiler = new Perl5Compiler();
    Pattern pattern =
        compiler.compile("CN=([^,]*)");

    PatternMatcherInput input =
        new PatternMatcherInput(username);
    Perl5Matcher m = new Perl5Matcher();

    // If there is no CN, abort
    if(!m.contains(input,pattern)) {
        return null;
    }

    MatchResult r = m.getMatch();
    String name   = r.group(1);
    User user     = database.findUser(name);
    if (user == null) {
        return (null);
    }

    ArrayList combined = new ArrayList();
    Iterator roles = user.getRoles();
    while (roles.hasNext()) {
        Role role = (Role) roles.next();
        String rolename = role.getRolename();
        if (!combined.contains(rolename)) {
```

```
                combined.add(rolename);
            }
        }

        Iterator groups = user.getGroups();
        while (groups.hasNext()) {
            Group group = (Group) groups.next();
            roles = group.getRoles();
            while (roles.hasNext()) {
                Role role = (Role) roles.next();
                String rolename = role.getRolename();
                if (!combined.contains(rolename)) {
                    combined.add(rolename);
                }
            }
        }

        return(new GenericPrincipal(parent,
                                    user.getUsername(),
                                    user.getPassword(),
                                    combined));

    }
```

This should do the trick, but regrettably it results in another error:

```
Sourced file: inline evaluation of:
"getPrincipal(username);" :
Typed variable declaration :
Class: User not found in namespace : at
Line: 58 : in file: realm .bsh : User
```

The `User` class, which is a class internal to Tomcat, cannot be found. This is a little more troubling.

The next step is to see where it is defined, and by exploring the jar files in both `common/lib` and `server/lib`, the class is discovered in `common/lib/catalina.jar`. It is tempting to try to fix this by copying it to `common/lib`, as was done with the ORO classes. Unfortunately, this breaks Tomcat to the point where it will no longer run. The other alternative is to copy all the jar files from `server/lib` to `common/ilb`. This is unquestionably an ugly solution, but it will do for the moment.

The good news is that that is the last thing that needs to be done. On the next browser reload "Jane Q. Websurfer" will successfully be granted access to the protected content, and this will happen securely, seamlessly, and without ever needing to type a password.

From here the new code could be rolled back into `ModifiedUserDatabaseRealm`, or even back into the original class.

17.9 Global Resources

To a large extent, Web applications are self-contained. All the configuration information, classes, jars, and other resources needed by an application can be held in a war file or in a directory, unknown to Tomcat as a whole. When developing an application for use only by a single individual or within a single company, it is perfectly satisfactory to draw a sharp distinction between Tomcat and the applications hosted within it. However, when a Web application is meant to be distributed and used by several people, some breaking of these boundaries is necessary.

The canonical example of a resource that breaks this boundary is a database. It is to be expected that a Web application that is meant to be run in many different places will also be run in conjunction with many different databases. One installation may use Microsoft SQL server, another MySQL, and a third Oracle. In addition, each installation will have its own usernames and passwords for database access.

Database connection information may be stored in a configuration file within the Web application, but this is inelegant because it requires the person installing the application to open the .war archive and poke around in the internals of the application. There is also no convention for how this information should be stored; it could be in the `web.xml`, a property file, a class, or jsp files.

The specification for Web applications provides a better solution that is fully supported by Tomcat. Web applications may refer to resources by name using the JNDI conventions. These resources may then be defined at the Tomcat level in the global `server.xml`. This provides for a consistent interface, eliminates the need to access the internals of a Web application, and makes it easier to share resources between several Web applications that may be running at the same time.

There are two categories of object that may be defined and used in this way: simple environment values such as strings and integers, and compound objects that are built from factories. There are three steps needed to use both, and these steps are basically the same for both types of resource. Environment variables are somewhat simpler, so they will be considered first.

An application that will use an environment variable must declare its intention to do so in its web.xml, through an env-entry node. For example, to use a string called theMessage, the following declaration would be needed:

```
<env-entry>
  <description>A simple text message</description>
  <env-entry-name>theMessage</env-entry-name>
  <env-entry-type>java.lang.String</env-entry-type>
</env-entry>
```

The second step is to define the variable in server.xml. To do this, a Context node must be defined for the application, and the variables can be declared within that node. Assuming that theMessage is to be used within the example Web application that has been used throughout this chapter, the declaration would consist of

```
<Context path="/example">
  <Environment
    name="theMessage"
    type="java.lang.String"
    value="This is the value of theMessage!"/>
</Context>
```

Alternately, if a variable is to be used by many applications, it may be defined globally and used by each application. First, the definition is made in the global resources section of server.xml:

```
<GlobalNamingResources>
  <Environment
    name="theMessage"
    type="java.lang.String"
    value="This is the value of theMessage!"/>
</GlobalNamingResources>
```

Then a reference to the global definition can be placed in the Context:

```
<Context path="/example">
  <ResourceLink
    name="theMessage"
    global="theMessage"
    type="java.lang.String"/>
</Context>
```

With these definitions any JSP page, servlet, or other code within the example application can access this value using the standard JNDI calls. Here is a JSP page that prints the value:

```
<%@page language="java"
        import="javax.naming.*" %>

<html>
<body>
The value of theMessage is

<%
try {
  Context initCtx = new InitialContext();
  Context envCtx =
    (Context) initCtx.lookup("java:comp/env");

  String message =
    (String) envCtx.lookup("theMessage");

  out.println(message);
} catch (Exception e) {
  out.println("Unable to access theMessage!");
  e.printStackTrace(System.out);
}
%>

</body>
</html>
```

The preceding example is enough for most usage within a Web application, noting that the base context as defined by Tomcat is `java:comp/env`.

Compound values are only slightly more complex than environment variables, and to illustrate this, a bean will be made available though JNDI. Listing 17.3 shows the bean.

Listing 17.3 A simple bean

```
package com.awl.toolbook.chapter17;

public class SampleBean {
    public SampleBean() {}
```

```
    private String message;
    public String getMessage() {return message;}
    public void setMessage(String message) {
        this.message = message;
    }

    private int intValue;
    public int getIntValue() {return intValue;}
    public void setIntValue(int intValue) {
        this.intValue = intValue;
    }

    public String toString() {
        return "[SampleBean: " +
            message + "," +
            intValue + "]";
    }
}
```

The definition in `server.xml` has two parts; the first defines the name and type of the resource:

```
<Resource
  name="beans/SampleBeanFactory"
  auth="Container"
  type="com.awl.toolbook.chapter17.SampleBean"/>
```

The second portion defines parameters for the resource. Bean values must be handled by a factory class, and Tomcat provides a bean factory that should be more than sufficient for most uses. The resource declarations name this class and provide values for the bean properties.

```
<ResourceParams name="beans/SampleBeanFactory">
  <parameter>
    <name>factory</name>
    <value>org.apache.naming.factory.BeanFactory</value>
  </parameter>
  <parameter>
    <name>message</name>
```

```
      <value>Hello, this is a message in a bean</value>
    </parameter>
    <parameter>
      <name>intValue</name>
      <value>288</value>
    </parameter>
  </ResourceParams>
```

The declaration of the resource and its parameters may be placed inside the `Context` definition to make the bean available only to the example application, or they may be defined in the global section and used in the `Context` with a `ResourceLink`.

```
<ResourceLink
  name="beans/SampleBeanFactory"
  global="beans/SampleBeanFactory"
  type="com.awl.toolbook.chapter17.SampleBean"/>
```

Regardless of how the resource is declared, it is imported into the application with another entry in `web.xml`.

```
<resource-env-ref>
  <description>Object factory beans</description>
  <resource-env-ref-name>
    beans/SampleBeanFactory
  </resource-env-ref-name>
  <resource-env-ref-type>
    com.awl.toolbook.chapter17.SampleBean
  </resource-env-ref-type>
</resource-env-ref>
```

The bean is now available to JSP pages and servlets through the same mechanism used to obtain `theMessage`, under the name `beans/SampleBeanFactory`.

JDBC data sources may be defined in exactly the same way. The type in this case would be a `javax.sql.DataSource`, and the resource parameters would use the `BasicDataSourceFactory`, from the `dbcp` package, which was discussed in Chapter 10. These are some other resource parameters:

- username: the username with which to connect
- password: the password with which to connect
- driverClassName: the name of the JDBC driver class
- url: the URL with which to connect

In addition, there are a number of tunable parameters for performance. See Chapter 10 for more information on these options.

17.10 Web-Based Management and Administration

Among the many other nice features provided with Tomcat are a complete set of Web-based monitoring and configuration tools. These are protected by security, so the first thing that must be done to use them is to create a user with the right security roles. Assuming the `UserDatabaseRealm` is being used, this can be done by adding

```
<user name="admin"
      password="admin"
      roles="standard,manager,admin" />
```

to `tomcat-users.xml`. There is nothing special about the username or password used here; any value could be chosen. Given the potential for abuse of these services, they should normally be disabled in a production server or at least protected by something stronger than a username and password. This is a good candidate for a client certificate.

The administration page is located at http://localhost:8080/admin and is shown in Figure 17.3. As the figure shows, much of Tomcat's configuration, both global and

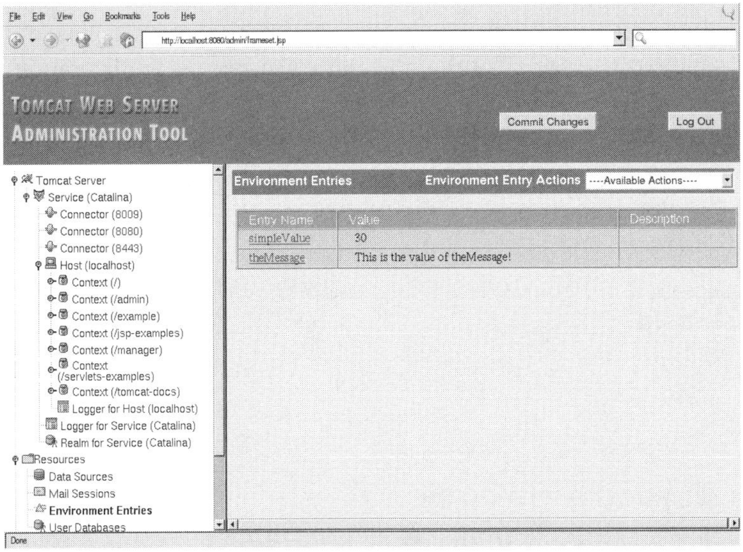

Figure 17.3. The administration page.

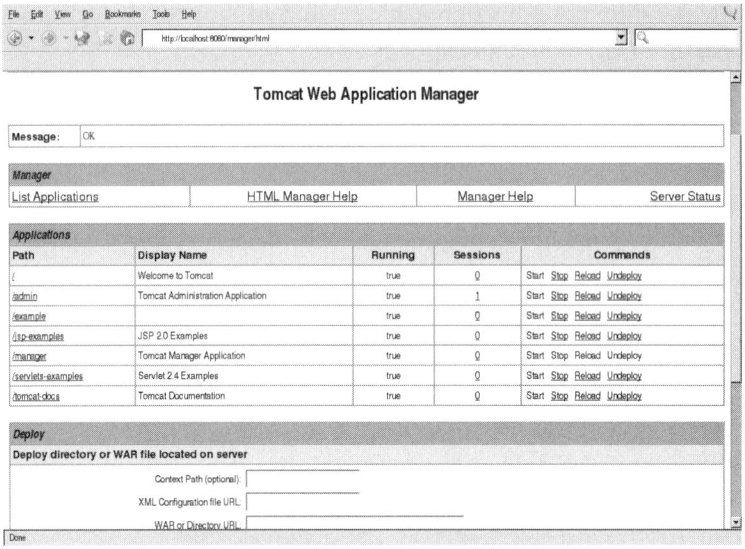

Figure 17.4. The control page.

that of individual Web applications, can be viewed from this screen. In particular the figure shows the values of the environment variables used in the previous section.

While the Web administration contains facilities to edit and add new values as well as view existing ones, the features are not working as of the current beta version of Tomcat 5. Saving a new value of `theMessage` will have no effect, and clicking the "Commit changes" button at the top will overwrite `server.xml`, losing comments and other information. Although fixes for these bugs are expected before the final version is released, the safest course of action when making configuration changes will always be to shut down Tomcat and edit the files by hand.

In addition to the administration screen there are also a number of management screens. The distinction between "management" and "administration" can be vague. For Tomcat management refers to the ability to monitor Tomcat's status and stop or restart services, while administration refers to control over system settings. The management control screen is available at http://localhost:8080/manager/html and is shown in Figure 17.4.

The management status is available at http://localhost:8080/manager/status and is shown in Figure 17.5.

17.11 Beyond This Book

This chapter has only begun to scratch the surface of Tomcat's features and abilities. For example, the management service makes it possible to deploy new applications by just entering the name of a war file and an XML descriptor. Tomcat can also

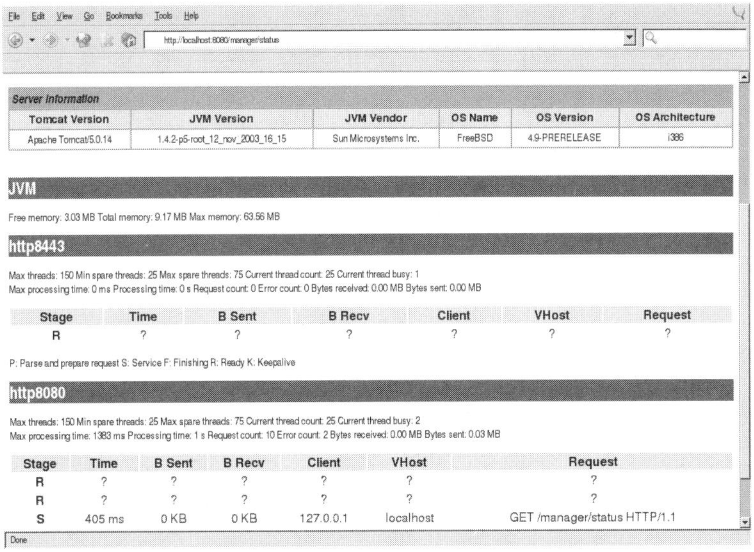

Figure 17.5. The status page.

be **clustered,** meaning several instances can work together so if one fails or is shut down, the end users will not be affected. It is also possible to install new management components though a system called **MBeans.** The Tomcat home page, http://jakarta.apache.org/tomcat, is a good place to start learning about all these additional abilities.

17.12 Summary

Tool: Tomcat
Purpose: Web and application server
Version covered: 5.0 beta
Home page: http://jakarta.apache.org/tomcat/
License: The Apache Software License, Version 1.1

Further Reading:

- *Web Security: A Step-by-Step Reference Guide,* by Lincoln D. Stein, Addison-Wesley, 1997.
- *Enterprise Java Servlets,* by Jeff M. Genender, Addison-Wesley, 2002.
- *JNDI API Tutorial and Reference: Building Directory-Enabled Java Applications,* by Rosanna Lee and Scott Seligman, Addison-Wesley, 2000.

CHAPTER 18

The Standard Tag Library

Chapter 17 covered what might be considered the outer layers of Tomcat. These included issues related to the way Tomcat offers and secures incoming requests, as well as how Tomcat can make global resources available to individual Web applications.

There is another view of Tomcat from the inner layers: the APIs and data structures that Tomcat offers to developers of Web applications. The most important of these APIs are the Servlet 2.4 and JavaServer Pages 2.0 specification. These APIs are large and complex, and covering them in full would require an entire book on each.

One of the most important features of JSP is the ability to create **tags,** code that may be invoked from pages using an HTML-like syntax. Such code has access to parameters passed from the page, chunks of text on the page that may include other tags, and the entire application environment.

Initially, after the tag functionality was introduced, almost everyone using tags developed their own set. This entailed a great deal of overlap and needless duplication of effort, so it was natural that a standard tag library would eventually be defined. This tag library is a separate standard from the Servlet and JSP specifications, but it rests on top of features introduced in JSP 2.0. It therefore is a natural enhancement to Tomcat, which at the time of this writing is the only application server that fully supports these features.

18.1 Tag Libraries

Before jumping into the full standard tag library, it helps to consider how pages load and use simpler tags. Listing 18.1 uses a simple tag that displays the date and time in a configurable format,

Listing 18.1 A JSP that uses a custom tag

```
<%@ taglib prefix="awl"
    uri="http://toolbook.awl.com/samples" %>
The time, in two different formats:<p>
<awl:date format="EEEE, MMMM dd yyyy 'at' hh:mm"/><br>
<awl:date format="hh:mm:ss MM/dd/yy"/><br>
```

The tag library is loaded with the first line. The URI specifies the location of the tag library definition, and the prefix specifies the name that will be used to access the tags. Here the prefix is `awl`, but it could be anything as long as it is used consistently. One of the tags from this library, `date`, is used twice in the last two lines. The name of the tag is prepended by the prefix specified at the top.[1]

The `awl:time` tag itself simply sends the current time to the page in a format specified by the `format` property. In one sense this is not a particularly good example. Tags are intrinsically part of the view portion of an application, and so dealing with issues such as formatting a time for presentation is perfectly valid. However, the tag in Listing 18.1 also generates data in the form of the current time, which ideally would be done by a JavaBean acting as a model component. With some effort the standard tag library can help make such separations of roles between tags and beans easier to manage, as will be seen later in this chapter.

18.2 Tags with Bodies

Custom tags can do more than just output data controlled by parameters. A custom tag can have a body, which it can control in arbitrary ways. Listing 18.2 shows such a custom tag that can be used to display its body, hide it, or even reverse it. The result is shown in Figure 18.1.

[1]Formally, the tag lives in an XML namespace specified by the prefix. Custom tags can be loaded with any namespace, so formally the portion before the colon is not part of the name. However, in the text this prefix will always be included to avoid possible confusion between tags such as c:param and sql:param.

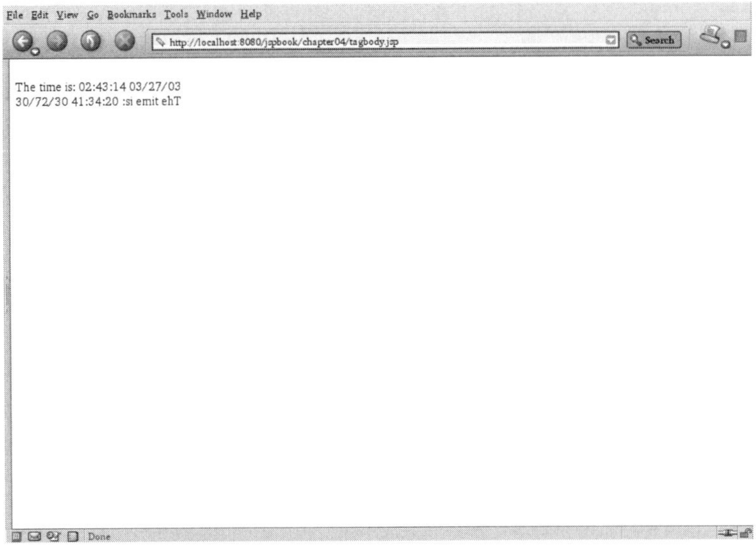

Figure 18.1. The result of a custom tag.

Listing 18.2 A custom tag with a body

```
<%@ taglib prefix="awl"
     uri="http://jspbook.awl.com/samples" %>
<awl:maybeShow show="no">
You can't see me!
</awl:maybeShow><br>

<awl:maybeShow show="yes">
  The time is:
  <awl:date format="hh:mm:ss MM/dd/yy"/>
</awl:maybeShow><br>

<awl:maybeShow show="reverse">
  The time is:
  <awl:date format="hh:mm:ss MM/dd/yy"/>
</awl:maybeShow><br>
```

This example loads the same tag library as used in Listing 18.1 and again specifies that it will be using the `awl` prefix to access the tags. The tag used this time is called `awl:maybeShow`, and it has a parameter called `show` that controls what the tag should do with its body. `show` may be set to "no," in which case the body is hidden from the page; "yes," in which case the body is displayed; or "reverse," in which case the body is shown backward.

Note that the body of the `awl:maybeShow` tag may include anything, including other JSP tags. This will be true of any custom tag that has been properly programmed. This property is described by saying that JSP tags can be **nested.** From here on it will be assumed that the body of any tag can contain any other tag unless otherwise noted.

18.3 Dynamic Attributes in Tags

For the standard tag library to be able to do all the things for which it was designed, the tags need to take parameters that are more complicated than simple orders like "yes" and "no." In fact, the parameters to the standard tag library comprise a full language, although one that is significantly simpler than Java itself and much better suited for building pages.

As of the latest version of the JSP specification this language is built into the very core of JSPs. This means that programmers creating new tags may use this language for their own purposes.

Expressions in this language are surrounded by curly braces and preceded by a dollar sign. The simplest kinds of expressions in the language are constants like strings or numbers. Here are some examples:

```
${23}
${98.6}
${'hello'}
```

These don't mean anything on their own, but when used as the value of a parameter, they are evaluated by the expression language before they are sent to the tag. Because numbers and strings evaluate to themselves, this means that

```
<awl:maybeShow show="${'yes'}">
```

means the same thing as

```
<awl:maybeShow show="yes">
```

Notice that within an expression literals are surrounded by single quotes, and the whole expression is surrounded by double quotes.

Errors to Watch For

If an expression is written incorrectly, such as leaving off a closing quote or a curly brace, a JSP page error will report an error like

```
An error occurred while parsing custom action
```

The scripting language can also refer to beans and properties of beans. A bean may be made available to a page through the use of the `jsp:useBean` tag. Tags in the `jsp` namespace are available automatically to any JSP, so there is no need to load this library explicitly. Listing 18.3 shows a simple bean that will be used for demonstration purposes.

Listing 18.3 A simple bean

```
package com.awl.toolbook.chapter18;

import java.text.*;
import java.util.*;

public class Bean1 implements java.io.Serializable {
    public String getName() {
        return "com.awl.toolbook.chapter18.Bean1";
    }

    public int getSeventhPrimeNumber() {
        return 17;
    }

    public String getColor() {
        return "#772266";
    }

    public String getCurrentTime() {
        SimpleDateFormat sdf =
            new SimpleDateFormat(
                "hh:mm 'and' s 'seconds'");
        return sdf.format(new Date());
    }
}
```

This bean may be loaded into a page with the following tag:

```
<jsp:useBean
  id="bean1"
  class="com.awl.toobook.chapter18.Bean1"/>
```

Once the bean has been loaded, the scripting language would refer to the seventh prime number property as

```
${bean1.seventhPrimeNumber}
```

Note the pattern: first the name of the bean as defined in the `jsp:useBean` tag, then a dot, then the name of the property. This very closely resembles the syntax used in BeanUtils, a toolkit discussed in Chapter 8. This is because the tag scripting language uses BeanUtils internally.

Errors to Watch For

If an attempt is made to access a property that does not exists, a page error will be generated that looks like

```
Unable to find a value for "property"
in object of class "beanClass"
```

As written the preceding example will not do anything interesting if placed in a page; it will just display `${bean1.seventhPrimeNumber}`. However, this code would serve perfectly as a way to send the seventh prime number to a custom tag, although the ability to send a constant value from a bean to a tag is not very useful. However, there is a close relationship between beans and HTML forms that becomes very powerful when combined with the scripting language.

Listing 18.4 shows a simple form that lets the user choose whether to show, hide, or reverse a block of text.

Listing 18.4 A form that will be used by a tag

```
<html>
<body>

<form action="show_result.jsp" method="post">
Shall I display the tag body?
<select name="shouldShow">
<option>yes
```

```
<option>no
<option>reverse
</select><br>

<input type="Submit" name="Go" value="Go">
</form>

</body>
</html>
```

Listing 18.5 shows a bean that will be used in conjunction with this form.

Listing 18.5 A bean used by a form

```
package com.awl.toolbook.chapter18;

public class FormBean {
    private String textField;
    public String getTextField() {return textField;}
    public void setTextField(String textField) {
        this.textField = textField;
    }

    private String color;
    public String getColor() {return color;}
    public void setColor(String color) {
        this.color = color;
    }

    private String cheese;
    public String getCheese() {return cheese;}
    public void setCheese(String cheese) {
        this.cheese = cheese;
    }

    private String shouldShow;
    public String getShouldShow() {return shouldShow;}
    public void setShouldShow(String shouldShow) {
        this.shouldShow = shouldShow;
    }
}
```

The target page that will use this bean is shown in Listing 18.6. It combines many of the things that have been discussed so far: a bean, the awl:maybeShow tag, and a scripted parameter.

Listing 18.6 Using a bean and a tag together

```
<%@ taglib prefix="awl"
    uri="http://jspbook.awl.com/samples" %>
<jsp:useBean
  id="form"
  class="com.awl.toolbook.chapter18.FormBean"/>

<jsp:setProperty name="form" property="*"/>

<awl:maybeShow show="${form.shouldShow}">
  The time is:
  <awl:date format="hh:mm:ss MM/dd/yy"/>
</awl:maybeShow>
```

The FormBean is first loaded by the jsp:useBean tag. The jsp:setProperty tag on the next line goes through all the properties of the named bean and all the values passed to this page from the form. When the names of a property and a value match, the appropriate set method in the bean is called. Conversion between types is done as expected because this functionality sits on top of the setProperty() method in PropertyUtils from the BeanUtils package.

The second part of the page uses the tag almost exactly as in Listing 18.2. The only difference is that the show parameter comes from the bean via a script rather than being a fixed value. Using a bean, a custom tag, and the scripting language, it is possible to dynamically control a whole block of text.

18.4 Displaying Expressions

The ability to use a bean to control a tag is certainly powerful, but often such values must be shown to the user rather than used by a tag. There is a standard tag called c:out that renders values to the page, and its use is quite straightforward. Listing 18.7 displays various values from Bean1.

Listing 18.7 The out tag

```
<%@ taglib prefix="c"
    uri="http://java.sun.com/jstl/core" %>
<jsp:useBean
```

```
  id="bean1"
  class="com.awl.toolbook.chapter18.Bean1"/>

<p>Here is some data that came from bean1:</p>

<ul>

<li>The name of this bean is:
<c:out value="${bean1.name}"/>

<li>The 7th prime number is:
<c:out value="${bean1.seventhPrimeNumber}"/>

<li>The current time is:
<c:out value="${bean1.currentTime}"/>

</ul>
```

Although the `c:out` tag is being used to display only a simple value, a great deal of power is offered due to the fact that what is being shown is the result of a script instead of just a simple property.

The Expression Language allows page developers to manipulate properties in many ways. For example, it is possible to write an expression that will add two numbers right in the page without needing to rely on any external mechanism. Listing 18.8 shows the first page of a simple calculator application.

Listing 18.8 Inputs to a calculator

```
<html>
<head><title>Calculator form</title></head>

<body>

<form action="calc_result.jsp" method="POST">
  First number: <input type="text" name="value1"><br>
  Second number: <input type="text" name="value2"><br>
  <input type="submit" name="Go!" value="Go!">
</form>

</body>
</html>
```

Listing 18.9 shows the bean that will be used by this application.

Listing 18.9 A simple calculator bean

```
package com.awl.toolbook.chapter18;

public class CalcBean implements java.io.Serializable {
    private int value1;
    public int getValue1() {return value1;}
    public void setValue1(int value1) {
        this.value1 = value1;
    }

    private int value2;
    public int getValue2() {return value2;}
    public void setValue2(int value2) {
        this.value2 = value2;
    }

    public int getSum() {
        return value1 + value2;
    }
}
```

Next, Listing 18.10 shows how a JSP can populate this bean and perform the calculation directly using the expression language.

Listing 18.10 Addition in the expression language

```
<%@ taglib prefix="c"
    uri="http://java.sun.com/jstl/core" %>
<jsp:useBean
  id="calc"
  class="com.awl.toolbook.chapter19.CalcBean"/>

<jsp:setProperty name="calc" property="*"/>

The sum is:
<c:out value="${calc.value1 + calc.value2}"/>
```

It is now possible to easily extend this to do more complex calculations, such as finding the average of the two numbers or raising one to the power of the other, and so on.

Note that although this is very powerful, it also breaks the model/view/controller paradigm because the model is now being manipulated directly from the view. There are times when this is worth doing, but as a general rule of thumb it is better to leave such calculations in the bean.

Another possibility offered by the `c:out` is that it can display things other than beans. Every JSP has access to a number of **implicit objects,** objects that the system provides without the developer needing to explicitly load or name them. One of these is the `pageContext` object, which contains a great deal of information about the action currently being performed. Among this information is the name of the page being generated, the name of the computer from which the request came, and so on. Listing 18.11 uses the `pageContext` object to display some of the available information.

Listing 18.11 The request object

```
<%@ taglib prefix="c"
    uri="http://java.sun.com/jstl/core" %>
<ul>

<li>Your computer is called
<c:out value="${pageContext.request.remoteHost}"/>

<li>This page came from server
<c:out value="${pageContext.request.serverName}"/>

<li>This page came from port
<c:out value="${pageContext.request.serverPort}"/>

</ul>
```

This example illustrates expressions with multiple dots. This follows directly from the use of BeanUtils. And compound expression handled by BeanUtils, including indexed and mapped properties, is valid in the JSP expression language.

Another important implicit variable is called `param`, and it holds all the values that have been sent to a page by a form. This acts like a special bean in that it does not have a predefined set of properties; instead, it has a property for every value in the form.

```
<input type="text" name="color">
```

The user's response could be displayed on a page using

```
<c:out value="${param.color}"/>
```

The availability of param also means the bean isn't actually needed in Listing 18.6. The whole page could be reduced to

```
<awl:maybeShow show="${param.shouldShow}">
  The time is:
  <awl:date format="hh:mm:ss MM/dd/yy"/>
</awl:maybeShow>
```

Likewise, the calculator could do without its bean, reducing the page to

```
The sum is:
<c:out value="${param.value1 + param.value2}"/>
```

This example may look familiar; it was used to create a testable page for use with HTTPUnit in Chapter 5.

Errors to Watch For

Trying to reference a property that a bean does not possess will result in an error. In addition, trying to reference a bean that does not exist, such as `c:out value="${someBean.someProperty}"` if `someBean` has not been loaded, will not result in an error but simply in nothing being displayed. This can cause problems that may be hard to fix—for example, if the name of a bean is simply misspelled.

Because `c:out` can obtain values from a bean, it is not surprising that there is also a tag that sets values called `c:set`. Unlike the `jsp:setProperty` tag, the `c:set` tag cannot set all properties in a bean at once by using the special property "*." However, each of the parameters to `c:set` may be a script that allows properties to be set with dynamic values.

```
<c:set
     target="bean"
     property="property name"
     value="property value" />
```

This sets the property called `property name` in the bean identified as `bean name` to `value`.

Errors to Watch For

When using the c:set tag, it is very important to keep in mind the distinction between something like target="bean" and target="${bean}." The former is just a name that has no properties; the latter is actually a bean obtained from the name by the expression language. This can be a natural source of confusion because the jsp:setProperty tag does use the name. Even if the reason is not completely clear at this point, just remember that target should always take an expression, not just a name.

18.5 Formatting Output

Once again, consider the calculator from Listing 18.10. If the user enters large numbers—say, 1264528 and 9273912—the sum will be 10538440. This is certainly the right answer, but it is not in a particularly readable format. It would be much better if it could be displayed as 10,538,440. The issue of formatting comes up frequently when designing Web pages because there are often particular rules about how numbers, currencies, and dates should be displayed.

There is another portion of the standard library that provides tags for displaying formatted values. This library can be imported using

```
<%@ taglib prefix="fmt"
    uri="http://java.sun.com/jstl/fmt" %>
```

Once loaded, a number of new tags are available, some of which work similarly to the c:out tag but allow a format to be specified. For example, the c:out tag from Listing 18.10 could be replaced with

```
<fmt:formatNumber
  value="${calc.value1 + calc.value2}"
  pattern="###,###"/>
```

The pattern indicates that there should be a comma after every three digits. It would also be legal to provide a decimal point, as in ###,###.##, which would indicate that there should be a comma every three digits and two digits following the decimal point.

This chapter started with an example that formatted dates and times. Finally, these is a more general solution to this problem: the fmt:formatDate tag. This works very much like fmt:formatNumber tag, except it expects its value to be a date. If the bean from Listing 18.7 were loaded with `jsp:useBean`, the `date` property could be formatted with

```
<fmt:formatDate
  value="${bean1.currentTime}"
  pattern="hh:mm:ss MM/dd/yy"/>
```

The valid expressions for `pattern` can be found in the documentation for the `java.text.SimpleDateFormat` class, but note for the moment that any of the expressions from Listing 18.1 would work. Also note that this is a more proper division between model and view elements.

The formatting tags can do a great deal more than has been shown here. Different countries have different standard ways to express numbers and dates, and the format tags can ensure that data is formatted in an appropriate way for country, through a mechanism called **internationalization.** The format tags can also be used to parse values, which would allow the calculator to accept inputs with commas and decimal points.

18.6 Iteration in a Page

It was mentioned previously that the expression language can handle compound values, meaning that an expression like

```
${aBean.values[1]}
```

would be legal if `aBean` has a property called `values` and that `values` is an array or `List` with at least two elements.

Errors to Watch For
If a request is made for an index beyond the number of elements in the array, the result will be empty.

It is unusual to need to access a particular element in an array, but it is more common to have to repeat some action for every element, regardless of how many there are. There is a tag in the standard library that handles such iteration, called `c:forEach`. Listing 18.12 uses the `c:forEach` tag to show some information from a serialized bean holding information about an album, including the set of tracks.

Listing 18.12 The forEach tag

```
<%@ taglib prefix="c"
    uri="http://java.sun.com/jstl/core" %>
<jsp:useBean
 id="album"
 beanName="tinderbox"
 type="com.awl.jspbook.chapter19.AlbumInfo"/>

<h1><c:out value="${album.name}"/></h1>

Artist: <jsp:getProperty name="album"
            property="artist"/><p>
Year: <c:out value="${album.year}"/></p>


Here are the tracks:
<ul>
<c:forEach items="${album.tracks}" var="track">
  <li><c:out value="${track}"/>
</c:forEach>
</ul>
```

This example also illustrates a new feature of the `jsp:useBean` tag: the ability to load a serialized bean. This is accomplished by specifying a `beanName`, which will cause `jsp:useBean` to load a file with that name ending in `.ser` from the CLASSPATH. The result of Listing 18.12 is shown in Figure 18.2.

The `c:forEach` tag takes a number of parameters. The first is the items to iterate over, which is specified by a script. The second is a name to use as a variable; within the body of the `c:forEach`, this variable will be set to each element in the array in turn. This variable can be accessed by the expression language just as a bean, which means among other things that the `c:out` tag can be used to display it.

Errors to Watch For

If a nonarray is used as the `items` parameter, the `c:forEach` tag will treat it as if it were an array with one element.

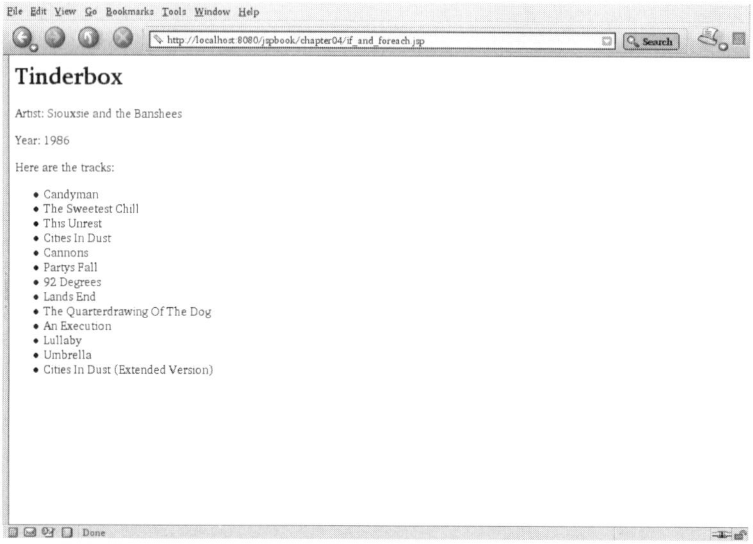

Figure 18.2. Iteration used to display every element in an array.

18.7 Conditionally Including Sections of a Page

Iteration allows a page to do one thing many times. A page may also need to be able to determine whether to do something at all. The custom `awl:maybeShow` tag introduced at the beginning of this chapter handled a limited version of that problem, but the standard tag library provides a number of much more general mechanisms collectively called the **conditional tags.** The most basic of these tags is called `c:if`.

In its most common form, the `c:if` tag takes a single parameter, `test`, whose value will be a script. This script should perform some logical check such as comparing two values. Facilities are provided to determine whether two values are equal to each other, the first is less than the second, the first is greater than the second, and a number of other possibilities.

Listing 18.13 shows how the `c:if` tag can work with a bean to determine whether to show a block of text.

Listing 18.13 The if tag

```
<%@ taglib prefix="c"
    uri="http://java.sun.com/jstl/core" %>
<%@ taglib prefix="awl"
    uri="http://jspbook.awl.com/samples" %>
<jsp:useBean
  id="form"
```

```
   class="com.awl.jspbook.chapter18.FormBean"/>
<jsp:setProperty name="form" property="*"/>

<c:if test="${form.shouldShow == 'yes'}">
 The time is:
 <awl:date format="hh:mm:ss MM/dd/yy"/>
</c:if>
```

Note the expression in the script for the test parameter. Two equal signs (==) are used to check two values for equality, just as in Java. Here the first value comes from a property and is obtained with the normal dotted notation. The second value, "yes," is a constant or **literal,** which is reflected by the quotes around it in the script. If these quotes were not present, the Expression Language would look for a bean called "yes," and because no such bean exists, the result would be an error.

Listing 18.13 is similar to Listing 18.6; the major difference is that this example uses the standard tag instead of the custom `awl:maybeShow`. The downside is there is no way that the `c:if` tag can reverse a block of text. All it can do is decide whether or not to include its body content in the final page.

While this may seem like a shortcoming, it in fact reflects a good design pattern. Note that `awl:maybeShow` does two completely unrelated things: It checks a value to see if it is "yes," "no," or "reverse," and it reverses a block of text. Rather than making one tag do two things, it is better to have two different tags. This represents an approach to software design often called the "Unix Philosophy," which states that each piece of code should do only one thing and do it well, and there should be easy ways to knit together these small pieces. In the case of tags, that means that each tag can be used independently or combined with other tags. In this case, if there were a `awl:reverse` tag that did nothing but reverse its body content, it could be combined with the `c:if` tag to do the same thing as Listing 18.1. This is shown in Listing 18.14.

Listing 18.14 Splitting tags

```
<%@ taglib prefix="c"
    uri="http://java.sun.com/jstl/core" %>
<%@ taglib prefix="awl"
    uri="http://jspbook.awl.com/samples" %>
<jsp:useBean
   id="form"
   class="com.awl.jspbook.chapter18.FormBean"/>
<jsp:setProperty name="form" property="*"/>
```

Listing 18.14 Splitting tags *(continued)*

```
<c:if test="${form.shouldShow == 'yes'}">
 The time is:
 <awl:date format="hh:mm:ss MM/dd/yy"/>
</c:if>

<c:if test="${form.shouldShow == 'reverse'}">
 <awl:reverse>
   The time is:
   <awl:date format="hh:mm:ss MM/dd/yy"/>
 </awl:reverse>
</c:if>
```

Note that two `c:if` tags are used here: one to check whether the value is "yes" and another to check if it is "reverse." The body content of both these tags is the same, which is rather wasteful. It means that if the body ever needs to change, it must be modified in two places to keep everything consistent. It would be better in this case to put the body in a common place, such as a separate file. If the contents were placed in a file called `body.jsp`, then they could be merged back into the original page using a tag called `jsp:include` as follows:

```
<c:if test="${form.shouldShow == 'yes'}">
  <jsp:include page="body.jsp"/>
</c:if>

<c:if test="${form.shouldShow == 'reverse'}">
 <awl:reverse>
  <jsp:include page="body.jsp"/>
 </awl:reverse>
</c:if>
```

Now that the functionality of `awl:maybeShow` has been divided into two pieces, the `c:if` tag can be used for many other things, and the `awl:reverse` tag can be used to unconditionally reverse a block of text, should that ever be desired.

Listing 18.14 imports two tag libraries: the standard one that is installed as `c` and that provides the `c:if` tag, and the custom one installed as `awl` that provides the `awl:reverse` tag. This is perfectly valid; often a page needs many different tags from different libraries, and it will then need to import all of them. The only catch is that each tag library must be given a different prefix.

18.8 Browser Detection

Web programmers face many difficult decisions, not the least of which is how to deal with the fairly horrible state of modern browsers. A popular Web site is likely to receive requests from versions of Internet Explorer 3 through 6, Mozilla, Netscape 4.7, Opera, various AOL browsers, and numerous custom browsers now available in consumer devices such as phones and PDAs. Each of these is likely to render HTML slightly differently, support different media types, and handle JavaScript differently, if at all.

One way of dealing with this is to use the "lowest common denominator"—that is, just those features that are supported and work the same in every browser. This makes development easier for the Web developer, but it means the user will be getting a site that looks like something from the early 1990s, which may disappoint many users. Alternately, Web developers may design a site for just one browser—perhaps Mozilla 1.5—and put up a note encouraging other users to switch to this browser. This is likely to infuriate many users who either don't want to or can't change browsers just to get to one site.

Finally, developers can create parallel versions of all the browser-specific HTML and JavaScript and so on, and send out the appropriate version based on which browser is being used. The browser makes this possible by identifying itself with every request, and JSPs make this possible through the conditional tags. A skeleton of code that accomplishes this is shown in Listing 18.15.

Listing 18.15 Browser detection

```
<%@ taglib prefix="c"
    uri="http://java.sun.com/jstl/core" %>
<jsp:useBean
  id="browser"
  class="com.awl.jspbook.ch04.BrowserBean"/>

<c:set
  target="${browser}"
  property="request"
  value="${pageContext.request}"/>

You are using a browser that identifies itself as
<c:out value="${browser.fullName}"/><p>

<c:if test="${browser.type == 'Gecko'}">
... include Mozilla code here ...
</c:if>
```

Listing 18.15 Browser detection *(continued)*

```
<c:if test="${browser.type == 'MSIE'}">
... include IE code here ...
</c:if>
```

This example uses a utility bean called `BrowserBean`, which is shown in Listing 18.16.

Listing 18.16 A bean that facilitates browser detection

```
package com.awl.toolbook.chapter18;

import java.text.*;
import java.util.*;
import javax.servlet.http.HttpServletRequest;

public class BrowserBean implements java.io.Serializable {
    private String fullName = null;
    public String getFullName() {return fullName;}

    private String type;
    public String getType() {return type;}

    public void setRequest(HttpServletRequest req) {
        fullName = req.getHeader("user-agent");

        if(fullName == null) {
            fullName = "";
        }

        if(fullName.indexOf("Gecko") != -1) {
            type = "Gecko";
        } else if(fullName.indexOf("MSIE") != -1) {
            type = "MSIE";
        }
    }
}
```

To obtain browser information, the `BrowserBean` must have access to the `request` object. This object is obtained from the `pageContext`, as was done in Listing 18.11, and passed to the bean with a `c:set` tag.

A bean such as `BrowserBean` is needed for two reasons. First, the browser name is not available as a simple property, such as the ones shown in listing 18.7. Second, the full name of the browser is likely to be something unwieldy, like "Mozilla/5.0 (X11; U; FreeBSD i386; en-US; rv:1.0rc3) Gecko/20020607," which contains information about the specific revision and operating system on which the browser is running. This is generally more information than is needed to select the appropriate browser-specific code for a page. This second problem is solved by having the bean recognize major browser types, and it is this type that is used by the `c:if` tags.

18.9 Combining Tags

It has been mentioned previously that the bodies of JSP tags can contain anything, including other JSP tags. There have already been a few examples of this, such as the `c:out` tag within the `c:forEach` tag in Listing 18.12. To demonstrate this further, here is an example of where the `c:if` and `c:forEach` tags work together.

If a `c:forEach` tag is given an empty array, it will not render its body content at all. This is fine, but on its own it can lead to some odd-looking pages. In Listing 18.12, if the CD is empty, the page will display "Here are the tracks" and then stop. This is technically correct, but to the user it may look like the page stopped generating halfway through. It would be better to inform the user that the CD is empty rather than show her a list with no elements.

This can be accomplished by putting the `c:forEach` tag inside a `c:if` tag, as shown in Listing 18.17.

Listing 18.17 Tags working together

```
<%@ taglib prefix="c"
    uri="http://java.sun.com/jstl/core" %>
<jsp:useBean id="album" beanName="tinderbox4"
 type="com.awl.jspbook.chapter18.AlbumInfo"/>
<h1><jsp:getProperty name="album" property="name"/></h1>

Artist: <jsp:getProperty name="album"
           property="artist"/><p>
Year: <jsp:getProperty name="album" property="year"/></p>
```

Listing 18.17 Tags working together *(continued)*

```
<c:if test="${empty album.tracks}">
There are no tracks!  What a boring CD.
</c:if>

<c:if test="${!(empty album.tracks)}">
  Here are the tracks:
  <ul>
  <c:forEach items="${album.tracks}" var="track">
    <li><c:out value="${track}"/>
  </c:forEach>
  </ul>
</c:if>
```

Conceptually the only new thing about this example is the check that is done in the `c:if` tag. The `empty` in the test checks whether the named property is equal to either `null` or an empty array. The exclamation point in the test should be read as "not," just as in Java.

18.10 Selecting between Multiple Choices

Once again, the preceding example had to use two `c:if` tags, although in this case the bodies are different. However, the need to perform the same check twice is still rather clumsy: once to see if it is true and once to see if the reverse is true. Although there is no tag equivalent to an `else` clause in the `c:if` tag, there is an equivalent of Java's `case` statement that allows multiway branching.

These tags work a little differently than the others seen so far in that there are three tags that work together to obtain the desired result. The outermost tag is called `c:choose`, and, surprisingly, it has no parameters. This is because this tag does not do anything on its own; it merely serves as a container for a collection of two other tags: `c:when` and `c:otherwise`. Each individual `c:when` tag acts much like an `c:if` tag. Both tags take a parameter called `test`, which should be a script and render their body content if the condition in the script is true. The difference is that multiple `c:if` tags will each be checked in turn, whereas a `c:choose` tag will stop after finding the first `c:when` tag with a test that is true.

Consider a set of possible values for a bean property such as the colors red, green, and blue. This snippet of code would check all three possibilities regardless of the value:

```
<c:if test="${bean.color == 'red'}">...</c:if>
<c:if test="${bean.color == 'green'}">...</c:if>
<c:if test="${bean.color == 'blue'}">...</c:if>
```

However, the following snippet will check to see if the color is red, and if so, it will stop without checking to see if it is green, and then blue:

```
<c:choose>
  <c:when test="${bean.color == 'red'}">...</c:when>
  <c:when test="${bean.color == 'green'}">...</c:when>
  <c:when test="${bean.color == 'blue'}">...</c:when>
</c:choose>
```

Clearly the second option is more efficient. In addition, using the `c:choose` tag groups related code in one place and so makes JSPs easier to read and understand.

The `c:choose` tag works with another tag called `c:otherwise`. This tag also has no parameters; its body will be evaluated if none of the `c:when` tags have a true condition.

It is now clear how it would be possible to avoid doing the check twice in Listing 18.17: by using one `c:when` and one `c:otherwise` rather than two `c:if` tags. This is shown in Listing 18.18.

Listing 18.18 The choose tag

```
<c:choose>
  <c:when test="${empty album.tracks}">
    There are no tracks!  What a boring CD.
  </c:when>

  <c:otherwise>
    Here are the tracks:
    <ul>
    <c:forEach items="${album.tracks}" var="track">
      <li><c:out value="${track}"/>
    </c:forEach>
    </ul>
  </c:otherwise>
</c:choose>
```

This is a little more verbose than Listing 18.17, but it does have the advantage of avoiding one redundant test. Using the `c:choose` tag also makes it clear that the conditions are mutually exclusive, and hence only one of the bodies will ever be rendered.

18.11 The SQL Tags

The iteration, conditional, and display tags seen so far have all been used with beans, but they may also be used with other kinds of data. In particular, there is a set of tags that allow JSPs to embed SQL, and the results of these queries can be manipulated using the same tags.

Before examining these tags a word of caution is in order. Embedding SQL directly in pages is highly error prone, requires a lot of duplicate effort throughout a site, and makes site maintenance extremely difficult. These tags are suitable only for "quick and dirty" one-shot pages. For anything more complex a bean-based solution is called for, and one will be discussed a little later in this chapter.

The most basic of the SQL tags is `sql:query`, which allows a page to perform a `select` and display the results. Its use is demonstrated in Listing 18.19. This example and subsequent ones in this chapter will use the CD database introduced in Chapter 10.

Listing 18.19 A page that gets data from a database

```
<%@ taglib prefix="c"
    uri="http://java.sun.com/jstl/core" %>
<%@ taglib prefix="sql"
    uri="http://java.sun.com/jstl/sql" %>

<sql:query
  dataSource="jdbc:hsqldb:toolbook,org.hsqldb.jdbcDriver,sa"
  sql="select * from artist"
  var="artists"/>


<ul>
<c:forEach items="${artists.rows}" var="artist">
<li><a href="<c:url value="show_cds.jsp">
  <c:param name="artist_id" value="${artist.artist_id}"/>
  <c:param name="name" value="${artist.name}"/>
```

```
</c:url>"><c:out escapeXml="false"
                  value="${artist.name}"/></a>
</c:forEach>
</ul>
```

This example starts by importing the core library and a new sql library that contains the new tags. Immediately after loading the library, the `query` tag is used to load data.

There are many options to the `query` tag, but the ones used here are the most common. First, the tag needs to be told how to connect to the database where the information lives, which is specified as the `dataSource` parameter. There are a few options for this parameter; here it is specified as the database URL, driver class, and username and password. It is also possible to specify the `dataSource` by using its JNDI name. See the section on resources in Chapter 17 for more on this option.

The `sql` parameter specifies the actual SQL to execute, which here is a simple select.

Finally, the `var` parameter names a variable in which the results of the query should be stored. This is somewhat similar to the `var` parameter in the `c:forEach` tag in that both make a value available elsewhere on the page.

Not coincidentally, the next place this variable is seen is in a `c:forEach` tag on the next line. Note that this variable is used as the `items` because this one variable contains something like an array, each element of which will be one row of data. The `artist` variable, defined in the `c:forEach` tag, will hold each row in turn.

Within the body of the `c:forEach` tag the `artist` variable acts like the `param` variable seen in conjunction with forms. Here `artist` will have one property for each column, which may be obtained using the normal 'dot' notation that has been used with beans. The artist name, therefore, is obtained with

```
<c:out value="${artist.name}" escapeXml="false"/>
```

The `escapeXml` option to the `c:out` tag is new. Some bands have non-ascii characters in their names, such as The Crüxshadows or Björk. Such names can be stored in the database using the HTML that encodes these characters—for example, `ü` represents the character 'ü.' However, by default the `c:out` tag will itself encode any special characters it encounters, including ampersands. If this were allowed to happen, it would turn `&#252` into `&#252`. Setting `escapeXml="false"` turns off this behavior and should be used whenever the `c:out` tag will be displaying data that has already been encoded for display.

The artist name should be a link to a page where all of that artist's albums will be shown. To do that, the `url` tag is used to construct a URL that will call the `show_cds.jsp` page, and pass along the `artist_id` of interest. The artist's name is also passed along so it can be displayed on the following page. This is not strictly necessary because once the artist ID is available, the name could be obtained through another `select`. However, because the name is already available, it may as well be used from here to save the effort of doing an extra call to the database.

Listing 18.20 shows the `show_cds.jsp` page, which will once again use the `sql:query` tag. Whereas in Listing 18.19 the query was always the same, here there must be some way to build a `where` clause that includes the `artist_id`. Fortunately, the tag library allows for this.

Listing 18.20 A parameterized query

```
<%@ taglib prefix="c"
    uri="http://java.sun.com/jstl/core" %>
<%@ taglib prefix="sql"
    uri="http://java.sun.com/jstl/sql" %>

<sql:query
  dataSource="jdbc:hsqldb:toolbook,org.hsqldb.jdbcDriver,sa"
  sql="select * from album where artist_id = ?"
  var="cds">

  <sql:param value="${param.artist_id}"/>
</sql:query>

<h2>Albums by <c:out escapeXml="false"
                    value="${param.name}"/></h2>

<ul>
<c:forEach items="${cds.rows}" var="cd">
<li><a href="<c:url value="show_tracks.jsp">
<c:param name="album_id" value="${cd.album_id}"/>
<c:param name="name" value="${cd.name}"/>
</c:url>"><c:out value="${cd.name}"/></a>
</c:forEach>
</ul>
```

The `sql:query` tag here looks very similar to the one in Listing 18.19; both specify a `dataSource`, `var`, and `sql` to run. However, in this example the `sql` has a question mark where the artist_id passed in from the previous page might be expected. Correspondingly, the sql:query tag has a body containing a sql:param tag, whose value is the very artist_id that was needed.

This is another feature of the sql:query tag. Question marks within the sql parameter may be filled in before the query is run with values from sql:param tags in the body. Because the values of the sql:param come from scripts, this allows queries to be dynamically altered as needed.

After the sql:query the rest of the page is straightforward—just another c:forEach that iterates over all the CDs and provides a link to see the tracks on another page.

18.11.1 Inserting Data from JSPs

To make the little CD application more useful, it can be expanded to allow the user to add new artists, CDs, and tracks. Not surprisingly, the standard tag library provides another tag to facilitate this; the sql:update tag. Before seeing how this tag is used, consider what must be done to add a new artist.

First, the user will specify the name in a form, which will be sent to another JSP, which will use the new tag to perform an insert. It would be reasonable to expect that a sql:param will be used to pass the name to the query. This is all straightforward enough. However, it is important to keep in mind that the artist table has an artist_id field in addition to the name. This ID will have to come from somewhere.

One possibility would be to force the user to provide it along with the name. This is far from satisfactory. Because this ID is only used internally by the system to track data, it has no intrinsic meaning to the user, and hence the user should never see it. Plus, there is no clear way in which the user would know what value to use.

It therefore seems that the system should keep track of IDs. That is perfectly fine, because such information can easily be added to the database. It is just necessary to create another table of IDs, which will be called sequence because it will provide sequences of ID values. Its definition is simple:

```
create table sequence (
  name  char(60),
  id    int)

insert into sequence values('artist',0);
insert into sequence values('album',0);
insert into sequence values('track',0);
```

With this table in place, creating a new artist would take the following steps:

1. Use a `select` to find the current ID where name is "artist."
2. Use an `update` to increment that ID so the next artist created will get a new number.
3. Use the obtained ID in an `insert` to create the artist.

There is actually a further complication to this. If two different users try to add an artist at the same time, they might both get the same ID in step 1 before either can get to step 2 to update the current ID. Most modern databases have a way to prevent this, and it is supported by the tag library through a tag called `jsp:transaction`, but this is beyond the scope of the book.

Listing 18.21 shows everything that must be done in a JSP to add an artist to the database with a proper ID.

Listing 18.21 Using a JSP to add data to a database

```
<%@ taglib prefix="sql"
    uri="http://java.sun.com/jstl/sql" %>

<sql:query
  dataSource="jdbc:hsqldb:toobook,org.hsqldb.jdbcDriver,sa"
  sql="select value from sequence where name='Artist'"
  var="ids"/>

<sql:update
  dataSource="jdbc:hsqldb:toobook,org.hsqldb.jdbcDriver,sa"
  sql="insert into artist(artist_id,name) values(?,?)">
<sql:param value="${ids.rows[0].id}"/>
<sql:param value="${param.name}"/>
</sql:update>

<sql:update
  dataSource="jdbc:hsqldb:toobook,org.hsqldb.jdbcDriver,sa"
  sql="update sequence set value=? where name='Artist'">
<sql:param value="${ids.rows[0].id + 1}"/>
</sql:update>

New artist has been added!<p>
<a href="show_artists.jsp">Return to the
artist list</a>
```

The example exactly follows the previous steps outlined. The only noteworthy point is that the ID obtained from the `select` is referred to as `ids.rows[0].id`. Recall that `rows` is an array-like object, suitable for using in `c:forEach` tags, so element 0 of this object will be the first row.

18.11.2 SQL and Beans

By now the disadvantages of using the SQL tags should be readily apparent. They require page developers to know the details of the database, they place way too much model code in the view layer, and they are verbose.

The solution, as always, is to move the model layer where it belongs, into some Java beans. Chapter 10 discussed OJB, a toolkit for hiding database structure and access within beans. The beans from that chapter could be used in a JSP without modification as long as they extend the `PersistentObject` object from Listing 10.11. The methods in this base class will make it possible for JSP to load and save beans by setting special methods, as shown in Listing 18.22.

Listing 18.22 Retrieving data through a bean

```
<%@ taglib prefix="c"
    uri="http://java.sun.com/jstl/core" %>

<jsp:useBean
  id="artist"
  class="com.awl.toolbook.chapter11.Artist"/>

<jsp:setProperty name="artist" property="artistId"/>

<h2>Albums by
<c:out escapeXml="false" value="${artist.matching[0].name}"/>
</h2>



<ul>
<c:forEach items="${artist.matching[0].albums}" var="cd">
<li><a href="<c:url value="show_tracks.jsp">
<c:param name="album_id" value="${cd.albumId}"/>
<c:param name="name" value="${cd.name}"/>
</c:url>"><c:out value="${cd.name}"/></a>
</c:forEach>
</ul>
```

The only difference between Listing 18.22 and the version that used the SQL tags are that the `sql:query` tag has been replaced by `jsp:useBean` and `jsp:setProperty` tags. Now the iteration goes over `cdBean.matching`, which implies the set of CDs with the given `artistId`. While this is no shorter than the database version, there is a huge conceptual difference. Now this page does not know whether the data is coming from a database or a serialized bean, or is connecting to some Web site to get its information. The details of the model have therefore been hidden from the view, which is as it should be.

The difference is even more pronounced in the bean version of the page that adds an artist, which is shown in Listing 18.23.

Listing 18.23 Storing data through a bean

```
<%@ taglib prefix="c"
    uri="http://java.sun.com/jstl/core" %>

<jsp:useBean
  id="artistBean"
  class="com.awl.toolbook.chapter11.Artist"/>

<jsp:setProperty name="artistBean" property="name"/>

<jsp:setProperty
  name="artistBean"
  property="save"
  value="true"/>

New artist has been added!<p>
<a href="show_artists_beans.jsp">Return to the
artist list</a>
```

Listing 18.23 does a much better job of hiding database and implementation details than Listing 18.21 did. All the view needs to do is load the data and then tell the model to save itself.

Note that OJB maintains its own version of the sequence table. Under no circumstances should a site mix OJB with pages that manually insert data because the difference in the way sequence numbers are maintained will inevitably lead to errors.

18.12 The XML Tags

XML, the Extensible Markup Language, is many things to many people. XML provides a mechanism to store documents in a format that is easy for both programs and humans to understand. XML provides the basis for programs running on different computers and operating systems to talk to each other over the Web. XML is also a language, on top of which a huge number of industry-specific data formats have been created, that describes data ranging from corporate workflow to warehouse inventories to geographic encyclopedias.

To support all these functions, and many more, a plethora of toolkits have become available to simplify the task of creating, processing, and manipulating XML documents. In an important sense XML provides another way to model data, and as such there are great benefits to be had by pairing XML with a view technology such as JSPs. The JSP specification itself, along with a number of tags from the standard tag library, make this pairing possible on a number of levels.

There are a number of JSP tags for manipulating XML, but before examining them, note that because an XML document is just a bunch of text, creating one through a JSP is no harder than creating an HTML document. Listing 18.24 shows a JSP that retrieves information from a database and generates an XML version of the CD collection.

Listing 18.24 Generating XML with a JSP

```
<%@ page contentType="text/xml" %>

<%@ taglib prefix="c"
    uri="http://java.sun.com/jstl/core" %>

<jsp:useBean
  id="artist"
  class="com.awl.jspbook.ch08.ArtistBean"/>

<jsp:setProperty
  name="artist"
  property="artistId"
  value="0"/>

<collection>
  <artist name="<c:out escapeXml="false"
                        value="${artist.name}"/>">
```

Listing 18.24 Generating XML with a JSP *(continued)*

```
    <c:forEach items="${artist.cds}" var="cd">
      <album name="<c:out value="${cd.name}"/>">
        <c:forEach items="${cd.tracks}" var="track">
        <track name="<c:out value="${track.name}"/>"/>
        </c:forEach>
      </album>
    </c:forEach>
    </artist>
</collection>
```

In almost all respects this example is identical to Listing 18.19, the major difference being the use of XML tags instead of HTML. Because this page will not be returning an HTML document, it is important that it notify the browser what kind of data to expect. This is accomplished by the use of the `page` directive at the top. Telling the browser that it will be getting an XML document allows the browser to present the data properly; for example, both Mozilla and Internet Explorer have special modes that allows users to interactively open and close portions of XML documents. Mozilla's view of such data is shown in Figure 18.3. In it a + in front of a node indicates that it may be expanded by clicking on it, and a - means the node can be collapsed.

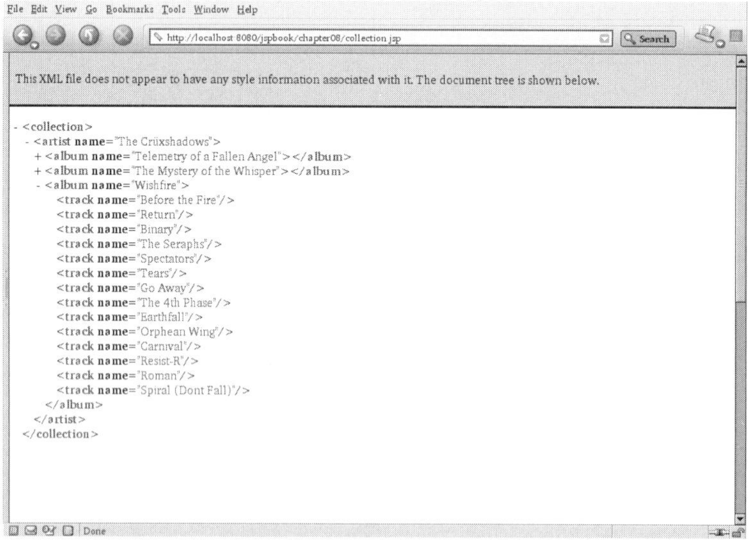

Figure 18.3. The browser view of an XML document.

18.12.1 Selecting Data from an XML Document

Just as the tags in the `core` package use BeanUtils, there are tags in an `xml` package that use JXPath, as discussed in Chapter 9. The most straightforward of these is illustrated in Listing 18.25.

Listing 18.25 Using XPath expressions in a JSP

```
<%@ taglib prefix="x"
    uri="http://java.sun.com/jstl/xml" %>
<%@ taglib prefix="c"
    uri="http://java.sun.com/jstl/core" %>

<c:import
url="http://localhost:8080/jspbook/chapter19/collection.jsp"
var="xml"/>

<x:parse xml="${xml}" var="doc"/>

Albums by <x:out select="$doc//artist[1]/@name"/>:<br>
<ul>
  <x:forEach select="$doc//artist[1]/album" var="album">
    <li><x:out select="$album/@name"/>
  </x:forEach>
</ul>
```

The first thing to notice in this example is that it loads a new portion of the standard tag library, which is imported with the prefix `x`. The first new tag used in this example, `c:import`, is not technically a part of the XML tags, but it is often used in conjunction with them. `c:import` imports the contents of one URL within another page. It can load data from *anywhere*, not just the site where the page lives. This makes it possible for sites to include content from other sites, although in general this should only be done with the other site's knowledge and permission. This ability works especially well in conjunction with XML, as will soon be demonstrated.

The `c:import` stores the data it has read in a variable rather than automatically sending it to the user. This makes it possible to process this data before the user sees it, which is what will be done here. In this case, the data from the collection page from Listing 18.24 has been placed into a variable called `xml`. This data could then be shown directly to the user with a simple `<c:out value="${xml}"/>`.

Rather than display this data, it is instead passed to another tag called `x:parse`, the first of the new XML tags. This tag takes a block of XML and processes it internally into a form that can be used more efficiently. The results of this conversion are stored in yet another variable, which has been called `doc`.

Next, data is extracted from this internal representation with the `x:out` tag. This tag works somewhat like `c:out`, but it obtains the value to display from a combination of the expression language and an XPath expression. The JSP XML tags allow the beginning of a `select` expression to start with a number of expression language identifiers, such as the variable `doc` that was created with the `x:parse` tag. Immediately following that can be any valid XPath expression, which will be used to pull data from the variable. Here the page gets the name of the first artist in the collection.

Following this is an `x:forEach` tag, which is to `c:forEach` what `x:out` is to `c:out`. `x:forEach` will repeat some action for every element returned by an XPath expression, which in this case is all albums from the first artist. As with `c:forEach`, each time through the loop the current value can be assigned to a variable—in this case, one called `album`.

Within the body of the `x:forEach` tag is another `x:out` that displays the value of the `name` attribute for each album. Because `album` holds each of the XML album tags, the XPath portion of this second `x:out` tag does not need the full path starting from the top; it only needs to know how to get to the `name` attribute from each `album` tag.

Note that it would also have been possible to write this loop as

```
<x:forEach select="$doc//artist[1]/album/@name"
           var="name">
  <li><x:out select="$name"/>
</x:forEach>
```

This would have the effect of looping over all album names instead of over all albums. This works because all the page will be showing is the name, but if the page had to show both the name and the year the album was released, it would have had to loop over the albums and then used two `x:out` tags to display the two different attributes.

There are also `x:if`, `x:choose`, `x:when`, and `x:otherwise` tags. These do essentially the same things as their counterparts from the `core` library except that each can take an XPath expression instead of a value from the expression language.

18.12.2 Formatting XML

Listing 18.25 does two separate but related things. It extracts a portion of an XML document using the XPath expression `//artist[1]/album`, and it builds HTML out of the values in the XML in the body of the `x:forEach`. This second part—translating XML into another format—is so common and so important that a whole new language was developed to make it easier. This language is called **XSLT.**

XSLT uses many of the ideas that have already been discussed. To begin, consider what would be needed to find every artists' name from a CD collection in an XML document and output the string "Albums for" followed by the name, enclosed in an `H1` tag. This would pose no challenge: Simply specify the set of nodes to loop over with an `x:forEach` tag, using `//artist` as the set of items. Then within the `x:forEach` tag, obtain the desired string using `<x:out select="@name"/>`.

XSLT takes these same concepts but replaces the idea of selecting a set of tags and then iterating over them with the notion of **patterns.** Each clause of an XSLT file specifies a pattern to find in the XML file, such as all artists, or all albums with a given name, or any other possibility XPath provides. An output template is also provided, which may include elements selected from the XML that matched the input. For example, the XSLT that will format artist names as desired is

```
<xsl:template match="artist">
  <h1>Albums by <xsl:value-of select="@name"/></h1>
</xsl:template>
```

This looks almost exactly like the corresponding JSP code, with `xsl:template` playing the role of the `x:forEach` and `xsl:value-of` replacing the `x:out`. It is important to note the conceptual difference, however. `xsl:template` is not an iteration operator; it does not perform an activity for every element of some set. Instead, it provides a rule, stating that whenever and wherever the XPath expression given as `match` is found, the body will be processed.

A similar clause could be added to put album names in level two headers:

```
<xsl:template match="album">
  <h2><xsl:value-of select="@name"/></h2>
</xsl:template>
```

However, there is one more thing that must be done to make both of these clauses fit together. The rule given for `artist` specifies that a certain string should result and no other actions should be taken. To get XSLT to continue examining the rest of the document, it must be told to do so, which can be done by adding

```
<xsl:apply-templates select="album"/>
```

after the string. This indicates that XSLT should continue processing the `album` elements within the `artist`. Order is important; if `xsl:apply-templates` appeared before the string, the result would **first** show the albums and then the artist.

Listing 18.26 rounds out the set of translations by putting track names in a bulleted list.

Listing 18.26 The full XSLT file

```
<xsl:stylesheet version="1.0"
     xmlns:xsl="http://www.w3.org/1999/XSL/Transform">

<xsl:template match="artist">
  <h1>Albums by <xsl:value-of select="@name"/></h1>
  <xsl:apply-templates select="album"/>
</xsl:template>

<xsl:template match="album">
  <h2><xsl:value-of select="@name"/></h2>
  <ul>
    <xsl:apply-templates select="track"/>
  </ul>
</xsl:template>


<xsl:template match="track">
  <li><xsl:value-of select="@name"/></li>
</xsl:template>

</xsl:stylesheet>
```

Notice that the rule for `album` also needs an `xsl:apply-templates` to process the tracks.

Once an XSLT file has been defined, using it from a JSP is quite easy. Such a page is shown in Listing 18.27.

Listing 18.27 Using XSLT from a JSP

```
<%@ taglib prefix="x"
    uri="http://java.sun.com/jstl/xml" %>
<%@ taglib prefix="c"
    uri="http://java.sun.com/jstl/core" %>
```

```
<c:import
url="http://localhost:8080/jspbook/chapter08/collection.jsp"
var="xml"/>

<c:import
  url="http://localhost:8080/jspbook/chapter08/style.xsl"
  var="xslt"/>

<html><body>
<x:transform xslt="${xslt}" xml="${xml}"/>
</body></html>
```

In this example the XML and XSLT files are loaded using `c:import` tags. Then the transformation is performed and the result displayed with the new `x:transform` tag. Because the final outcome of the transformation is HTML, there is no need to set the content type, and a browser will be able to render it in the usual way, as shown in Figure 18.4.

In a sense, this process has split the view layer into two smaller components: the XML, which provides data from the model to the view, and the XSLT, which contains all the presentation information. Using pure JSPs, these two actions are typically intertwined, with some bean tags getting data from the model and various iteration and conditional tags munging that data into the desired presentation.

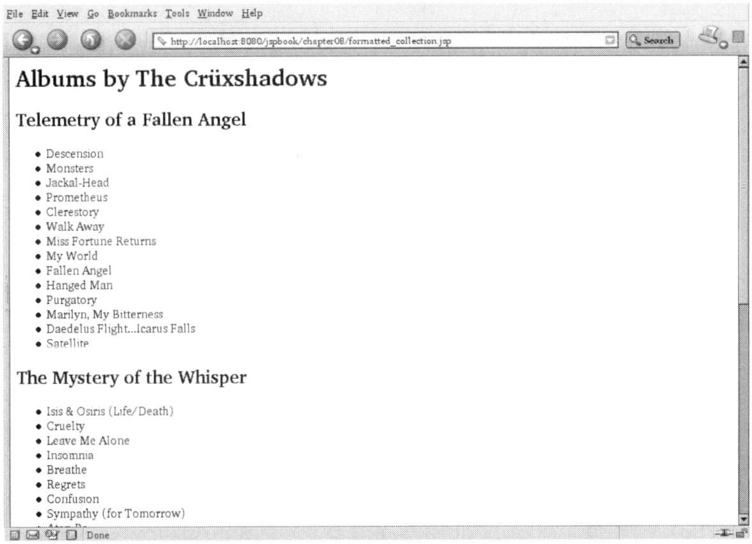

Figure 18.4. The result of an XSLT translation.

Both of these operations may legitimately be considered part of the view, and so having them in the same JSP is not a bad design. However, splitting them into separate components offers some new possibilities. It is often true that splitting pieces of a complex system into separate modules makes it easy to add new functionality.

In this case, one new piece of functionality is the ability to easily change the apparence of a page without changing any of the underlying implementation. Listing 18.28 shows an alternate XSLT file that uses tables to format a CD collection instead of itemized lists.

Listing 18.28 An alternate style

```
<xsl:stylesheet version="1.0"
     xmlns:xsl="http://www.w3.org/1999/XSL/Transform">

<xsl:template match="album">
  <table border="1">
    <tr>
      <td><xsl:value-of select="parent::artist/@name"/></td>
      <td><xsl:value-of select="@name"/></td>
    </tr>
    <xsl:apply-templates select="track"/>
  </table><p></p>
</xsl:template>

<xsl:template match="track">
  <tr><td colspan="2"><xsl:value-of select="@name"/></td></tr>
</xsl:template>

</xsl:stylesheet>
```

This XSLT file does nothing for artist nodes. When it encounters an album, it creates a new table, the first row of which will have a column for the artist name and another for the album name. The artist name is obtained with a new kind of XSLT expression: `parent::artist/@name`. The `parent::` portion indicates that the value should be obtained from the parent node—that is, the node that contains the current one. Because album nodes are contained within artist nodes, this will get the artist, and from there getting the name is done as usual.

Now that a second style has been defined, Listing 18.27 can be easily modified to switch between them, based on user preference, as shown in Listing 18.29.

Listing 18.29 Allowing the user to choose a style

```
<%@ taglib prefix="x"
    uri="http://java.sun.com/jstl/xml" %>
<%@ taglib prefix="c"
    uri="http://java.sun.com/jstl/core" %>

<c:import
url="http://localhost:8080/jspbook/chapter08/collection.jsp"
var="xml"/>

<c:choose>
  <c:when test="${param.style == 'list'}">
    <c:import
    url="http://localhost:8080/jspbook/chapter08/style.xsl"
    var="xslt"/>
  </c:when>
  <c:otherwise>
    <c:import
   url="http://localhost:8080/jspbook/chapter08/tablestyle.xsl"
   var="xslt"/>
  </c:otherwise>
</c:choose>

<html><body>
<x:transform xslt="${xslt}" xml="${xml}"/>
</body></html>
```

This example simply uses a `c:choose` tag to load one of two XSLT files into the `xslt` variable, which will then be used by the `x:transform` tag. The result of formatting with the table-based XSLT file is shown in Figure 18.5.

18.13 Beyond This Book

Of necessity this chapter introduced only a very small portion of the custom tag library. In addition to the tags that were not covered, there is the whole infrastructure of the servlet and JSP specifications. Anyone doing serious development with JSPs should take the time to become familiar with the full specifications. Like the best toolkits, these tags can greatly facilitate development.

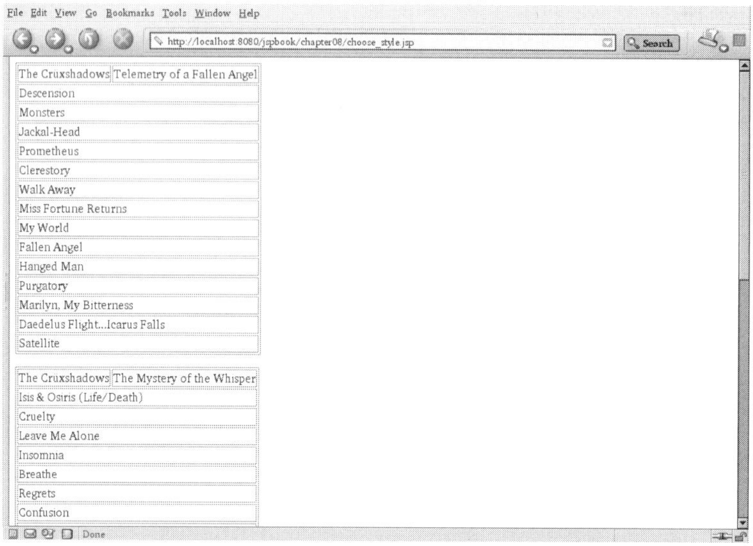

Figure 18.5. An alternate XSLT translation.

18.14 Summary

Tool: Jakarta Taglibs
Purpose: Implementation of the JSP standard tags
Version covered: 1.1
Home page: http://jakarta.apache.org/taglibs/
License: The Apache Software License, Version 1.1

Further Reading:

- The official JSTL specification: http://java.sun.com/products/jsp/jstl/
- *JavaServer Pages*, Second Edition, by Larne Pekowsky, Addison-Wesley, 2003. This is an overview of JSPs aimed at developers with no previous Java experience, but readers of this book may find the information on creating new tags and using the JSTL of interest. (In the interest of full disclosure it should be noted that *JavaServer Pages* was written by the author of this book.)

CHAPTER 19

Struts

The preceding chapter covered the standard tag library, which consists of a set of components with which to build views. Beans, as used throughout this book, comprise the model layer of any application. That leaves only the issue of the controller, which is addressed in this chapter.

19.1 Some Common Controller Tasks

Before building a controller it is necessary to identify what it should do. This can be determined by examining what has been placed in the model and see what might not belong there. Some of the JSPs in Chapter 18 followed a similar pattern. A form (part of the view) has a number of fields for a user to fill in; when the form is submitted, the values are loaded into a bean (the model) via `jsp:setProperty` tags. Then another `jsp:setProperty` may set a "pseudo property," which causes the bean to perform an action. An example of this latter aspect is the `save` property in the `Artist` bean, which when set causes the data to be written to a database.

In this system the beans are doing two unrelated things. They model the conceptual entity being manipulated, which is good, but they also talk to forms, which is bad. This requires that the model and view must look pretty similar. At the very least, form field names must match property names. More generally, the dual use of beans requires that developers must think of these two very different tasks as in some way connected.

It would therefore make sense to more cleanly separate the model from the view. One way to approach this would be to split the bean into two beans: one that will model the system and another that will talk to the form. The view elements would then consist of the JSP containing the form and the form bean, and the model will consist of another bean that manages the data.

Looking at the boundary between model and view in this way provides an opportunity to start thinking about error conditions. So far, all the examples have been lax about the form inputs. Users have been permitted to enter any values into fields, even when these values might not make sense. For example, if a letter like 'q' were provided to the calculator from Listing 18.8, a JSP error would result. This error would arise even if the value looks like a number to humans but not to Java, such as "8,442.23." The standard converters used by BeanUtils, and hence by the standard tags, are not equipped to parse numbers with commas. Worst of all, the error displayed is one that is meant to be useful to JSP developers but will be incomprehensible to any end users.

The general form of this problem is called **form validation,** ensuring that the values provided by users are both syntactically valid and sensible for the particulars of the application. There will also need to be a means to report problems back to users in a useful and friendly way. The question then becomes whether this validation should be done in the beans making up the model or the new form beans that are part of the view.

There is a perhaps surprising amount of debate about this issue. Because it is the model's job to store and act on the data, it should usually be responsible for all validation as well. Certainly some kinds of validation can *only* be done by the model, such as an inventory check for an item ordered through an online catalog. Likewise, a bean modeling a calculator that can do division should be responsible for ensuring that the denominator is not zero.

However, there are a very few kinds of validation that are not intrinsic to the model but arise as part of the way the model and view communicate. Again, consider a calculator model that may have a method called `add()` that takes two integers as arguments. When used directly by a Java program there would be no way to invoke this with the letter 'a' as an argument. In essence, the Java compiler would do the validation before the model was ever used. However, the dynamic nature of JSPs bypasses this check by the compiler. This check could be put into the calculator bean by adding a version of the `add()` method that takes strings as arguments and ensures they look like numbers before proceeding. However, this approach violates the distinction between model and view in a different way. It is often stressed that a view should not need to know the details of how the model works, yet here the model would be changed based on the details of the view. One reasonable compromise is to note that all **semantic** validation must be done in the model because it is the only part of the system that knows what the data means but that simple **syntactic** validation can be done by the view, which in this case means by the new form beans.

The controller's role should now be clear. It will be the controller's job to take values from the form and provide them to the form bean and then ask that bean to validate them. If the validation fails, the controller will send the user back to the original form and report the validation errors. The form can then display these errors and ask the user to correct them. Once the validation succeeds, the controller will pass data from the form bean to the model bean.

At this stage the controller can also populate the model with additional global information. Recall the discussion of the `awl:date` tag in Chapter 18. It was pointed out that this tag dealt with both model information (the current time) and view information (how the time should be formatted). A cleaner division would be to use the controller to place the current time in beans or tags that needed it.

After populating the model, the controller will then perform the desired action on it, such as invoking a `save()` method, and then send the user to the appropriate page from which to continue activities.

19.2 Struts: An Application Toolkit

From the preceding discussion it is clear that a great deal of new infrastructure is needed to support controllers. There must be some means to associate form beans and controller actions with forms. These controller actions must know where to send users after successfully completing an action. There also must be a mechanism to send validation errors to users. The Java classes to implement the controller actions must also be written.

This is a lot of work, but much of it has already been done by a toolkit called **struts.** Struts is much more than a way to build controllers; it is a complete application framework containing custom tags, a controller framework, and much more.

Among the many other services it provides, struts adds another layer between data and presentation. Up until now content on a page could come from one of two places: either hard-coded in the page or from a bean. A typical example is the CD database from Chapter 18, where the name of the artist was provided by a bean, but the preceding string "Albums by: " was in the page itself.

Struts takes the approach that the only elements that should be part of a JSP are the structural ones such as table cells, paragraph breaks, and so on. All other text, such as messages to users, labels for form elements, and so on, should live in a common file separate from all JSPs. Separating content from structure ensures some level of consistency because a message used on several pages is defined in one place. It also makes it easier to make changes because there is no question about where to find a particular message.

Most importantly, isolating all of a site's text in one file makes it possible to easily support multiple languages and locales. A site might have multiple versions of such a file—one for English that contains

```
message.entry=Welcome
message.departure=Goodbye
```

and another for German that contains

```
message.entry=Willkommen
message.departure=Auf Wiedersehen
```

Using tags from the struts library or a utility class, a developer can just refer to "message.entry," and the appropriate text will be retrieved depending on whether the location has been set to an English-speaking or German-speaking locale. Note that the dots in the names do not necessarily imply that there is any sort of hierarchy as the dots in bean properties do. Here the dots are just a convenient way to mentally group messages into convenient units.

19.3 Using Struts

The entry point to struts is a servlet called `ActionServlet`. This servlet is typically configured in `web.xml` (see Chapter 17) to handle all URLs ending in ".do," as in the following:

```
<servlet>
  <servlet-name>action</servlet-name>
  <servlet-class>
    org.apache.struts.action.ActionServlet
  </servlet-class>

  <init-param>
    <param-name>application</param-name>
    <param-value>
      config.ApplicationResources
```

```
    </param-value>
  </init-param>

  <init-param>
    <param-name>config</param-name>
    <param-value>
      /WEB-INF/classes/config/struts-config.xml
    </param-value>
  </init-param>

  <init-param>
    <param-name>validate</param-name>
    <param-value>true</param-value>
  </init-param>
  <load-on-startup>1</load-on-startup>
</servlet>

<servlet-mapping>
  <servlet-name>action</servlet-name>
  <url-pattern>*.do</url-pattern>
</servlet-mapping>
```

The `applicaton` parameter names the location of the property file with the messages. This is relative to the effective CLASSPATH, so a typical place for this file is under `WEB-INF/classes`. Dots in this name represent subdirectories just as they do in package names, so the file will be found in the `config` directory. Note that although this is a property file, adding the `.properties` extension will cause `ApplicationResources` to be treated as a subdirectory. Hence the entry in `web.xml` should not include the extension.

The `config` parameter points to a file with additional struts configuration; this file will be examined in more detail shortly. Note that the location of this file is relative to the top level of the Web application, not to the CLASSPATH.

The `validate` flag tells struts to perform input validation, and the `load-on-startup` flag tells Tomcat to load and initialize the servlet as soon as the Web application starts up.

The next several examples will rebuild the calculator application from Chapter 18. The `ApplicationResources` with the full set of messages used by this little application is shown in Listing 19.1.

Listing 19.1 The application messages

```
prompt.number1=First number
prompt.number2=Second number
button.save=Add
button.reset=Reset
button.cancel=Cancel
error.calculator.missing1=\
<li>Please provide a value for the first number</li>
error.calculator.missing2=\
<li>Please provide a value for the second number</li>
error.calculator.bad1=\
<li>The first value does not look like a number</li>
error.calculator.bad2=\
<li>The second value does not look like a number</li>
errors.required={0} is a required field
testform.whuh={0} is improperly formatted
```

Next the model needs to be defined, which is quite simple and shown in Listing 19.2.

Listing 19.2 The calculator model

```
package com.awl.toolbook.chapter19;

public class Calculator {
    private double number1;
    public double getNumber1() {return number1;}
    public void setNumber1(double number1) {
        this.number1 = number1;
    }

    private double number2;
    public double getNumber2() {return number2;}
    public void setNumber2(double number2) {
        this.number2 = number2;
    }

    private double sum;
    public double getSum() {return sum;}
    public void setSum(double sum) {this.sum = sum;}
```

```
    public void computeSum() {
        sum = number1 + number2;
    }
}
```

This class has simple properties for the two inputs and the resulting sum. It also has a method called `computeSum()` that will perform the computation. In this case it would be easy enough to have the controller compute the sum and store it by calling `setSum()`, but that would be inappropriate because the model should be responsible for managing all of its data. Note that nothing in this bean knows anything about taking values from a form or parsing numbers with commas or anything else.

The bean that will directly interface with the HTML form is shown in Listing 19.3.

Listing 19.3 The calculator form

```
package com.awl.toolbook.chapter19;

import java.text.DecimalFormat;
import javax.servlet.http.HttpServletRequest;
import org.apache.struts.action.ActionError;
import org.apache.struts.action.ActionErrors;
import org.apache.struts.action.ActionForm;
import org.apache.struts.action.ActionMapping;


public class CalculatorForm extends ActionForm {
    private String number1;
    public String getNumber1() {return number1;}
    public void setNumber1(String number1) {
        this.number1 = number1;
    }

    private String number2;
    public String getNumber2() {return number2;}
    public void setNumber2(String number2) {
        this.number2 = number2;
    }
```

Listing 19.3 The calculator form *(continued)*

```
public ActionErrors validate(ActionMapping mapping,
                             HttpServletRequest request)
{
    ActionErrors errors = new ActionErrors();
    DecimalFormat f     =
        new DecimalFormat("###,###.##");

    if(empty(number1)) {
        errors.add("number1",
                   new ActionError(
                       "error.calculator.missing1"));
    } else {
        try {
            f.parse(number1);
        } catch (Exception e) {
            errors.add("number1",
                       new ActionError(
                           "error.calculator.bad1"));
        }
    }

    if(empty(number2)) {
        errors.add("number2",
                   new ActionError(
                       "error.calculator.missing2"));
    } else {
        try {
            f.parse(number2);
        } catch (Exception e) {
            errors.add("number2",
                       new ActionError(
                           "error.calculator.bad2"));
        }
    }

    return errors;
}
```

```
    private boolean empty(String s) {
        return s == null || s.trim().length() == 0;
    }
}
```

The first thing to notice about this class is that it extends a struts class called `ActionForm`. In struts terms everything the controller does is considered an `Action`, and data is made available to an `Action` via an `ActionForm`.

The `CalculatorForm` contains two simple properties to hold the inputs from the form. Notice that these properties are `Strings`, whereas those in the model are `doubles`. This makes sense because a calculator can add numbers, but the form should allow the user to enter arbitrary text including representations of numbers with commas.

The `CalculatorForm` allows the inputs to be validated through the `validate()` method, which is defined in the `ActionForm` base class. Setting the `validate` flag in `web.xml` instructs struts to call this method when the form is submitted.

The `validate()` method is passed an `ActionMapping` object, which is a struts class containing information about the application, and an `HttpServlet-Request`, which is a part of the servlet specification and contains information about the request. Neither of these parameters is used in this example, but they are available for more sophisticated kinds of validation.

The `validate()` method itself checks that values have been provided for both inputs and that Java is able to turn the inputs into numbers. This latter test is done by attempting to parse the data by using the `DecimalFormat` class, which here has been told to allow numbers with commas. For more information about this class and how it is used, consult the JDK documentation.

If a value is missing or malformed, a new `ActionError` is added to the set maintained by the `ActionErrors` object, called `errors`. The exact text of these error messages comes from the file in Listing 19.1, which means it would be possible to report these errors in any language for which such a file had been built.

The `errors` are returned at the end of the message. Internally struts will check this return value, and if it is empty, it means there were no problems and the form can be processed. Otherwise, the user must be informed of the errors and given the opportunity to fix them.

Now that the form bean is completed, it is time to write the class that will actually implement the action. This is shown in Listing 19.4.

Listing 19.4 The action handler

```
package com.awl.toolbook.chapter19;

import java.io.IOException;
import java.lang.reflect.InvocationTargetException;
import java.text.DecimalFormat;
import java.util.Locale;

import javax.servlet.RequestDispatcher;
import javax.servlet.ServletException;
import javax.servlet.http.*;
import org.apache.struts.action.*;
import org.apache.struts.util.*;

public final class CalculatorAction extends Action {
    public ActionForward perform(ActionMapping mapping,
                 ActionForm form,
                 HttpServletRequest request,
                 HttpServletResponse response)
        throws IOException, ServletException
    {
        // Populate the input form
        if (form == null) {
            form = new CalculatorForm();
            request.setAttribute(mapping.getAttribute(),
                                 form);
        }

        CalculatorForm calcForm = (CalculatorForm) form;

        // Build the model
        Calculator calc          = new Calculator();
        calc.setNumber1(getNumber(calcForm.getNumber1()));
        calc.setNumber2(getNumber(calcForm.getNumber2()));
        calc.computeSum();
```

```
        // Store the model in the request so the result
        // page can get to it
        request.setAttribute("calc",calc);

        return (mapping.findForward("success"));
    }


    private double getNumber(String s) {
        DecimalFormat d = new DecimalFormat("###,###.##");
        try {
            Number n = d.parse(s);
            return n.doubleValue();
        } catch (Exception e) {
            // No need to worry about parse errors, the
            // check in the form bean ensures us of that!
        }

        return 0.0;
    }
}
```

This class extends another struts class—`Action`—whose `perform()` method will be called after the form bean successfully validates the inputs. This method is invoked with the form bean, the same `ActionHandler` that was passed to the `validate()` method, and the request and response. The method ensures there is a valid form bean, constructs an instance of the `Calculator` model bean, populates it, and then finishes the process by calling `computeSum()`. In a more complicated example the model bean might come from a database or some other repository rather than being constructed within the action. Finally, the calculator is stored in the request, which sets up everything for the result page to display the sum, and the name of the result page is returned. This name is not hard-coded; rather, it is kept in the `ActionMapping` under a key called `success`.

Now that the classes are completed, struts needs to be told how to use them. This is accomplished though the file specified as the `config` parameter in `web.xml`. A minimal version of this file is shown in Listing 19.5.

Listing 19.5 The struts configuration file

```
<?xml version="1.0" encoding="ISO-8859-1" ?>

<struts-config>
  <form-beans>
    <form-bean name="calculatorForm"
            type="com.awl.toolbook.chapter19.CalculatorForm"/>
  </form-beans>

  <action-mappings>
    <action path="/calculator"
            type="com.awl.toolbook.chapter19.CalculatorAction"
            name="calculatorForm"
            scope="request"
            validate="true"
            input="/chapter19/calculator.jsp">
      <forward name="success"
               path="/chapter19/calc_result.jsp"/>
    </action>
  </action-mappings>
</struts-config>
```

The first section defines all the form beans the application will use, which here is just the `CalculatorForm` just defined. It is given a name—`calculatorForm`—which will be used to reference it from JSP pages and elsewhere in the file.

The next section defines the actions that the application will perform. The `path` attribute defines the URL for which this action will be taken. Recall that by convention the `ActionServlet` is configured to handle all URLs ending in ".do," so this clause of the configuration file indicates that `CalculatorAction` will be invoked when the user accesses "/calculator.do." The `name` parameter indicates the name of the form class to use, which here is the name given to the `CalculatorForm` in the previous section. The `scope` parameter names the scope in which the form bean should be stored. Using the session scope would allow one bean to collect inputs from a number of different forms spread across many JSP pages. This is useful for applications that must collect a great deal of information before they can perform their actions. The `validate` flags indicates whether the `validate()` method of the form bean should be called before calling the `perform()` method of the handler. Finally, the `input` parameter indicates the JSP file that contains the form. This value is used if there are any errors validating the form, and the user must be sent back to correct them.

The action tag may contain any number of forward tags that give symbolic names to pages. In this example there is only one called success, which matches the name used in the CalculatorAction. Using symbolic names like this makes it much easier to modify the way sites behave. If it was ever decided that after successfully computing a sum the calculator should send the user somewhere other than calc_result.jsp, it would just be necessary to change the configuration file. Neither the Java nor JSP files would need to be altered.

Struts has been configured with two pages: calculator.jsp, which is marked as the input, and calc_result.jsp, which is marked as the success URL. Struts will determine which of these pages is appropriate based on the input it has received and will then use a RequestDispatcher to include the contents of that page. This means that the URL will be calculator.do regardless of whether the user is looking at the input or result pages. This one URL thus "controls" access to these two pages, further justifying the use of the term controller.

The model and controller have now been fully constructed, and struts will even simplify the task of completing the view. The input page is shown in Listing 19.6.

Listing 19.6 The input page

```
<%@ taglib prefix="bean"
    uri="http://jakarta.apache.org/struts/bean" %>
<%@ taglib prefix="html"
    uri="http://jakarta.apache.org/struts/html" %>


<html:html>
<head>
  <title>Calculator</title>
  <html:base/>
</head>

<body>
<html:form action="/calculator">

<bean:message key="prompt.number1"/>
<html:text property="number1"/><br>

<bean:message key="prompt.number2"/>
<html:text property="number2"/><br>
```

Listing 19.6 The input page *(continued)*

```
<html:submit>
  <bean:message key="button.save"/>
</html:submit>

<html:reset>
  <bean:message key="button.reset"/>
</html:reset>

<html:cancel>
  <bean:message key="button.cancel"/>
</html:cancel>

</html:form>


<html:errors/>

</body>
</html:html>
```

This example imports two tag libraries from struts, installed as `bean` and `html`. The `bean` tag library supports a number of tags that simplify working with beans and in particular for connecting beans to forms. The `html` tag library provides a number of tags that simplify the creation of HTML: Of particular interest is a set of tags that simplify the construction of forms and add some very useful functionality.

The first use of these tags is encountered at the top of the page, with the `html:html` tag. This tag doesn't render any output beyond a standard HTML tag, but it does set up a context that other struts tags will use internally. This is also true of the `html:base` tag a few lines down, which establishes the current URL from which URLs to the action and result pages can be built.

The `html:errors` tag displays all the messages that have been added to the `ActionErrors` object by the `CalculatorForm` in Listing 19.2. The first time a user accesses this page it will not yet have been through the `CalculatorForm`, so the `html:errors` will not render any output. If there are errors, the `html:errors` will first display the value of the `errors.header` property from Listing 19.1, then each of the errors, then `errors.footer`. This makes it as easy to change the format of the errors as it is to change their text.

The form itself starts a little lower and begins with another new tag called `html:form`. This renders as a regular HTML form tag but ensures that the action points to the right place. In particular, it will ensure that the form gets sent to the `ActionSeverlet` by pointing the URL at `calculator.do`. This in turn will allow the servlet to use the name `calculator` to look up the correct form bean and action handler in the configuration file.

There are then a number of `bean:message` and `html:text` tags. `bean:message` simply looks up a message in the resource file from Listing 19.1—once again allowing the messages to be configured, changed, or localized. The `html:text` tags render a standard HTML input of type text, but in addition struts can use the name of the provided property, plus what it knows about the form bean, to provide values for these fields as the form is rendered.

Consider what will happen if a user provides a value for the first number but leaves the second one blank. As previously noted the `validate()` method will fail, and the user will be returned to this input form. The `html:errors` tag will display the appropriate error message, informing the user to provide a value for the second number. However, because the user already filled in the first number, it would not be friendly to make them fill it out again. The `html:text` tag will be able to get the value for the first number back out of the form bean and make it the default value, so the user will not need to reenter it. Conceptually this is similar to writing

```
<input
  type="text"
  name="number1"
  value="<c:out value="${calculatorForm.number1}"/>">
```

The `html:text` tag hides all the details about which bean and property are used, and it is therefore much easier to work with. Struts provides similar tags that handle check boxes, text areas, and all the rest. It even provides tags to handle form submit and reset buttons, as shown at the bottom of Listing 19.6.

This is possible because JSP is invoked by the servlet. The servlet sets up the `CalculatorForm` bean and places it in the request, so when validation fails and the servlet passes control to `calculator.jsp` the bean and hence the user's original inputs are still available.

The only remaining piece of the calculator is the result page, which is shown in Listing 19.7.

Listing 19.7 The result page

```
<%@ taglib prefix="c"
    uri="http://java.sun.com/jstl/core" %>

<%@ taglib prefix="bean"
    uri="http://jakarta.apache.org/struts/bean" %>

<bean:message key="message.result"/>:
<c:out value="${calc.sum}"/>
```

There is no need for the page to load the `Calculator` because this was already done by the `CalculatorAction`. The page is thus reduced to pure view with no controller or model elements at all.

19.4 Simplifying Form Beans with the Validator

There are a number of validation tests that arise very frequently, such as ensuring values are provided and are of the correct form. Both of these were encountered in the calculator example, which required both fields to be provided and be parsable as numbers.

As of version 1.1 struts provides a set of tools that eliminate the need to repeatedly write code for many common validation conditions. The first step to using these tools is to enable the `ValidatorPlugIn`, which is done by adding the following to `struts-config.xml`:

```
<plug-in
    className="org.apache.struts.validator.ValidatorPlugIn">
  <set-property
    property="pathnames"
    value="/WEB-INF/classes/config/validator-rules.xml,
           /WEB-INF/classes/config/validation.xml"/>
</plug-in>
```

The `pathnames` argument is a list of files that contain XML definitions of validation rules and how those rules should be applied to various forms and fields. `validator-rules.xml` is provided as part of struts and contains definitions for many common validations. It is usually not necessary for users to modify this file. `validation.xml` specifies which tests are to be performed on which fields and can best be understood through an example.

```
<form-validation>
  <formset>
    <form name="calculatorForm2">
      <field  property="number1" depends="required,double">
        <arg0 key="calculatorForm2.number1"/>
      </field>

      <field  property="number2" depends="required,double">
        <arg0 key="calculatorForm2.number2"/>
      </field>

    </form>
  </formset>
</form-validation>
```

The `name` in the `form` tag must match a corresponding `form-bean` in `struts-config.xml`. Here, `calculatorForm2` is used, which will be defined shortly. Each `field` node specifies a field for which validation should be done. The `depends` attribute is a comma-separated list of validations that should be performed. Each entry is defined in `validator-rules.xml` and behaves as the name implies. `requires` demands that the field is not empty, and `double` indicates that the field must be parsable as a number.

The `key` value names an entry in the application resources that specifies the name of the field. Additionally, the validator uses a number of properties to contain error messages. The full set of properties that must be added to the resources file for this example are

```
calculatorForm2.number1=The first number
calculatorForm2.number2=The second number

errors.required=<li>{0} is a required field</li>
errors.double=<li>{0} is improperly formatted</li>
```

The `errors.required` entry is the message that the validator will use when a required field is not provided. Within this message `{0}` will be replaced by the property named by `arg0` from the field. If the first number is not provided, the result will be, as expected,

```
<li>The first number is a required field</li>
```

Messages can have any number of such parameters that will be called `arg1`, `arg2`, and so on, and will appear in error declarations as `{1}`, `{2}`, and so on.

Using the validator the form bean becomes much simpler, and it is shown in Listing 19.8.

Listing 19.8 A simpler calculator form bean

```
package com.awl.toolbook.chapter19;

import org.apache.struts.validator.ValidatorForm;

public class CalculatorForm2 extends ValidatorForm {
    private double number1;
    public double getNumber1() {return number1;}
    public void setNumber1(double number1) {
        this.number1 = number1;
    }

    private double number2;
    public double getNumber2() {return number2;}
    public void setNumber2(double number2) {
        this.number2 = number2;
    }
}
```

Note that Listing 19.8 extends `ValidatorForm` instead of `actionForm`. `ValidatorForm` provides a `validate()` method that performs all the validations specified in `validations.xml`. It is legal to override this method in derived classes as long as `super.validate()` is called first. This makes it possible to mix built-in and custom validations.

The action form also becomes simpler, as shown in Listing 19.9.

Listing 19.9 A simpler calculator action

```
package com.awl.toolbook.chapter19;

import java.io.IOException;
import java.lang.reflect.InvocationTargetException;
import java.text.DecimalFormat;
import java.util.Locale;

import javax.servlet.RequestDispatcher;
import javax.servlet.ServletException;
```

```
import javax.servlet.http.*;
import org.apache.struts.action.*;
import org.apache.struts.util.*;

public final class CalculatorAction2 extends Action {
    public ActionForward perform(ActionMapping mapping,
                 ActionForm form,
                 HttpServletRequest request,
                 HttpServletResponse response)
        throws IOException, ServletException
    {
        CalculatorForm2 calcForm = (CalculatorForm2) form;

        // Build the model
        Calculator calc          = new Calculator();
        calc.setNumber1(calcForm.getNumber1());
        calc.setNumber2(calcForm.getNumber2());
        calc.computeSum();

        // Store the model in the request so the result
        // page can get to it
        request.setAttribute("calc",calc);

        return (mapping.findForward("success"));
    }
}
```

None of the parsing is necessary this time because by the time this action is called, struts will have ensured that the inputs are of the correct form and populated the `double` fields in `CalculatorForm2`.

All that remains is to connect everything together in `struts-config.xml`:

```
<form-bean name="calculatorForm2"
           type="com.awl.toolbook.chapter19.CalculatorForm2"/>

<action path="/calculator2"
        type="com.awl.toolbook.chapter19.CalculatorAction2"
        name="calculatorForm2"
        scope="request"
        validate="true"
```

```
        input="/chapter19/calculator2.jsp">
    <forward name="success"
             path="/chapter19/calc_result2.jsp"/>
</action>
```

These exactly parallel the entries for the first version of the calculator, but different pages and classes are used so the two examples can coexist.

There are many other validations in addition to `required` and `double`. One particularly useful one is called `mask`, which requires that the specified field matches a particular regular expression. For example, a required field that allows only alphabetic characters could be represented as

```
<field  property="someField" depends="required,mask">
  <arg0 key="testForm.someField"/>
    <var>
      <var-name>mask</var-name>
      <var-value>^[A-Za-z]*$</var-value>
    </var>
  </arg0>
</field>
```

The use of `mask` in the `depends` attribute indicates that the regular expression test should be performed, and the entries in the `var` node indicate what that regular expression is. The struts validator uses the ORO Perl5 expression library covered in Chapter 13.

There are a number of other validations that require parameters. Such parameters are specified by a `var` node whose `var-name` matches the name of the validation and whose `var-value` holds the parameter.

19.5 Eliminating Form Beans

The form bean used in Listing 19.8 had no code and was reduced to a simple value container. This happens fairly often when using the validator because the provided validations cover all common situations. In this case the bean can be eliminated through the use of a `DynaBean`, as covered in Chapter 8. Recall from that chapter that such beans are somewhat like `Maps`, except that values have a type as well as a name.

A DynaBean can be used as a form bean by replacing the definition of the `form-bean` in `struts-config.xml` with an entry defining the properties of the bean. `CalculatorForm2` could be completely replaced with the following entry:

```
<form-bean
    name="calculatorForm3"
    type="org.apache.struts.validator.DynaValidatorForm">
  <form-property name="number1" type="java.lang.Double"/>
  <form-property name="number2" type="java.lang.Double"/>
</form-bean>
```

The action handler needs only a slight modification to use this DynaBean, which is shown in Listing 19.10.

Listing 19.10 Using a dynamic bean

```
package com.awl.toolbook.chapter19;

import java.io.IOException;
import java.lang.reflect.InvocationTargetException;
import java.text.DecimalFormat;
import java.util.Locale;

import javax.servlet.RequestDispatcher;
import javax.servlet.ServletException;
import javax.servlet.http.*;
import org.apache.struts.action.*;
import org.apache.struts.util.*;
import org.apache.struts.validator.DynaValidatorForm;

public final class CalculatorAction3 extends Action {
    public ActionForward perform(ActionMapping mapping,
                 ActionForm form,
                 HttpServletRequest request,
                 HttpServletResponse response)
        throws IOException, ServletException
    {
        DynaValidatorForm f = (DynaValidatorForm) form;

        // Build the model
        Calculator calc         = new Calculator();
        calc.setNumber1(
            ((Double) f.get("number1")).doubleValue());
```

Listing 19.10 Using a dynamic bean *(continued)*

```
        calc.setNumber2(
            ((Double) f.get("number2")).doubleValue());

        calc.computeSum();

        // Store the model in the request so the result
        // page can get to it
        request.setAttribute("calc",calc);

        return (mapping.findForward("success"));
    }
}
```

As this example illustrates, values are obtained from a dynamic bean through the `DynaValidatorForm` class. Individual values are obtained via called to `get()`, just as they are with a `Map`. Here the values are cast to `Doubles`, and then `doubleValue()` is used to get the primitive value to hand off to the bean.

19.6 The Pros and Cons of Struts

It should be clear at this point that struts provides a very clean, very sharp distinction between model, view, and controller. It also simplifies some aspects of creating the view by communicating problems to the user in a flexible way and maintaining valid inputs as errors are corrected. These are undeniably good things.

However, these benefits are not without their costs. It is also clear that using struts adds a great deal of overhead. Creating a new form requires creation of at least an action handler, plus possibly a form bean, plus several entries in several different files. On sites with many forms the configuration files may become overwhelming.

In the process of adding a new page and fine-tuning the entries in the XML file it is likely that Tomcat, or at least the particular Web application, will need to be restarted several times. This may take only thirty seconds each time, but those delays quickly add up.

It must also be said that struts's error reporting leaves a very great deal to be desired. Any mistake in the configuration, including mistyping the location of the `application` or `config` files, omitting the `load-on-startup` flag or any syntactic errors will result in the utterly unhelpful error message "Cannot find ActionMappings or ActionFormBeans collection." There is no way to narrow down what might be the cause of the problem short of very carefully reviewing the structure and all the values in all the configuration files. Any problems with the validator, including misconfiguration or a dependency on classes that are not available, result in the system failing to perform validations without reporting any error message at all!

While it is true that having the source to struts makes it possible to track down even the most obscure problems; it is also true that the poor quality of error reporting can make working with struts extremely frustrating.

In the final analysis the benefits of using struts must be weighed against the difficulties of developing with it on a project-by-project basis.

19.7 Beyond This Book

There is much more to struts than could possibly be covered in a single chapter. It is possible to add new validators to the set provided out of the box. It is also possible to add completely new components through the plug-in architecture. There are also many more tags in the `bean` and `html` libraries, as well as a library of logic tags that provides similar functionality to the standard tag libraries but is designed with struts integration in mind.

19.8 Summary

Tool: Jakarta Struts
Purpose: Web application framework, including controller tools
Version covered: 1.1
Home page: http://jakarta.apache.org/struts/
License: The Apache Software License, Version 1.1

Further Reading:

- *Programming Jakarta Struts,* by Chuck Cavaness, O'Reilly, 2002.

CHAPTER 20

Cocoon

Chapter 18 included an overview of the XML portion of the Java tag library. Several of the examples in that chapter illustrated a two-stage approach to building pages. In the first stage a JavaServer Page builds an XML document containing the data, and in the second stage XSLT is used to transform the document into a form suitable for presentation.

Cocoon takes this idea and expands on it by several orders of magnitude. Cocoon provides a complete XML-based publishing suite that provides dozens of tools for the generation, manipulation, and rendering of XML. The basic two-stage approach is augmented into an XML **pipeline** that may build and transform a document in several steps.

20.1 Building and Configuring Cocoon

Cocoon is unlike any tool examined in this book so far. Because it is so large and contains so many features, distributing and using a binary-only release would be impractical. Therefore, Cocoon is only distributed as source code plus a number of of Ant-based build utilities. Although Ant was covered in Chapter 2, it is not necessary to be intimately familiar with Ant in order to build Cocoon. It is just necessary to have the `JAVA_HOME` environment variable set and then run the provided `build.sh` on Unix or `build.bat` on Windows.

By default the build includes all of Cocoon, which is likely to be more than any particular site will need. The set of components to build is controlled by two files: `build.properties` and `blocks.properties`. These files should be copied to `local.build.properties` and `local.blocks.properties`, respectively; any changes made to the local files will override the defaults in the standard files.

`local.build.properties` controls supplementary elements such as documentation, javadocs, and deprecated portions of Cocoon. `local.blocks.properties` controls which elements of Cocoon itself will be built. There is a very long list of elements, grouped into units called "blocks." These elements include support for various kinds of databases, profiling, demos, different kinds of form handling, and much more.

A sensible approach for those just getting to know Cocoon for the first time is to use the defaults to build everything.

The result of the build process is a Web application, which will be in the `build/webapp` directory. This application can be run directly from its currently location using the servlet runner provided with Cocoon. This can be started by running `cocoon.bat servlet` from the command line or `cocoon.sh servlet` for those using Unix. Once this application starts up, access `http://localhost:8888` will bring up the page in Figure 20.1.

Of particular interest is the "samples" link, which brings up the screen in Figure 20.2. Demonstrations and documentation for all compiled blocks are

Figure 20.1. The Cocoon start page.

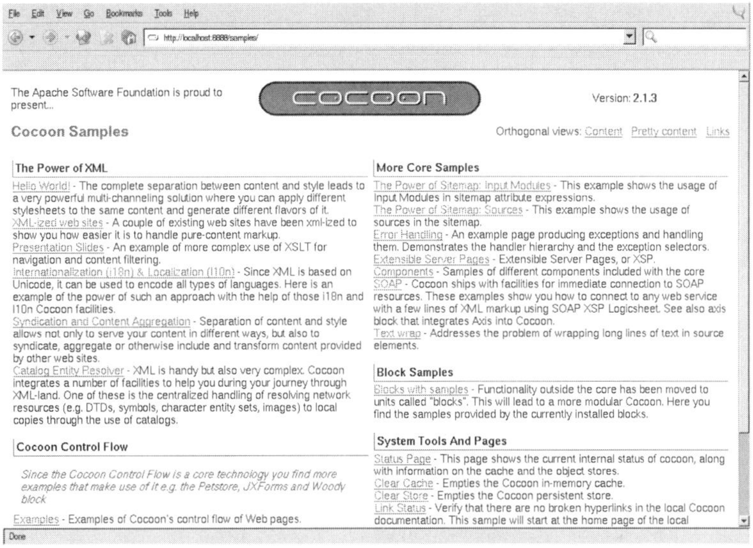

Figure 20.2. The Cocoon sample page.

accessible from this page. The number of links on this screen should give some sense of how much functionality is built into Cocoon.

The Cocoon Web application can also be run under Tomcat by copying or moving the `webapp` directory from the Cocoon `build` directory to Tomcat's `webapps` directory. The Web application will behave exactly the same way, and all the examples will be available.

This Web application is a great way to learn about Cocoon's capabilities, and it also provides a framework to begin to experiment with these capabilities. The next step is using Cocoon in new applications, which requires additional setup.

To do this, a skeletal Web application must be set up as described in Chapter 17. Next, all the jar files from the Cocoon application must be copied into the `lib` directory of the new application. Note that there may be many such jar files—a full Cocoon installation requires over 130.

Cocoon configuration begins with an entry in `web.xml` that defines a master servlet and many of its parameters. This can also be taken from the Cocoon Web application and modified as needed. Here is a portion of the configuration as used on the example CD-ROM:

```
<servlet>
  <servlet-name>Cocoon</servlet-name>
  <display-name>Cocoon</display-name>
  <description>Cocoon</description>
```

```
    <servlet-class>
      org.apache.cocoon.servlet.CocoonServlet
    </servlet-class>

    <init-param>
      <param-name>configurations</param-name>
      <param-value>
        /WEB-INF/classes/config/cocoon.xconf
      </param-value>
    </init-param>

    <init-param>
      <param-name>logkit-config</param-name>
      <param-value>
        /WEB-INF/classes/config/logkit.xconf
      </param-value>
    </init-param>

    <load-on-startup>1</load-on-startup>
  </servlet>
```

As with any servlet definition this starts with the class and continues with values for initialization parameters. The `configurations` parameter is the single most important because this names a file that installs all available components into Cocoon and initializes a number of global attributes.

The `logkit-config` names a file with detailed logging information. Because Cocoon is so large and complex, there are many logging options that can be tweaked to give appropriate levels of information for all of its subsystems. A number of other log-related parameters follow the `logkit-config`; these are omitted here in the interest of space.

`load-on-startup` tells Tomcat to start the servlet as soon as the Web application loads. This parameter was also used with struts.

There are many other parameters that configure character sets, upload handling, temporary file storage, and much more. The configuration that is built with the Cocoon Web application has sensible values for many of these, which can be copied directly.

In addition to the definition of the servlet a mapping must be provided. Very often Cocoon is given complete control of a site, and a single mapping is specified to pass all requests through Cocoon. For the purpose of this book Cocoon is only given control over the examples from this chapter with the following entry:

```
<servlet-mapping>
  <servlet-name>Cocoon</servlet-name>
  <url-pattern>/chapter20/*</url-pattern>
</servlet-mapping>
```

After setting up `web.xml`, the secondary configuration files, `cocoon.xconf` and `logkit.xconf`, must be copied from the Cocoon Web application. It is essential that these be placed in the locations named in `web.xml`, or Cocoon will be unable to run.

`cocoon.xconf` is constructed by the Cocoon build process and under normal circumstances should not be altered. If Cocoon is ever rebuilt to add or remove blocks, the generated `cocoon.xconf` must be recopied.

The only change to this file that should be made is the addition of database connection information. The configuration for the examples in this chapter is

```
<datasources>
  <jdbc name="toolbook">
    <pool-controller max="10" min="5"/>
    <driver>org.hsqldb.jdbcDriver</driver>
    <dburl>jdbc:hsqldb:toolbook</dburl>
    <user>sa</user>
    <password/>
  </jdbc>
</datasources>
```

This creates a data source called `toolbook`, which will be used throughout the examples in this chapter. Multiple data sources can be defined.

`web.xml` defines Cocoon's connection to Tomcat, and `cocoon.xconf` configures Cocoon's internals. The final configuration file is `sitemap.xmap`, which must be located at the top level of the Web application. This file configures pages and is the file that developers will interact with most directly. This will be examined in more detail in the next section.

20.2 Using Cocoon

The central concept in Cocoon is that of an **XML pipeline.** A pipeline starts with a **generator,** a class that generates XML. Typically this is done by reading a file, but XML can also be obtained from a remote URL, read from a database, or generated from other data.

Following generation the XML can be sent through any number of **transformers,** which convert from one form of XML to another. The obvious example of such a transformer is one that performs XSLT transformations, as discussed in Chapter 18. Such a transformer is provided, along with many others that do less obvious things. Some of these will be covered in following sections.

After passing through transformers the XML is given to a **serializer,** which puts it in a final form that may not be XML. There are serializers that generate HTML and other standard Web formats, but there are also serializers that produce files such as zip archives, OpenOffice spreadsheets, and even images.

This provides a very flexible architecture for building applications. A complex report can be built to generate XML, and this report can then be deployed on the Web as HTML and to users' desktops as a spreadsheet by specifying two pipelines with different serializers. In addition, backend developers can concentrate on the model by building tools that create minimalistic XML, and page developers can concentrate on the view by writing XSLT transformers and style sheets. Cocoon calls this the "separation of concerns."

The set of available generators, transformers, and serializers is controlled by the `sitemap.xmap` file, as are the pipelines themselves. This file is large and complex and cannot be covered in detail; see the Cocoon documentation and the sample on the CD-ROM for details. An overview of the most important elements follows.

Generators, transformers, serializers, and other pluggable elements are called **components** and are defined in the `map:components` section of `sitemap.xmap`. Here is a minimal set of definitions:

```
<map:components>
  <map:generators default="file">
    <map:generator
      name="file"
      src="org.apache.cocoon.generation.FileGenerator"/>
  </map:generators>

  <map:transformers default="xslt">
    <map:transformer
      name="xslt"
      src="org.apache.cocoon.transformation.TraxTransformer"/>
  </map:transformers>
```

```
    <map:serializers default="html">
      <map:serializer
        mime-type="text/html"
        name="html"
        src="org.apache.cocoon.serialization.HTMLSerializer"/>
    </map:serializers>
  </map:components>
```

Each of the three categories—`map:generators`, `map:transformers`, and `map:serializers`—contains individual entries of the appropriate type. Each may also specify a default, which can be used to appreciate the definition of the pipelines.

Within each category individual entries are defined by a name and an implementing class. These classes must reside in the usual Tomcat directories to be available. Classes that rely on underlying Cocoon blocks may also require configuration in `cocoon.xmap`.

There are other elements that may be configured in this file, although they will not be covered here. The next piece of immediate interest is the pipelines. Each pipeline consists of a set of URLs to match against and a set of steps that should be performed in response to requests for that URL. For the purposes of this book, there is only a single pipeline defined in the global `sitemap.xmap` in the top-level directory, which is as follows:

```
<map:pipelines>
  <map:pipeline>

    <map:match pattern="*/**">
      <map:mount check-reload="yes"
                 src="{1}/"
                 uri-prefix="{1}"/>
    </map:match>

  </map:pipeline>
</map:pipelines>
```

This pipeline says that when a request comes in for a file in a subdirectory, as indicated by the presence of a slash, pass control to the `sitemap.xmap` within that subdirectory. Note that even though `web.xml` specified that only requests for files under `chapter20` should be handled by Cocoon, Cocoon will still get its master configuration information from the global `sitemap.xmap`. The `mount` entry will pass control to a `sitemap.xmap` within the `chapter20` directory.

The pipeline entries in `chapter20/sitemap.xmap` are more interesting. Here is one that generates a basic page with some information about Cocoon:

```
<map:match pattern="sample.html">
  <map:generate src="sample1.xml"/>
  <map:transform src="sample1.xslt"/>
  <map:serialize type="xhtml"/>
</map:match>
```

This entry specifies that requests for `sample.html` should be handled by performing the following steps:

- Use the default generator (file) with a src of `sample1.xml` to obtain the initial XML.
- Use the default transformer (xslt) to transform this XML, using the `sample1.xslt` file.
- Use the `xhtml` serializer to generate XHTML to send to the user.

`sample1.xml`, which contains the data for this page, is shown in Listing 20.1. `sample1.xslt`, which contains the transformation rules, is shown in Listing 20.2.[1] The resulting page as viewed in a browser is shown in Figure 20.3.

Listing 20.1 A sample XML page

```
<tools>
  <tool name="Coccoon" publisher="Apache">
    <description>
      XML publishing framework
    </description>
    <features>
      <feature>Generate XML from many sources</feature>
      <feature>Manipulate XML in many ways</feature>
    </features>
  </tool>
</tools>
```

[1]Readers who are not familiar with XSLT may wish to review the overview of this technology in Chapter 18.

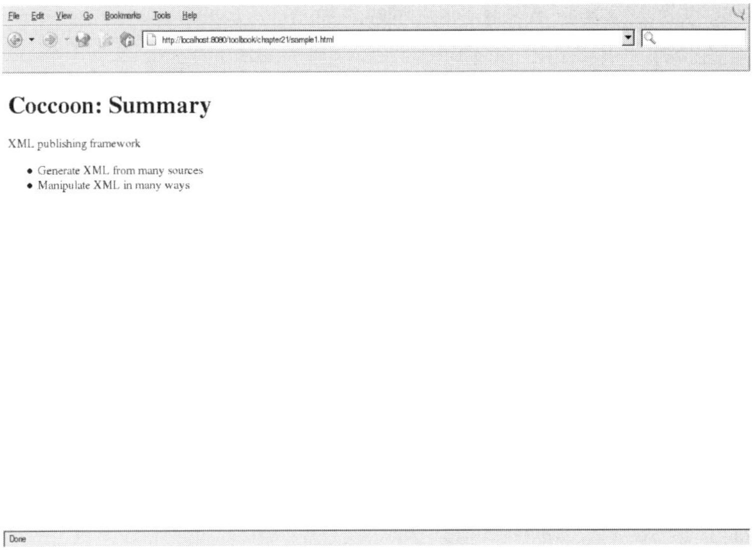

Figure 20.3. A simple page generated by Cocoon.

Listing 20.2 An XSLT file to transform data into HTML

```
<?xml version="1.0" encoding="UTF-8"?>

<xsl:stylesheet
  version="1.0"
  xmlns:xsl="http://www.w3.org/1999/XSL/Transform"
  xmlns="http://www.w3.org/1999/xhtml">

  <xsl:param name="contextPath" select="'/cocoon'"/>

  <xsl:template match="tool">
    <html>
      <head>
        <title>
          Toolkit: <xsl:value-of select="@name"/>
        </title>
      </head>
      <body>
        <h1>
          <xsl:value-of select="@name"/>: Summary
        </h1>
```

Listing 20.2 An XSLT file to transform data into HTML *(continued)*

```
        <xsl:apply-templates/>
      </body>
    </html>
  </xsl:template>

  <xsl:template match="description">
    <p><xsl:apply-templates/></p>
  </xsl:template>

  <xsl:template match="features">
    <ul><xsl:apply-templates/></ul>
  </xsl:template>

  <xsl:template match="feature">
    <li><xsl:apply-templates/></li>
  </xsl:template>
</xsl:stylesheet>
```

To repurpose this page as plain text, it is just necessary to create another entry in the pipeline with a different serializer:

```
<map:match pattern="sample1.txt">
  <map:generate src="sample1.xml"/>
  <map:serialize type="text"/>
</map:match>
```

The result is shown in Figure 20.4.

Note that the name of the toolkit does not appear in the text version of the page. This is due to the way the `text` serializer works; it emits all CDATA between tags and ignores all attributes. If this is not what is desired, it could be remedied by introducing a new XSLT file that would pull the `name` from the attribute and place it within the body of a tag.

An interesting and important feature of the `file` generator is that it can pull data from remote sources as well as from local files. Recall the discussion of the `c:import` tag from the standard tag library, which performed a similar function. This feature makes it easy to build pages that gather syndicated content. For example, www.slashdot.org offers their news stories as an XML stream that could be obtained

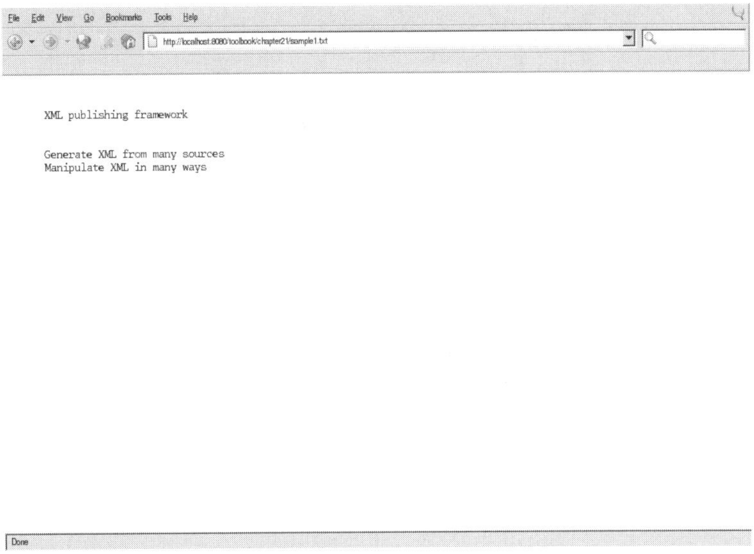

Figure 20.4. An alternate text version of the simple page.

with the following pipeline element:

```
<map:match pattern="slashfeed.xml">
  <map:generate src="http://slashdot.org/slashdot.xml"/>
  <map:serialize type="xml"/>
</map:match>
```

Because no transformation is done here, and the result is serialized as XML, browsers will render this according to their own internal XML visualization. Mozilla renders it as in Figure 20.5.

It would be a simple matter to create an XSLT transformation to turn this into HTML, allowing a site to include slashdot stories in a way that is consistent with their own look and feel.

Another important transformer, `xinclude`, allows one file to include another. A simple example of this reads one file, processes the includes, and sends the result as HTML.

```
<map:match pattern="includer.html">
  <map:generate src="includer.xml"/>
  <map:transform type="xinclude"/>
  <map:serialize type="xhtml"/>
</map:match>
```

The master file, `includer.xml`, is shown in Listing 20.3.

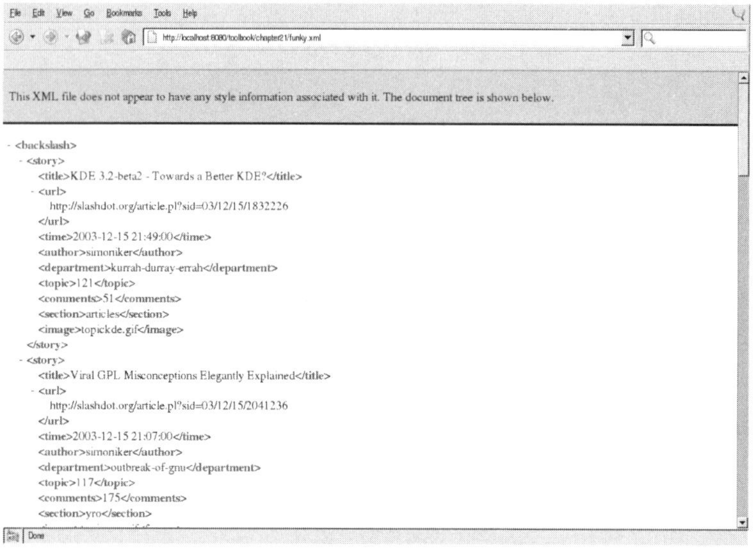

Figure 20.5. The slashdot feed.

Listing 20.3 A file that includes another

```
<?xml version="1.0" encoding="UTF-8"?>
<html xmlns:xi="http://www.w3.org/2001/XInclude">
  <head>
    <title>File that includes another</title>
  </head>

  <body>
    <p>This is from the master file</p>
    <xi:include href="included.xml"/>
  </body>
</html>
```

Note that the file to be included is specified in the including file, even though it is processed by the transformer specified in `sitemap.xmap`. Also note the import and use of the `xi` namespace, which is necessary for `xinclude` to function properly. This is a common theme in Cocoon; files to be transformed may need to import certain namespaces that the transformers will use to find the tags on which they act.

The included file contains the text "<p>This is some text from the included file</p>," and the result is a page with both paragraphs.

Like the `file` generator, `xinclude` can handle remote URLs as well as local files. Listing 20.4 shows a possible XML file that combines news from two sources.

Listing 20.4 A news portal page

```
<?xml version="1.0" encoding="UTF-8"?>
<page
  xmlns:xi="http://www.w3.org/2001/XInclude">
  <title>Latest news</title>
  <content>
    <newsboxes>
      <newsbox title="Stories from Computerworld">
        <xi:include href=
"http://www.computerworld.com/news/xml/6/0,5009,,00.xml"
/>
      </newsbox>

      <newsbox title="Stories from slashdot">
        <xi:include
href="http://slashdot.org/slashdot.xml"/>
      </newsbox>
    </newsboxes>
  </content>
</page>
```

Combined with the proper XSLT file, Listing 20.4 could be the beginning of a comprehensive news page.

20.3 Accessing Databases

Cocoon offers a few different mechanisms for database access; the simplest of these uses another transformer. The general idea is that this transformer replaces SQL commands within special tags by XML representing the rows and columns of the results. The entry in `sitemap.xmap` will specify the transformer and provide the name of the connection to use. The name of this connection should match one provided in `cocoon.xconf`. The next example will generate a page of artist names pulled from the CD database discussed in Chapter 10 and elsewhere. The first step is once again to add the entry in `sitemap.xmap`:

```
<map:match pattern="artists.html">
  <map:generate src="artists.xml"/>
  <map:transform type="sql">
    <map:parameter name="use-connection" value="toolbook"/>
  </map:transform>
  <map:transform src="sql2html.xsl"/>
  <map:serialize type="xhtml"/>
</map:match>
```

The `artist.xml` page is shown in Listing 20.5.

Listing 20.5 A Cocoon page with embedded SQL

```
<?xml version="1.0"?>

<page xmlns:sql="http://apache.org/cocoon/SQL/2.0">
  <title>Artists</title>
  <content>
    <sql:execute-query>
      <sql:query name="artists">
          select * from artist
      </sql:query>
    </sql:execute-query>
  </content>
</page>
```

Note the use of the `sql` namespace and the `select` statement enclosed within the `sql:query` tags.

After passing through the `sql` transformer, the SQL tags in this page will be replaced with XML resembling the following:

```
<rowset name="artists"
        xmlns="http://apache.org/cocoon/SQL/2.0">
  <row>
    <artist_id>1</artist_id>
    <name>The Cr&#252;xshadows</name>
  </row>
```

```
    <row>
      <artist_id>2</artist_id>
      <name>VNV Nation</name>
  </rowset>
```

All that remains is to transform this into HTML. This is accomplished by `sql2html.xsl`, which is shown in Listing 20.6.

Listing 20.6 XSLT to convert rowsets to html

```
<?xml version="1.0"?>

<xsl:stylesheet
 version="1.0" xmlns:xsl="http://www.w3.org/1999/XSL/Transform"
               xmlns:sql="http://apache.org/cocoon/SQL/2.0">


  <xsl:import href="simple-page2html.xsl"/>

  <xsl:template match="sql:rowset">
   <xsl:choose>
    <xsl:when test="ancestor::sql:rowset">
     <tr>
      <td>
       <table border="1">
        <xsl:apply-templates/>
       </table>
      </td>
     </tr>
    </xsl:when>
    <xsl:otherwise>
     <table border="1">
      <xsl:apply-templates/>
     </table>
    </xsl:otherwise>
   </xsl:choose>
  </xsl:template>
```

Listing 20.6 XSLT to convert rowsets to html *(continued)*

```
  <xsl:template match="sql:row">
   <tr>
     <td><xsl:value-of select="sql:artist_id"/></td>
     <td><a href="albums.html?artist_id={./sql:artist_id}">
       <xsl:value-of select="sql:name"/></a></td>
   </tr>
  </xsl:template>

</xsl:stylesheet>
```

The included simple-page2html.xsl file is included with Cocoon and handles tags such as page and content. The remaining transformation rules build an HTML table with two columns: one showing the ids and the other showing the names. The names are linked to the albums.html page, passing along the artist id.

The next task is to build the albums.html page that will show a list of albums for the selected artist. It is clear that this page will need to use the sql transformer in order to obtain the data. What is not yet clear is how the page will use the provided value for artist_id.

Request values from hrefs and forms is available through another transformer called session. There are tags that may refer to values in session and request objects, and the session transformer will replace these tags with their values. Listing 20.7 shows the albums.xml page that uses this session capability.

Listing 20.7 The albums page

```
<?xml version="1.0"?>

<page xmlns:session="http://apache.org/cocoon/session/1.0"
      xmlns:sql="http://apache.org/cocoon/SQL/2.0">

  <title>Albums</title>
  <content>
    <sql:execute-query>
      <sql:query name="albums">
          select * from album
          where artist_id=<session:getxml
                              context="request"
                              path="/parameter/artist_id"/>
      </sql:query>
```

```
    </sql:execute-query>
  </content>
</page>
```

Note the new `session` namespace and the `getxml` tag. The `request` context refers to values associated with the current request, much like the `request` object in JSPs. The `path` attribute references a value in a hierarchy associated with each context; in this case, it is used to obtain the value of the parameter.

Here is the entry in `sitemap.xmap` that drives this page:

```
<map:match pattern="albums.html">
  <map:generate src="albums.xml"/>
  <map:transform type="session"/>
  <map:transform type="sql">
    <map:parameter name="use-connection" value="toolbook"/>
  </map:transform>
  <map:transform src="sql2html.xsl"/>
  <map:serialize type="xhtml"/>
</map:match>
```

Requests for `albums.html` are handled by first using a generator to load `albums.xml`. The resulting XML is then fed through the `session` transformer, which will replace the `getxml` tag with the value of the `artist_id` parameter. After this transformer is finished, the text within the `sql:query` tag will resemble

```
select * from album where artist_id=1
```

The transformed page with this complete SQL statement is then passed to the `sql` transformer, which will process the query and replace it with `rowset` data, just as in the artist example. The XML is then processed by another XSLT transformation and sent to the user as XHTML.

20.4 Writing to Databases

It would be possible to use the `session` transformer to populate an SQL `insert` statement with values from a form and then use the `sql` transformer to execute that statement. However, Cocoon provides a much more powerful and flexible technique based on the idea of **actions.**

Actions are classes that are invoked prior to the beginning of a pipeline, and they are usually used to process form data. They serve a controller role in Cocoon very similar to that served by struts `Actions`, and it is no coincidence that they have the same name. However, Cocoon actions work very differently, and a number of classes are provided that are more general than classes written to work with struts.

Actions must be declared in `sitemap.xmap`, just like generators and transformers. The following entry loads a built-in class called `DatabaseAddAction` that can add a row to any table:

```
<map:actions>
  <map:action
    name="dbAdd"
    src="org.apache.cocoon.acting.DatabaseAddAction"/>
</map:actions>
```

It is also necessary to declare one or more **action sets** that will use these actions. An action set is simply a group of actions where the group as a whole has a name, as does each action within the group. For the purposes of this example the following definition will be sufficient:

```
<map:action-sets>
  <map:action-set name="process">
    <map:act type="dbAdd" action="CreateArtist"/>
  </map:action-set>
</map:action-sets>
```

The group as a whole is called `process`, and the `dbAdd` action within this group is called `CreateArtist`. If this were a more complete application, there would likely also be entries called `DeleteArtist` and `UpdateArtist` within the `process` group. There would likely also be another `action-set` that would handle creation, deletion, and update of albums.

There also must be a pipeline entry that uses this action:

```
<map:match pattern="process-artist.html">
  <map:act set="process">
    <map:parameter name="descriptor"
                   value="artist_table.xml"/>
    <map:generate src="success.xml"/>
      <map:serialize type="html"/>
  </map:act>

  <!-- If not invoked from page, show the form -->
  <map:generate src="artist_form.xml"/>
  <map:serialize type="html"/>
</map:match>
```

This entry states that when the URL process-artist.html is invoked, Cocoon should look for request parameters that invoke any action in the process action set. If any of these actions are being invoked, the implementing class will look for a property called descriptor, which here is set to artist_table.xml. This is a file that describes the table to be updated, and it will be examined shortly. After completing the action, the pipeline will start processing by generating the success.xml file, which will then be serialized as HTML.

Alternately, if no action in the process set is invoked from the page, the pipeline will start with artist_form.xml, which will be rendered as HTML.

The descriptor used by the database actions is an XML description of the table that is being used. Conceptually, it is rather like the XML descriptions used by OJB in Chapter 10, although the syntax is significantly different. The definition for the artist table is shown in Listing 20.8.

Listing 20.8 The definition of the artist table

```
<?xml version="1.0"?>

<artist>
  <connection>toolbook</connection>
  <table name="artist">
    <keys>
      <key param="artist_id"
           dbcol="artist_id"
           type="int"
           mode="manual"/>
    </keys>
    <values>
      <value param="name" dbcol="name" type="string"/>
    </values>
  </table>
</artist>
```

Conceptually, this description is straightforward. The data source and table are both specified at the top. Within the table definition each value names a simple row and specifies its type. Each key represents a key in the table and specifies how it should be populated when new data is entered. A value of manual tells Cocoon to find the current maximum value of the column in the table, add one to that value, and use the result as the value for the new row. This is a form of **auto increment,** which is similar to that provided by OJB, although it is important to note that the two methods are incompatible and hence OJB cannot be easily used with Cocoon.

The only remaining question is how Cocoon knows whether a form is invoking an action and, if so, which one. This is done by passing a specially named value through the form, which can be illustrated by `artist_form.xml`, shown in Listing 20.9.

Listing 20.9 The artist input form

```
<html>
  <head><title>Create artist</title></head>
  <body>
    <form action="process-artist.html" method="GET">
      <input type="text" name="name"/>
      <input type="submit" name="cocoon-action-CreateArtist"
             value="CreateArtist"/>
    </form>
  </body>
</html>
```

The text input of this form is perfectly standard. The submit name, `cocoon-action-CreateArtist`, is the key that tells Cocoon how to proceed. Cocoon knows from the entry in `sitemap.xmap` that the action set called `process` is being used. Cocoon will then look for any submitted value whose name starts with `cocoon-action-`. When one is found, the portion of the name following the second dash is taken to be the name of an entry in the specified set. In this case it will determine that the name is specifying an action called `CreateArtist` and will find that name in the definition of the `process` set, pointing at the action called `dbAdd`. This action will then be invoked with the `name` value from the form and the table `descriptor`. This is everything the action needs to construct an `insert` statement and update the database.

The `success.xml` file contains a message and a link back to `artist.html`. The page itself doesn't need to do anything because everything has been handled by the action.

It is important to note that although this accurately describes the way in which Cocoon works, it is *not* how Cocoon is typically used. Cocoon sites that use actions and perform database access are usually written in XSP—Extensible Server Pages—a page language used by Cocoon that in many ways provides a complete replacement for JSPs, the standard tag library, and struts. XSP contains logic and iteration tags, a form validation mechanism, and more. Using XSP, there would be no need to know how Cocoon names its submit values because the creation of these form handlers would be populated by XSP translators. However, XSP is far too large a topic to be able to address in a single chapter, and the techniques used here are sufficient to build simple database applications using Cocoon.

20.5 The Pros and Cons of Cocoon

Many of the examples in this chapter exactly mimic examples from Chapter 18 on the XML tags in the Java standard tag library. Indeed, it is possible to accomplish many of the things that Cocoon does using JSPs and these XML tags: XML generation, XSLT transformations, and accessing remote content. Database access can be done with the SQL tags or, better yet, an object-relational mapping tool like OJB.

There are two immediately obvious differences between the examples in Chapter 18 and those in this chapter. The first is the overall architecture; although both JSPs and Cocoon have notions of a model, a view, and a controller, they are very different notions. In addition, the concept of a pipeline of transformations is unique to Cocoon. The second obvious difference is how much more overhead there is to doing things with Cocoon. There is a toolkit to build, multiple configuration files to maintain, a set of namespaces, and new tags to learn.

Considering this overhead, it is safe to say that if all a site needs to support are a few XML pages, plus some Web pages and forms that access a database, then JSP, combined with the XML tags and OJB, will always be a better choice. They are easier to use, there is less to learn, and these tools are more standard than Cocoon.

However, it is also worth stressing that Cocoon is intended to be far more than just a tool to do the things discussed in this chapter. It is meant to be a complete publishing suite that controls all aspects of a site. Once a site has been built in Cocoon, it is trivially easy to publish pages to other formats, such as PDF or lightweight HTML for cell phones, simply by invoking a new serializer. If a site already has a large XML-based infrastructure and needs to deploy this content in many ways, then Cocoon may be the right tool.

20.6 Beyond This Book

As already mentioned, this chapter has barely touched the tip of the Cocoon iceberg. In addition to XSP, Cocoon also comes with a wealth of publishing features, including a scheduler that can periodically rebuild a few pages or an entire site, and much more. The information in this chapter should serve as a guide to get over the initial hump of figuring out how to use Cocoon and start exploring the examples provided with the Cocoon Web application.

This concludes our tour through some of the more common and more useful open source tools. Any one of these tools, when used properly, can make development faster, less error-prone, more productive, and perhaps even more fun. The comparison to physical tools is a good one. Think of this book as a well-stocked workshop with saws, screwdrivers, and hammers. It is possible that no one person will ever need all of these, but it is good to know that a tool is sitting nearby on a shelf if it ever is needed. It is even possible for a tool to suggest a whole new project.

There are many, many other open source toolkits available on the Web of widely varying quality. The only thing they have in common is the idea that a tool's usefulness is significantly magnified when it comes with the source code. Hopefully, this book has lent support to that idea.

20.7 Summary

Tool: Cocoon
Purpose: XML-based publishing suite
Version covered: 2.1
Home page: http://cocoon.apache.org/
License: The Apache Software License, Version 1.1

APPENDIX A

A.1 Dynamic Proxies

It is well known that a class can implement any number of interfaces at compile time by specifying the list of interface names and providing implementations of the required methods. Any class that implements an interface may be cast to the interface type at run time. A typical, if simple, example is shown in Listing A.1.

Listing A.1 A simple interface and its use

```
public Interface MyInterface {
     public void sayHello();
}

pubilc class MyClass implements MyInterface {
    public void sayHello() {
        System.out.println("Hello, world");
    }
}

public class MyDemo {
    public static void main(String argv[]) {
        MyClass c     = new MyClass();
```

Listing A.1 A simple interface and its use *(continued)*

```
        MyInterface i = (MyInterface) c;
        i.sayHello();
    }
}
```

In this example the cast to `MyInterface` is not necessary, but it is included for clarity.

What is somewhat less known is that as of JDK 1.3, it is possible for a class to declare that it implements any number of interfaces dynamically at run time. Such classes are called **dynamic proxies.**

Dynamic proxies can best be understood by using slightly different terminology to talk about object-oriented programming. Today a line of code like

```
i.sayHello();
```

is thought of as a **method invocation**—that is, it runs a piece of code inside `i` called `sayHello`. However, in the early days of object-oriented programming[1] a line like this would be thought of as *sending a message*—in particular sending the message `sayHello` to the object `i`. The object would be expected to understand this message and respond by performing the appropriate action.

Viewed in this way an interface definition is nothing more than a guarantee that a certain kind of object will respond to a certain kind of message. Similarly a line like

```
i instanceof MyInterface
```

can be thought of as asking `i` whether it understands the `sayHello` message. The important distinction here is that an object may be able to respond to a message without providing a method with the same name. This is important because it is impossible for an object to add new methods after it has been compiled, but it *is* possible for an object to decide to accept new kinds of messages.

In Java this is done in two stages. First, an object must declare that it will accept new messages, which is the same as saying that it will implement a new interface. This is done with a method in the `Proxy` class in the `java.lang.reflect` package. Second, an object must handle the new messages. This is done by providing a method with the following signature:

```
public Object invoke(Object proxy, Method m, Object[] args)
```

[1] In particular in a language called Smalltalk, developed at Xerox Parc in 1971.

This method will be invoked for all messages in the interface. The first argument will be the proxy itself, the second is an object representing the method being invoked, and the third is an array of arguments to that method. Any primitive types such as integers in the original call will automatically be converted to their object counterparts.

To make these ideas more concrete, consider an interface definition for a simple calculator that can add and subtract, as shown in Listing A.2.

Listing A.2 A calculator interface

```
package com.awl.toolbook.appendix_a;

public interface CalcInterface {
    public int add(int num1,int num2);
    public int sub(int num1,int num2);
}
```

Again, it may help to think of this as defining two messages, `add` and `subtract`, rather than two methods.

The interface shown in Listing A.2 could be satisfied dynamically by the class shown in Listing A.3.

Listing A.3 A dynamic handler for the calculator

```
package com.awl.toolbook.appendix_a;

import java.lang.reflect.*;

public class CalcImpl implements InvocationHandler {
    public static CalcInterface newInstance() {
        CalcImpl handler = new CalcImpl();

return (CalcInterface) Proxy.newProxyInstance(
                   handler.getClass().getClassLoader(),
                   new Class[] {CalcInterface.class},
                   handler);
    }
```

Listing A.3 A dynamic handler for the calculator *(continued)*

```
    private CalcImpl() {}
    public Object invoke(Object proxy,
                         Method m,
                         Object[] args)
throws Throwable
    {
        String name = m.getName();

        if(name.equals("add")) {
            Integer num1 = (Integer) args[0];
            Integer num2 = (Integer) args[1];

            return new Integer(num1.intValue() +
                               num2.intValue());
        } else if(name.equals("sub")) {
            Integer num1 = (Integer) args[0];
            Integer num2 = (Integer) args[1];

            return new Integer(num1.intValue() -
                               num2.intValue());
        }

        throw new NoSuchMethodException();
    }
}
```

The `newInstance()` method uses the `newProxyInstance()` from the `Proxy` class to declare that the `handler` object will respond to the `add` and `subtract` messages. The first argument is a class loader, which is needed to ensure that the proxy and handler live in the same class namespace. The third argument is the object to which proxied requests will be sent. The second argument is the most interesting: It is an array of interfaces that the object should handle. There is no limit to what this array may contain, as long as the interfaces themselves are accessible.

The `invoke()` method is what handles the messages. It does so by checking the name of the message, converting the arguments as appropriate, and performing the arithmetic.

Listing A.4 shows how this proxy can be used, and also provides a JUnit test (see Chapter 4) to ensure it works.

Listing A.4 A test for the calculator

```
package com.awl.toolbook.appendix_a;

import junit.framework.*;

public class CalcTest extends TestCase {
    public void testCalc() throws Exception {
        CalcInterface calc = CalcImpl.newInstance();

        assertEquals(88,calc.add(53,35));
        assertEquals(-4,calc.sub(24,28));
    }
}
```

There are no surprises here; the `newInstance()` method is used to obtain an instance of the proxy, which is then used just like any class that implements the `CalcInterface` would be.

This is a rather artificial example because clearly it would be far easier to simply implement the `CalcInterface`. A more realistic and common use for the dynamic proxy feature is to modify or extend the abilities of existing classes. This is conceptually how proxies in OJB (see Chapter 10) work. The idea is that a means is needed to load data from a database only when required. This can be done by trapping all the methods that request data and loading up the data if necessary before passing control to the requested method. An outline of how this might work is shown in Listing A.5.

Listing A.5 The skeleton of an OJB-like proxy

```
package com.awl.toolbook.appendix_a;

import java.lang.reflect.*;

public class SampleOJBProxy implements InvocationHandler {
    private Object dataBean = null;
    private boolean loaded  = false;

    public static Object newInstance(Object dataBean) {
        SampleOJBProxy handler = new SampleOJBProxy();

return Proxy.newProxyInstance(
                        dataBean.getClass().getClassLoader(),
```

Listing A.5 The skeleton of an OJB-like proxy *(continued)*

```
                    dataBean.getClass().getInterfaces(),
                    handler);
    }

    private SampleOJBProxy() {}

    public Object invoke(Object proxy,
                         Method m,
                         Object[] args)
throws Throwable
    {
        if(!loaded) {
            // ... Load the data here ...
            loaded = true;
        }

        return m.invoke(dataBean,args);
    }
}
```

Here the `newInstance()` method takes as an argument an instance of the data bean. This might be something like the `Album` from Chapter 10. The set of interfaces for the call to `newProxyInstance()` comes from the object, ensuring that the `handler` will handle all of that class's interfaces. Then the `invoke()` method simply loads the data, if necessary, before passing the request on to the data bean.

Another use for dynamic proxies is in building "virtual objects" that look like regular Java objects to any code that uses them but internally implement methods through calls to a scripting language or by invoking external programs or Web services. This model is called **dispatching,** and it is how BeanShell (see Chapter 16) is able to dynamically create interface instances. An outline of such a handler is shown in Listing A.6

Listing A.6 The skeleton of an script proxy

```
package com.awl.toolbook.appendix_a;

import java.lang.reflect.*;
import java.util.HashMap;

public class SampleScriptProxy
    implements InvocationHandler
```

```
{
    private HashMap handlers = new HashMap();

    public static Object newInstance(
                            Class interfaceToImplement)
    {
        SampleScriptProxy handler =
            new SampleScriptProxy();

return Proxy.newProxyInstance(
                handler.getClass().getClassLoader(),
                new Class[] {interfaceToImplement},
                handler);
    }

    private SampleScriptProxy() {}

    public void addHandler(String name,Script handler) {
        handlers.put(name,handler);
    }


    public Object invoke(Object proxy,
                         Method m,
                         Object[] args)
throws Throwable
    {
        String name = m.getName();

        Script handler = (Script) handlers.get(name);

        if(handler == null) {
            throw new NoSuchMethodException(name +
                  " not implemented by virtual object");
        }

        return handler.run(args);
    }
}
```

This time the call to `newInstance()` is explicitly passed to the interface to implement. Once the instance has been created, methods can be added to it by calling `addHandler()`. `invoke` then obtains the name of the method that has been called, looks up the script, and calls it.

There is a great deal more that can be done with dynamic proxies. More information is available from http://java.sun.com/j2se/1.4.2/docs/guide/reflection/proxy.html.

Readers who are interested in Smalltalk or the history of object-oriented programming can find a great deal of information at http://www.squeak.org/.

Index

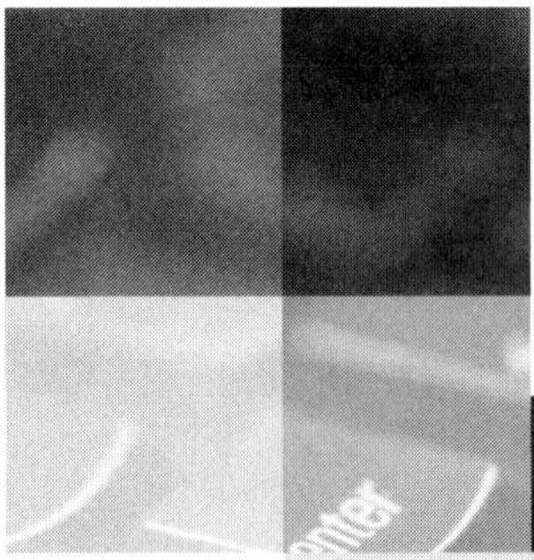

CD-ROM Warranty

Addison-Wesley warrants the enclosed CD-ROM to be free of defects in materials and faulty workmanship under normal use for a period of ninety days after purchase (when purchased new). If a defect is discovered in the CD-ROM during this warranty period, a replacement CD-ROM can be obtained at no charge by sending the defective CD-ROM, postage prepaid, with proof of purchase to:

Disc Exchange
Addison-Wesley Professional
Pearson Technology Group
75 Arlington Street, Suite 300
Boston, MA 02116
Email: AWPro@aw.com

Addison-Wesley makes no warranty or representation, either expressed or implied, with respect to this software, its quality, performance, merchantability, or fitness for a particular purpose. In no event will Addison-Wesley, its distributors, or dealers be liable for direct, indirect, special, incidental, or consequential damages arising out of the use or inability to use the software. The exclusion of implied warranties is not permitted in some states. Therefore, the above exclusion may not apply to you. This warranty provides you with specific legal rights. There may be other rights that you may have that vary from state to state. The contents of this CD-ROM are intended for personal use only.

More information and updates are available at:
http://www.awprofessional.com/